An Introduction to Computable Languages and Abstract Machines

An Introduction to Computable Languages and Abstract Machines

Alan Parkes
School of Engineering
Computing and Mathematical Sciences
Lancaster University

INTERNATIONAL THOMSON COMPUTER PRESS
I(T)P An International Thomson Publishing Company

London • Bonn • Johannesburg • Madrid • Melbourne • Mexico City • New York • Paris
Singapore • Tokyo • Toronto • Albany, NY • Belmont, CA • Cincinnati, OH • Detroit, MI

An Introduction to Computable Languages and Abstract Machines

I(T)P A division of International Thomson Publishing Inc.
The ITP logo is a trademark under licence.

For more information, contact:

International Thomson Computer Press
Berkshire House
168-173 High Holborn
London WC1V 7AA
UK

International Thomson Computer Press
20 Park Plaza
Suite 1001
Boston, MA 02116
USA

Imprints of International Thomson Publishing

International Thomson Publishing GmbH
Königswinterer Straße 418
53227 Bonn
Germany

International Thomson Publishing Asia
221 Henderson Road #05–10
Henderson Building
Singapore 0315

Thomas Nelson Australia
102 Dodds Street
South Melbourne, 3205
Victoria
Australia

International Thomson Publishing Japan
Hirakawacho Kyowa Building, 3F
2-2-1 Hirakawacho
Chiyoda-ku, 102 Tokyo
Japan

Nelson Canada
1120 Birchmount Road
Scarborough, Ontario
Canada M1K 5G4

International Thomson Editores
Campos Eliseos 385, Piso 7
Col. Polenco
11560 Mexico D. F. Mexico

International Thomson Publishing South Africa
PO Box 2459
Halfway House
1685 South Africa

International Thomson Publishing France
1, rue St. Georges
75 009 Paris
France

British Library Cataloguing-in-Publication Data
A catalogue record for this book is available from the British Library

Library of Congress Cataloging-in-Publication Data
A catalog record for this book is available from the Library of Congress

First Printed 1996

ISBN 1-85032-181-7

Commissioning Editor: Samantha Whittaker
Typeset by Lorraine Hodghton
Printed in the UK by The Alden Press, Oxford

Contents

Part Two: From computation to languages

Preface

At the time of writing, I have taught an undergraduate computer science course in Formal Languages and Automata for seven years. For the first two or three years, writing a book in the subject did not enter my thoughts. However, during this time I was becoming increasingly aware that my students found the recommended books very dry and heavy going. In a conversation with a sales representative (from another publishing company) I expressed my disenchantment with the books on offer, and received in return an invitation to submit a proposal to write one. The project eventually came to be supported by International Thomson Computer Press, and led to this book.

I would like to thank various people who contributed in some way to the production of this book. Tony Llewellyn, when head of the Computing Department at Lancaster University, asked me to teach the course on Formal Languages when I joined the staff as a new lecturer. If this had not happened, this book would most probably have never been written. Other people contributed greatly to this book. Two of these were the anonymous reviewers of the first draft of the book, for Chapman & Hall. Despite my initial reaction to their highly critical reviews, I incorporated most of the suggestions they made into the second draft. In connection with the production of the second draft, I would also like to thank Eliane Wigzell of Chapman & Hall, who encouraged me to continue when I was sure it would be best to abandon the book altogether. Then there is the anonymous reviewer for International Thomson, who made comments about the final draft that restored my faith in myself. Samantha Whittaker of International Thomson Computer Press is also to be praised for her encouragement and patience with regard to deadlines.

The greatest contribution of all came from my wife, Anna, and my daughter, Betty, to whom I dedicate this book.

Lancaster 1995

1 Introduction

AIMS

To describe

- what this book is about
- what this book tries to do
- what this book tries not to do
- two useful features of the book: the Glossary, and the Exercises

1.1 WHAT THIS BOOK IS ABOUT

This book is about two key topics of computer science, namely **computable languages**[1] and **abstract machines**. Computable languages are related to what are usually known as '**formal languages**'. I avoided using the latter phrase in the title of the book, because later on in the book I make a distinction between *formal* languages and *computable* languages. In fact, computable languages are a special type of formal language, namely formal languages that can be processed, in ways considered in this book, by computers, or rather abstract machines that represent computers. Abstract machines are formal computing devices that we use to investigate properties of real computing devices. The term that is sometimes used to describe abstract machines is *automata*, but that sounds too much like real machines, in particular the type of machines we call *robots*.

This book assumes that you are a layperson, in terms of computer science. If you are a computer science undergraduate, as you might be if you are reading this book, you may by now have written many programs. So, in this introduction we will draw on your experience of programming to illustrate some of the issues related to formal languages introduced in this book.

The programs that you write are written in a formal language. They are expressed in text which is presented as input to another program, a compiler or perhaps an interpreter. To the compiler, your program text represents a code, which the compiler knows exactly how to handle, as the rules by which that code is constructed are completely specified inside the compiler. The type of language in which we write our programs (the programming language) has such a well defined **syntax** (rules for forming acceptable programs) that a machine can decide whether or not the program you enter has the right even to be considered as a proper program. This is only part of the task of a compiler, but it's the part in which we are most interested.

For whoever wrote the compiler, and whoever uses it, it is very important that the compiler does its job properly in terms of deciding that your program is syntactically valid. The compiler writer would also like to be sure that the compiler will always reject syntactically invalid programs as well as accepting those that are syntactically valid. Finally, the compiler writer would like to know that his or her compiler is not wasteful in terms of precious resources: if the compiler is more complex than it needs to be, if it carries out many tasks that are unnecessary, and so on. In this book we see that the solutions to such problems depend on the type of language being considered.

Now, because your program is written in a formal language in such a way that another program can decide if your program *is* a program, the programming language is a computable language. A computable language then, is a formal language that is such that a computer can understand its syntax. Note that we have not discussed what your program will actually do when it's run: the compiler doesn't really understand

[1] Terms in bold, **like this**, are described in the 'Glossary' (described later in this chapter).

that at all. The compiler is just as happy to compile a program that *doesn't* do what you intended as it is to compile one that *does* (as you'll know, if you've ever done any programming).

The book is in two parts. *Part 1: From languages to computation* is concerned with the relationship between different types of formal languages and different types of theoretical machines (abstract machines) that can serve to process those languages, in ways we consider later. So, the book isn't really directly concerned with programming languages at all. However, much of the material in the first part of the book is highly relevant to programming languages, especially in terms of providing a useful theoretical background for compiler writing, and even programming language design. For that reason, some of the examples used in the book are from programming languages (particularly Pascal, but you need not be familiar with the language to appreciate the examples).

In Part 1, we study four different types of formal languages, and see that each of these types is associated with a particular type of abstract machine. The four types of language we consider were actually defined by the American linguist Noam Chomsky, and the classification of formal languages he defined has come to be called the **Chomsky hierarchy**. It's a hierarchy since it defines a general type of language (**type 0**), then a restricted version of that general type (**type 1**), then a restricted version of that type (**type 2**), and then finally the most restricted type of all (**type 3**).

The types of language considered are very simple to define, and even the most complex of abstract machines is also quite simple. What's more, all the types of abstract machine we consider in this book can be represented in diagrammatic form. The most complex abstract machine we look at is called the **Turing machine (TM)**. The TM is, in some senses, the most powerful computational device possible, as you will see in Part 2 of the book. The chapters of Part 1 are shown in Figure 1.1.

By the end of Part 1 of the book you should have an intuitive appreciation of computable languages. *Part 2: From computation to languages* investigates computation in a wider sense. We see that we can discuss the types of computation carried out by real computers in terms of our abstract machines. We see that a machine, called a **finite state transducer**, that appears to share some properties with real computers is not really a suitable general model of real computers. Part of the reason for this is that this machine cannot do *multiplication* or *division*. We see that the Turing machine is capable of multiplication and division, and any other tasks that real computers can do. We even see that the Turing machine can run programs. What is more, since the Turing machine effectively has unlimited storage capacity, it turns out to be more powerful than any real computer could ever be.

One interesting property of Turing machines is that we cannot make them any more powerful than they are by adding extra computational facilities. Nevertheless, TMs use only one data structure, a potentially infinite one-dimensional array of symbols, called a **tape**, and only one type of instruction. A TM can simply read a symbol from its tape, replace that symbol by another, and then move to the next symbol on the right or left

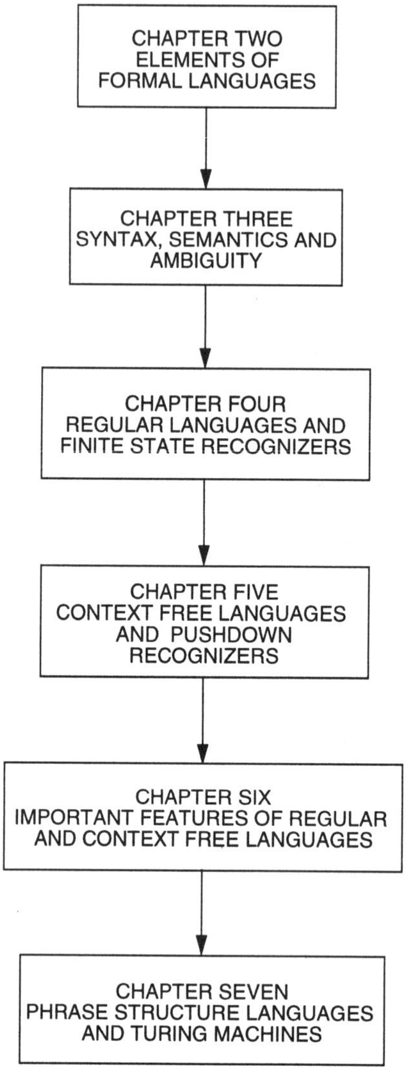

Figure 1.1 Part 1 of the book

in the tape. We find that if a TM is designed so that it carries out many processes simultaneously, or uses many additional tapes, it cannot perform any more computational tasks than the basic serial one-tape version. In fact, it has been established that no other formalisms we might create for representing computation give us any more functional power than does a TM. This assertion is known as **Turing's thesis**.

Finally, we see that we can actually take any Turing machine, code it and its data structure (tape) as a sequence of zeros and ones, and then let another TM run the original TM as if it were a program. This second TM can carry out the computation

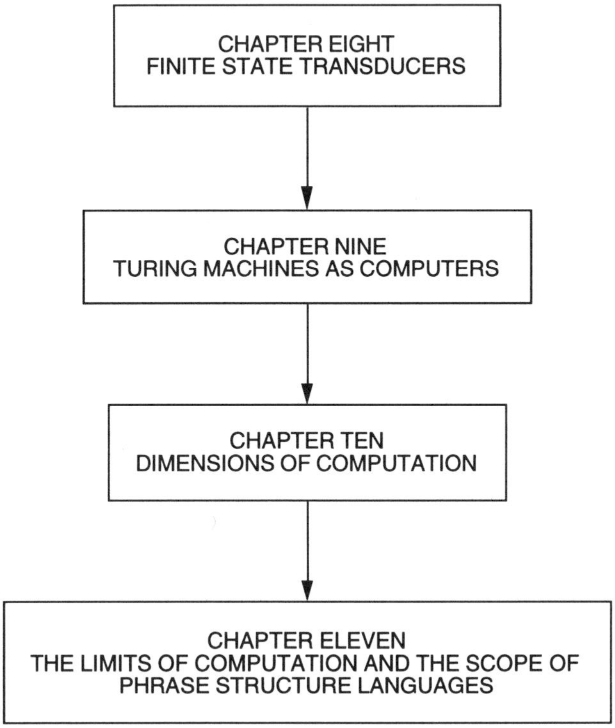

Figure 1.2 Part 2 of the book

described by any TM. We thus call it the **Universal Turing machine** (**UTM**). However, it is simply a standard TM, which, because of the coding scheme used, only needs to expect either a zero or a one every time it examines a symbol on its tape. The UTM is an abstract counterpart of the real computer.

The UTM has unlimited storage, so no real computer can exceed its power. We use this fact as the basis of some extremely important results of computer science, one of which is to see that the following problem cannot be solved, in the general case:

Given any program, and appropriate input values to that program, will that program terminate when run on that input?

In terms of TMs, rather than programs, this problem is known as the **halting problem**. We see that the halting problem is unsolvable[2], which has implications both to the real world of computing, and to the nature of formal languages. The book ends by using the result of the halting problem to convince us that there are formal languages that cannot be processed by any TM, and thus by any program. This enables us to finally define the relationship between computable languages and abstract machines. Figure 1.2 shows the chapters of Part 2 of the book.

[2] You have probably realized that the halting problem is solvable in certain cases.

1.2 WHAT THIS BOOK TRIES TO DO

This book tries to present formal computer science in a way that you, the student, can understand. This book does not assume that you are a mathematician. It assumes that you are not particularly familiar with formal notation, set theory, and so on. As far as is possible, excessive formal notation is avoided. When formal notation or jargon is unavoidable, the formal definitions are usually accompanied by short explanations, at least for the first few times they appear. Many technical terms are defined in the '**Glossary**', of which more later.

Overall, this book represents an understanding of computable languages and abstract machines which lies somewhere beyond that of a layperson, but is considerably less than that of a mathematician. There is a certain core of material in the subject of which any student of computer science or related disciplines should be aware. Nevertheless, many students do not become aware of this important, and often useful material, as they are discouraged by the way it is presented.

1.3 WHAT THIS BOOK TRIES NOT TO DO

This book tries not to be too formal. References to a small number of formal books are included in the section '*Further reading*', at the end of the book. In those books you will find many theorems, usually proved conclusively by logical proof techniques. The 'proofs' appearing in this book are included usually to establish something absolutely central, or something we need to assume for subsequent discussion. Where possible, such 'proofs' are presented in an intuitive way.

This is not to say that proofs are unimportant. I assume that, like me, you are the type of person who needs to be convinced that something is right before you really accept it. However, the proofs in this book are presented in a way that is different from the usual. Many results are established 'beyond a reasonable doubt' by presenting particular examples and encouraging the reader to appreciate ways in which the examples can be generalized. Of course, this is not *really* sound logic, as it does not argue throughout in terms of the general case. However, some of the end-of-chapter exercises give you an opportunity to practise or complete proofs. Such exercises often include hints and/or sample answers.

1.4 SOME USEFUL FEATURES OF THIS BOOK

1.4.1 The glossary

Throughout the book, words and phrases appear in bold, **like this**. Such phrases are defined in the Glossary. A given glossary term does not look **like this** every time it appears in the book, but will be emphasised the first time it appears in each chapter, and sometimes on other occasions within a chapter. Glossary terms are always defined in the text itself the first time they are used, but the explanation in the Glossary may be useful for subsequent reference. In particular, the Glossary makes it easier for you to refer to the definition of a term without having to search for it in the main text.

1.4.2 The exercises

At the end of each of Chapters 2–11, you will find a small number of exercises to test and develop your knowledge of the material covered in that chapter. Most of the exercises are of the 'pencil and paper' type, though some of them are medium scale programming problems. Any exercise marked with a dagger (†) has a sample solution in the 'Solutions to Selected Exercises' section near the end of the book. You do not need to attempt any of the exercises to fully understand the book. However, although the book attempts to make the subject matter as informal as possible, in one very important respect it is very much like maths: you need to practise applying the knowledge and skills you learn or you will not retain them.

Finally, some of the exercises give you an opportunity to cover additional material that is not covered in the chapters themselves.

1.4.3 Further reading

A small section called 'Further reading' appears towards the end of the book. This is not meant to be an exhaustive list of reading material; there are many other books on formal computer science than are cited here. The *Further reading* list also refers to books concerned with other fields of computer science (e.g. computer networks) where certain of the formal techniques in this book have been applied.

Brief notes accompany each title cited in the *Further reading* section.

1.5 SOME ADVICE

Most of the material in this book is very straightforward, though some requires a little thought the first time it is encountered. Students of limited formal mathematical ability should find most of the subject matter of the book reasonably accessible. You should use the opportunity to practise provided by the exercises, if possible. If you find a section really difficult, ignore it and go on to the next. You will probably find that an appreciation of the overall result of a section will enable you to follow the subsequent material. Sections you omit on first reading may become more comprehensible when studied again later.

You should not allow yourself to be put off if you cannot see immediate applications of the subject matter. There have been many applications of grammars and abstract machines in computing and related disciplines, some of which are referred to by books in the *Further reading* section.

This book should be interesting and relevant to any intelligent reader who has an interest in computer science and approaches the subject matter with an open mind. Such a reader may then see the subject of computable languages and abstract machines as an explanation of the simple yet powerful and profound abstract computational processes beneath the surface of the digital computer.

PART I

From languages to computation

2 Elements of formal languages

AIMS

To describe

- the building blocks of formal languages: alphabets and strings
- grammars and languages
- a way of classifying grammars and languages: the Chomsky hierarchy
- how formal languages relate to the definition of programming languages
- how to write definitions of sets of strings
- how to produce sentences from grammars
- how to use the notation of formal languages

2.1 ALPHABETS

An alphabet is a **finite** collection (or set) of symbols. The symbols in the alphabet are entities which cannot be taken apart in any meaningful way, a property which leads to them being sometimes referred to as **atomic**. The symbols of an alphabet are simply the 'characters', from which we build our 'words'. As already said, an alphabet is finite. That means we could define a program which would print out its **elements** (or **members**) one by one, and (this last part is very important) the program would terminate sometime, having printed out each and every element.

So, for example, the small letters you use to form words of your own language (e.g. English) could be regarded as an alphabet, in the formal sense, if written down as follows:

$\{a, b, c, d, e, .. , x, y, z\}.$

The digits of the (base 10) number system we use can also be presented as an alphabet:

$\{0, 1, 2, 3, 4, 5, 6, 7, 8, 9\}.$

2.2 STRINGS

A **string** is a finite **sequence** of zero or more symbols taken from a formal alphabet. We write down strings just as we write the words of this sentence, so the word 'strings' itself could be regarded as a string taken from the alphabet of letters, above. Mathematicians sometimes say that a string taken from a given alphabet is a string *over* that alphabet, but we will say that the string is **taken from** the alphabet.

Let us consider some more examples. The string *abc* is one of the many strings which can be taken from the alphabet $\{a, b, c, d\}$. So is *aabacab*. Note that duplicate symbols are allowed in strings (unlike in sets). If there are no symbols in a string it is called the **empty string**, and we write it as ε (the Greek letter **epsilon**), though some write it as λ (the Greek letter **lambda**).

2.2.1 Functions applying to strings

We now know enough about strings to describe some important functions that we can use to manipulate strings or obtain information about them. Table 2.1 shows the basic string operations (note that x and y stand for any strings).

Those of you who are familiar with Pascal may have noticed that strings have certain features in common with *arrays* in that we can index them. To index a string, we use the notation x_i, as opposed to something like *x*[i]. However, strings actually have more in common with the *list* data structures of programming languages such as LISP or PROLOG, in that we can concatenate two strings, creating a new string. This

Table 2.1 Basic String Operations

Name of op.	Written as	Meaning	Examples and comments
length	$\mid x \mid$	the number of symbols in the string x	$\mid abcabca \mid = 7$ $\mid a \mid = 1$ $\mid \varepsilon \mid = 0$
concatenation	xy	the string formed by writing down the string x followed immediately by the string y concatenating the empty string to any string makes no difference	let $x = abca$ let $y = ca$ $xy = abcaca$ let x = any string $x\varepsilon = x$ $\varepsilon x = x$
power	x^n where n is a whole number ≥ 0	the string formed by writing down n copies of the string x	let $x = abca$ $x^3 = abcaabcaabca$ $x^1 = x$ Note: $x^0 = \varepsilon$
index	x_n where n is whole number	the nth symbol in the string x (i.e. treats the string as if it were an array of symbols)	let $x = abca$ $x_1 = a$ $x_2 = b$ $x_3 = c$ $x_4 = a$

is like the *append* function in LISP, with strings corresponding to lists, and the empty string corresponding to the empty list. It is only possible to perform such operations on arrays if the programming language allows arrays to be of dynamic size (which Pascal, for example, does not)[1].

2.2.2 *Useful notation for describing strings*

As described above, a string is a sequence of symbols taken from some alphabet. Later, we will need to say such things as:

[1] However, many versions of Pascal now provide a special dynamic 'string' data type, on which operations such as concatenation can be carried out.

'suppose x stands for some string taken from the alphabet A'.

This is a rather clumsy phrase to have to use. A more accurate, though even clumsier, way of saying it is:

'*x* is an element of the set of all strings which can be formed using zero or more symbols of the alphabet *A*'.

A convenient and simple notational device to represent this statement is as follows:

$x \in A^*$,

which relates to the English version as shown in Figure 2.1.

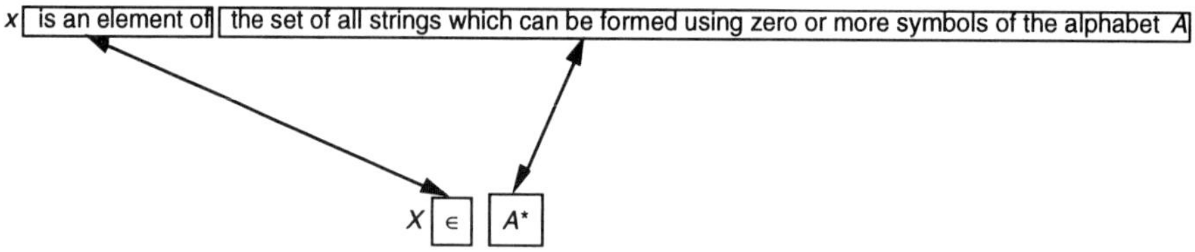

Figure 2.1 How we specify an unknown (possibly empty) string

On other occasions, we may wish to say something like:

'*x* is an element of the set of all strings which can be formed using one or more symbols of the alphabet *A*',

for which we write:

$x \in A^+$

which relates to the associated verbal description as shown in Figure 2.2.

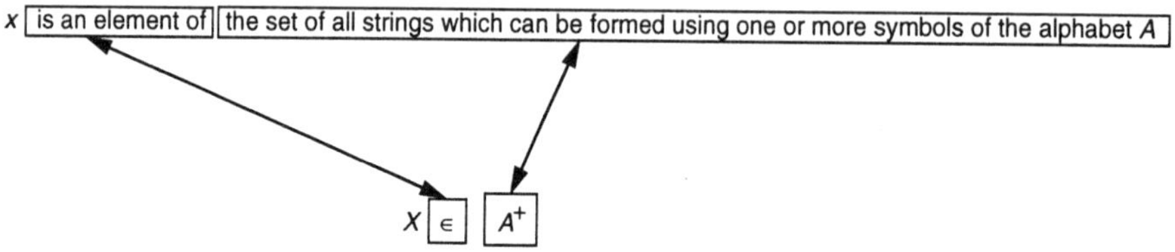

Figure 2.2 How we specify an unknown (non empty) string

Suppose we have the alphabet $\{a, b, c\}$. Then $\{a, b, c\}^*$ is the set

$\{\varepsilon, a, b, c, aa, ab, ac, ba, bb, bc, ca, cb, cc, aaa, aab, aac, aba, abb, abc \ldots\}$.

Clearly, for any non empty alphabet (i.e. an alphabet consisting of one or more symbols), the set so defined will be **infinite**.

Earlier in the chapter, we discussed the notion of a program printing out the elements of a finite set, one by one, terminating when all the elements of the set had been printed. If A is some alphabet, we could write a program to print out all the strings in A^*, one by one, such that each string only gets printed out once. Obviously, such a program would never terminate (because A^* is an infinite set), but we could design the program so that any string in A^* would appear within a finite period of time. Table 2.2 shows a possible method for doing this (as an exercise, you might like to develop the method into a program in your favourite programming language). The method is suggested by the way the first few elements of the set A^*, for $A = \{a, b, c\}$ were written down, above.

Table 2.2 Systematically printing out A^*

```
begin
        <print whatever symbol we use to represent the empty string>;
        i := 1;
        while i >= 0 do
                <print all strings that can be formed of length i>
                i := i + 1
        endwhile
end.
```

An infinite set for which we can print out any given element within a finite time of starting the program is known as a **countably infinite** set. I suggest you think carefully about the program in Table 2.2, as it may help you to appreciate just what is meant by the terms 'infinite' and 'finite'. Clearly, the program specified in Table 2.2 would never terminate. However, on each iteration of the loop i would have a *finite* value, and so any string printed out would be *finite in length* (a necessary condition for a string). Moreover, any string in A^* would appear after a finite period of time.

2.3 FORMAL LANGUAGES

Now we know how to express the notion of all of the strings that can be formed by using symbols from an alphabet, we are in a position to describe what is meant by the term formal language. Essentially, a **formal language** is simply any set of strings formed using the symbols from any alphabet. In set parlance, given some alphabet A,

> a formal language is 'any (**proper** or **non proper**) subset of the set of all strings which can be formed using zero or more symbols of the alphabet A'.

The formal expression of the above statement can be seen in Figure 2.3.

A proper subset of a set is not allowed to be the whole of a given set. For example, the set $\{a, b, c\}$ is a *proper* subset of the set $\{a, b, c, d\}$, but the set $\{a, b, c, d\}$ is not.

A *non proper* subset is a subset that can possibly be the whole of a set.

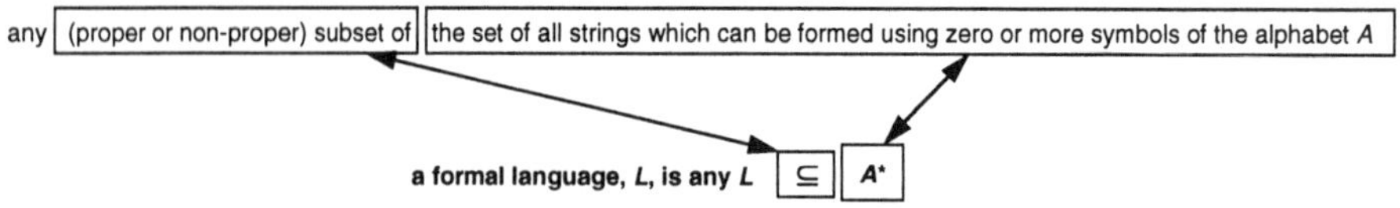

Figure 2.3 The definition of a 'formal language'

So, the above definition says that, for a given alphabet, A, A^* is a formal language, and so is any subset of A^*. Note that this also means that the **empty set**, written { } is also a formal language, since it's a subset of A^* (it is a subset of *any* set).

A formal language, then, is any set of strings. To indicate that the strings are part of a language, we usually call them **sentences**. In some books, sentences are called **words**. However, while the strings we have seen so far are similar to English words, in that they are unbroken sequences of alphabetic symbols (e.g. *abca*), later we will see strings that are statements in a programming language, such as **if** $i > 1$ **then** $x := x + 1$. It seems peculiar to call a statement such as this a 'word'.

2.4 METHODS FOR DEFINING FORMAL LANGUAGES

Our definition of a formal language as being a set of strings (called *sentences*) is extremely simple. However, it does not allow us to say anything about the form of sentences in a particular language.

For example, in terms of our definition, the Pascal programming language, by which we mean 'the set of all syntactically correct Pascal programs', is a subset of the set of all strings which can be formed using symbols found in the character set of a typical computer. This definition, though true, is not particularly helpful if we want to write Pascal programs, because it tells us nothing about what makes one string a Pascal program, and another string *not* a Pascal program, except in the trivial sense that we can immediately rule out any strings containing symbols that are not in the character set of the computer. You would be most displeased if you opened the Pascal manual and it consisted entirely of one statement which said: 'Let C be the set of all characters available on the computer. Then the set of compilable Pascal programs, P, is a subset of C^*'.

One way of informing you what constitutes 'proper' Pascal programs would be to write all the proper ones out for you. However, this would also be unhelpful, albeit in a different way, since such a manual would be infinite, and thus could never be completed.

In this section we discover three approaches to defining a formal language. Following this, every formal language we meet in this book will be defined according to one or more of these approaches.

2.4.1 Set definitions of languages

Since a language is a *set* of strings, the obvious way to describe some language is by providing a **set definition**. Set definitions of the formal languages in which we are interested are of three different types, as now discussed.

The first type of set definition we consider is only used for the smallest **finite languages**, and consists of writing the language out in its entirety. For example,

$\{\varepsilon, abc, abbba, abca\}$

is a language consisting of exactly four strings.

The second method is used for **infinite languages**, but those in which there is some obvious pattern in all of the strings that we can assume the reader will induce when presented with sufficient instances of that pattern. In this case, we write enough sentences out for the pattern to be made clear, then indicate that the pattern should be allowed to continue indefinitely, by using three dots '…'. For example,

$\{ab, aabb, aaabbb, aaaabbbb, \ldots\}$

suggests the infinite language consisting of all strings which consist of one or more *a*s followed by one or more *b*s and in which the number of *a*s equals the number of *b*s.

The final method, used for many finite and infinite languages, is to use a set definition to specify how to construct the sentences in the language, i.e. provide a **function** to deliver the sentences as its *output*. In addition to the function itself, we must provide a specification of how many strings should be constructed. Such set definitions have the format shown in Figure 2.4.

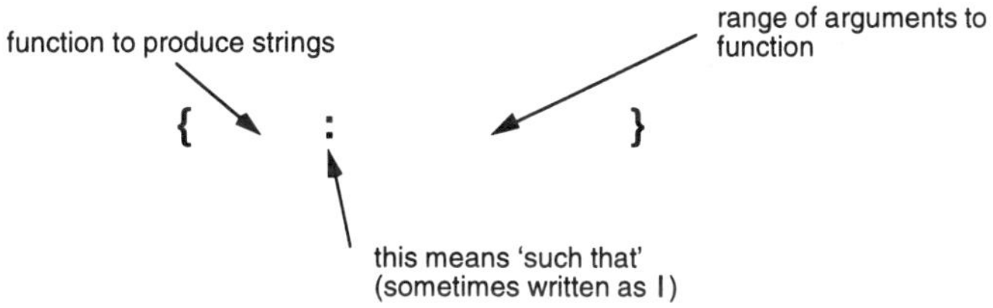

Figure 2.4 Understanding a set definition of a formal language

For the 'function to produce strings', of Figure 2.4, we use combinations of the string functions we considered earlier (**index**, **power**, and **concatenation**). A language that was defined immediately above,

> 'all strings which consist of one or more *a*s followed by one or more *b*s and in which the number of *a*s equals the number of *b*s'

can be defined using our latest method as:

$\{a^i b^i : i \geq 1\}$

The above definition is explained in Table 2.3.

Table 2.3 Understanding the set definition of the language $\{a^ib^i : i \geq 1\}$

Notation	String function	Meaning
a	N/A	'the string a'
b	N/A	'the string b'
a^i	power	'the string formed by writing down i copies of the string a'
b^i	power	'the string formed by writing down i copies of the string b'
a^ib^i	concatenation	'the string formed by writing down i copies of a followed by i copies of b'
$: i \geq 1$	N/A	'such that i is allowed to take on the value of each and every whole number value greater than or equal to 1 (we could have written $i > 0$)'

From Table 2.3 we can see that $\{a^ib^i : i \geq 1\}$ means:

> 'the set of all strings consisting of i copies of a followed by i copies of b such that i is allowed to take on the value of each and every whole number value greater than or equal to 1'.

Changing the right hand side of the set definition can change the language defined. For example $\{a^ib^i : i \geq 0\}$ defines:

> 'the set of all strings consisting of i copies of a followed by i copies of b such that i is allowed to take on the value of each and every whole number value greater than or equal to 0'.

This latter set is our original set, along with the empty string (since $a^0 = \varepsilon$, $b^0 = \varepsilon$, and therefore $a^0 b^0 = \varepsilon\varepsilon = \varepsilon$). In set parlance, $\{a^ib^i : i \geq 0\}$ is the **union** of the set $\{a^ib^i : i \geq 1\}$ with the set $\{\varepsilon\}$, which is written:

$$\{a^ib^i : i \geq 0\} = \{a^ib^i : i \geq 1\} \cup \{\varepsilon\}.$$

This last example illustrates a further useful feature of sets. We can often simplify the definition of a language by creating several sets and using the union, **intersection** and **set difference** operators to combine them into one. This sometimes removes the need for a complicated expression in the right hand side of our set definition. For example, this definition:

$$\{a^ib^jc^k : i \geq 1, j \geq 0\ , k \geq 0, \text{if } i \geq 3 \text{ then } j = 0 \text{ else } k = 0\}$$

is probably better represented as:

$\{a^i c^j : i \geq 3, j \geq 0\} \cup \{a^i b^j : 1 \leq i < 3, j \geq 0\}$, which means
'the set of strings consisting of three or more *a*s followed by zero or more *c*s, or consisting of one or two *a*s followed by zero or more *b*s'.

2.4.2 *Decision programs for languages*

We have seen how to define a language by using a formal set definition. Another way of describing a language is to provide a *program* which tells us whether or not any given string of symbols is one of its sentences. Such a program is called a **decision program.** If the program always tells us whether or not any one string is a sentence, then the program in an implicit sense defines the language, in that the language is the set containing each and every string that the program tells us is a sentence. That is why we use a special term, 'sentences', to describe the strings in a language. A string input to the program may or may not be a sentence of the language; the program should tell us. For an alphabet A, a language is any subset of A^*. For any interesting language, then, there will be many strings in A^* which are not sentences.

Later in this book we will be more precise about the form these decision programs take, and what can actually be achieved with them. For now, however, we will consider an example to show the basic idea.

If you have done any programming at all, you will have used a decision program many times. The decision program you have used is a component of the *compiler.* If you write programs in a language such as Pascal, you submit your program text to a compiler, and the compiler tells you if the text is a syntactically correct Pascal program. Of course, the compiler does a lot more than this, but a very important part of its job is to tell us if the source text (string) is a syntactically correct Pascal program.

Consider again the language

$\{a^i c^j : i \geq 3, j \geq 0\} \cup \{a^i b^j : 1 \leq i < 3, j \geq 0\}$,

i.e.

all strings consisting of three or more *a*s followed by zero or more *c*s, or consisting of one or two *a*s followed by zero or more *b*s'.

Table 2.4 shows a decision program for the language.

The program of Table 2.4 is purely for illustration. In the next chapter we consider formal languages for which the above type of decision program can be created automatically. For now, examine the program to convince yourself that it correctly meets its specification, which can be stated:

'given any string in $\{a, b, c\}^*$, tell us whether or not that string is a sentence of the language
$\{a^i c^j : i \geq 3, j \geq 0\} \cup \{a^i b^j : 1 \leq i < 3, j \geq 0\}$'.

Table 2.4 A decision program for a formal language

```
1:  read(sym);      {assume read just gives us the next symbol in the string being examined}
    case sym of
        eos:        goto N;   {assume read returns special symbol 'eos' if at end of string}
        'a':        goto 2;
        'b'         goto N;
        'c'         goto N;
    endcase;                  {case statement selects between alternatives as in Pascal}

2:  read(sym);
    case sym of
        eos:        goto Y;   {if we get here we have a string of one a which is OK}
        'a':        goto 3;
        'b':        goto 6;   {we can have a b after one a}
        'c':        goto N    {any cs must follow three or more as – here we've only had one}
    endcase;

3:  read(sym);
    case sym of
        eos:        goto Y;   {if we get here we've read a string of two as which is OK}
        'a':        goto 4;
        'b':        goto 6;
        'c':        goto N;   {any cs must follow three or more as – here we've only had two}
    endcase;

4:  read(sym);
    case sym of
        eos:        goto Y;   {if we get here we've read a string of three or more as which is OK}
        'a':        goto 4;   {we loop here because we allow any number of as ≥ 3}
        'b':        goto N;   {b can only follow one or two as}
        'c':        goto 5;   {cs are OK after three or more as}
    endcase;

5:  read(sym);
    case sym of
        eos:        goto Y;   {if we get here we've read ≥ 3 as followed by ≥ 1 cs which is OK}
        'a':        goto N;   {as after cs are not allowed}
        'b':        goto N;   {bs are only allowed after one or two as}
        'c':        goto 5;   {we loop here because we allow any number of cs after ≥ 3 as}
    endcase;

6:  read(sym);
    case sym of
        eos:        goto Y;   {we get here if we've read 1 or 2 as followed by ≥ 0 bs – OK}
        'a':        goto N;   {no as allowed after bs}
        'b':        goto 6;   {we loop here because we allow any number of bs after 1 or 2 as}
        'c':        goto N;   {no cs are allowed after bs}
    endcase;

Y:  write('yes');
    goto E;
N:  write('no');
    goto E;
E:  {end of program}
```

2.4.3 *Rules for generating languages*

We have seen how to describe formal languages by providing *set definitions*, and we have encountered the notion of a *decision program* for a language. The third method, which is the basis for the remainder of this chapter, defines a language by providing a set of rules to generate sentences of a language. We require that such rules are able to generate every one of the sentences of a language, and no others. In a similar way, a set definition describes every one of the sentences, and no others, and a decision program says 'yes' to every one of the sentences, and to no others.

There are several ways of specifying rules to generate sentences of a language. One popular form is the **syntax diagram**. Such diagrams are often used to show the structure of programming languages, and thus inform you how to write syntactically correct programs (*syntax* is considered in more detail in Chapter 3).

Figure 2.5. shows a syntax diagram for the top level syntax of the Pascal 'program' construct:

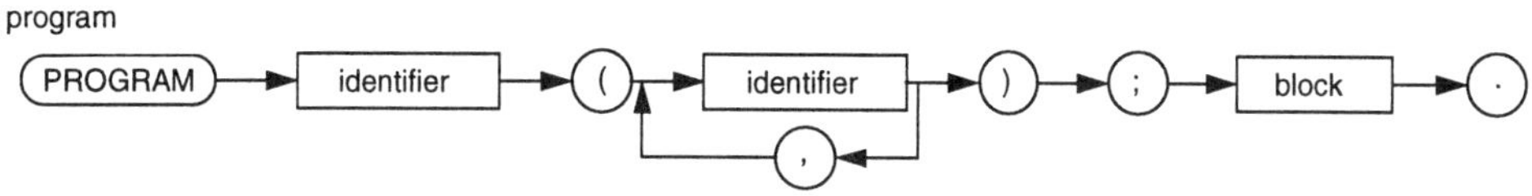

Figure 2.5 Syntax diagram for Pascal 'program'

The diagram in Figure 2.5 tells us that the syntactic element called a 'program' consists of

the string 'PROGRAM' (entities in rounded boxes and circles represent actual strings that are required at a given point),

followed by something called

an 'identifier' (entities in rectangles are those which need elaborating in some way),

followed by

an open bracket '(',

followed by

a list of one or more 'identifiers, in which every one except the last is followed by a comma, ',', followed by a semi-colon, ';', followed by something called a 'block', followed by a full stop, '.'.

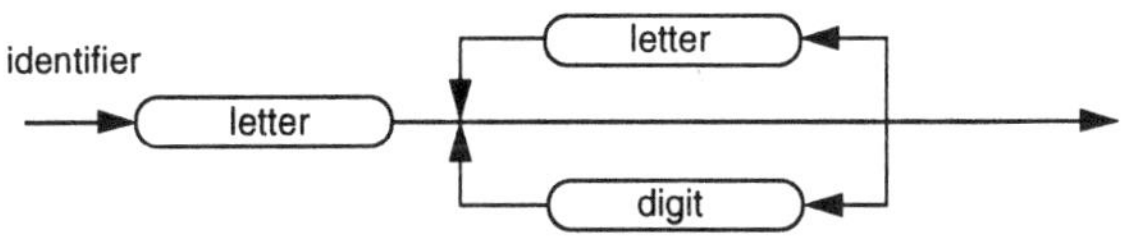

Figure 2.6 Syntax diagram for Pascal 'identifier'

In Figure 2.6. we see the syntax diagram for the entity 'identifier'.

Figure 2.6. shows us that an 'identifier' consists of a letter followed by zero or more letters and/or digits.

The following fragment of Pascal:

program calc(input, output, infile26, outfile23);

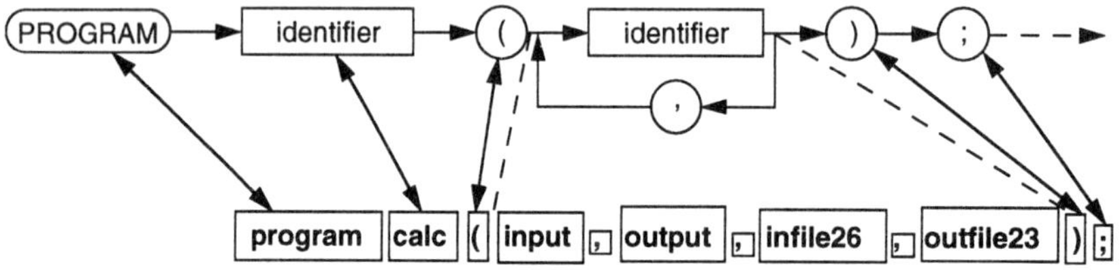

Figure 2.7 A syntax diagram describes a Pascal statement

associates with the syntax diagram for 'program' as shown in Figure 2.7.

Of course, the diagrams in Figures 2.5–2.7, together with all the other diagrams defining the syntax of Pascal, cannot tell us how to write a program to solve a given problem. That is a **semantic** consideration, relating to the meaning of the program text, not only its form. The diagrams merely describe the syntactic structure of sentences of the Pascal language.

An alternative method of specifying the syntax of a programming language is to use a notation called **Backus-Naur form (BNF)**[2]. Table 2.5 presents a BNF version of our

Table 2.5 The BNF version of Figures 2.5–7

<program> ::= <program heading> <block> .
<program heading> ::= program <identifier> (<file identifier> { ,<file identifier> }) ;
<file identifier> ::= <identifier>
<identifier> ::= <letter> {<letter or digit>}
<letter or digit> ::= <letter> | <digit>

syntax diagrams from above.

The meaning of the notation in Table 2.5 should be reasonably clear when you see its correspondence with syntax diagrams, as shown in Figure 2.8.

Formalisms such as syntax diagrams and BNF are excellent ways of defining the syntax of a language. If you were taught to use a programming language, you may never have looked at a formal definition of its syntax. Analogously, you probably did not learn your own 'natural' language by studying a book describing its grammar.

[2] The formalism we describe here is actually Extended BNF (EBNF). The original BNF did not include the repetition construct found in Table 2.5.

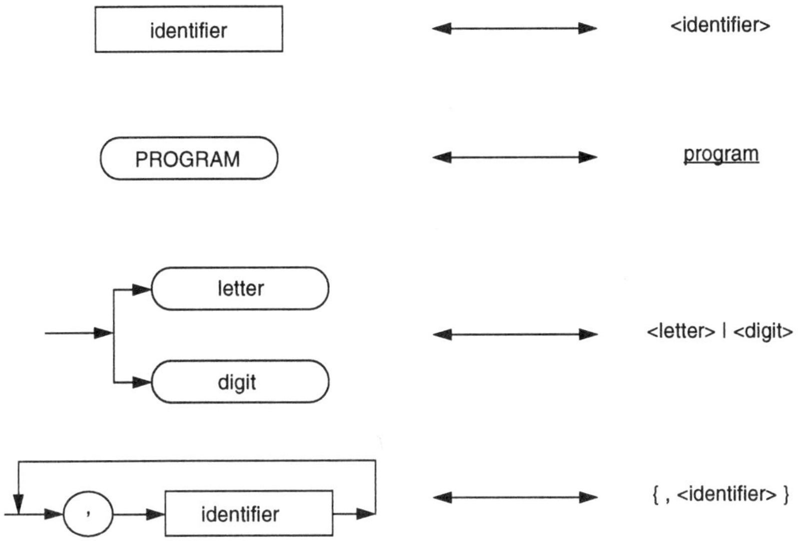

Figure 2.8 The correspondence between syntax diagrams and BNF

However, many programming languages are similar to each other in many respects, and learning a subsequent programming language is made easier if the syntax is concisely explained. Moreover, syntax descriptions can be useful for refreshing your memory about the syntax of a programming language you are familiar with, particularly for types of statements you rarely use.

If you want to see how concisely a whole programming language can be described in BNF, see the original definition of the Pascal language[3], from where the above Pascal syntax diagrams and BNF descriptions were obtained. The BNF definitions for the whole Pascal language are presented in only five pages.

2.5 FORMAL GRAMMARS

A **grammar** is a set of rules for generating strings. The type of grammars used in the remainder of this book are called **phrase structure grammars** (**PSGs**). Our formal definitions are illustrated by reference to the following grammar:

$$S \rightarrow aS \mid bB$$
$$B \rightarrow bB \mid bC \mid cC$$
$$C \rightarrow cC \mid c$$

In order to use our grammar, we need to know something about the status of the symbols that we have used. Table 2.6 gives an informal description of the symbols that appear in grammars such as the one above.

[3] Jensen and Wirth (1975) – see *Further Reading* section.

Table 2.6 The symbols in a phrase structure grammar

Symbols	Name and meaning
S, B, C	**non terminal** symbols [BNF: things in angled brackets e.g. <identifier>]
S	special non terminal, called a **start,** or sentence, symbol [BNF: in our example above, <program>]
a, b, c	**terminal** symbols: only these symbols can appear in sentences [BNF: the underlined terms (e.g. program) and punctuation symbols (e.g. ';')]
$\rightarrow$	**production arrow** [BNF: the symbol '::=']
$S \rightarrow aS$	production rule, usually called simply a production (or sometimes we'll just use the word rule). Means 'S produces aS', or 'S can be replaced by aS'. The string to the left of $\rightarrow$ is called the left hand side of the production, the string to the right of $\rightarrow$ is called the right hand side. [BNF: this rule would be written as <S> ::= *a* <S>]
$\mid$	'or', so $B \rightarrow bB \mid bC \mid cC$ means 'B produces bB or bC or cC'. Note that this means that $B \rightarrow bB \mid bC \mid cC$ is really **three** production rules i.e. $B \rightarrow bB$, $B \rightarrow bC$, and $B \rightarrow cC$. So there are **seven** production rules altogether in the example grammar above. [BNF: exactly the same]

2.5.1 An informal look at grammars, derivations and languages

Table 2.7 presents an informal description, supported by examples using our grammar above, of how we use a grammar to generate a sentence.

As you can see from Table 2.7, there is often a choice as to which rule to apply at a given stage. For example, when the resulting string was aaS, we could have applied the rule $S \rightarrow aS$ as many times as we wished. A similar observation can be made for the applicability of the $C \rightarrow cC$ rule when the resulting string was $aabcC$, for example.

Here are some other strings we could create, by applying the rules in various ways:

$abcc$
$bbbbc$
$a^3b^2c^5$

Table 2.7 Using a phrase structure grammar

Action taken	Resulting string	Prod^n applied
Start with S, the start symbol	S	
If a substring of the resulting string matches the left hand side of one or more productions, replace that substring by the right hand side of any one of those productions	aS	$S \rightarrow aS$
"	aaS	$S \rightarrow aS$
"	$aabB$	$S \rightarrow bB$
"	$aabcC$	$B \rightarrow cC$
"	$aabccC$	$C \rightarrow cC$
"	$aabccc$	$C \rightarrow c$
If the result string consists entirely of terminals, then stop.		

You may like to see if you can apply the rules yourself to create these strings. You must always begin with a rule that has S on its **left hand side** (that is why S is called the **start symbol**).

So, once we have written down the S symbol to start the process, we merely repeat the process described in Table 2.7 as:

if a **substring** *of the resulting string matches the left hand side of one or more productions, replace that substring by the right hand side of any one of those productions*

until the following becomes true:

if the result string consists entirely of terminals,

at which point we:

stop.

You may wonder why the process of matching the substring was not presented as:

if a non terminal symbol in the resulting string matches the left hand side of one or more productions, replace that non terminal symbol by the right hand side of any one of those productions.

This would clearly work for the example grammar given. However, as discussed in the next section, grammars are not necessarily restricted to having single non terminals on the left hand sides of their productions.

The process of creating strings using a grammar is called **deriving** them, so when we show how we've used the grammar to derive a string (as was done in Table 2.7), we're showing a **derivation** for that string.

Let us now consider all the '**terminal strings**' – strings consisting entirely of terminal symbols, also known as *sentences* – we can derive using the example grammar. As this is a simple grammar, it's not too difficult to work out what they are.

Figure 2.9 shows the choice of rules possible for deriving terminal strings from the example grammar:

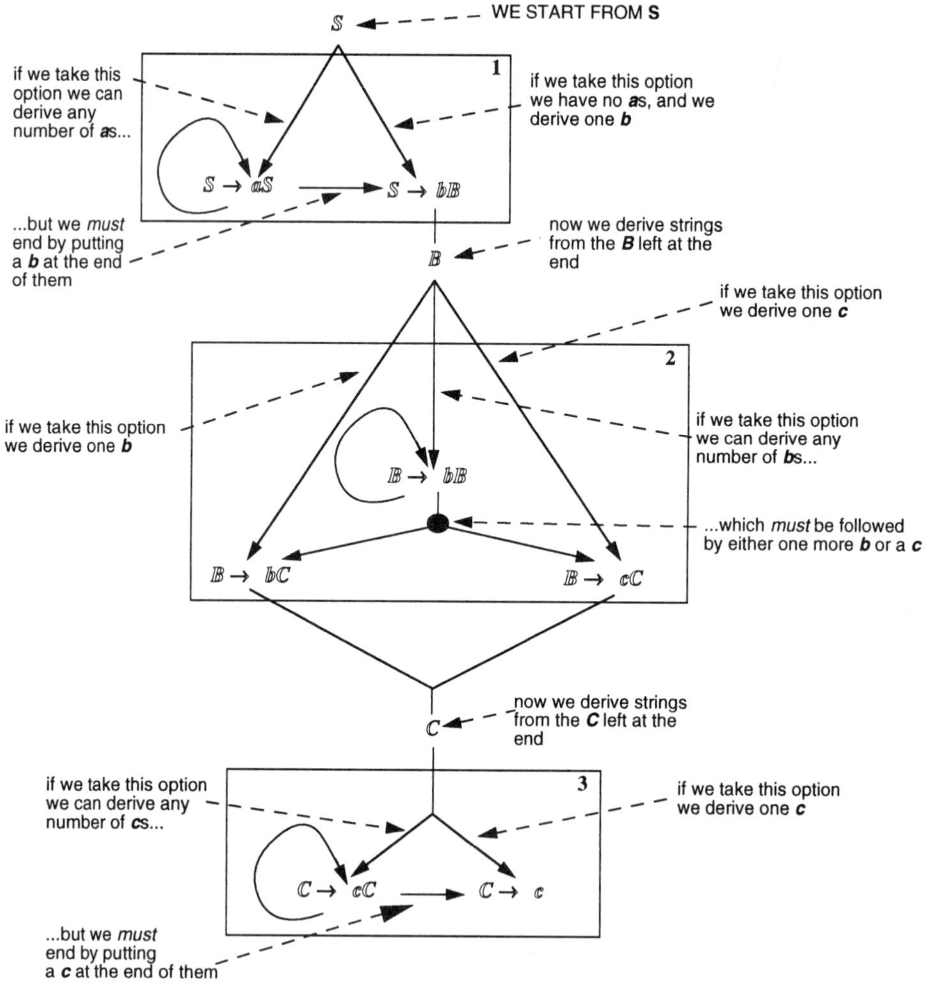

Figure 2.9 Working out all the terminal strings generated by a grammar

Any 'legal' application of our production rules, starting with S, the start symbol, alone, and resulting in a terminal string, would involve us in following a path through the diagram in Figure 2.9 starting in box 1, passing through box 2, and ending up in box 3. The boxes in Figure 2.9 are annotated with the strings produced by taking given options in applying the rules. Table 2.8 summarizes the strings described in Figure 2.9.

Table 2.8 The language generated by a grammar

Box in diagram of Figure 2.9	Informal description of derived strings	Formal description of derived strings
1 i.e. productions $S \rightarrow aS \mid S \rightarrow bB$ ...is expanded in box 2...	'any non zero number of *a*s followed by *bB*' or 'just *bB*' which is the same as saying 'zero or more *a*s followed by *bB*'	$a^i bB,\ i \geq 0$ ...the B at the end...
2 i.e. productions $B \rightarrow bB \mid bC \mid cC$ ...is expanded in box 3...	'any non zero number of *b*s followed by either *bC* or *cC*' or 'just *bC*' or 'just *cC*'	$b^jC,\ j \geq 1$ or $b^jcC,\ j \geq 0$ ...the C at the end...
3 i.e. productions $C \rightarrow cC \mid c$	'any non zero number of *c*s followed by one *c*' or 'just one *c*' which is the same as saying 'one or more *c*s'	$c^k,\ k \geq 1$

We now define a set which contains all the terminal strings (and only those strings) that can be derived from the example grammar. The set will contain all strings defined as follows:

> A string taken from the set $\{a^ib : i \geq 0\}$ concatenated with a string taken from the set $\{b^j : j \geq 1\} \cup \{b^jc, j \geq 0\}$ concatenated with a string taken from the set $\{c^k : k \geq 1\}$

which could be written as:

$$\{a^ibb^jck : i \geq 0, j \geq 1, k \geq 1\} \cup \{a^ibb^jcc^k : i \geq 0, j \geq 0, k \geq 1\}$$

$bb^j, j \geq 1$ is the same as $b^j, j \geq 2$, and $bb^j, j \geq 0$ is the same as $b^j, j \geq 1$, and $cc^k, k \geq 1$ is the same as $c^k, k \geq 2$, so we could write:

$$\{a^ib^jc^k : i \geq 0, j \geq 2, k \geq 1\} \cup \{a^ib^jc^k : i \geq 0, j \geq 1, k \geq 2\}$$

This looks rather complicated, but essentially there is only one awkward case, which is that if there is only one b then there must be two or more cs (any more than one b and we can have 1 or more cs). So we could have written:

$$\{a^i b^j c^k : i \geq 0, j \geq 1, k \geq 1, \text{if } j = 1 \text{ then } k \geq 2 \text{ else } k \geq 1\}.$$

Whichever way we write the set, one point should be made clear: the set is a set of strings formed from symbols in the alphabet $\{a, b, c\}$, that is to say, the set is a *formal language*. As we saw earlier, the terminal strings are called sentences of the language. We are now ready to give an intuitive definition of the relationship between grammars and languages:

> The **language generated by a grammar** is the set of all terminal strings that can be derived using the productions of that grammar, each derivation beginning with the start symbol of that grammar.

Our example grammar, when written like this:

$S \to aS \mid bB$
$B \to bB \mid bC \mid cC$
$C \to cC \mid c$

is only partly defined. A grammar is only fully specified when we know which symbols are terminals, which are non terminals, and which of the non terminals is the start symbol. Then the grammar is fully defined. In this book, we will usually see only the productions of a grammar, and we will assume the following:

- capitalized letters are non terminal symbols
- non capitalized letters are terminal symbols
- the capital letter S is the start symbol.

This will always be the case unless explicitly stated otherwise.

2.1 PHRASE STRUCTURE GRAMMARS AND THE CHOMSKY HIERARCHY

The production rules of the example grammar from the preceding section are simple in format. For example, the left hand sides of all the productions consist of lone **non terminals**. As we see later in the book, restricting the form of productions allowed in a grammar in certain ways simplifies certain language processing tasks, but it also reduces the sophistication of the languages that such grammars can generate. For now, we will define a scheme for classifying grammars according to the 'shape' of their productions which will form the basis of our subsequent discussion of grammars and languages. The classification scheme is called the **Chomsky hierarchy**, named after Noam Chomsky, an influential American linguist.

2.6.1 *Formal definition of phrase structure grammars*

To prepare for specifying the Chomsky hierarchy, we first need to define precisely the term **phrase structure grammar (PSG)**, as described in Table 2.9.

Table 2.9 The formal definition of a phrase structure grammar

Any PSG, G, consists of the following:		
N	a set of non terminal symbols	an alphabet, containing no symbols that can appear in sentences
T	a set of terminal symbols	also an alphabet, containing only symbols that **can** appear in sentences
P	a set of production rules of the form $x \rightarrow y$, where $x \in (N \cup T)+$, and $y \in (N \cup T)^*$	this specification uses the notation for specifying strings from an alphabet we looked at earlier. *x* is the left hand side of a production, *y* the right hand side. The definition of *y* means: the right hand side of each production is a possibly empty string of terminals and/or non terminals. The only difference between the specification above and the one for *x* (the left hand side) is that the one for *x* uses + rather than *. So the specification for *x* means: the left hand side of each production is a non empty string of terminals and/or non terminals.
S	a member of *N*, designated as the start, or sentence symbol	the non terminal symbol with which we always begin a derivation

Formally, then, a PSG, *G*, is specified as (*N*, *T*, *P*, *S*). This is what mathematicians call a '**tuple**' (of four elements).

The definition in Table 2.9 makes it clear that the **empty string**, ε, cannot appear alone on the left hand side of any of the productions of a PSG. Moreover, the definition tells us that ε is allowed on the right hand side. Otherwise, any strings of terminals and/or non terminals can appear on either side of productions. However, in most grammars we usually find that there are one or more non terminals on the left hand side of each production.

As we always start a derivation with a lone *S* (**the start symbol**), for a grammar to derive anything it must have at least one production with *S* alone on its left hand side. This last piece of information is not specified in the definition above, as there is nothing in the formal definition of PSGs that says they must generate anything.

To refer to our earlier example grammar, its full formal description would be as shown in Table 2.10.

Table 2.10 The (N, T, P, S) form of a grammar

Productions	**(N, T, P, S)**		
	(	$\{S, B, C\}$,	— N
$S \to aS \mid bB$		$\{a, b, c\}$,	— T
$B \to bB \mid bC \mid cC$		$\{S \to aS, S \to bB, B \to bB, B \to bC,$	— P
$C \to cC \mid c$		$B \to cC, C \to cC, C \to c\}$,	
		S	— S
	)		

2.6.2 Derivations, sentential forms, sentences and 'L(G)'

We have formalized the definition of a phrase structure grammar (PSG). We now formalize our notion of **derivation**, and introduce some useful terminology to support subsequent discussion. To do this, we consider a new grammar:

$S \to aB \mid bA \mid \varepsilon$
$A \to aS \mid bAA$
$B \to bS \mid aBB$

Using the conventions outlined earlier, we know that S is the start symbol, $\{S, A, B\}$ is the set of non terminals, and $\{a, b\}$ is the set of terminals. So we need not provide the full (N, T, P, S) definition of the grammar.

As in our earlier example, the left hand sides of the above productions all consist of single non terminals. We see an example grammar that differs from this later in the chapter.

Here is a string in $(N \cup T)^+$ that the above productions can be used to derive, as you might like to verify for yourself:

abbbaSA.

This is not a terminal string, since it contains non terminals (S and A). Therefore it is not a sentence. The next step could be, say, to apply the production $A \to bAA$, which would give us:

abbbaSbAA

We now have two strings, *abbbaSA* and *abbbaSbAA* that are such that the former can be used as a basis for the derivation of the latter by the application of one production rule of the grammar. This is rather a mouthful, even if we replace 'by the application of one production rule of the grammar' by the phrase 'in one step', so we introduce a symbol to represent this relationship. We write:

$abbbaSA \Rightarrow abbbaSbAA$.

To be absolutely correct, we should give our grammar a name, say G, and write:

$$abbbaSA \overset{G}{\Rightarrow} abbbaSbAA$$

to denote which particular grammar is being used. Since it is usually clear in our examples which grammar is being used, we will simply use $\Rightarrow$. We now use this symbol to show how our example grammar derives the string *abbbaSbAA*:

$S \Rightarrow aB$
$aB \Rightarrow abS$
$abS \Rightarrow abbA$
$abbA \Rightarrow abbbAA$
$abbbAA \Rightarrow abbbaSA$
$abbbaSA \Rightarrow abbbaSbAA$

As it is tedious to write out each stage twice, apart from the first (S) and the last (*abbbaSbAA*), we allow an abbreviated form of such a derivation as follows:

$$S \Rightarrow aB \Rightarrow abS \Rightarrow abbA \Rightarrow abbbAA \Rightarrow abbbaSA \Rightarrow abbbaSbAA.$$

We now use our new symbol as the basis of some additional useful notation, as shown in Table 2.11.

Table 2.11 Useful notation for discussing derivations

Notation	Meaning	Example true statements
$x \Rightarrow y$	the application of one production rule results in the string x becoming the string y also expressed as 'x generates y in one step', or 'x produces y in one step', or 'y is derived from x in one step'	$aB \Rightarrow abS$ $S \Rightarrow \varepsilon$ $abbbaSA \Rightarrow abbbaSbAA$
$x \overset{*}{\Rightarrow} y$	x generates y in zero or more steps, or just 'x generates y', or 'x produces y', or 'y is derived from x'	$S \overset{*}{\Rightarrow} S$ $S \overset{*}{\Rightarrow} abbbaSA$ $aB \overset{*}{\Rightarrow} abbbaa$
$x \overset{+}{\Rightarrow} y$	x generates y in one or more steps, or just 'x generates y', or 'x produces y', or 'y is derived from x'	$S \overset{+}{\Rightarrow} abbbaSA$ $abbbaSbAA \overset{+}{\Rightarrow} abbbabaa$

A new term is now introduced, to simplify references to the intermediate stages in a derivation. We call these intermediate stages **sentential forms**. Formally, given any grammar, G, a sentential form is any string that can be derived in zero or more steps from the start symbol, S. By 'any string', we mean exactly that; not only terminal strings, but any string of terminals and/or non terminals. Thus, *a sentence is a sentential form, but a sentential form is not necessarily a sentence*. Given the simple grammar

$S \rightarrow aS \mid a,$

some sentential forms are: S, $aaaaaaS$, and a^{10}. Only one of these sentential forms (a^{10}) is a sentence, as it's the only one that consists entirely of terminal symbols.

Formally, using our new notation,

if $S \stackrel{*}{\Rightarrow} x$, then x is a sentential form.
If $S \stackrel{*}{\Rightarrow} x$, and x is a terminal string, then x is a sentence.

We now formalize the definition above, this being the statement that

> the language generated by a grammar is the set of all terminal strings that can be derived using the productions of that grammar, each derivation beginning with the start symbol of that grammar.

Using various aspects of the notation introduced in this chapter, this becomes:

Given a **PSG**, G, $L(G) = \{x : x \in T^* \text{ and } S \stackrel{*}{\Rightarrow} x\}$.

(Note that the definition assumes that we have specified the set of terminals and the start symbol of the grammar, which as we said earlier is done implicitly in our examples).

So, if G is some PSG, $L(G)$ means *the language generated by G*. As the set definition of $L(G)$ clearly states, the set $L(G)$ contains *all* of the terminal strings generated by G, but *only* the strings that G generates. It is very important to realise that this is what it means when we say the language generated by the grammar.

We now consider three examples, to reinforce these notions. The first is an example grammar encountered above, now labelled G_1:

$S \rightarrow aS \mid bB$
$B \rightarrow bB \mid bC \mid cC$
$C \rightarrow cC \mid c$

We have already provided a set definition of $L(G)_1$; it was:

$$L(G_1) = \{a^i b^j c^k : i \geq 0, j \geq 1, k \geq 1, \text{ if } j = 1 \text{ then } k \geq 2 \text{ else } k \geq 1\}.$$

Another grammar we have already encountered, which we now call G_2, is:

$S \rightarrow aB \mid bA \mid \varepsilon$

$A \to aS \mid bAA$
$B \to bS \mid aBB.$

This is more complex than G_1, in the sense that some of G_2's productions have more than one non terminal on their right hand sides.

$L(G_2) = \{x : x \in \{a, b\}^*$ and
the number of as in x equals the number of bs$\}$.

I leave it to you to establish that the above statement is true.
Note that $L(G_2)$ is not the same as a set that we came across earlier, i.e.

$\{a^i b^i : i \geq 1\}$,

which we will call set A.

In fact, set A is a **proper subset** of $L(G_2)$. G_2 can generate all the strings in A, but it generates many more besides (such as ε, *bbabbbaaaaab*, and so on). A grammar, G_3, such that $L(G_3) = A$ is:

$S \to ab \mid aSb.$

2.6.3 The Chomsky hierarchy

This section describes a classification scheme for PSGs, and the corresponding **phrase structure languages** (**PSLs**) that they generate, which is of the utmost importance in determining certain of their computational features. PSGs can be classified in a hierarchy, the location of a PSG in that hierarchy being an indicator of certain characteristics required by a decision program for the corresponding language. We saw above how one example language could be processed by an extremely simple decision program. Much of this book is devoted to investigating the computational nature of formal languages. We use as the basis of our investigation the classification scheme for PSGs and PSLs called the **Chomsky hierarchy**.

Classifying a grammar according to the Chomsky hierarchy is based solely on the presence of certain patterns in the productions. Table 2.12 tells us how to make the classification. The types of grammar in the Chomsky hierarchy are labelled **type 0** to **3**, with 0 as the most general type. Each type from 1 to 3 is defined according to one or more restrictions on the definition of the type numerically preceding it, which is why the scheme qualifies as a hierarchy.

If you are observant, you may have noticed an anomaly in Table 2.12. **Context sensitive** grammars are not allowed to have the empty string on the right hand side of productions, whereas all of the other types are. This means that, for example, our grammar G_2, which can be classified as **unrestricted** and as **context free** (but not as **regular**) cannot be classified as context sensitive. However, every grammar that can be classified as regular can be classified as context free, and every grammar that can be classified as context free can be classified as unrestricted.

Table 2.12 The Chomsky hierarchy

Type No	Type name	Patterns which ALL productions must conform to	Informal description and examples
0	unrestricted	$x \rightarrow y$, $x \in (N \cup T)+$, $y \in (N \cup T)^*$	The definition of PSGs we have already seen. Anything allowed on the left hand side (except for ε), anything allowed on the right. All of our example grammars considered so far conform to this. example type 0 production: $aXYpq \rightarrow aZpq$ (all productions of G_1, G_2 and G_3 conform – but see below).
1	context sensitive	$x \rightarrow y$, $x \in (N \cup T)+$, $y \in (N \cup T)+$, $\mid x \mid \leq \mid y \mid$	As for type 0, but we are not allowed to have ε on the left **or the right hand sides**. Note that the example production given for type 0 is **not** a context sensitive production, as the length of the left hand side is **greater** than the length of the right. example type 1 production: $aXYpq \rightarrow aZwpq$ (all productions of G_1 and G_3 conform, but not all of those of G_2 do).
2	context free	$x \rightarrow y$, $x \in N$, $y \in (N \cup T)^*$	Single non terminal on left, any mixture on the right. Also, ε is allowed on the right. example type 2 production: $X \rightarrow XapZQ$ (all productions of G_1, G_2 and G_3 conform).
3	regular	$w \rightarrow x$, or $w \rightarrow yz$ $w \in N$, $x \in T \cup \{\varepsilon\}$, $y \in T$, $z \in N$	Single non terminal on left, and either • ε or a single terminal, or • a single terminal followed by a single non terminal, on the right. example type 3 productions: $P \rightarrow pQ$ $F \rightarrow a$ (all productions of G_1 conform to this, but G_2 and G_3 DO NOT).

When classifying a grammar according to the Chomsky hierarchy, you should remember the following:

> For a grammar to be classified as being of a certain type, *each and every production of that grammar must match the pattern specified for productions of that type*.

Which means that the grammar:

$S \rightarrow aS \mid aA \mid AA$
$A \rightarrow aA \mid a$

is classified as context free, since the production $S \rightarrow AA$ does not conform to the pattern for regular productions, even though all the other productions do.

So, given the above rule that all productions must conform to the pattern, you classify a grammar, G, according to the procedure in Table 2.13.

Table 2.13 The order in which to attempt the classification of a grammar in the Chomsky hierarchy

```
if G is regular
then return('regular')
else
    if G is context free
    then return('context free')
    else
        if G is context sensitive
        then return('context sensitive')
        else return('unrestricted')
        endif
    endif
endif
```

Table 2.13 tells us to begin attempting to classify G at the most restricted type in the hierarchy. This means that, as indicated by Table 2.12, G_1 is a regular grammar, and G_2 and G_3 are context free grammars. Of course, we know that as all regular grammars are context free grammars, G_1 is *also* context free. Similarly, we know that they can all be classified as unrestricted. But we make the classification as specific as possible.

From the above, it can be seen that classifying a PSG is done simply by seeing if its productions match a given pattern. As we already know, grammars generate languages. In terms of the Chomsky hierarchy, *a language is of a given type if it is generated by a grammar of that type*. So, for example,

$\{a^i b^i : i \geq 1\}$ (the set A mentioned above)

is a context free *language*, since it is generated by G_3, which is classified as a context free *grammar*. However, how can we be sure that there is not a *regular* grammar that could generate A? We see later on that the more restricted the language (in the Chomsky hierarchy), the simpler the decision program for the language. It would therefore be useful to be able to define the simplest type of grammar for a given language. In the meantime, you might like to see if you can create a regular grammar to generate A (clue: do not devote too much time to this!).

From a theoretical perspective, the immediately preceding discussion is very important. If we can establish that there are languages that can be generated by grammars at some level of the hierarchy and *cannot* be generated by more restricted grammars, then we are sure that we do indeed have a genuine hierarchy. However, there are also practical issues at stake, for as mentioned above, and discussed in more detail in Chapters 4, 5 and 7, each type of grammar has associated with it a type of decision program, in the form of an abstract machine. The more restricted a language is, the simpler the type of decision program we need to write for that language.

In terms of the Chomsky hierarchy, our main interest is in context free languages, as it turns out that the syntactic structure of most programming languages is represented by context free grammars. The grammars and languages we have looked at so far in this book have all been context free (remember that any regular grammar or language is, by definition, also context free).

2.7 A TYPE 0 GRAMMAR: COMPUTATION AS SYMBOL MANIPULATION

We close this chapter by considering a grammar that is more complex than our previous examples. The grammar, which we label G_4, has productions as follows (each row of productions has been numbered, to help us to refer to them later).

$S \rightarrow AS \mid AB$	(1)
$B \rightarrow BB \mid C$	(2)
$AB \rightarrow HXNB$	(3)
$NB \rightarrow BN$	(4)
$BM \rightarrow MB$	(5)
$NC \rightarrow Mc$	(6)
$Nc \rightarrow Mcc$	(7)
$XMBB \rightarrow BXNB$	(8)
$XBMc \rightarrow Bc$	(9)
$AH \rightarrow HA$	(10)
$H \rightarrow a$	(11)
$B \rightarrow b$	(12)

G_4 is a **type 0**, or **unrestricted grammar**. It would be **context sensitive**, but for the production $XBMc \rightarrow Bc$, which is the only production with a right hand side *shorter* than its left hand side.

Table 2.14 represents the derivation of a particular sentence using this grammar. It is presented step by step. Each sentential form, apart from the sentence itself, is followed by the number of the row in G_4 from which the production used to achieve the next step was taken. Table 2.14 should be read row by row, left to right.

Table 2.14 A type 0 derivation

STAGE	row	STAGE	row	STAGE	row
S	(1)	AS	(1)	AAB	(2)
AABB	(2)	AABBB	(2)	AABBBC	(3)
AHXNBBBC	(4)	AHXBNBBC	(4)	AHXBBNBC	(4)
AHXBBBNC	(6)	AHXBBBMc	(5)	AHXBBMBc	(5)
AHXBMBBc	(5)	AHXMBBBc	(8)	AHBXNBBc	(4)
AHBXBNBc	(4)	AHBXBBNc	(7)	AHBXBBMcc	(5)
AHBXBMBcc	(5)	AHBXMBBcc	(8)	AHBBXNBcc	(4)
AHBBXBNcc	(7)	AHBBXBMccc	(9)	AHBBBccc	(10)
HABBBccc	(3)	HHXNBBBccc	(4)	HHXBNBBccc	(4)
HHXBBNBccc	(4)	HHXBBBNccc	(7)	HHXBBBMcccc	(5)
HHXBBMBcccc	(5)	HHXBMBBcccc	(5)	HHXMBBBcccc	(8)
HHBXNBBcccc	(4)	HHBXBNBcccc	(4)	HHBXBBNcccc	(7)
HHBXBBMccccc	(5)	HHBXBMBccccc	(5)	HHBXMBBccccc	(8)
HHBBXNBccccc	(4)	HHBBXBNccccc	(7)	HHBBXBMcccccc	(9)
HHBBBcccccc	(11)	aHBBBcccccc	(11)	aaBBBcccccc	(12)
aabBBcccccc	(12)	aabbBcccccc	(12)	aabbbcccccc	

The sentence derived is $a^2b^3c^6$. Notice how in Table 2.14 the grammar replaces each A in the sentential form $AABBBC$ by H, and each time it does this it places one c at the rightmost end for each B. Note also how the grammar uses non terminals as 'markers' of various types:

- H is used to replace the As that have been accounted for;
- X is used to indicate how far along the Bs we have reached;
- N is used to move right along the Bs, each time ending in a c being added to the end of the sentential form;
- M is used to move left back along the Bs.

You may also notice that at many points in the derivation several productions are applicable. However, many of these productions lead eventually to 'dead ends', i.e., *sentential forms that can do not lead eventually to sentences.*

The language generated by G_4, i.e. $L(G_4)$, is $\{a^i b^j c^{i \times j} : i, j \geq 1\}$. This is the set of

> 'all strings of the form one or more *a*s followed by one or more *b*s followed by *c*s in which the number of *c*s is the number of *a*s multiplied by the number of *b*s'.

You may wish to convince yourself that this is the case.

G_4 is rather a complicated grammar compared to our earlier examples. You may be wondering if there is a simpler type of grammar, perhaps a context free grammar, that can do the same job. In fact there is not. However, while the grammar is comparatively complex, the method it embodies in the generation of the sentences is quite simple. Essentially, like all grammars, it simply replaces one string by another at each stage in the derivation.

An interesting way of thinking about G_4 is in terms of it performing a kind of **computation**. Once a sentential form like $A^i B^j C$ is reached, the productions then ensure that $i \times j$ *c*s are appended to the end by essentially modelling the simple **algorithm** in Table 2.15.

Table 2.15 The algorithm embodied in grammar G_4

```
for each A do
        for each B do
                put a c at the end of the sentential form
        endfor
endfor
```

The question that arises is: what range of *computational* tasks can we carry out using such purely syntactic transformations? We see from our example that the type 0 grammar simply specifies string substitutions. If we take our strings of *a*s and *b*s as representing numbers, so that, say, a^6 represents the number 6, we see that each sentence of $L(G_4)$ represents the modelling by G_4 of the multiplication of arbitrary length numbers. Later in this book, we encounter an abstract machine, called a **Turing machine**, that specifies string operations, each operation involving the replacing of only one symbol by another, and we see that the machine is actually as powerful as the type 0 grammars. Indeed, the machine is capable of performing a wider range of computational tasks than even the most powerful real computer.

However, we will not concern ourselves with these issues until much later in the book. In the next chapter, we encounter more of the fundamental concepts of formal languages: **syntax**, **semantics**, and **ambiguity**.

EXERCISES

For exercises marked '†', solutions, partial solutions, or hints to get you started appear in '*Solutions to selected exercises*' at the rear of the book.

1 Classify the following grammars according to the **Chomsky hierarchy**. In all cases, briefly justify your answer.

(a)† $S \to aA$
$A \to aS \mid aB$
$B \to bC$
$C \to bD$
$D \to b \mid bB$

(b)† $S \to aS \mid aAbb$
$A \to \varepsilon \mid aAbb$

(c) $S \to XYZ \mid aB$
$B \to PQ \mid S$
$Z \to aS$

(d) $S \to \varepsilon$

2† Construct **set definitions** of each of the languages generated by the four grammars in exercise 1.
Hint: the language generated by 1(c) is not the same as that generated by 1(d), as one of them contains no strings at all, whereas the other contains only one string.

3† It was pointed out above that we usually insist that one or more non terminals must be included in the left hand side of **type 0 productions**. Write down a formal expression representing this constraint. Assume that N is the set of **non terminals**, and T the set of **terminals**.

4 Construct **regular grammars**, G_v, G_w and G_x such that
(a) $L(G_v) = \{c^j : j > 0, \text{ and } j \text{ does not divide exactly by } 3\}$
(b) $L(G_w) = \{a^i b^j [cd]^k : i, k \geq 0, 0 \leq j \leq 1\}$
Notes: as we are dealing only with *whole numbers*, the expression $0 \leq j \leq 1$, which is short for $0 \leq j$ and $j \leq 1$, is thc samc as writing: $j = 0$ or $j = 1$.
(c) $L(G_x) = \{a, b, c\}^*$

5† Use your answer to 4(c) as the basis for sketching out an intuitive justification that A^* is a regular language, for any alphabet, A.

6 Use the symbol $\Rightarrow$ in showing the step by step **derivation** of the string c^5 using
(a) G_v
and
(b) G_x
from exercise 4.

7 Construct **context free grammars**, G_y and G_z such that
(a) $L(G_y) = \{a^{2i+1}c^jb^{2i+1} : i \geq 0, 0 \leq j \leq 1\}$
Note: if $i \geq 0$, a^{2i+1} means 'all odd numbers of *a*s'
(b)† $L(G_z)$ = all Boolean expressions in your favourite programming language

8 Use the symbol $\Rightarrow$ in showing the step by step derivation of a^3b^3 using
(a) G_y from exercise 7,
and the grammar
(b) G_3 from Chapter 2, i.e. $S \rightarrow ab \mid aSb$

9 Provide a regular grammar to generate the language $\{ab, abc, cd\}$.
Hint: make sure your grammar generates *only* the three given strings, and no others.

10† Use your answer to exercise 9 as the basis for sketching out an intuitive justification that any **finite language** is regular.
Note: the converse, i.e. that every regular language is finite, is certainly not true. All of the regular languages we have encountered so far, except for the one in exercise 9, have been **infinite**.

3 Syntax, semantics and ambiguity

AIMS

In this chapter, you learn about the following aspects of formal languages, and their particular relevance to programming languages:

- the syntax, or grammatical structure, of a sentence
- the semantics, or meaning, of a sentence
- the graphical representation of derivations by structures called derivation trees
- parsing, or trying to discover the grammatical structure of a given sentence
- ambiguity, when a sentence in a formal language could have more than one meaning

3.1 SYNTAX VS. SEMANTICS

Phrase structure grammars (PSGs) describe the **syntax** of a language. The syntax of a language is the set of rules by which 'well formed' phrases, which we call **sentences**, come about. The **BNF** definitions or **syntax charts** for Pascal to which we referred in the previous chapter tell us about the correct *form* of Pascal statements, but do not tell us what the statements cause the machine to do after they have been compiled. They do not tell us how to write a program to compute a particular function, or solve a given problem. To write programs to do these things requires us to know about the meaning of the program constructs, i.e. their **semantics**.

Some of the languages we looked at in Chapter 2 had no semantics whatsoever (or at least none that we referred to). For semantics is not form alone, but also 'interpretation', and, like syntax, requires that we have access to a set of rules which tell us how to make this interpretation. For natural languages such as English these rules of interpretation are extremely complex, and not completely understood. Moreover, the rules of natural languages are not necessarily universal, and are subject to constant revision, especially in artistic usage.

The *semantics* of a sentence (or 'program') then, is its *meaning*. For a program, the term semantics refers to the computation carried out after the program source code has been compiled, when the program actually *runs*. In **formal languages**, meaning is inextricably linked to form. The grammatical structure of a sentence, by which we mean an account of how the **productions** were applied to obtain the sentence, is assumed to determine the meaning that we attribute to that sentence. We shall see certain implications of this below, but first we provide a foundation for our discussion by investigating a very useful way of representing the structure of a context free **derivation**.

3.2 DERIVATION TREES

As we know, context free grammars have productions where every left hand side consists of a single **non terminal**, a property also shared by the **regular grammars**. In each step (application of one production) of the derivation, therefore, a single non terminal in the sentential form will have been replaced by a string of zero or more **terminals** and/or non terminals to yield the next sentential form. Any **derivation** of a **sentential form** begins with S, the **start symbol**, alone. These features mean that we can represent the derivation of any sentential form as a **tree**, and a very useful feature of trees is that they can be represented graphically, and therefore be used to express the derivation in a visually useful way. Trees used to represent derivations are called **derivation trees** (or sometimes **parse trees**, as we see later).

Let us describe how derivation trees are constructed by using examples. First, a simple tree, featuring grammar G_3 from Chapter 2:

$S \rightarrow ab \mid aSb.$

Consider the derivation:

$S \Rightarrow aSb \Rightarrow aaSbb \Rightarrow aaabbb$

This can be represented as the tree in Figure 3.1.

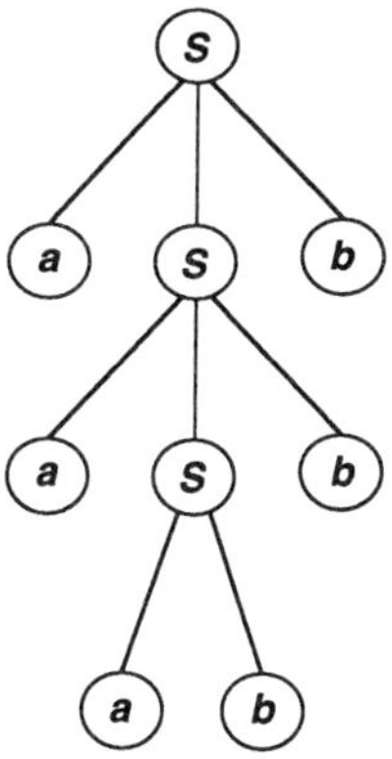

Figure 3.1 A derivation tree

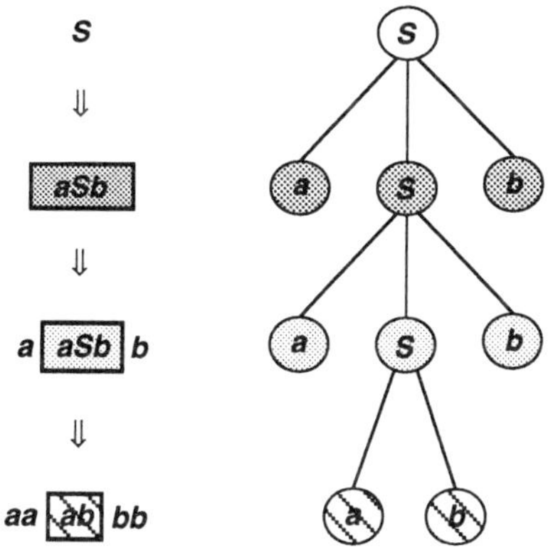

Figure 3.2 A derivation and its corresponding derivation tree

Figure 3.2 shows how the derivation tree relates to the derivation itself.

In a tree, the circles are called **nodes**. The nodes that have no nodes attached beneath them are called **leaf** nodes, or sometimes **terminal nodes**. In such a tree, the resulting string is taken by reading the leaf nodes in left to right order.

A slightly more complex example is based on grammar G_2, also from Chapter 2:

$S \rightarrow aB \mid bA \mid \varepsilon$
$A \rightarrow aS \mid bAA$
$B \rightarrow bS \mid aBB$

The derivation

$$S \Rightarrow aB \Rightarrow aaBB \Rightarrow aabSB \Rightarrow aabB \Rightarrow aabaBB \Rightarrow aababSB \Rightarrow aababB \Rightarrow aababbS \Rightarrow aababb$$

is represented by the tree in Figure 3.3.

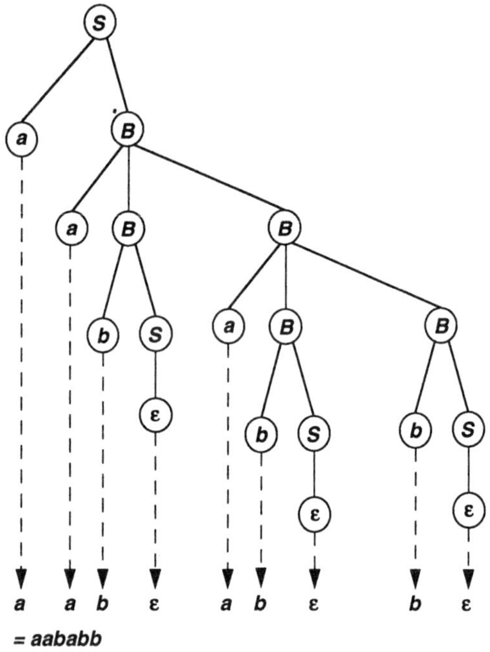

Figure 3.3 A more complex derivation tree

Dashed lines have been included in Figure 3.3 to clarify the order in which we read the terminal symbols from the tree.

Note how, for the purposes of drawing the derivation tree, the **empty string**, ε, is treated exactly as any other symbol. However, remember that the final string *aababb* does not show the εs, as they disappear when **concatenated** into the resulting string.

3.3 PARSING

The derivation of a string, as described in Chapter 2, is the process of applying various productions to produce that string. In the immediately preceding example, we derived the string *aababb* using the productions of grammar G_2. **Parsing**, on the other hand, is the creation of a structural account of the string according to a grammar. The term parsing relates to the Latin for the phrase *parts of speech*. As for *derivation* trees, we also have **parse trees**, and the derivation trees shown above are also parse trees for the corresponding strings (i.e. they provide an account of the grammatical structure of the strings).

Parsing is an important part of (formal and natural) language understanding. For the compilation of source programs it is absolutely crucial, since unless the compiler can arrive at an appropriate parse of a statement, it cannot be expected to produce the appropriate object code.

For now, we look at the two overall approaches to parsing, these being **top-down** and **bottom-up**. The treatment given here to this subject is purely abstract, and takes a somewhat extreme position. There are actually many different approaches to parsing, and it is common to find methods that embody elements of both top-down and bottom-up approaches.

The essence of parsing is that we start with a grammar, G, and a terminal string, x, and we say:

> construct a derivation (parse) tree for x which would be produced by the grammar G.

Now, while x is a terminal string, it may not be a sentence, so we may need to precede the above instruction with 'find out if x is a sentence and if so, ...'.

As previously stated, there are two overall approaches to parsing, these being top-down and bottom-up. We now briefly describe the two approaches.

In top-down parsing, we build the parse tree for the terminal string x, starting from the top, i.e. from S, the start symbol. The most purely top-down approach would be to use the grammar to repeatedly generate different sentences until x was produced.

Bottom-up parsing begins from the terminal string x itself, trying to build the parse tree from the sentence upwards, finishing when the tree is fully formed, with S, the start symbol, at the top.

To clarify bottom-up parsing, we will consider one bottom-up approach, known as the **reduction** method of parsing. We begin with our grammar, G, and make a grammar G_{red}, by swapping over the left and right hand sides of all of the productions in G. We call the resulting 'productions' **reductions**. The goal then becomes to use the reductions to eventually arrive at S after starting with the string x.

We again consider grammar G_3, i.e.

$$S \rightarrow aSb \mid ab$$

and the problem of producing the parse tree for *aaabbb*. The 'reductions' version of G_3, called G_{3red}, is as follows:

$$aSb \rightarrow S$$
$$ab \rightarrow S$$

We start with our sentence x, and look for a left hand side of one of the reductions that matches some **substring** of x. We replace that substring by the right hand side of the chosen reduction, and so on. We terminate when we reach a string consisting only of S. Parsing is simple in our example, which is shown in Figure 3.4, since only one reduction will be applicable at each stage.

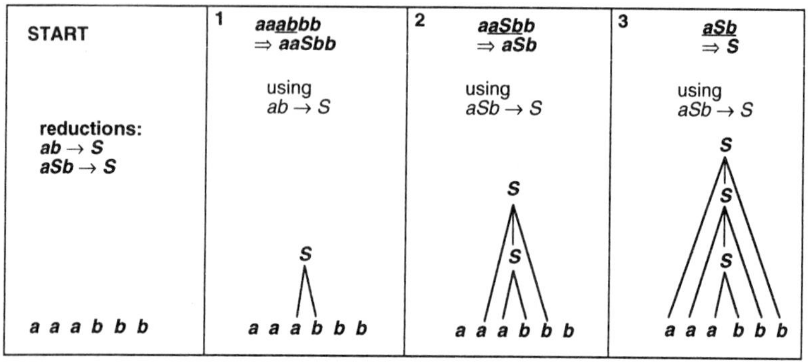

Figure 3.4 Reduction parsing

In the example in Figure 3.4, there was never a point at which we had to make a choice between several applicable reductions. In general, however, a grammar may be such that at many points in the process there may be several applicable reductions, and several substrings within the current string which match the left hand sides of various reductions.

As a more complex example, consider using the reduction method to produce a parse tree for the string *aababb*. This is a sentence we derived using grammar G_2 above. For G_2, the reductions $G_{2\text{red}}$ are:

$\varepsilon \to S$
$aB \to S$
$bA \to S$
$aS \to A$
$bAA \to A$
$bS \to B$
$aBB \to B$

We have to begin with the $\varepsilon \to S$ reduction, to place an S somewhere in our string so that one of the other reductions will apply. However, if we place the S after the first a, for example, we will be unable to complete the tree (you should convince yourself of this). The same applies if we place the S after the *second a* in the string. In fact, you will appreciate that a reduction rule with an ε on its left hand side can be applied at *any* stage in the parse. Moreover, suppose that later on in the parse we reach, say, *aabSaBB*. How do we choose between $aBB \to B$ and $aB \to S$?

We shall see in Chapters 4 and 5 how some of the problems of parsing can be simplified for certain classes of grammars, i.e. the **regular** grammars and (some of) the **context free** grammars. We do this by establishing that, associated with these grammars, are **abstract machines**. We then see that such machines can be used as a basis for designing parsing programs for the languages in question. For now, however, we look at an extremely important concept that relates to languages in general.

3.4 AMBIGUITY

Now that we have familiarized ourselves with the notion, and some of the problems, of parsing, we are going to consider one of the most important related concepts of formal languages, i.e. that of **ambiguity**. Natural language permits, and indeed in some respects actually thrives on, ambiguity. In talking of natural language, we usually say a statement is ambiguous if it has more than one possible meaning. The somewhat contrived example often used to demonstrate this is the phrase:

'Fruit flies like a banana.'

Does this mean 'the insects called fruit flies are positively disposed to bananas'? Or does it mean 'something called fruit is capable of the same type of trajectory as a banana'? These two potential meanings are partly based on the (at least) two ways in which the phrase can be parsed. The former meaning assumes that 'fruit flies' is a *single noun*, while the latter assumes that the same phrase is a *noun followed by a verb*.

The point of the above example is to show that while our intuitive description of what constitutes ambiguity makes reference to meaning, the different meanings can in fact be regarded as the *implication* of the ambiguity. Formally, ambiguity in a language is reflected in *the existence of more than one parse tree for a sentence in that language*.

To illustrate this point, let us consider an example which relates to a programming language called Algol60, a language that influenced the designers of Pascal. The example also applies to Pascal itself, and is based on the following fragment of a programming language definition, for which we revert, for convenience, to the BNF notation introduced in Chapter 2.

<statement> ::= <if statement> | <arithmetic expression> | ...

<if statement> ::= **if** <boolean expression> **then** <statement> |
if <boolean expression> **then** <statement> **else** <statement>

Remember that the terms in *angled* brackets ('<statement>', etc.) are non terminals, and that other items (**if**, **then** and **else**) are regarded as terminals.

Now consider the following statement:

if $x > y$ **then if** $y < z$ **then** $x := x + 1$ **else** $x := x - 1$

Suppose that $x > y$ and $y < z$ are <Boolean expression>s, and that $x := x + 1$ and $x := x - 1$ are <arithmetic expression>s. The following two different parse trees can be constructed for our statement. The first is shown in Figure 3.5, and is labelled PARSE TREE 1.

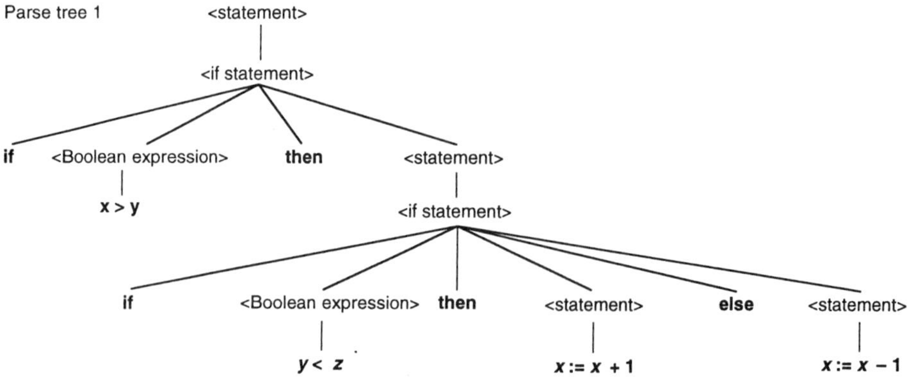

Figure 3.5 A derivation tree for an 'if statement'

PARSE TREE 2, an alternative parse tree for the same statement is shown in Figure 3.6.

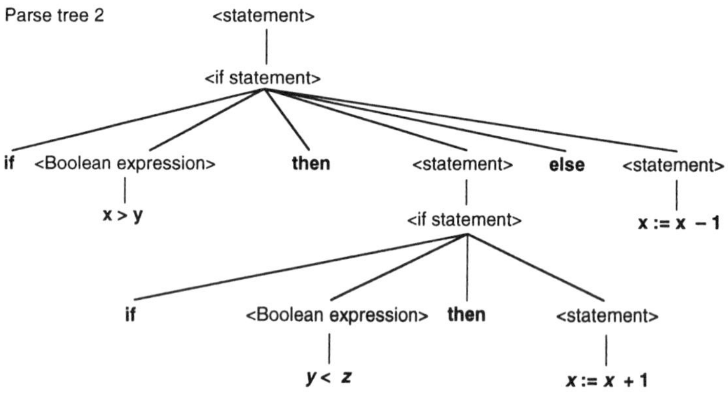

Figure 3.6 Another derivation tree for the same 'if statement' as that in Figure 3.5

We have two distinct structural accounts of a single sentence. This tells us that the grammar is **ambiguous**.

Now, suppose that the compiler for our language used the structure of the parse tree to indicate the order in which the parts of the statement were executed. Let us write out the statement again, but this time indicate (by inserting '[' and ']' into the statement) the *interpretation* suggested by the structure of each of the two trees:

PARSE TREE 1 suggests: **if** $x > y$ **then** [**if** $y < z$ **then** $x := x + 1$ **else** $x := x - 1$],

while

PARSE TREE 2 suggests: **if** $x > y$ **then** [**if** $y < z$ **then** $x := x + 1$] **else** $x := x - 1$.

The 'else part' belongs to different 'if parts' in the two interpretations. This would clearly yield different results according to which interpretation our compiler made. For example, if $x = 1$, $y = 1$ and $z = 2$, then in case 1 the execution of our statement would result in x still having the value 1, while after execution in case 2, x would have the value 0.

More seriously, a compiler for our language on one manufacturer's machine may create PARSE TREE 1 (Figure 3.5), while a compiler for another type of machine creates PARSE TREE 2 (Figure 3.6). What is more, a note would probably have to be added to the syntax descriptions of our programming language, e.g. in the manual, to explain which interpretation was assumed by the particular compiler. This is not a good policy to adopt in programming language definition, as the syntax for the programming language ought to be specified in a way that is subject to a single interpretation, and that interpretation should be obvious from looking at the formal definition of the syntax. That is to say, the language should be **unambiguous**.

Now, our example statement above is actually syntactically correct Pascal, as an 'if' statement is not a compound statement in Pascal, and therefore the subordinate if statement ('**if** $y < z$ **then** ...') does not need to be bracketed with **begin** and **end**. Thus, there is ambiguity in the standard definition of Pascal. The solution to this in the original Pascal manual was to inform the reader (in an additional note) which interpretation would be taken. The solution adopted for ALGOL was to change a later version of the language (Algol68) by introducing 'bracketing tokens', sometimes called 'guards' (similar to the **endifs** used in the algorithms in this book).

If we have bracketing tokens, and we would like the interpretation specified by PARSE TREE 1 (Figure 3.5), we write:

if $x > y$ **then if** $y < z$ **then** $x := x + 1$ **else** $x := x - 1$ **endif endif**

and if we want the PARSE TREE 2 (Figure 3.6) interpretation we write:

if $x > y$ **then if** $y > z$ **then** $x := x + 1$ **endif** else $x := x - 1$ **endif**

While ambiguity is, as mentioned above, an accepted part of natural languages, it cannot be accepted in programming languages, where the consequences of ambiguity can be serious. However, ambiguity in natural language can also lead to problems on some occasions. Krushchev, a president of the former Soviet Union (now the CIS), spoke a phrase to western politicians that was translated into English literally as 'Communism will bury you'. This was interpreted to be a threat that the Soviet Union would destroy the west, but in Russia the original phrase also has the meaning 'Communism will outlast you'!

To complete this introduction to ambiguity, we will state precisely the definition of ambiguity in formal grammars.

> A Phrase Structure Grammar (PSG), G, is ambiguous if $L(G)$ contains *any* sentence which has two or more distinct derivation trees.

And, correspondingly:

> A PSG, G, is unambiguous if $L(G)$ contains *no* sentences which have two or more distinct derivation trees.

If we find *any* sentence in $L(G)$ which has two or more derivation trees, we have established that our grammar is ambiguous. Sometimes, an ambiguous grammar can be replaced by an *un*ambiguous grammar which does the same job (i.e. generates exactly the same language). This was not done to solve the Algol60 problem described above, since in that case new terminal symbols were introduced (the bracketing terms), and so the new grammar generated different sentences from the original grammar, and therefore the language was changed.

Ambiguity is problematic as there is no general solution to the problem of determining whether or not an arbitrary PSG is ambiguous. There are some individual cases where we can show that a grammar is unambiguous, and there are some cases where we can show that a given grammar is ambiguous (exactly what happened in the case of Algol60). However, there is no general solution to the ambiguity problem, since establishing that a grammar is unambiguous could require that we make sure that there is absolutely no sentence that the grammar generates for which we can construct more than one derivation tree.

In programming languages, ambiguity is a great cause for concern, as stated above. The main reason for this is that the compiler is usually designed to use the parse tree of a program to derive the structure of the object code that is generated. It is obvious therefore, that the programmer must be able to write his or her program in the knowledge that there is only one possible interpretation of that program. Being unable to predict the behaviour of a statement in a program directly from the text of that statement could result in dire consequences both for the programmer and the user.

EXERCISES

For exercises marked '†', solutions, partial solutions, or hints to get you started appear in '*Solutions to selected exercises*' at the rear of the book.

1 Given the following grammar, G:

$S \rightarrow XC \mid AY$
$X \rightarrow aXb \mid ab$
$Y \rightarrow bYc \mid bc$
$A \rightarrow a \mid aA$
$C \rightarrow c \mid cC$

(a) Classify G according to the **Chomsky hierarchy**
(b)† Write a **set definition** of $L(G)$
(c)† Using the sentence $a^3b^3c^3$ in $L(G)$, show that G is an **ambiguous grammar**.

Note: $L(G)$ is known as an 'inherently ambiguous language', as any context free grammar that generates it is necessarily ambiguous. You might like to justify this for yourself (hint: think about the derivation of sentences of the form $a^i b^i c^i$).

2 Given the following productions of a grammar, G:

$S \rightarrow E$
$E \rightarrow T \mid E + T \mid T - E$
$T \rightarrow 1 \mid 2 \mid 3$

(note that 1, 2, 3, +, – are terminal symbols); and the following sentence in $L(G)$:

3 – 2 + 1

(a) use the sentence to show that G is an ambiguous grammar
(b)† assuming the standard arithmetic interpretation of the terminal symbols, and with particular reference to the example sentence, discuss the **semantic** implications of the ambiguity.

3 Discuss the semantic implications of the ambiguity in the grammar:

$P \rightarrow P$ or $P \mid P$ and $P \mid x \mid y \mid z$

(where 'or' and 'and' are terminals), assuming the usual Boolean logic interpretation of 'or' and 'and'. Introduce new terminals '(' and ')' in such a way as to produce a grammar that generates similar, but unambiguous logical expressions.

4 Given the following ambiguous grammar:

$S \rightarrow T \mid A \mid T$ or $S \mid A$ or S
$A \rightarrow T$ and $T \mid T$ and $A \mid$ not A
$T \rightarrow a \mid b \mid c \mid$ not T

(where or, and, not, a, b, and c are terminal symbols).
Discuss possible problems that the ambiguity might cause when interpreting the sentence a or not b and c (assuming the usual Boolean logic interpretation of the symbols and, or and not).

4 Regular languages and finite state recognizers

AIMS

To learn about the most restricted class of languages in the Chomsky hierarchy: the regular languages. In particular, you are introduced to our first, and most simple, type of abstract machine, the Finite State Recognizer (FSR), and learn

- how to convert a regular grammar into a FSR
- how any FSR can be made deterministic so it never has to make a choice when parsing a regular language
- how a deterministic FSR converts directly into a simple parsing program
- how to make an FSR as small as possible
- about the limitations of the regular languages

4.1 REGULAR GRAMMARS

As we saw in Chapter 2, a **regular grammar** is one in which every **production** conforms to one of the following patterns:

$X \rightarrow xY$ where X and Y are each single **non terminals**, x is a
$X \rightarrow y$ **terminal**, and y is either the **empty string** (ε), or a single terminal.

Here are some productions that all conform to this specification (A and B are non terminals, a and b are terminals):

$A \rightarrow \varepsilon$
$A \rightarrow aB$
$B \rightarrow bB$
$A \rightarrow bA$
$A \rightarrow b$
$B \rightarrow a.$

When we discussed **reduction parsing** in Chapter 3, we saw that productions such as $A \rightarrow \varepsilon$, with ε, the empty string on the right hand side can cause problems in parsing. However, for reasons to be discussed later, we can ignore them for the present, and assume for now that regular grammars contain no productions with ε on the right hand side.

Here is an example of (the productions of) a regular grammar, G_5:

$S \rightarrow aS \mid aA \mid bB \mid bC$
$A \rightarrow aC$
$B \rightarrow aC$
$C \rightarrow a \mid aC$

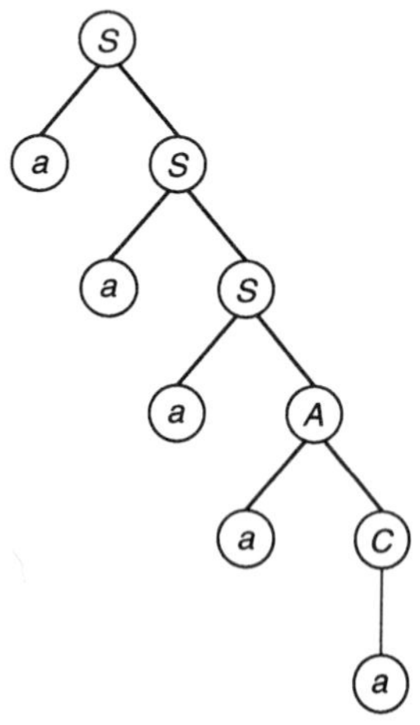

Figure 4.1 A derivation tree produced by a regular grammar

and here is an example derivation of a sentence:

$$S \Rightarrow aS \Rightarrow aaS \Rightarrow aaaA \Rightarrow aaaaC \Rightarrow aaaaa.$$

An equivalent **derivation tree**, can be seen in Figure 4.1.

You may have observed that the above grammar is also **ambiguous** (ambiguity was discussed in Chapter 3), since there is at least one alternative derivation tree for the given sentence. Try to construct one, if you wish.

In this chapter, we use G_5 to illustrate some important features of regular languages. For now, you might like to try to write a **set definition** of the language generated by the grammar. You can assess your attempt later in the chapter, when $L(G_5)$ is defined.

4.2 SOME PROBLEMS WITH GRAMMARS

It is not always straightforward to define a language by examining the corresponding grammar. Take our example grammar G_5 above: one obvious problem is that various symbols representing the same entity are scattered throughout the productions (the non terminal C, for example). Another problem is that, as computer scientists, we are not usually satisfied by merely designing and writing down a grammar, we usually want to write a **parser** for the language it generates. This leads to questions that grammars do not conveniently allow us to address. Will our grammar yield an *efficient* parser (in terms of **space** and **time**)? If we design another grammar with fewer productions, say, to generate the same language, is there a way of being sure that it does indeed do this? What about the design of grammars themselves: is there a more convenient design notation which we can use prior to, or even instead of, the textual form? What about productions such as $S \rightarrow aS$ and $S \rightarrow aA$: these may cause problems in the parsing of the language, as was discussed in Chapter 3. Can we eliminate situations where there is a *choice*, like these?

For the regular grammars, the answer to all of the above questions is 'yes'.

4.3 FINITE STATE RECOGNIZERS AND FINITE STATE GENERATORS

For the regular grammars there is a corresponding **abstract machine** that can achieve the same tasks (*parsing* and *generating*) as those supported by the grammar. Moreover, as the structure of the regular grammar is so simple, the corresponding machine is also simple. We call the machine the **finite state recognizer** (**FSR**). It is called a **recognizer** because it 'recognizes' if a string presented to it as input belongs to a given language. If we were using the machine to *produce*, rather than *analyse*, strings, we would call it a **finite state generator**.

4.3.1 Creating an FSR

We can devise an **equivalent** FSR from any regular grammar, by following the simple rules in Table 4.1.

Table 4.1 Constructing an FSR from the productions of a regular grammar

X and *Y* denote any non terminals, *y* denotes any terminal

(a) Convert all productions using whichever of the following three rules applies, in each case:

1. a production of the form: $X \rightarrow yY \quad (Y \neq X)$

   becomes a drawing of the form: 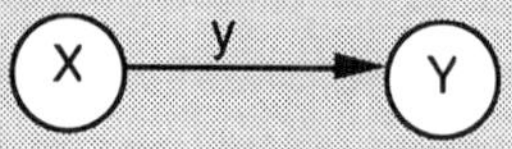

2. a production of the form: $X \rightarrow yX$

   becomes a drawing of the form: 

3. a production of the form: $X \rightarrow y$

   becomes a drawing of the form: 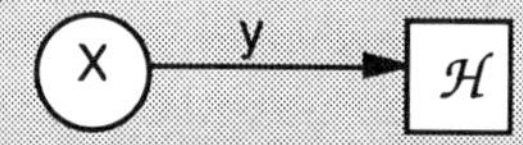

   where $\mathcal{H}$ is not a **non** terminal of the grammar

   [Note: we use the label $\mathcal{H}$ every time this rule applies]

(b) Take all the drawings produced in (a), and join all of the circles and squares with the same labels together

(c) The circle: 

becomes 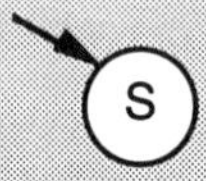

, where *S* is the start symbol of the grammar

The result is a pictorial representation of a directed graph ('digraph') which represents a finite state recognizer.

Figure 4.2 demonstrates the application of part (a) of the instructions in Table 4.1 to our example grammar G_5.

Figure 4.3 shows the machine that is produced after parts (b) and (c) of the procedure in Table 4.1 have been carried out.

To show its correspondence with the grammar from which it was constructed (G_5), we will call our new machine M_5.

To support a discussion of how our machines operate, we need some new terminology, which is provided by Table 4.2.

Part (a):

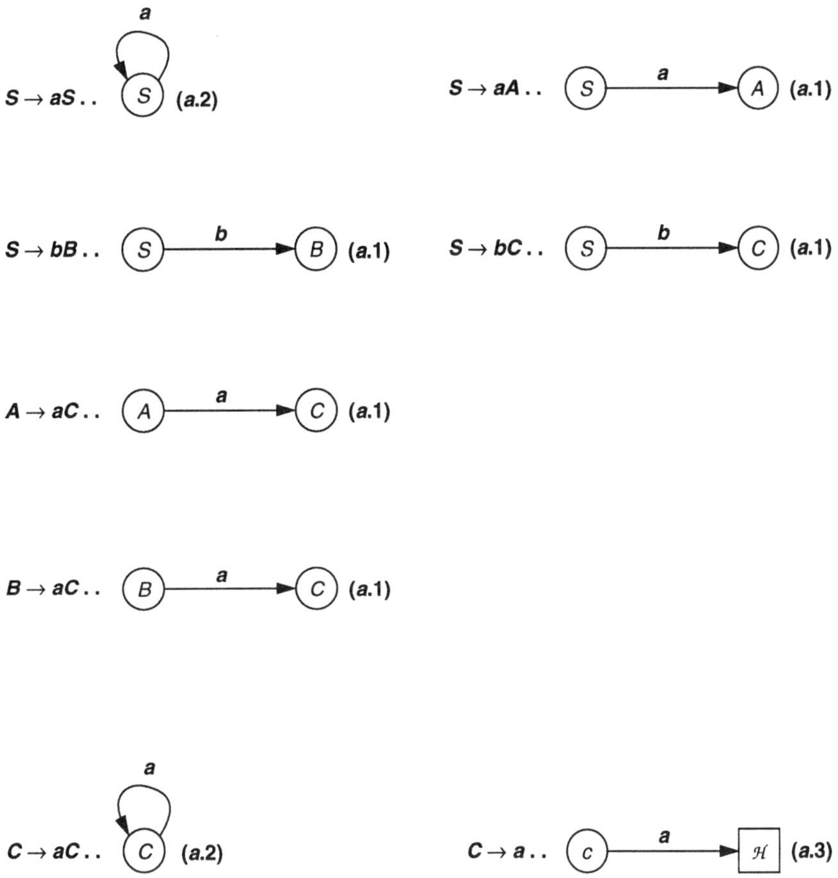

Figure 4.2 Example regular grammar to FSR conversion

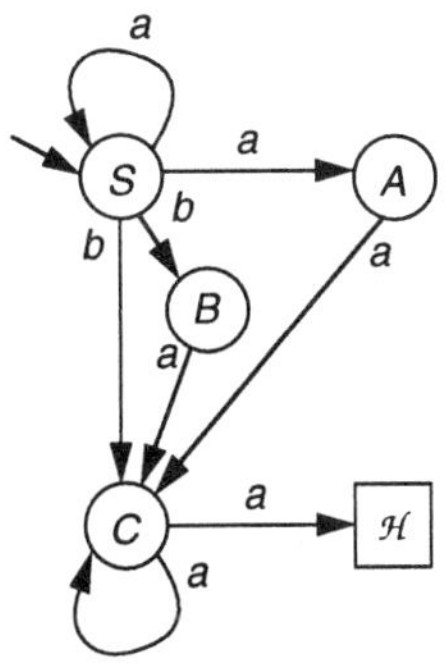

Figure 4.3 The machine M_5

Table 4.2 Terminology relating to FSRs

the labelled circles and squares are called states

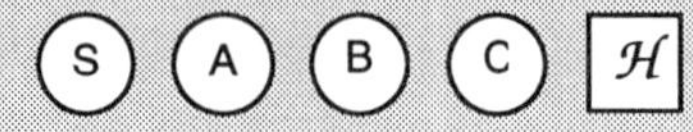

the arrows are called arcs

an arc can be labelled (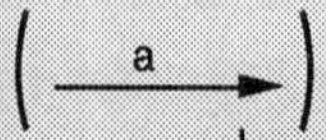

) [a is the label], or unlabelled ()

states can have ingoing arcs (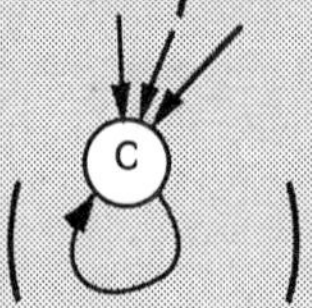

) and/or outgoing arcs (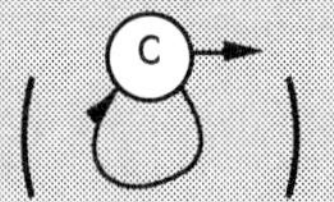

)

a state with an ingoing arc coming from nowhere is called a start state (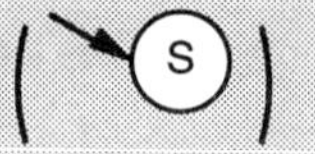

)

a square state is called a halt state or acceptance state (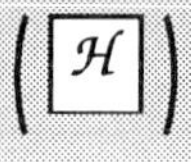

)

4.3.2 *The behaviour of the FSR*

A machine is of little use if it does not do something. Our machines are abstract, so we need to specify their rules of operation. Table 4.3 provides us with these rules.

Table 4.3 The rules governing the behaviour of the FSR

RULE 1. It begins its operation from any start state. It is said to be in the start state. It has available to it any string of terminal symbols, called the input string. If the input string is non empty, its leftmost symbol is called the current input symbol.

RULE 2. When in any state, q (the symbol q is often used to denote states in abstract machines) it can make a move, called a transition (or state transition) *to any other (possibly the same) single state*, q_1, if and only if there is an arc as follows:

(i) 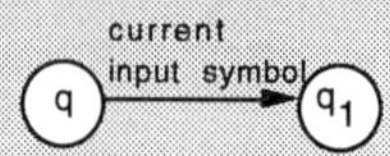

and/or (ii) 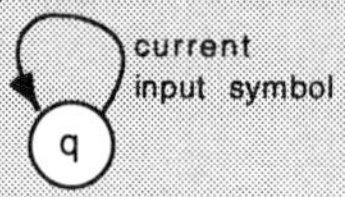

[in this case $q = q_1$]

After making a transition, the following conditions hold:
- the machine is in state q_1(or state q in case (ii))
- the symbol in the input string immediately to the right of the current input symbol now becomes the current input symbol. If there is no such symbol we say that the input is exhausted.

If any transitions are possible, the machine *must* make one of them.
We sometimes refer to the machine reading the current input symbol as it makes a transition.

RULE 3. When the machine is in a given state, and can make no transitions whatsoever, it is said to have halted in that state, and no more processing takes place.

It can be seen from Table 4.3 that there are two possible conditions which cause the **halting** of the machine:

(1) the input is **exhausted**, so no **transitions** can be made;
(2) the input is not exhausted, but no transitions are possible.

It can also be seen that one of two possible additional conditions must prevail when the machine halts:

(a) it is in an **acceptance state**,
(b) it is in a non acceptance state.

Our machine is very simple, and does not produce output as a program might, and so, if we imagine that we are blessed with the power to observe the internal workings of the machine, the situation that we observe at the time of halting is of critical importance. What we will observe when the machine stops is the situation 'inside' the machine with respect to the combination of (1) or (2) with (a) or (b) from above, as represented in Table 4.4.

Table 4.4 Possible state × input string configurations when the FSR halts

	input exhausted	input not exhausted
acceptance (halt) state	accepted	rejected
non acceptance state	rejected	rejected

Table 4.5 defines the **acceptance** and **rejection** conditions of the FSR.

Table 4.5 Acceptance and rejection conditions of the FSR

If the machine halts, with the input exhausted, in an acceptance state we say that the input string is accepted by the machine
If any other conditions prevail when the machine halts, we say that the input string is rejected by the machine

We now consider examples of the machine M_5 in operation. These examples are shown in Figures 4.4–4.6. In each case, we show the initial configuration of the machine and input, followed by the sequence of transitions. In each of Figures 4.4–4.6, the emboldened state in the transitions represents the state that the machine reaches on making that transition. The arrow beneath the input string shows the new current input symbol, also after a transition is made.

Example 1: Input string: *aaba*. This is shown in Figure 4.4.

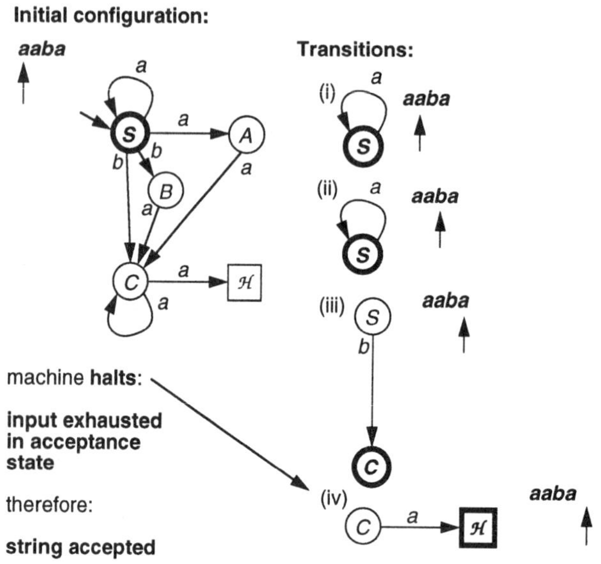

Figure 4.4 An FSR accepts an input string

Example 1 (Figure 4.4) shows how the string *aaba* can be accepted by M_5. You can observe that several choices were made, as if by magic, as to which transition to take in a given situation. In fact, you could show a sequence of transitions which lead to *aaba* being *rejected*. This appears to be a problem with Rule 2 in Table 4.3, to which we return later. First, another example:

Example 2: Input string: *aabb*. This is illustrated in Figure 4.5.

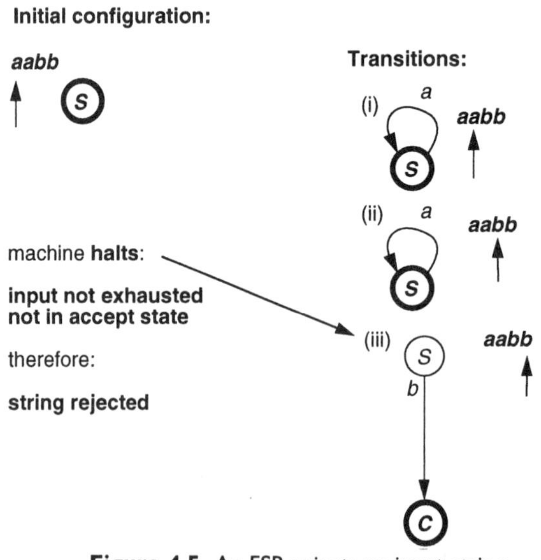

Figure 4.5 An FSR rejects an input string

In Figure 4.5, we see the string *aabb* being rejected by M_5. Although choices were made at several points, you can easily establish that there is *no* sequence of transitions which will lead to the string *aabb* being *accepted* by M_5.

The next example, shown in Figure 4.6, shows another string being rejected under different halting conditions.

Example 3: Input string: *aaabb*

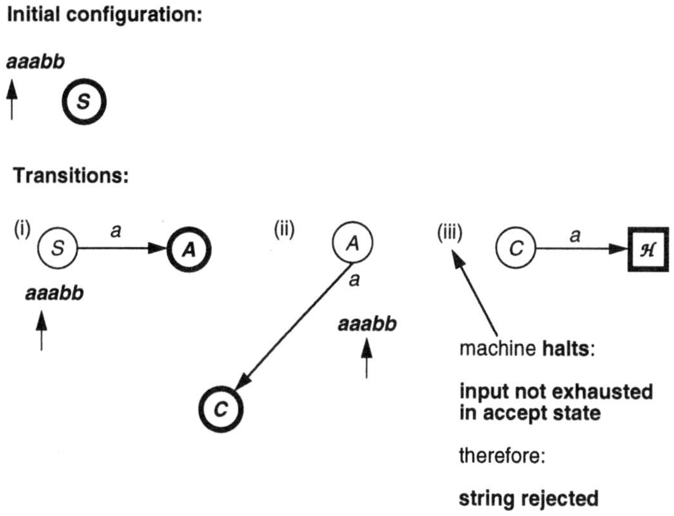

Figure 4.6 An FSR rejects an input string

As in Example 2 (Figure 4.5), you can see that no sequence of transitions can be found that would result in the input string in Figure 4.6 being accepted by M_5.

The final combination of halting conditions (*input exhausted, not in accept state*) can be achieved for the string *aaba*, which we saw being accepted above (Example 1). We see a sequence of transitions which will achieve these rejection conditions for the same string later. For the moment, you may wish to discover such a sequence for yourself.

4.3.3 The FSR as equivalent to the regular grammar

Let us remind ourselves why we created the machine in the first place. Recall the earlier statement about the machine being *equivalent* to the original grammar. What this ought to mean is that all strings accepted by the machine are in the language generated by the grammar (and vice versa). The problem is that, according to the particular transition chosen in the application of Rule 2 (Table 4.3.), the machine can sometimes *reject* a string which (like *aaba* in Example 1, above) *is* generated by the grammar. We need to be able to say something like: 'all strings that *can* be accepted by the machine are in the language generated by the grammar, and all strings that are generated by the grammar *can* be accepted by the machine'. That is exactly what we do next.

First we say this:

a string is **acceptable** if there is some sequence of transitions which lead to that string being **accepted**

Thus, *aaba*, from Example 1, is *acceptable*, even though we could provide an alternative sequence of transitions which would lead to the string being *rejected.* On the other hand, the strings from Examples 2 and 3 are not acceptable, and also cannot be generated by the grammar. You may wish to convince yourself that the preceding statement is true.

Suppose that G_z is any regular grammar, and we call the finite state recognizer derived from G_z's productions M_z, we can say that the set of acceptable strings of M_z is exactly the same as $L(G_z)$, the language generated by the grammar G_z. The rules we followed to produce M_z from G_z ensure that this is the case, but to convince ourselves, let us argue the case thoroughly.

To prove that two sets (in this case, the set of acceptable strings of M_z, and $L(G_z)$) are equal, we have to show that all members of one set are members of the other, and vice versa. If we carry out the first part only, we are merely showing that the first set is a **subset** of the second. We need to show that each set is a subset of the other. Only then can we be sure that the two sets are equal.

In the following, L_z is an abbreviation for $L(G_z)$,

Part 1: All strings in L_z are acceptable to M_z

Let x be any sentence of L_z, such that $|x| = n$, where $n \geq 1$, i.e. x is a non-empty string of **length** n. We can index the symbols of x, as discussed in chapter 2, and we write it $x_1, x_2, \ldots, x_n$. We show that a derivation tree for x directly represents a part of the machine M_z. A derivation tree for x is of the form shown in Figure 4.7.

The derivation tree in Figure 4.7 can be transformed, by the application of an obvious set of rules, to the diagram shown in Figure 4.8.

We can do this because each part of the derivation tree like this:

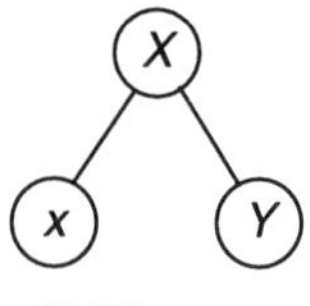

used a production of the form $X \rightarrow xY$. The expansion of the lowest non terminal node in the tree will look like this:

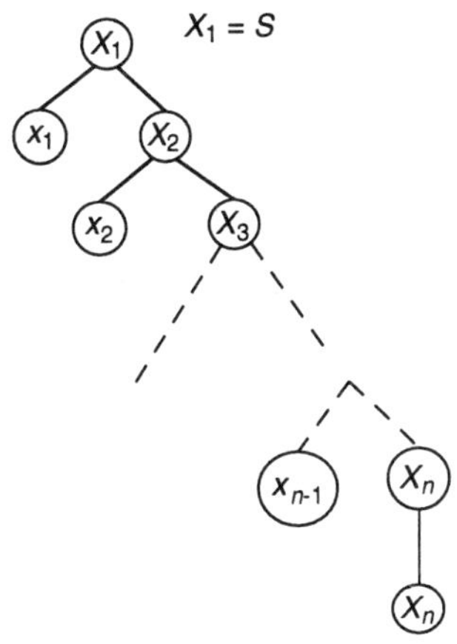

Figure 4.7 An abstract representation of a derivation tree

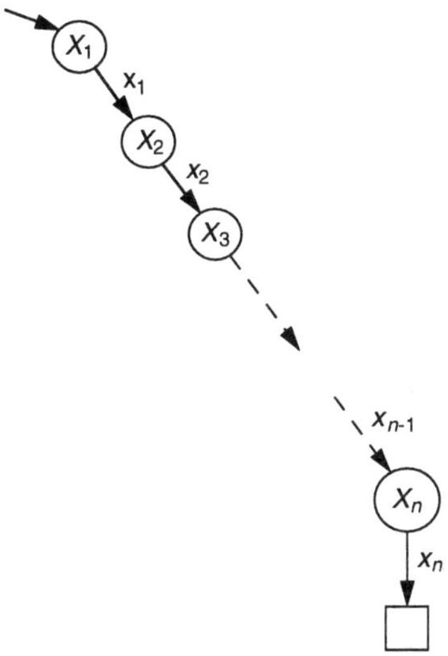

Figure 4.8 Conversion of the tree in Figure 4.7 into an FSR

which used a production of the form $X \rightarrow x$ (single **non terminal** to single **terminal**). The sequence of productions used in Figure 4.7 become, if the conversion algorithm is applied, the FSR of Figure 4.8, since $X_1 = S$ (the **start symbol** of the grammar), and a production of the form $X \rightarrow x$ becomes an arc:

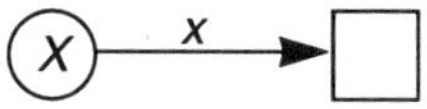

Some of the non terminals may, of course, appear more than once in the derivation tree, and may have to be joined together (as specified in part (b) of Table 4.1). For any sentence, x, of the language there will thus be a path in the FSR which will accept that sentence – x is an acceptable string to M_Z.

Part 2: All acceptable strings of M_z are in L_z

Let x be any acceptable string of M_z. Choose any path through M_z which accepts x. We can write out this path so that it is has no loops in it (as in Figure 4.8). We then convert this version into a tree using the converse of the rules applied to the derivation tree in Figure 4.7. You can easily justify that the resulting tree will be a derivation tree for x which uses only productions of G_z. Thus, any acceptable string of M_z can be generated by G_z and is thus in L_z.

We have shown (Part 1) that every string generated by G_z is acceptable to M_z, and (Part 2) that every string acceptable to M_z is generated by G_z. We have thus established the equivalence of M_z and G_z.

4.4 NON DETERMINISM IN FINITE STATE RECOGNIZERS

As was pointed out above, Rule 2 of the rules governing the behaviour of an FSR (see Table 4.3) implies that there may be a choice of transitions to make when the machine is in a given state, with a given current input symbol. As we saw in the case of Example 1, a wrong choice of transition in a given state may result in an *acceptable string being rejected*. It is not Rule 2 itself which is at fault, it is the type of machine that we may produce from a given set of productions. We will now state this more formally.

- If a finite state recognizer/generator contains any state with two or more identically labelled outgoing arcs, we call it a **non deterministic finite state recognizer**.
- If a finite state recognizer/generator contains no states with two or more identically labelled outgoing arcs, we call it a **deterministic finite state recognizer**.

It should be clear from this that M_5, our example machine, is non deterministic.

If a machine is deterministic, then in the process of accepting or rejecting a string, it *never has to make a choice as to which transition to take, for a given current input symbol, when in a given state: there is only one possible transition which can be made at that point*. This considerably simplifies the processes of **parsing**, as we shall see in the next section. Incidentally, we can still use the same rules for FSR behaviour as those above, for deterministic FSRs: the 'choice' of transitions will at each point consist of only one option.

In following our rules to produce an FSR from the productions of a regular grammar, we may create a non deterministic machine. Remember our machine M_5 (see Figure 4.3), and in particular our discussion about input string *aaba*. If the wrong sequence of transitions is chosen, for example

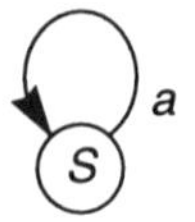

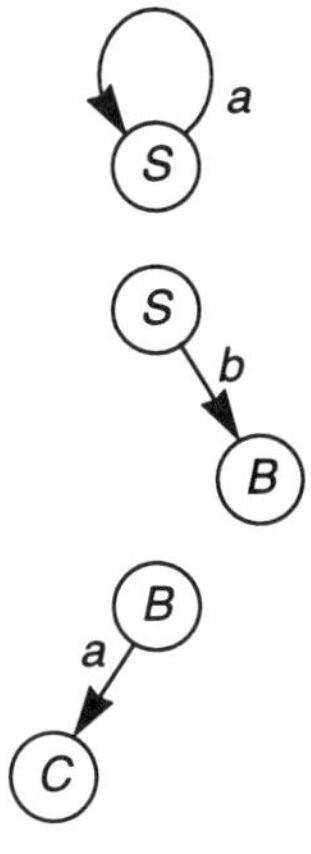

the machine's halting conditions are known as 'input exhausted, not in halt state', indicating a rejection of what we know to be an acceptable string. This implies that a parser which behaves similarly to a non deterministic FSR might have to try many sequences of applicable transitions to establish whether or not a string was acceptable. Worse than this, for a non acceptable string, the parser might have to try all possible sequences of applicable transitions of length equal to the length of the string before being sure that the string could indeed be rejected.

The main problem associated with non determinism, therefore, is that it may result in parsers that have to **backtrack**. Backtracking means returning to a state of affairs (for FSRs this means to a given *state* and *input symbol*) at which a choice between applicable transitions was made, in order to try an alternative. Backtracking is undesirable (and as we shall see, for regular languages it is also *unnecessary*), since

- a backtracking parser would have to save arbitrarily long input strings in case it made the wrong choice at any of the choice points (as it may have made several transitions since the choice point), and
- backtracking uses up a lot of time.

If an FSR is deterministic there is, in any given state, only one choice of transition for any particular input symbol, which means that a corresponding parser *never* has to backtrack.

4.4.1 Constructing deterministic FSRs

It may surprise you to learn that for every set of regular productions we can produce an equivalent *deterministic* FSR. As we will see, we can then use that FSR to produce a simple, but efficient, deterministic *parsing program* for the language. First, we consider a procedure to convert any non deterministic FSR into an equivalent deterministic FSR. We will call the old machine M and the new deterministic machine M^d.

Table 4.6 presents the procedure, which is called the **subset construction algorithm**. Our machine M_5 will be used to illustrate the steps of the procedure. Table 4.6, followed by Figures 4.9–4.14 show how the new machine $M_5{}^d$ is built up.

Table 4.6 The subset construction algorithm

1. (a) Copy out all of the start states of *M*.
   [Note: if *M* were derived from productions, it would have only one start state: we include this step for generality]

   (b) If any of M's states that you just copied out is a halt state, put a square (or rectangle) around all the states you just drew, else put a circle (ellipse) around them

   (c) Draw an unlabelled arrow pointing to the edge of the shape you drew in (b)

   [For M_5:

   ]

2. choose any state of M^d with no outgoing arcs

   for each state, *q*, of *M* inside the chosen state of M^d do
       for each terminal, *t*, in the alphabet of *M* do
           (a) copy out each state of *M* which has an entering arc labelled *t* leaving *q*
           (NOTE: only copy out any given state once)
       endfor
   endfor;

   (b) if you just copied out NO states, draw an empty circle else do step 1(b)

   (c) if the state of M^d you've just drawn contains exactly the same states of M as an existing state of M^d, rub out the state of M^d you've just drawn

   (d) Draw an arc labelled t from the chosen state of M^d to either
   (i) the shape you just drew at (b)
   or (ii) the state of M^d which was the same as the one you rubbed out

   [The first time we do the above step on M_5 we get $M_5{}^d$ =

   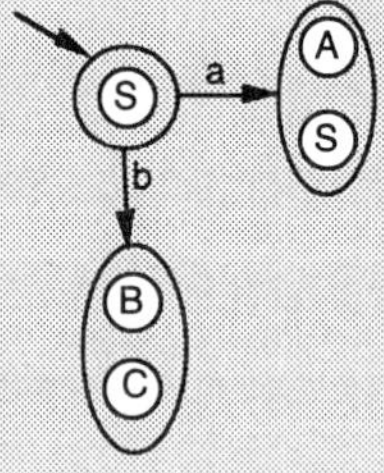

   ]

3. Repeat step two until every state of M^d has exactly one outgoing arc for each terminal in *M*'s alphabet

Continuing the execution of step 2, we will choose the state of $M_5{}^d$ with A and S in it. This results in the partial machine shown in Figure 4.9.

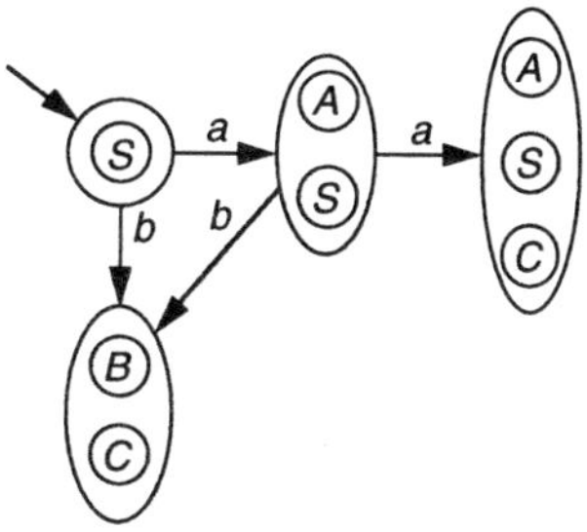

Figure 4.9 Subset algorithm in action (1)

We still have states of $M_5{}^d$ with no outgoing arcs in Figure 4.9, so we choose one (in this case, the one with B and C inside it). The result is shown in Figure 4.10.

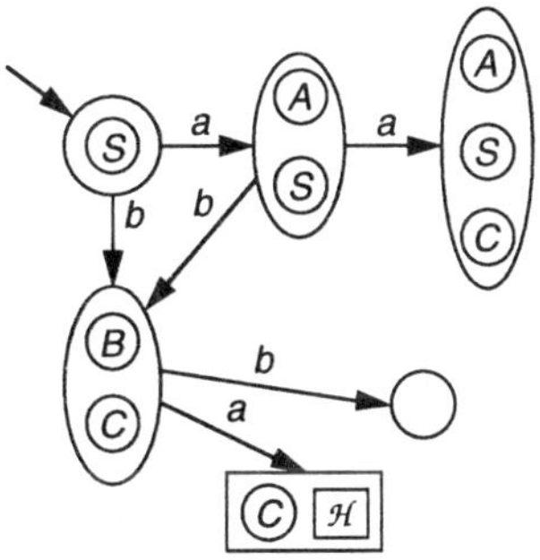

Figure 4.10 Subset algorithm in action (2)

Now from Figure 4.10 we choose the state containing A, S and C, resulting in Figure 4.11.

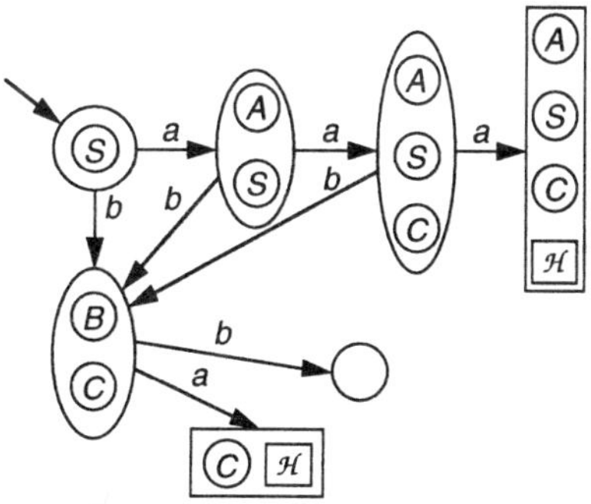

Figure 4.11 Subset algorithm in action (3)

From Figure 4.11, we choose the state that contains A, S, C and $\mathcal{H}$. The result can be seen in Figure 4.12.

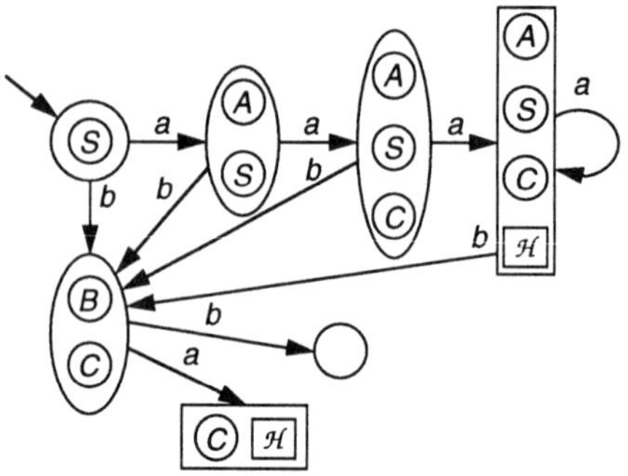

Figure 4.12 Subset algorithm in action (4)

Then we choose the state in Figure 4.12 containing only C and $\mathcal{H}$. Figure 4.13 shows the outcome.

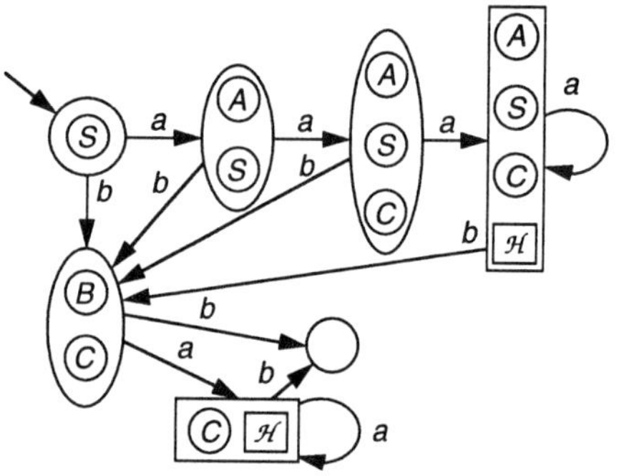

Figure 4.13 Subset algorithm in action (5)

Finally, from Figure 4.13 we choose the empty state of $M_5{}^d$. This state represents unrecognized input in certain states of M_5. Thus, if $M_5{}^d$ finds itself in this state it is reading a string not in the language. To make $M_5{}^d$ totally deterministic, we need to cater for the remainder (if any) of the string that caused $M_5{}^d$ to reach this **'null' state**. Thus we draw an arc, for each terminal in M's alphabet, leaving and immediately re-entering the null state. The final machine is as shown in Figure 4.14.

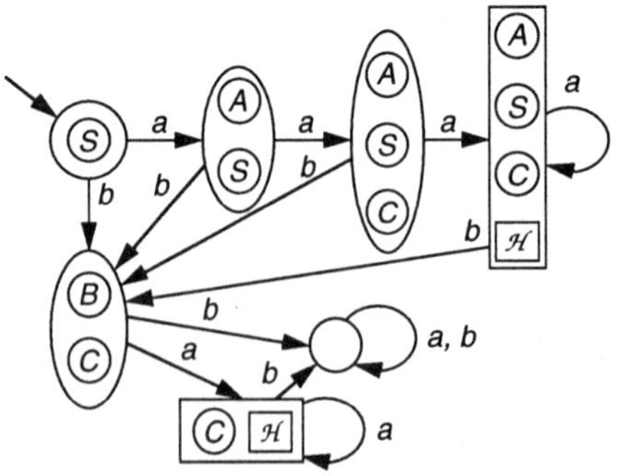

Figure 4.14 The result of the subset algorithm

If the machine ever finds itself in the null state, it will never leave it, but will continue to process the input string until the input is exhausted. It will not accept such a string, however, since *the null state is not a halt state.*

The subset algorithm now terminates (see step 3 of Table 4.6), leaving us with a totally deterministic machine, $M_5{}^d$ (shown in Figure 4.14) which is equivalent to M_5 (Figure 4.3).

We can now tidy up $M_5{}^d$ by renaming its states so that the names consist of single symbols, resulting in the machine we see in Figure 4.15.

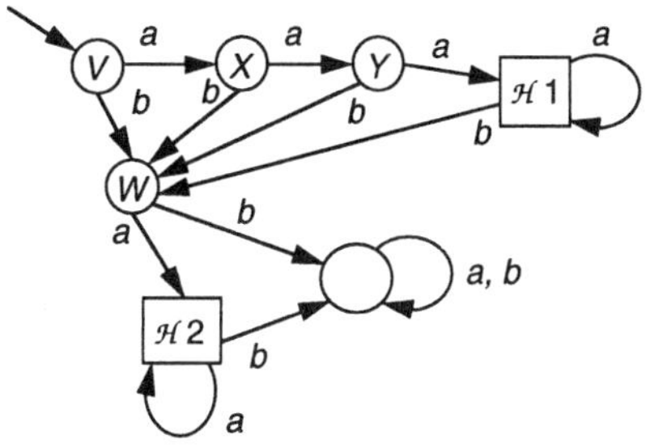

Figure 4.15 The FSR of Figure 4.14 with renamed states $M_5{}^d$

This renaming of states illustrates that the names of states in an FSR are insignificant (as long as each label is distinct). What is important in this case is that there is a one-to-one association between the states and arcs of the old $M_5{}^d$ and the states and arcs of the one with the renamed states.

The null state and its **ingoing** and **outgoing arcs** are sometimes removed from the deterministic machine, their presence being assumed. Later, we will see that the null state in the deterministic FSR has its uses.

4.4.2 The deterministic FSR as equivalent to the non deterministic FSR

We will now convince ourselves that M_5 and $M_5{}^d$ are equivalent. From $M_5{}^d$, we observe the following properties of acceptable strings:

- if they consist of *a*s alone, then they consist of three or more *a*s
- they can consist of any number (≥ 0) of *a*s, followed by exactly one *b*, followed by one or more *a*s.

This can be described in set form:

$$\{a^n : n \geq 3\} \cup \{a^n b a^m : n \geq 0, m \geq 1\}$$

You can verify for yourself that all strings accepted by the original machine (M_5) are also described by one of the above statements.

If we establish that for any non deterministic FSR, M we can produce an equivalent deterministic machine, M^d, we will, for the remainder of our discussion about regular languages, *be able to assume that any FSR we discuss is deterministic.* This is extremely useful, as we will see.

Suppose that M is any FSR, and that M^d is the machine produced when we applied our subset method to M. We will establish two things: (1) every string which is *acceptable* to M is *accepted* by M^d; (2) every string which is *accepted* by M^d is *acceptable* to M.[1]

Part 1: Every acceptable string of M is accepted by M^d.

Let x be an acceptable string of M. Suppose x has **length** n, where $n \geq 1$. We can index the symbols in x, as discussed in Chapter 2: $x_1, x_2.. x_n$. x is acceptable to M, so there is a path through M, from a start state, S, to a halt state, $\mathcal{H}$, as represented in Figure 4.16.

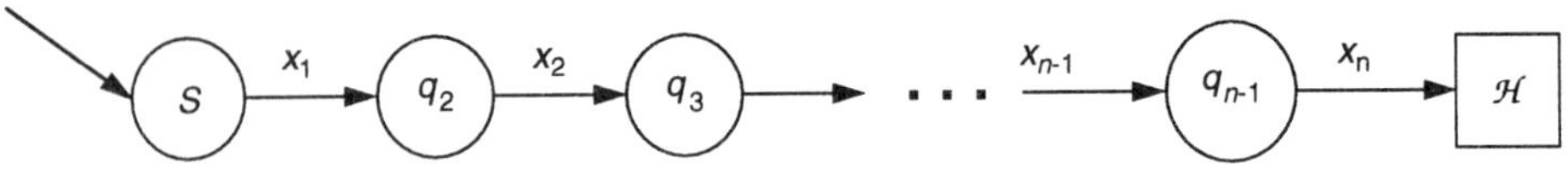

Figure 4.16 How a string is accepted by an FSR

The states on the path in Figure 4.16 are not necessarily all distinct. Also, if $n = 1$, the path looks like this:

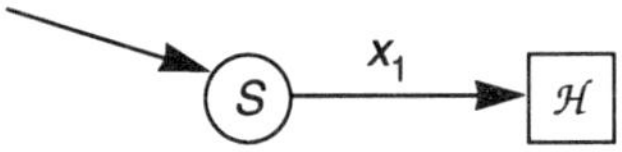

With respect to the above path through M, M^d will be as represented in Figure 4.17.

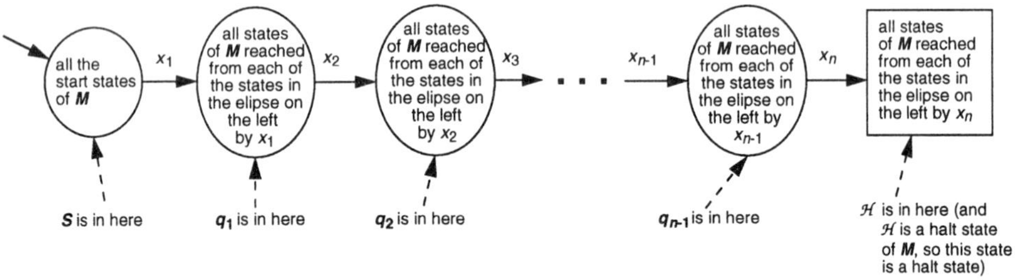

Figure 4.17 How a deterministic FSR accepts the string of Figure 4.16

The string x, which was acceptable to M, is thus accepted by M^d. The above representation of the path taken by the string x through M^d may also incorporate any paths for the same string which result in the situations:

- input exhausted, not in halt state (the non halt state of M reached will be incorporated into the halt state of M^d),

[1] Note that this is not the only way of doing this: we could show (1) and then for (2) show that every string that is non-acceptable to M is rejected by M^d. You might like to try this approach.

- input not exhausted, in halt state (other states of M^d on the path in Figure 4.17 may be halt states),

and

- input not exhausted, not in halt state (M would have stopped in one of the states contained in the non halt states of Figure 4.17, but M^d will be able to proceed to the rightmost state with the remainder of the string).

Part 2: Every string accepted by M^d is acceptable to M.

If a string, x, is accepted by M^d, the way the machine was constructed ensures that there is only one path through M^d for that string, as represented in Figure 4.17, if, again, we index the symbols of x as $x_1, x_2 .. x_n$. There obviously exist one or more paths in M which will accept the string x. I leave it to you to convince yourself of this.

We have seen (Part 1) that every string accepted by M, the non deterministic FSR, is accepted by M^d, the deterministic version of M. Moreover, we have seen (Part 2) that every string accepted by M^d is acceptable to M. M and its deterministic counterpart, M^d, are equivalent FSRs.

4.5 A SIMPLE DETERMINISTIC DECISION PROGRAM

The FSR is not only a more convenient representation of the productions of a regular grammar in some respects, but, if deterministic, also represents a simple **parsing** program for the corresponding language. It is straightforward to convert a deterministic FSR into an equivalent decision program. Here, we will produce a 'pseudo-Pascal' version. A similar program was presented in Chapter 2; you may like to examine it again.

Figure 4.18 illustrates the conversion of a deterministic FSR into a parsing program by associating parts of our deterministic machine $M_5{}^d$ with modules of the program. The example should be sufficient to enable you to infer the rules being used in the conversion.

Note that the use of quoted characters 'a' and 'b' in the program in Figure 4.18 is not meant to suggest that data types such as Pascal's 'char' are generally suitable to represent terminal symbols. (A related discussion can be found in the *Solutions to selected exercises* section in the comments on Exercise 3 of this chapter.)

You should appreciate the importance of the null state to the construction of our parser: without it, our program may have had no defined action in one or more of the 'case' statements. Whether or not the program continues to process the input string when it reaches the **null state** (the code segment labelled *NLL*), as does our program in Figure 4.18, is a matter of preference. One may require, in certain circumstances, for the program to abort immediately (with a suitable message), as soon as this

```
begin
V: read(x);
 case x of
  eos: goto NO;
  'a': goto X;
  'b': goto W
 endcase;
X: read(x);
 case x of
  eos: goto NO;
  'a': goto Y;
  'b': goto W
 endcase;
Y: read(x);
 case x of
  eos: goto NO;
  'a': goto H1;
  'b': goto W
 endcase;
W: read(x);
 case x of
  eos: goto NO;
  'a': goto H2;
  'b': goto NLL
 endcase;
H1: read(x);
 case x of
  eos: goto YES;
  'a': goto H1;
  'b': goto W
 endcase;
H2: read(x);
 case x of
  eos: goto YES;
  'a': goto H2;
  'b': goto NLL
 endcase;
YES: write('string accepted');
 goto exit;
NO: write('string rejected');
 goto exit;
NLL: read(x);
 case x of
  eos: goto NO;
  'a': goto NLL;
  'b': goto NLL
 endcase
end.
```

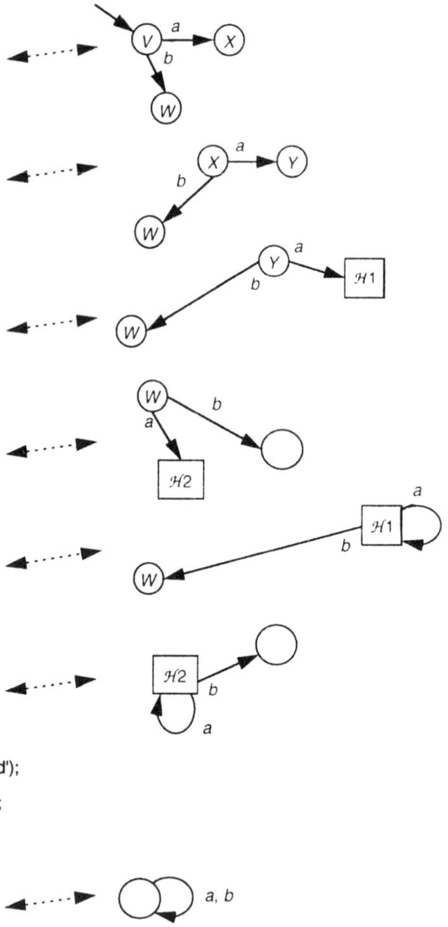

Figure 4.18 The correspondence between a DFSR and a decision program

segment is entered, not bothering with the rest (as do some compilers). On the other hand, it may be desirable to clear the input stream of the remainder of the symbols of the rejected string.

4.6 MINIMAL FSRs

Each boxed segment of the program in Figure 4.18 represents one **state** in the corresponding FSR, $M_5{}^d$. In general, if we were to build such a parser for a regular language, we would like to know that our parser did not feature an unnecessarily large number of such segments.

The above program is structured, notwithstanding misgivings often expressed about the use of unconditional jumps. If an equally structured program consisting of fewer such segments, but doing the same job could be derived, then we would prefer, for obvious and sound reasons, to use that one. In terms of a given FSR, the question is this: can we find an equivalent machine which features fewer states? We will go beyond this however: we will discover a method for producing a machine, from a given FSR, which is deterministic and uses *the smallest number of states necessary for a deterministic FSR to recognize the same language as that recognized by the original machine*. We call such a machine the **minimal FSR**.

If we produce such a minimal FSR, we can be confident that the corresponding parsing program uses the smallest number of segments possible to perform the parsing task. Of course, there may be other methods for reducing the amount of code, but these are not of interest here.

4.6.1 Constructing a minimal FSR

To demonstrate our method for producing minimal FSRs, we will use an FSR derived from a new example grammar, G_6, with productions:

$S \rightarrow aA \mid bB$
$A \rightarrow aA \mid bB \mid bD$
$B \rightarrow bC \mid bB \mid bD$
$C \rightarrow cC \mid c$
$D \rightarrow bC \mid bD$

From G_6, we derive the non-deterministic FSR, M_6, which is shown in Figure 4.19.

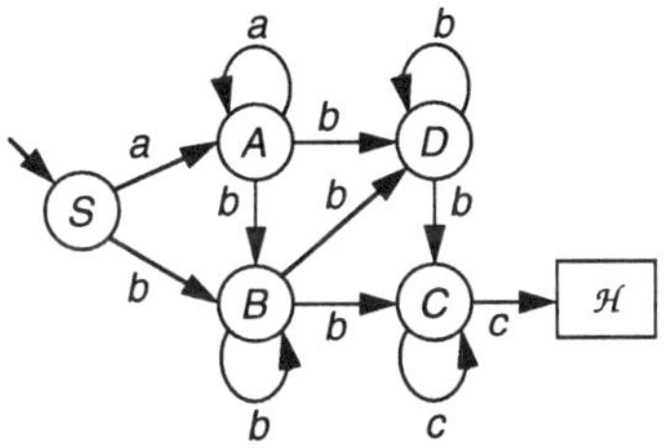

Figure 4.19 The non deterministic FSR, M_6

We practise our **subset algorithm** on the machine in Figure 4.19, to obtain the machine in Figure 4.20(a). For convenience, we rename the states of this deterministic machine to give us the machine in Figure 4.20(b), and which we call $M_6{}^d$.

The *null state* is irrelevant in this section, and has been omitted from our deterministic machines.

Suppose we wished to produce a parsing program for $M_6{}^d$, as we did for $M_5{}^d$ in the previous section. Our program would have seven segments of the type discussed

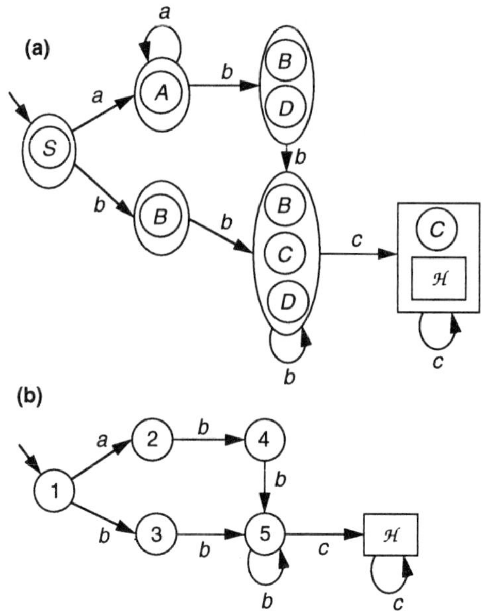

Figure 4.20 (a) The output of the subset algorithm for input M_6; (b) the machine in (a) with renamed states, $M_6{}^d$

earlier, as our machine $M_6{}^d$ has seven states including the null state. We will shortly see that we can produce an equivalent machine which has only five states, but first, we present, in Table 4.7, a simple procedure for creating the 'reverse' machine, which will be used in our minimization method.

Table 4.7 'Reversing' an FSR

(i) M_{rev} is initially an exact copy of M

(ii) modify states and arcs in M_{rev} according to the following rules:

(a) states of the form  in M become states of the form  in M_{rev}

(b) states of the form  in M become states of the form 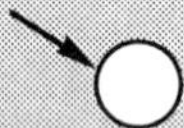 in M_{rev}

(c) arcs of the form 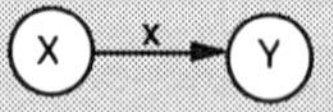 in M become arcs of the form 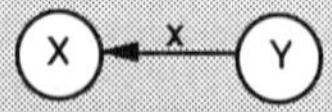 in M_{rev}

Note: all other parts of M_{rev} remain unaltered.

If L is the language recognized by M, then the language L_{rev} recognized by M_{rev} is L with each and every sentence reversed.

Table 4.8 Minimizing an FSR, M.

(1) reverse M
(2) make the result of (1) deterministic (using the subset method)
(3) reverse the result of (2)
(4) make the result of (3) deterministic (using the subset method)

The result of (4), called M_{min}, is the minimal finite state recognizer for the language recognized by M.

Table 4.8 specifies an algorithm that uses our reverse (Table 4.7) and subset (Table 4.6) procedures to produce a minimal machine, M_{min}, from a deterministic FSR, M.

We can demonstrate the operation of the above method on our example machine $M_6{}^d$ from above (we use the one with the renamed states):

Step 1: Reverse $M_6{}^d$ (Figure 4.20(b)), giving the machine shown in Figure 4.21.

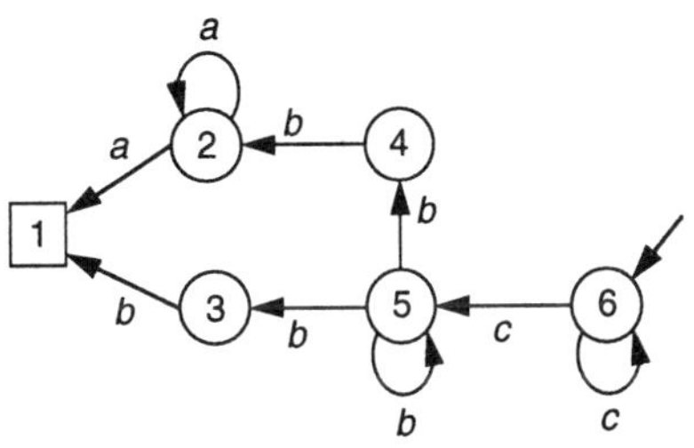

Figure 4.21 $M_6{}^d$ of Figure 4.20 reversed

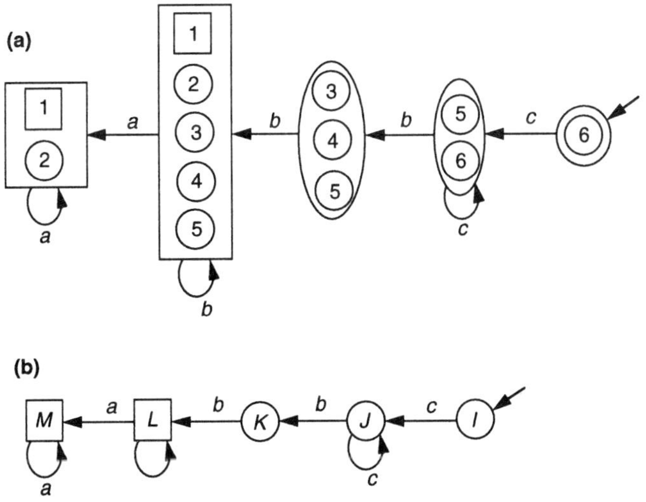

Figure 4.22 (a) The deterministic version of Figure 4.21; (b) The machine (a) with renamed states

Step 2: Make the result of step 1 (Figure 4.21) deterministic. The result of step 2, after renaming the states, can be seen in Figure 4.22(b).

Step 3: Reverse the result of step 2. The reversed version of Figure 4.22(b) can be seen in Figure 4.23.

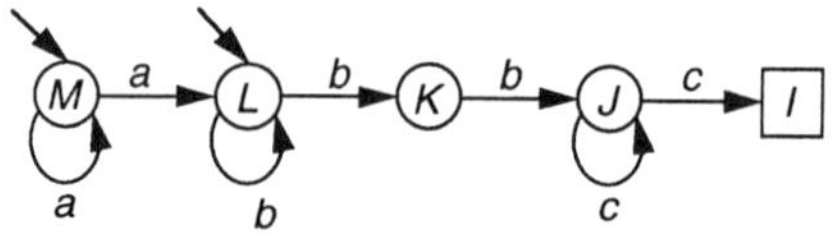

Figure 4.23 The reverse of Figure 4.22(b)

Note that the machine in Figure 4.23 has two **start states**; this is permitted in our rules for FSR behaviour, and in rule 1 of the subset algorithm. However, this represents a *non deterministic* situation, since *such a machine effectively has a choice as to which state it starts in.*

Step 4: Make the result of step 3 (Figure 4.23) deterministic. We obtain the machine depicted in Figure 4.24(a).

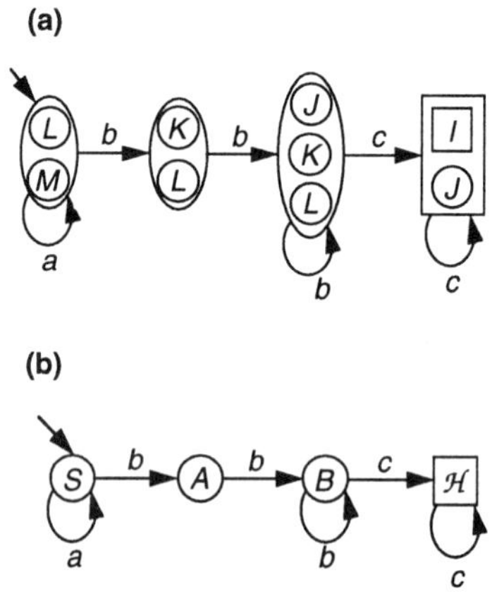

Figure 4.24 (a) Deterministic version of Figure 4.23;
(b) with renamed states giving the minimal FSR for M_6, M_{6min}

The machine in Figure 4.24(b), resulting from renaming the states of the machine in Figure 4.24(a), has been called M_{6min}. It is *the minimal deterministic FSR for the language recognized by* M_6^d.

We now see clearly that the language recognized by M_{6min} (and, of course, M_6 and M_6^d), is:

$\{a^i b^j c^k \mid i \geq 0, j \geq 2, k \geq 1\}$,

i.e. all sentences are of the form:

zero or more *a*s, followed by two or more *b*s, followed by one or more *c*s.

With a little thought, we can easily justify that the machine is minimal. We must have one state for the 'zero or more as' part, a further two states for the 'two or more bs' part, and an extra state to ensure the 'one or more *c*s' part.

4.6.2 How minimization works

The minimization algorithm of Table 4.8 simply uses the *subset algorithm* twice, first applying it to the *reversed form* of the original machine, and then to the *reversed form* of the *deterministic reversed form*. Let us consider why this approach produces the correct result. To do this, we focus on the example FSR in Figure 4.25.

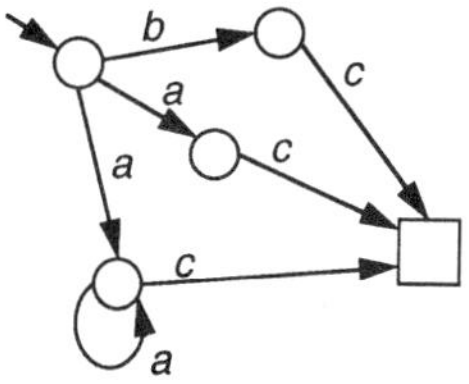

Figure 4.25 An FSR that is also non deterministic when in reverse

Making the machine in Figure 4.25 deterministic, by using our subset algorithm, we merge the two paths labelled *a* into one. We then obtain the machine in Figure 4.26.

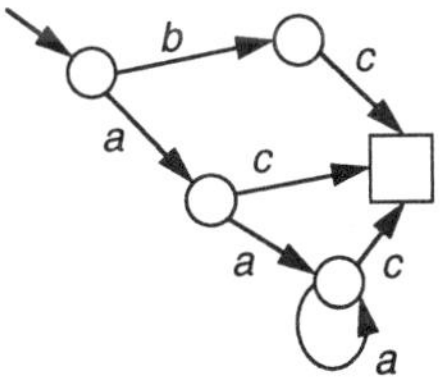

Figure 4.26 Subset method applied to Figure 4.25

Now, while the machine in Figure 4.26 is deterministic, it is *not* minimal. It seems that we ought to be able to do something about the fact that regardless of whether the first symbol is an *a* or a *b*, the machine could get to its halt state given one *c*. However, as this is not a non deterministic situation, the subset algorithm has ignored it.

Now, reversing the machine in Figure 4.26 gives us the machine in Figure 4.27.

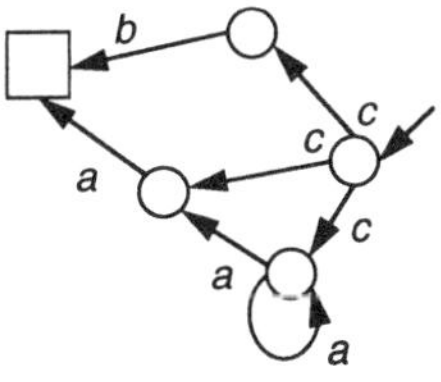

Figure 4.27 Reverse of Figure 4.26

The 'three *c*s situation' has become non deterministic in Figure 4.27. The subset algorithm will now deal with this, resulting in the machine of Figure 4.28.

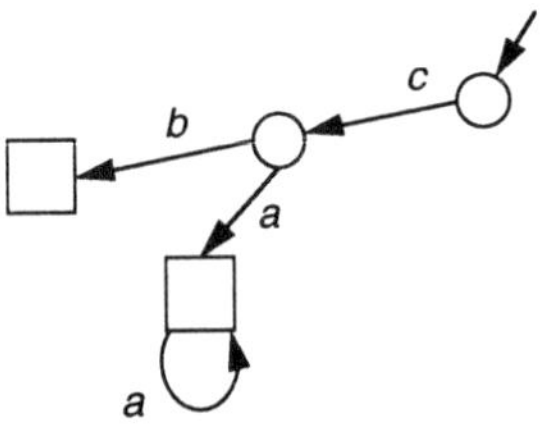

Figure 4.28 Deterministic version of Figure 4.27

While the machine in Figure 4.28 now consists of only *four* states, and is deterministic, it unfortunately recognizes our original language *in reverse*, so we must reverse it again, giving Figure 4.29.

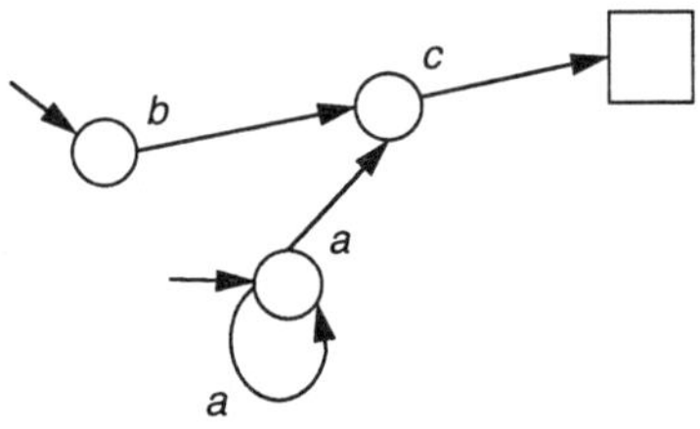

Figure 4.29 The reverse of Figure 4.28

The Figure 4.29 machine now recognizes our original language, but is *non deterministic* (it has *two* start states and *a state with two outgoing arcs labelled a*). So, we make it deterministic again, giving the machine of Figure 4.30.

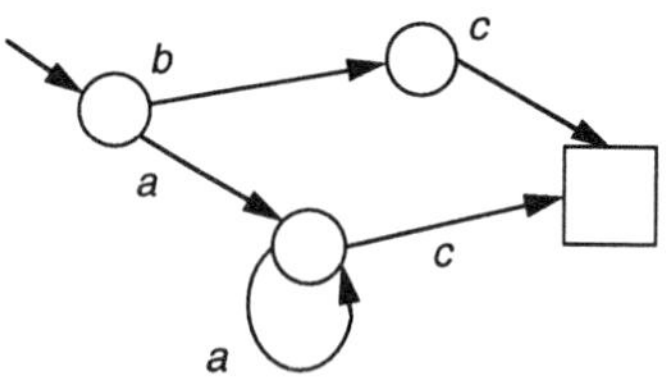

Figure 4.30 Deterministic and minimal version of Figure 4.29

The machine in Figure 4.30 is the *minimal (deterministic) machine.*

The algorithm thus removes non determinism 'in both directions' through the machine. Reversing a machine creates a machine that recognizes the original language with each and every string reversed, and the subset algorithm always results in a machine that accepts exactly the same strings as the machine to which it is applied. Thus, making the reversed machine deterministic and then reversing the result will not change the language recognized by the machine.

There are other ways of creating a minimal FSR. One of the most popular is based on *equivalence sets*. The beauty of the method we use here is that it is very simple to specify, and makes use of a method we defined earlier, i.e. the subset algorithm. Thus, the minimization method we have used here has a pleasing modularity. It uses the *subset* and *reverse* methods as *subroutines*, so to speak.

4.7 THE GENERAL EQUIVALENCE OF REGULAR LANGUAGES AND FSRs

We saw above that any regular grammar can be converted into an equivalent FSR. In fact, the converse is also true, i.e.,

every FSR can be converted into a regular grammar.

We will consider an example showing the conversion of an FSR into regular productions. The interesting thing about our example is that the particular machine in question has transitions labelled ε. These are called **empty moves** or **ε-moves**, and enable an FSR to make a transition without **reading** its input. As we will see, they produce slightly different **productions** from the ones we have seen up to now. We consider this observation in more detail after working through the following example, which is based on the machine M shown in Figure 4.31.

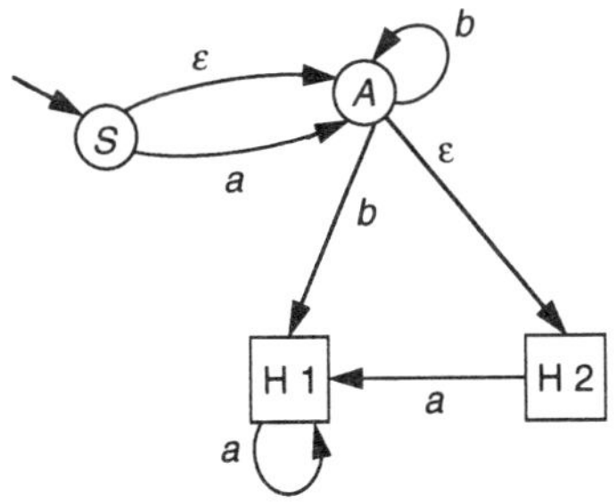

Figure 4.31 An FSR, *M*, with 'empty moves'

The grammar that we obtain from M, in Figure 4.31, which we will call G_m, is as follows:

$S \to aA \mid A$
$A \to bA \mid bX \mid Y$
$X \to aX \mid \varepsilon$
$Y \to aX \mid \varepsilon$

Some issues are raised by this construction:

- M can get to its halt state $H1$ without reading any input. Thus, ε is in the language accepted by M. As we would therefore expect, G_m generates ε ($S \Rightarrow A \Rightarrow Y \Rightarrow \varepsilon$). The empty move from S to A becomes a production $S \rightarrow A$. Productions of the form $x \rightarrow y$ where x and y are both non terminals are called **unit productions**, and are actually prohibited by the definition of regular grammar productions with which we began this chapter. However, we see in Chapter 5 that there is a method for removing these productions, leaving a grammar that *does* conform to our specification of regular grammar productions, and generates the same language as the original.
- M has arcs *leaving* halt states, and *has more than one halt state*. We saw above that the subset algorithm produces machines with these characteristics. In any case, there is nothing in the definition of the FSR that precludes multiple halt *or* start states. Where there is an arc leaving a halt state, such as the arc labelled a leaving $H2$, the machine could either halt or read an a. Halting in such a situation is exactly the same as an empty move, so in the grammar the $H2$ situation becomes $Y \rightarrow aX \mid \varepsilon$, where Y represents $H2$, and X represents $H1$.

I leave it to you to convince yourself that $L(G_m)$ is identical to the language accepted by M, and that the way the productions of G_m were obtained from M could be applied to any FSR, no matter how complex, and no matter how many empty moves it has. In the above machine, the start state was conveniently labelled S. We can always label the states of an FSR how we please; a point made earlier in this chapter. The only other potential problem that arises is for FSRs with more than one start state: in this case we can simply introduce a new *single* start state, with outgoing arcs labelled ε leaving it and directly entering each state that was a start state of the original machine (which we then no longer class as start states). Then the machine can be converted into productions, as was M, above.

The above should convince you that the following statement is true.

> for any FSR M, there exists a regular grammar, G, which is such that $L(G)$, the language generated by G, is equal to the set of strings accepted by M.

Our earlier result that for every regular grammar there is an **equivalent** FSR means that if we come across a language that *cannot* be accepted by an FSR, we know that we are wasting our time trying to create a regular grammar to generate that language. As we will see in Chapter 6, there are properties of the FSR that we can exploit to establish that certain languages could not be accepted by the FSR. We now know that if we do this, we have also established that we could not define a regular grammar to generate that language. Conversely, if we can establish that there is no regular grammar to generate a given language, we know it is pointless attempting to create an FSR, or a parser of 'FSR-level-power', like the parsing program earlier in the chapter, to accept that language.

4.8 OBSERVATIONS ON REGULAR GRAMMARS AND LANGUAGES

The properties of regular languages described in this chapter make them very useful in a computational sense. We have seen that simple parsers can be written for a language generated by a regular grammar. We have also seen how we can make our parsers extremely efficient, by ensuring that they are deterministic and reduced to the smallest possible form, while reflecting a modular structure. We have also seen that there is a general equivalence between the FSRs and the regular languages.

Unfortunately, the simple structure of regular grammars means that they can only be used to represent simple constructs in programming languages, for example, basic objects such as *identifiers* (variable names) in Pascal programs. In fact, the definition of Pascal 'identifiers' given in **context free** form in Chapter 2 could be represented as a regular grammar. An alternative representation of the regular languages are symbolic statements known as the *regular expressions*. These are not only a purely formal device, but are also implemented in text editors such as the Unix 'vi' editor, and the 'emacs' text editor.

We will defer more detailed discussion of the limitations of regular grammars until Chapter 6. In that chapter we show that even a language as simple as $\{a^ib^i : i \geq 1\}$, generated by the two-production context free grammar $S \rightarrow aSb \mid ab$ (grammar G3 of Chapters 2 and 3) is not regular. If such a language cannot be generated by a regular grammar, then a regular grammar is not likely to be capable of specifying syntactically valid Pascal programs, where, for example, a parser has to ensure that the number of **begins** is the same as the number of **ends**. In fact, when it comes to programming languages, the context free grammars as a whole are much more important[2]. Context free grammars and context free languages are the subject of the next chapter.

EXERCISES

For exercises marked '†', solutions, partial solutions, or hints to get you started appear in *Solutions to selected exercises* at the rear of the book.

1 Construct **FSRs** equivalent to the following grammars. For each FSR briefly justify whether or not the machine is **deterministic**. If the machine is **non deterministic**, convert it into an equivalent deterministic machine.

(a)† $S \rightarrow aA$
$A \rightarrow aS \mid aB$
$B \rightarrow bC$
$C \rightarrow bD$

[2] Bear in mind that the class of the context free grammars **includes** the class of the regular grammars.

$D \rightarrow b \mid bB$

Note: This is the grammar from Chapter 2, Exercise 1 (a)

(b) $S \rightarrow aA \mid aB \mid aC$
$A \rightarrow aA \mid aC \mid bC$
$B \rightarrow aB \mid cC \mid c$
$C \rightarrow cC \mid c$

(c) Grammar G_1 from Chapter 2, i.e.
$S \rightarrow aS \mid bB$
$B \rightarrow bB \mid bC \mid cC$
$C \rightarrow cC \mid c$

2 Given the FSR in Figure 4.32

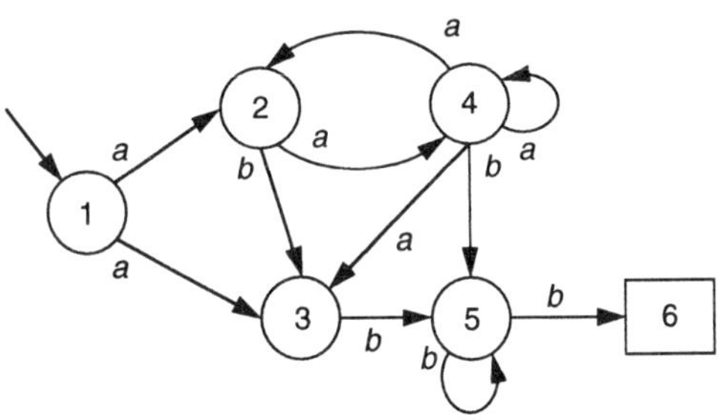

Figure 4.32 An FSR

produce a **minimal** version.
Construct an **equivalent** regular grammar.
Hint: it is often more straightforward to use the original, non deterministic machine (in this case the one above) to obtain the productions of the grammar, i.e., we write down the productions that would have given us the above machine according to our conversion rules.

3 Design suitable data structures to represent FSRs. Design a program to apply operations such as the subset method and the minimization algorithm to FSRs.

4 The **subset algorithm** is so called because each new state of M^d, the deterministic machine, produced contains a subset of the states of M. An algorithm is a procedure that always terminates for valid inputs. Consider why we can be sure that the subset procedure will terminate given any non deterministic machine as its input, and thus deserves to be called an algorithm.

5 Context free languages and pushdown recognizers

AIMS

To consider the context free grammars (CFGs) and context free languages, including learning

- how to remove the empty string (ε) from a CFG
- how to convert a CFG into Chomsky Normal form
- how to create a non deterministic PDR from a CFG
- about deterministic PDRs
- about the deterministic and non deterministic CFLs
- the implications of the fact that not all CFLs are deterministic

5.1 CONTEXT FREE GRAMMARS AND CONTEXT FREE LANGUAGES

Recall from Chapter 2 that the context free grammars (type 2 in the **Chomsky hierarchy**) are **Phrase Structure Grammars (PSGs)** in which each and every production conforms to the following pattern:

$x \rightarrow y,\ x \in N,\ y \in (N \cup T)^*$

i.e. x is a single **non terminal**, and y is an arbitrary (possibly empty) mixture of **terminals** and/or non terminals.

So, the grammar G_2 of Chapter 2, i.e.:

$S \rightarrow aB \mid bA \mid \varepsilon$
$A \rightarrow aS \mid bAA$
$B \rightarrow bS \mid aBB$

is context free. If G is a CFG, then $L(G)$, the **language generated by the grammar** G, is a **context free language (CFL)**. We will consider a further example CFG, G_7:

$S \rightarrow ABC$
$A \rightarrow aAb \mid B$
$B \rightarrow bB \mid \varepsilon$
$C \rightarrow ccC \mid B$

$L(G_7) = \{a^h b^i c^{2j} b^k : h, j, k \geq 0,\ i \geq h\}$

i.e. 0 or more *a*s followed by at least as many *b*s, followed by an *even* number of (or no) *c*s, followed by 0 or more *b*s as you may like to justify for yourself. You may arrive at a different, though equivalent, **set definition**; if so, check that it describes the same set as the one above.

5.2 CHANGING G WITHOUT CHANGING $L(G)$

The purpose of this section is to show how one can modify the productions of a CFG in various ways *without changing the language the CFG generates*. There are more ways of modifying CFGs than are featured here, but the two methods below are relatively simple to apply. The results of this section serve also to simplify various proofs in Chapter 6.

5.2.1 The empty string

Our example grammar G_7, above, features the **empty string** (ε) on the **right hand side** of one of its productions. The empty string often causes problems in **parsing**, as was noted in Chapter 3, and again in the context of **empty moves** in **finite state recognizers (FSRs)**. Ideally, then, for parsing purposes, we would not like the empty string to feature in our grammars. Indeed, you may wonder whether the empty string actually features in any 'real world' situations, or if it is included for mathematical reasons. In string concatenation for example, ε could be regarded as playing a similar role as does 0 in addition, or 1 in multiplication.

However, it is quite common to find the empty string in the definition of programming languages. Pascal, for example, allows a <statement> to be *empty*, and such 'empty' statements have their practical uses. For example, the programmer may leave empty 'actions' in a 'case' statement, or an empty 'else' part of an 'if' statement, so that additional code can be entered later. Note, however, that the empty string is not a sentence of the Pascal language. The Pascal syntax does not allow for an empty <program>, and thus, according to the definition of the language, an empty source code file should not compile.

It turns out, however, that for CFGs we can deal with the empty string in one of two ways. Firstly, for any PSG, G, we can, by applying the rules we are about to see, remove it altogether from the productions, except for one special case which we discuss later. We will need the terminology defined in Table 5.1 to discuss the empty string in CFGs.

Table 5.1 Terminology relevant to the empty string in grammars

Term	Definition	Examples from G_7
ε production	any production with ε on the right hand side	$B \rightarrow \varepsilon$
ε generating non terminal	any non terminal, X, which is such that $X \stackrel{*}{\Rightarrow} \varepsilon$ (i.e, any non terminal from which we can generate the empty string)	S, A, B and C since we can have: $S \Rightarrow ABC$ and $A \Rightarrow B \Rightarrow \varepsilon$ and $C \Rightarrow B \Rightarrow \varepsilon$
ε free production	any production which does not have ε on the right hand side	all productions except $B \rightarrow \varepsilon$

The method for removing ε productions from a grammar is described in Table 5.2. On the right of Table 5.2 we see the method applied to our grammar G_7.

You may like to verify for yourself that the new grammar, which in Table 5.2 has been called G_8, generates exactly the same set of strings as the grammar with which we started (G_7).

Table 5.2 How to remove ε from a CFG

Op No	Operation Description	As applied to G_7
1	Put all the ε generating non terminals into a set, call the set X	S, A, B, C – set X
2	Put all the ε free productions into another set, call the set Y	$S \rightarrow ABC$ $A \rightarrow aAb \mid B$ $B \rightarrow bB$ $C \rightarrow ccC \mid B$ – set Y
3	for each production, p, in Y, add to Y any ε free productions we can make by omitting one or more of the non terminals in X from p's right hand side	$S \rightarrow ABC \mid AB \mid AC \mid BC \mid A \mid B \mid C$ $A \rightarrow aAb \mid B$ $B \rightarrow bB \mid b$ $C \rightarrow ccC \mid cc \mid B$ – new set Y (G_8)
(4)	WE ONLY DO THIS IF S IS MEMBER OF SET X:	
	4.1 replace the non terminal S throughout the set Y by a new non terminal, A, which is not in any of the productions of Y	$S \rightarrow Z \mid \varepsilon$ $Z \rightarrow ABC \mid AB \mid AC \mid BC \mid A \mid B \mid C$ $A \rightarrow aAb \mid B$ $B \rightarrow bB \mid b$ $C \rightarrow ccC \mid cc \mid B$ – new set Y
	4.2 put the productions $S \rightarrow A \mid \varepsilon$ into Y	

Referring to Table 5.2, at stage 3, the productions added to the set Y were necessary to deal with cases where one or more non terminals in the original productions could have been used to generate ε. For example, we have the production $S \rightarrow ABC$. Now in G_7, the B could have been used to generate ε, so we need to cater for this by introducing the production $S \rightarrow AC$. Similarly, both the A and the C could have been used to generate ε, so we need a production $S \rightarrow B$, and so on. Of course, we still need to include $S \rightarrow ABC$ itself, because, in general, the ε **generating** non terminals may generate other things apart from ε (as they do in our example).

As for stage 4, it is important to remember that we only do this if ε is in the language generated by the grammar (in formal parlance, if $\varepsilon \in L(G)$). This occurs only when S itself is an ε generating non terminal, as it is in the case of G_7. If S is an ε generating non terminal for a grammar G, then obviously ε is in $L(G)$. Conversely, if S is not such a non terminal, then ε cannot be in the language. If we applied step 4 to a grammar for which ε is not in the corresponding language, the result would be a new grammar that did not generate the same language (it would generate the same set of strings along with ε, formally $L(G) \cup \{\varepsilon\}$).

Alternatively, if we did not apply step 4 to a grammar in which S *is* an ε generating non terminal, then we would produce a grammar which generated all the strings in $L(G)$ except for the string ε (formally $L(G) - \{\varepsilon\}$). We must always take care to preserve exactly the set of strings generated by the original grammar.

If we were to apply the above rules to a *regular* grammar, *the resulting grammar would also be regular*. That is why Chapter 4 explained that dealing with the empty string in regular grammars would be best left to this chapter.

For **parsing**, the grammars produced by the above rules are useful, since at most they contain one ε production, and if they do, it is $S \to \varepsilon$. This means that when we parse a string x:

- if x is non empty, our parser need no longer consider the empty string; it will not feature in any of the productions that could have been used in the derivation of x;
- if, on the other hand, $x = \varepsilon$, either our grammar has the one ε production $S \to \varepsilon$, in which case we accept x, or it has no ε productions, and we simply reject it.

However, while for parsing purposes our amended grammars may be useful, there may be reasons for leaving the empty string in a grammar showing us the structure of, say, a programming language. One of these reasons is readability. As we can see, G_8 consists of many more productions (16) than does the equivalent G_7 (seven), and thus it could be argued that G_7 is easier for us to read. A format for grammars useful for a parser may not necessarily support one of the other purposes of grammars, i.e. to show us the structure of languages.

To complete this section, we consider a further example of the removal of ε productions from a CFG. In this case ε is not in the language generated by the grammar. Only a sketch of the process will be given; you should be able to follow the procedure by referring to the rules in Table 5.2.

The example grammar, G_9, is as follows:

$S \to aCb$
$C \to aSb \mid cC \mid \varepsilon$

In this case, the only ε generating non terminal is C. S cannot generate ε as any string it generates *must* contain at least one a and one b. The new productions we would add are $S \to ab$ and $C \to c$, both resulting from the omission of C. Step 4 should *not* be applied in this case, as S is not ε generating. The final amended productions would be:

$S \to aCb \mid ab$
$C \to aSb \mid cC \mid c.$

A set definition of the language generated by this grammar, which, of course, is exactly the same as $L(G_9)$, is:

$$\{a^{2i+1}c^jb^{2i+1} : i, j \geq 0\}$$

i.e. a non zero *odd* number of *a*s, followed by 0 or more *c*s, followed by the same number of *b*s as there were *a*s.

5.2.2 Chomsky normal form

Once we have removed the empty string (ε) from a context free grammar, isolating it if necessary in one production, $S \rightarrow \varepsilon$, there are various methods for transforming the ε free part of *G* while leaving *L*(*G*) unchanged. One of the most important of these methods results in the productions being in a form we call **Chomsky Normal Form** (CNF). This section briefly describes the method for converting a CFG into CNF by presenting a worked example. That we can assume that *any CFG can be converted into CNF* is useful in Chapter 6.

As an example grammar, we use part of G_8 (the ε free version of G_7), and assume in this case that *Z* is the start symbol:

$Z \rightarrow ABC \mid AB \mid AC \mid BC \mid A \mid B \mid C$
$A \rightarrow aAb \mid B \mid A$
$B \rightarrow bB \mid B \mid b$
$C \rightarrow ccC \mid cc \mid B$

The method to 'Chomskyfy' a grammar is as follows. There are three steps:

Step 1: Unit productions

Unit productions were briefly introduced in Chapter 4. A unit production is a production of the form: $x \rightarrow y$, where *x* and *y* are single non terminals. Thus, G_8 has the following unit productions:

$Z \rightarrow A \mid B \mid C$
$A \rightarrow B$
$C \rightarrow B$

To help us deal with the unit productions of G_8, we draw the structure shown in Figure 5.1, representing all derivations that begin with the application of a unit production and end with a string that does not consist of a single non terminal (each path stops the first time such a string is encountered).

The structure in Figure 5.1 is not a tree, but a **graph**. We can call the structure a **unit production graph**. It could be drawn as a tree if we repeated some nodes at lower levels (in the graph in Figure 5.1 we would repeat *B* beneath *A* and beneath *C*). However, such a representation would not be so useful in the procedure for creating new non unit productions described below.

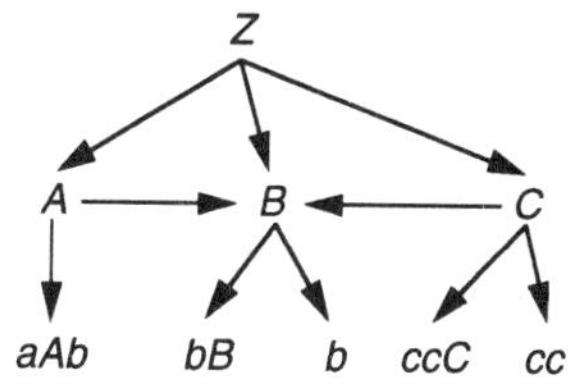

Figure 5.1 A unit production graph

Some unit production graphs we draw may lead to even more circular (known as cyclical) situations, as in the example in Table 5.3.

Table 5.3 Example productions and a corresponding unit production graph

Example productions	Resulting graph
$S \to aS \mid B$ $B \to bS \mid A \mid C$ $A \to a \mid C$ $C \to bA \mid S \mid B$	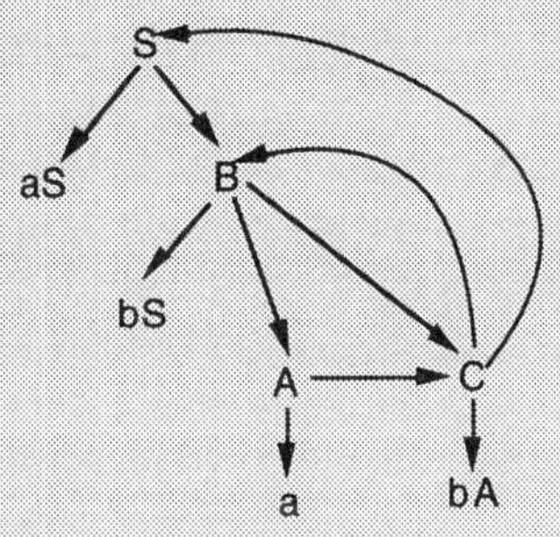

We now continue with our initial example. From the unit production graph for G_8, (Figure 5.1), we obtain:

> every possible non-unit production we can obtain by following a directed path from every non terminal to every node that does not consist of a single non terminal, where each production we make has a left hand side that is the non terminal we started at, and a right hand side that is the string where we stopped.

So, from our unit production graph for G_8 in Figure 5.1, we obtain the following productions (those crossed out are already in G_8, so we need not add them):

$Z \to bB \mid b \mid aAb \mid ccC \mid cc$	{by following all paths from Z}
$A \to$ ~~aAb~~ $\mid bB \mid b$	{by following all paths from A}
$B \to$ ~~bB~~ $\mid b$	{...from B}
$C \to$ ~~ccC~~ $\mid$ ~~cc~~ $\mid bB \mid b$	{...and from C}

We remove all the unit productions from the grammar and add the new productions to it, giving $G_{8(a)}$ (new parts are underlined):

$\underline{Z} \rightarrow ABC \mid AB \mid AC \mid BC \mid \underline{bB} \mid \underline{b} \mid \underline{aAb} \mid \underline{ccC} \mid \underline{cc}$
$\underline{A} \rightarrow aAb \mid \underline{bB} \mid \underline{b}$
$B \rightarrow bB \mid b$
$C \rightarrow ccC \mid cc \mid \underline{bB} \mid \underline{b}$

You should perhaps take a moment to convince yourself that the terminal strings we can generate from $G_{8(a)}$ (remember Z is currently assumed to be the start symbol) are exactly the same as those we can generate starting from Z in G_8. Observe, for example, that from the initial grammar, we could perform the derivation $Z \Rightarrow A \Rightarrow B \Rightarrow C \Rightarrow ccC \Rightarrow cccc$. With $G_{8(a)}$ this derivation is simply $Z \Rightarrow ccC \Rightarrow cccc$.

In Chapter 4, with reference to the conversion of an arbitrary finite state recognizer into regular grammar productions, we noted that *empty moves in an FSR correspond to unit productions*. You can now see that if we applied step 1 of 'Chomskyfication' to the ε free part of a regular grammar containing unit productions, we would obtain a grammar that was also regular.

Step 1 is now complete, as unit productions have been removed. We turn now to step 2.

Step 2: Productions with terminals and non terminals on the right hand side, or with more than one terminal on the right hand side

Our grammar $G_{8(a)}$ now contains no unit productions. We now focus on the productions in $G_{8(a)}$ described in the title to this step. These productions we call *secondary productions*:

$Z \rightarrow bB \mid aAb \mid ccC \mid cc$
$A \rightarrow aAb \mid bB$
$B \rightarrow bB$
$C \rightarrow ccC \mid cc \mid bB$

To these productions we do the following:

> replace each terminal, t, by a new non terminal, N, and introduce a new production $N \rightarrow t$, in each case

So, for example, from $A \rightarrow aAb \mid bB$, we get:

$A \rightarrow JAK \mid KB$
$J \rightarrow a$
$K \rightarrow b$

Now we can use J and K to represent a and b, respectively, throughout our step 2 productions, adding all our new productions to $G_{8(a)}$ in place of the original step 2 productions. Then we replace c by L in all the appropriate productions, and introduce a new production $L \rightarrow c$. The result of this we will label $G_{8(b)}$:

$\underline{Z} \rightarrow ABC \mid AB \mid AC \mid BC \mid b \mid \underline{KB} \mid \underline{JAK} \mid \underline{LLC} \mid \underline{LL}$
$\underline{A} \rightarrow \underline{JAK} \mid \underline{KB} \mid b$
$\underline{B} \rightarrow \underline{KB} \mid b$
$\underline{C} \rightarrow \underline{LLC} \mid \underline{LL} \mid \underline{KB} \mid b$
$\underline{J \rightarrow a}$
$\underline{K \rightarrow b}$
$\underline{L \rightarrow c}$

The new productions are again underlined. You can verify that what we have done has not changed the terminal strings that can be generated from Z.

We are now ready for the final step.

Step 3: Productions with more than two non terminals on the right hand side

After steps 1 and 2, all our productions will be of the form:

$x \rightarrow y$ or where y consists of two or more non terminals, and
$x \rightarrow z$ z is a single terminal.

As the step 3 heading suggests, we now focus on the following productions of $G_{8(b)}$:

$Z \rightarrow ABC \mid JAK \mid LLC$
$A \rightarrow JAK$
$C \rightarrow LLC.$

As an example, consider $Z \rightarrow ABC$. It will not affect things if we introduce a new non terminal, say P, and replace $Z \rightarrow ABC$ by:

$Z \rightarrow AP$
$P \rightarrow BC.$

The $G_{8(b)}$ derivation $Z \Rightarrow ABC$ would then involve doing: $Z \Rightarrow AP \Rightarrow ABC$. As P is not found anywhere else in the grammar, this will not change any of the terminal strings that can be derived. We treat the rest of our step 3 productions analogously, again replacing the old productions by our new ones, and using a new non terminal in each case. This gives us the grammar $G_{8(c)}$:

$\underline{Z} \rightarrow \underline{AP} \mid AB \mid AC \mid BC \mid KB \mid b \mid \underline{JQ} \mid LR \mid LL$
$\underline{P \rightarrow BC}$
$\underline{Q \rightarrow AK}$
$\underline{R \rightarrow LC}$
$\underline{A} \rightarrow \underline{JT} \mid KB \mid b$
$\underline{T \rightarrow AK}$
$B \rightarrow KB \mid b$
$\underline{C \rightarrow LU} \mid LL \mid KB \mid b$
$\underline{U \rightarrow LC}$

$J \to a$
$K \to b$
$L \to c$

Changes have again been indicated by underlining.

The resulting grammar, $G_{8(c)}$, is in Chomsky normal form.

It is important to appreciate that, unlike in G_8, step 3 productions may include *right hand sides of more than three non terminals*. For example, we may have a production such as:

$E \to DEFGH.$

In such cases, we split the production up into productions as follows:

$E \to DW$	where W, X, and Y are new non terminals, not found
$W \to EX$	anywhere else in the grammar.
$X \to FY$	
$Y \to GH.$	

So the old derivation $E \Rightarrow DEFGH$ now becomes the new derivation:

$E \Rightarrow DW \Rightarrow DEX \Rightarrow DEFY \Rightarrow DEFGH.$

From the final example, you should be able to induce the general rule for creating several 'two-non-terminals-on-the-right-hand-side' productions from one 'more-than-two-non-terminals-on-the-right-hand-side' production.

If we apply steps 1, 2 and 3 to any ε free CFG, we obtain a CFG where all productions are of the form:

$x \to y$ or	where y is a single terminal,
$x \to uv$	where u and v are single non terminals.

A CFG like this is said to be in Chomsky normal form (CNF).
So, it should be clear that

any ε free CFG can be converted into CNF.

Once the ε free part of the grammar has been converted into CNF, we need to include the two productions that resulted from step 4 of the method for removing the empty string (Table 5.2), *but only if step 4 was carried out for the grammar*. In the case of G_8, step 4 *was* carried out. To arrive at a grammar equivalent to G_8 we need to add the productions $S \to \varepsilon \mid Z$ to $G_{8(c)}$, and designate S as the start symbol again.

It is very useful to know that any CFG can be converted into CNF. For example, we will use this 'CNF assumption' to facilitate an important proof in the next chapter. In a CFG in CNF, all **reductions** will be considerably simplified, as the right hand sides of productions consist of single terminals or two non terminals. A parser using such a grammar need only examine two adjacent non terminals or a single terminal symbol in the **sentential form** at a time. This simplifies things considerably, since a non-CNF CFG could have a large number of terminals and/or non terminals on the right hand side of some of its productions.

A final point is that if the CFG is in CNF, any **parse tree** will be such that every non terminal node expands into either two non terminal nodes or a single terminal node. So, for example, a parser written in Pascal could use a three field *record* to hold details of each non terminal node that expands into two non terminals (one field for the node's label, and two pointers to the two non terminals into which the non terminal expands). A single type of record structure would therefore be sufficient to represent all the non terminal nodes of the parse tree.

5.3 PUSHDOWN RECOGNIZERS

We saw in Chapter 4, that from any **regular grammar** we can build an abstract machine called a **finite state recognizer**. The machine is such that it recognizes all (and not any other) strings that are generated by the corresponding grammar. Moreover, for any finite state recognizer we invent we can produce an **equivalent** regular grammar. It was also said (though it will not be proved until Chapter 6) that there is at least one language, $\{a^i b^i : i \geq 1\}$, that *cannot* be recognized by any finite state recognizer (and therefore cannot be generated by a regular grammar), which nevertheless we have seen to be context free.

In terms of the processing of the context free languages, the problem with the finite state recognizer is that it has no memory device: it has no way of 'remembering' details about the part of the string it has processed at a given moment in time. This observation is crucial in several results considered in this book. The FSR's only memory is in terms of the state it is in, which provides limited information. For example, if a finite state recognizer wishes to 'count' n symbols, it has to have n states with which to do it. This immediately makes it unsuitable even for a simple context free language such as $\{a^i b^i : i \geq 1\}$, that requires a recognizer to be able to 'count' a number of as that cannot be predicted in advance, so that it can make sure that an equal number of bs follows.

It turns out that with the addition of a rudimentary memory device called a **stack**, the finite state recognizer can do the job for context free languages that the basic finite state recognizer can do for regular languages. We call such an augmented finite state recognizer a **pushdown recognizer** (**PDR**). Before we examine these machines in detail, we need to be clear about what is meant by a *stack*.

5.3.1 The stack

A stack is simply a linear data structure that consists of a pile of symbols. The stack can only be accessed by putting a symbol on top of, or removing a symbol from the top of, the pile. The stack has a special marker (⊥), called the **stack bottom marker** which is always at the bottom of the pile. We use a diagrammatic representation of a stack as shown in Figure 5.2. If you prefer formal definitions, our stacks are really *strings* with the symbol ⊥ at the rightmost end.

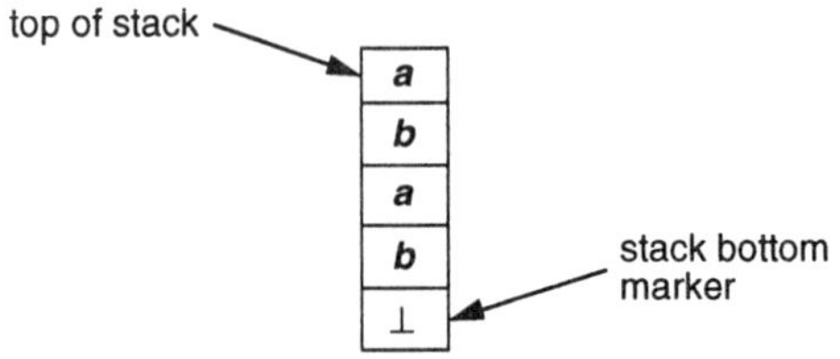

Figure 5.2 A stack

Figure 5.3 specifies the operations **push** and **pop**, which will be needed by our machines.

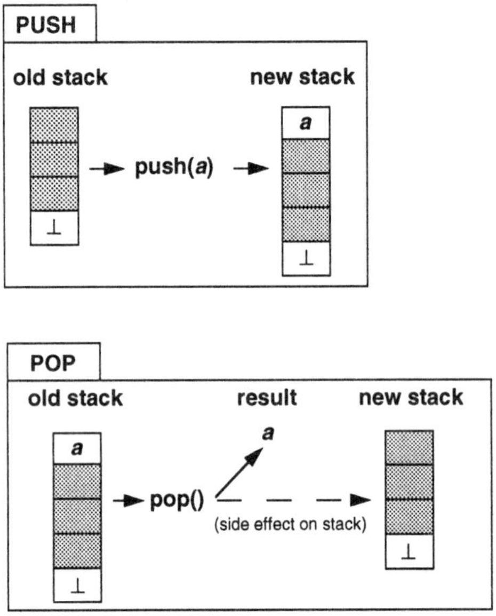

Figure 5.3 'Push' and 'Pop'

However,

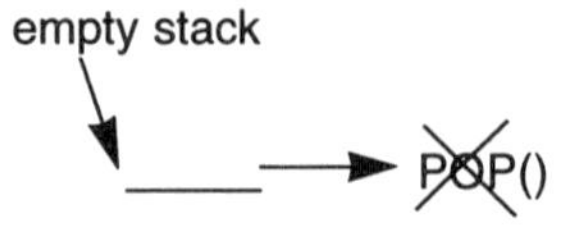

i.e. we cannot pop anything from an empty stack. Also note that we have defined a destructive pop, in that its result is the top element of the stack, but its side effect is to remove that element from the stack. Finally, observe from Figure 5.4. that pushing the empty string onto the stack leaves the stack unchanged.

Table 5.4 How to create an NPDR from a CFG

Step	Actions	Comments
1	We always begin with  where S is the start symbol of the grammar.	Note that state 1 is the start state. The meaning of the labels on the arcs can be appreciated from the following: 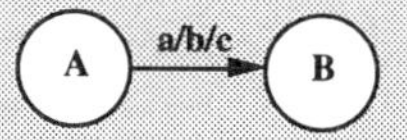 which means: if in state *A*, about to read a, and there is a b on top of the stack, a transition can be made to state B, with the symbol b being popped off the stack, and then the string c being pushed onto the stack. When strings are PUSHed, PUSH(efg) is interpreted as PUSH(g) then PUSH(f) then PUSH(e). So, the transition introduced on the left means: 'when in state 1, without reading any input, and POPping the stack bottom marker off the stack, PUSH the stack bottom marker back on the stack, then push S onto the stack, then go to state 2'
2a	For each production of *G*, $x \rightarrow y$, introduce a transition:  	So, in state 2, we will have a situation where the left hand side (i.e. non terminal symbol) of any production of G that is at the top of the stack can be replaced by the right hand side of that production. Again, all these transitions are made without affecting the input string. As you may be able to see, the machine will operate by modelling derivations that could be carried out using the grammar.
2b	For each terminal symbol, *t*, found in the grammar *G*, introduce a transition:  	Still in state 2, we now will have a situation where if a given terminal symbol is next in the input, and also on top of the stack, we can read the symbol from the input, and remove the one from the top of the stack (i.e. the effect of POPping the symbol off and then PUSHing ε). These transitions allow us to read input symbols only if they are in the order that would have been produced by derivations made by the grammar (ensured by the transitions introduced by rule 2a).
3	Introduce a transition: 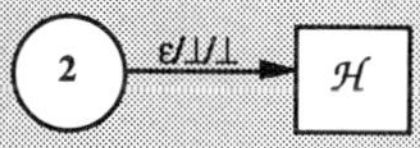 	In state 2, we can move to the halt state (again represented as a box) only if the stack is empty. We make this move without reading any input, and we ensure that the stack bottom marker is replaced on the stack.

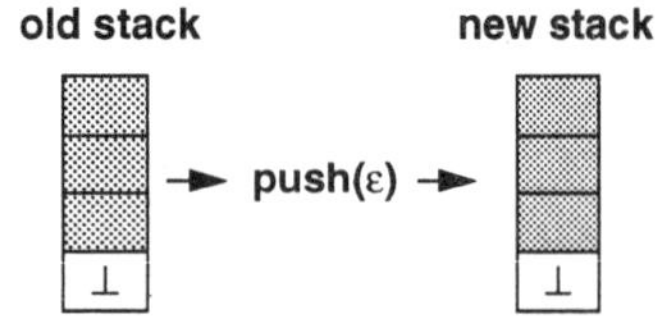

Figure 5.4 Pushing the empty string leaves the stack unchanged

The stacks in this chapter are used to store strings of terminals and non terminals, such that each symbol in the string constitutes one element of the stack. For convenience, we allow PUSH(abc), for example, as an abbreviation of PUSH(c) followed by PUSH(b) followed by PUSH(a). Given that, as stated above, our stacks are really strings, we could have defined POP and PUSH as formal string functions.

Stacks are important data structures, and have many applications. A related data structure you may encounter (though we have no cause to use it in this book) is called a queue. A **queue** is like a stack, except that, as its name suggests, items are added to one end, but taken from the other.

5.3.2 Constructing a non deterministic PDR

The rules we introduce in this section (in Table 5.4) will produce a **non deterministic PDR** (**NPDR**) from the productions of any context free grammar. As for finite state recognizers, the PDR has a pictorial representation. However, due to the additional complexity of the PDR resulting from the addition of the stack, the pictorial form does not provide such a succinct description of the language accepted by a PDR as it does in the case of the FSR. The rules in Table 5.4 convert any CFG, G, into a three-state NPDR.

The **acceptance conditions** for the NPDR, given some input string x, are specified in Table 5.5.

Table 5.5 The acceptance conditions of the NPDR

The machine begins in state 1, with the stack containing only the stack bottom marker, ⊥.
If there is some sequence of transitions by which the machine can reach the halt state $\mathcal{H}$, and on doing so, the input is exhausted and the stack contains only the stack bottom marker ⊥, then the string x is said to be acceptable.

As for FSRs, in Chapter 4 we assert that the set of all **acceptable** strings of an NPDR derived from a grammar, G, is exactly the same as $L(G)$. We are not going to prove this, however, because as you will be able to see from the examples we consider next, it is reasonably obvious that any PDR constructed by using rules in Table 5.4 will be capable of reproducing any **derivation** that the grammar could have produced, and, moreover, will reach a **halt state** only if its input string is a sentence that the grammar could derive. However, if you want to try to prove this, it makes a useful exercise.

5.3.3 Example NPDRs, M_3 and M_{10}

Let us now produce an NPDR from the grammar G_3. Figure 5.5 shows the **transitions** produced by each rule (the rule number applied is in the upper right hand corner of each box).

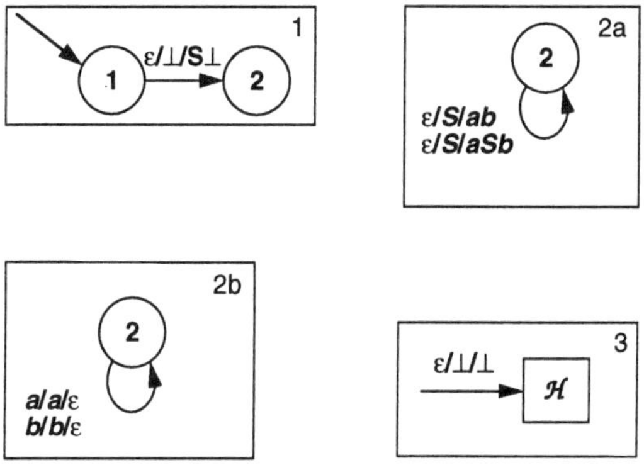

Figure 5.5 Creating a non deterministic PDR

Figure 5.6 shows the connected machine (we have simply joined the appropriate circles together[1]):

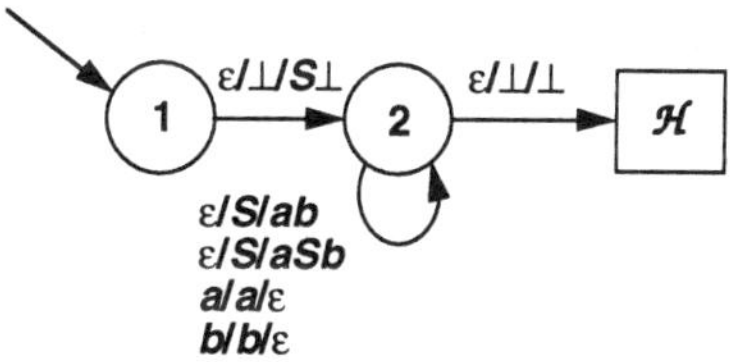

Figure 5.6 The NPDR, M_3

As in the previous chapter, we show the correspondence between the grammar and the machine by using the same subscript number in the name of both. We now investigate the operation of such a machine, by presenting M_3 with the input string a^3b^3. G_3 can generate this string, so M_3 should accept it. The operation of M_3 on the example string is shown in Table 5.6. Table 5.6(a) shows M_3's initial configuration, while Tables 5.6(b) and (c) show the machine's behaviour, eventually accepting the string in Table 5.6(c).

[1] As for the FSRs in Chapter 4, once you understand the process of constructing the machine you can draw it directly in its connected form.

Table 5.6(a) An initial configuration of the NPDR, M_3

Initial state	Initial stack	Input
	⊥	aaabbb

Table 5.6(b) Trace of M_3's behaviour (part 1)

Transition	Resulting stack	Input
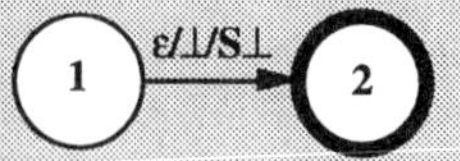	S ⊥	aaabbb
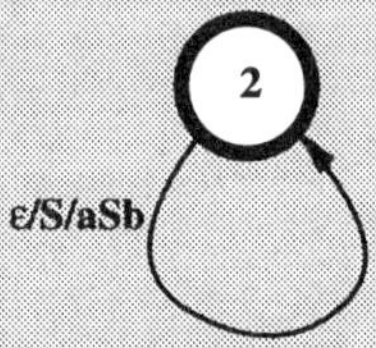	a S b ⊥	aaabbb
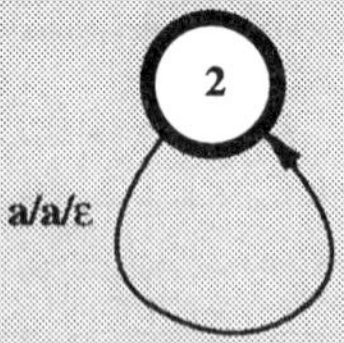	S b ⊥	aaabbb
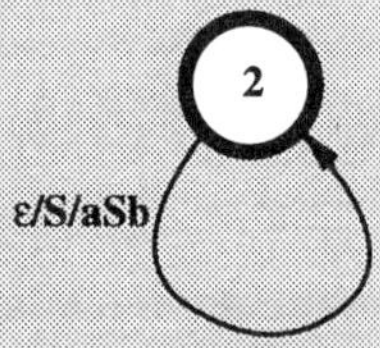	a S b b ⊥	aaabbb
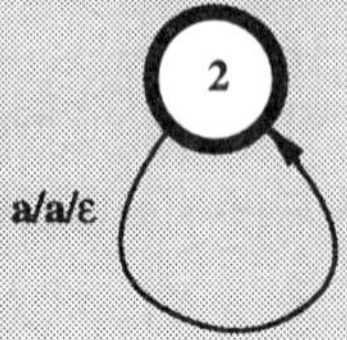	S b b ⊥	aaabbb

Table 5.6(c) Trace of M_3's behaviour (part 2)

Transition	Resulting stack	Input
ε/S/ab 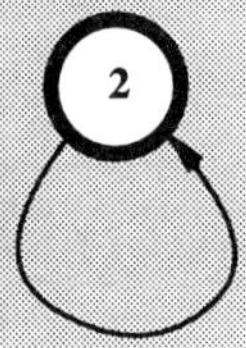	a b b b ⊥	aaabbb ↑
a/a/ε 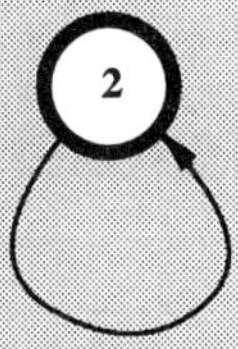	b b b ⊥	aaabbb ↑
b/b/ε 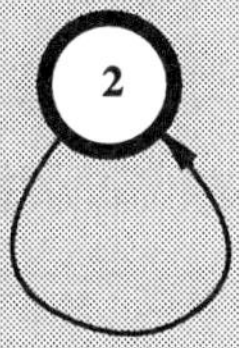	b b ⊥	aaabbb ↑
b/b/ε 	b ⊥	aaabbb ↑
b/b/ε 	⊥	aaabbb ↑
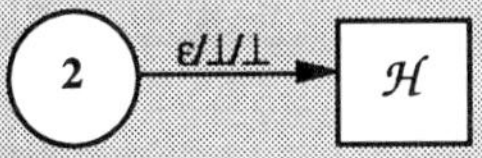 ε/⊥/⊥	⊥	aaabbb ↑

Input exhausted, in halt state, stack empty, therefore string accepted.

Notice in Tables 5.6(b) and (c) how either of the transitions derived from the productions $S \to aSb$ and $S \to ab$ can be applied any time we have S on the top of the stack. There are in fact (infinitely) many sequences of transitions that can be followed, but most of them will lead to a non acceptance state.

We complete this section by considering a further example, this time a grammar that is **equivalent** to grammar G_2, of Chapters 2 and 3. G_2 is:

$S \to aB \mid bA \mid \varepsilon$
$A \to aS \mid bAA$
$B \to bS \mid aBB.$

However, the example, G_{10}, has been constructed by applying our rules for removing the empty string (Table 5.2) to G_2. You should attempt this construction as an exercise.

G_{10}'s productions are as follows:

$S \to \varepsilon \mid X$
$X \to aB \mid bA$
$A \to aS \mid a \mid bAA$
$B \to bS \mid b \mid aBB$

We now apply the rules for creating the equivalent NPDR, resulting in the machine M_{10}, shown in Figure 5.7.

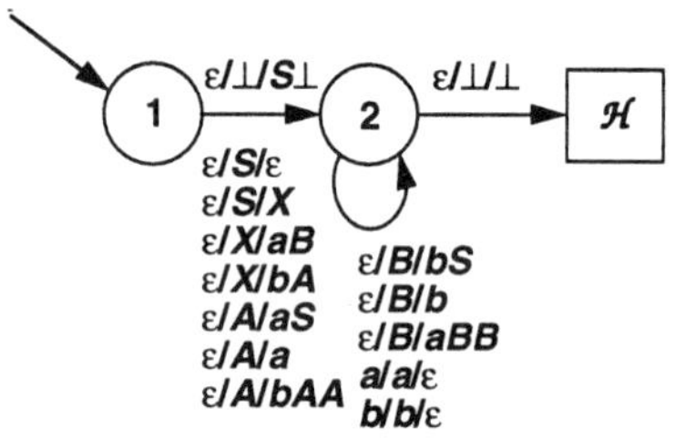

Figure 5.7 The NPDR, M_{10}

Note that, unlike M_3, M_{10} **will accept the empty string** (since it allows S at the top of the stack to be replaced by ε), as indeed it should, since $\varepsilon \in L(G_{10})$. The empty string can be derived by G_{10}. However, $\varepsilon \notin L(G_3)$, i.e. the empty string is *not* one of the strings that can be derived from the start symbol of G_3.

I now leave it to you to follow the M_{10}'s behaviour on some example strings. You are reminded that $L(G_{10})$ is the set of all strings of *as* and *bs* in which the number of *as* is equal to the number of *bs*.

5.4 DETERMINISTIC PUSHDOWN RECOGNIZERS

For the FSRs, non determinism was not a problem, since we discovered that for any non deterministic machine we could construct an equivalent, deterministic FSR. In Chapter 4, we also discussed the problems inherent in parsing by non deterministic methods. First, let us clarify how non determinism manifests itself in PDRs. In PDRs the next move that can be made from a given state is determined by two things:

1. The next symbol to be read from the input.
2. The symbol currently on top of the stack.

If, given a particular instance of 1 and 2, the machine has transitions which would allow it to:

- make a choice as to which state to move to
  or
- make a choice as to which string to push onto the stack
  (or both),

then the PDR is *non deterministic.*

On the other hand, a *deterministic* pushdown recognizer (DPDR), is such that

> in any state, given a particular input symbol and particular stack top symbol, the machine has only *one* applicable transition.

The question thus arises: *for any NPDR, can we always construct an equivalent DPDR*? We saw in Chapter 4 that the answer to the corresponding question for FSRs was 'yes'. For the PDRs however, the answer is more like: 'in general no, but in many cases, yes'. We shall see that the 'many cases' includes *all* the regular languages and *some* of the proper CFLs (i.e. those that are *context free but not regular*). However, we shall also see that there are some languages that are certainly context free, but *cannot* be recognized by a DPDR.

5.4.1 M_3^d, a deterministic version of M_3

First, we consider context free languages that *can* be recognized by a DPDR. The language:

$$A = \{a^i b^i : i \geq 1\},$$

is not regular (this is proved in Chapter 6). However, A is *certainly* context free, since it is generated by the CFG G_3. Above, we constructed an NPDR (M_3) for A, from the productions of G_3 (see Figure 5.6). However, we can see that any sentence in the language A consists of a number of as followed by the same number of bs. A deterministic method for accepting strings of this form might be:

> PUSH each a in the input string onto the stack until a b is encountered, then POP an a off the stack for each b in the input string.

The above method is used by the DPDR M_3^d, shown in Figure 5.8.

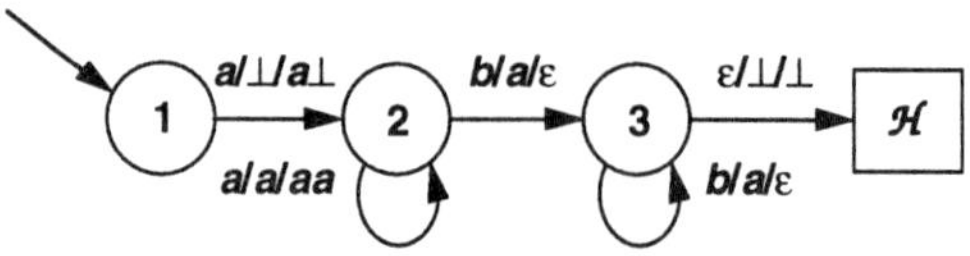

Figure 5.8 The DPDR, M_3^d

In Table 5.6 we saw a trace of the operation of the NPDR M_3 for the input a^3b^3. We now trace the operation of M_3^d for the same input. Table 5.7(a) shows the initial configuration of M_3^d, while Table 5.7(b) shows the behaviour of the machine until it accepts the string.

Table 5.7(a) An initial configuration of the DPDR, M_3^d

Initial state	Initial stack	Input
1	⊥	aaabbb ↑

5.4.2 *More deterministic PDRs*

Two more example DPDRs follow (Figures 5.9 and 5.10). It is suggested that you trace their behaviour for various valid and invalid input strings.

First, Figure 5.9 shows a DPDR for the language $L(G_{10})$, the set of all strings of as and bs in which the number of as is equal to the number of bs. This is the same

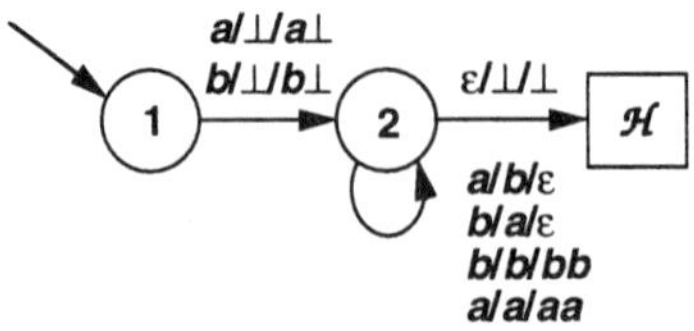

Figure 5.9 A DPDR for the language $L(G_{10}) - \{\varepsilon\}$.

Table 5.7(b) Trace of M_3^d's behaviour

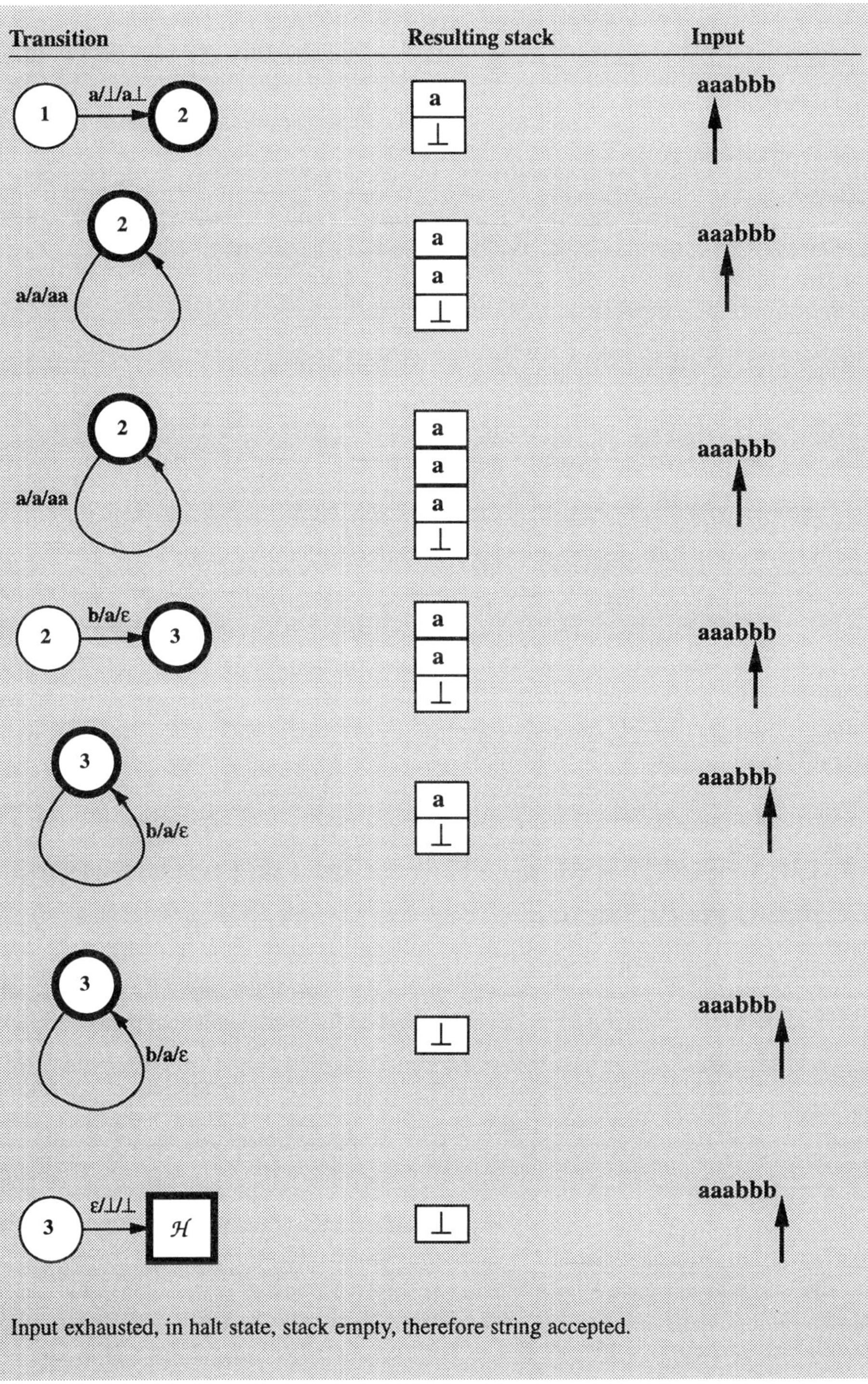

Input exhausted, in halt state, stack empty, therefore string accepted.

language as $L(G_2)$, as we obtained the productions for G_{10} by applying our procedure for removing ε productions to G_2. Let us consider $L(G_{10})$ without the empty string (using the **set difference** operator, $L(G_{10}) - \{\varepsilon\}$), which is obviously the set of all *non empty* strings of *a*s and *b*s in which the number of *a*s is equal to the number of *b*s. The DPDR shown in Figure 5.10 recognizes the language $L(G_9)$, which is:

$$\{a^{2i+1}c^jb^{2i+1} : i, j \geq 0\}$$

a non zero *odd* number of *a*s, followed by 0 or more *c*s, followed by the same number of *b*s as there were *a*s.

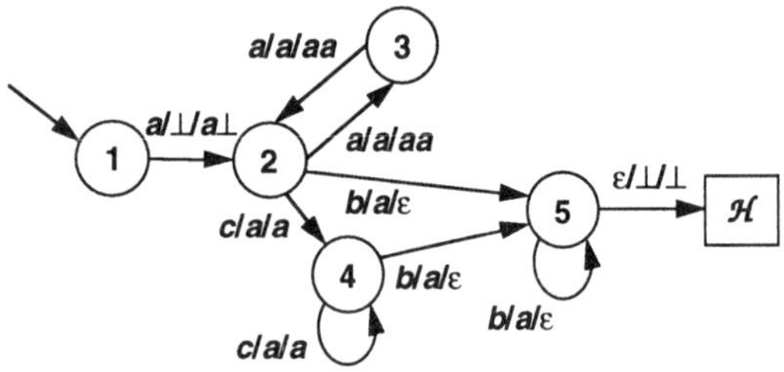

Figure 5.10 A DPDR for the language $L(G_9)$

Clearly, then, there are CFLs that can be recognized by DPDRs. Here, we have encountered but a few. However, there are, as you can probably imagine, an infinite number of them. If a CFL can be recognized by a DPDR, we call it a **deterministic context free language**.

5.5 DETERMINISTIC AND NON DETERMINISTIC CONTEXT FREE LANGUAGES

In this section, we discover that *there are context free languages that cannot be recognized by a deterministic PDR*. There is no general equivalence between the non deterministic and the deterministic PDRs, as there is for FSRs. We begin our investigation with the regular languages, which we find to be wholly contained within the deterministic CFLs.

5.5.1 *Every regular language is a deterministic CFL*

Any regular language is generated by a regular grammar without ε productions (apart from the one ε production $S \rightarrow \varepsilon$, if it is necessary). Such a grammar can be represented as a non deterministic FSR, which can, if necessary, be represented as a deterministic FSR (DFSR).

Now, any DFSR can be represented as a DPDR which effectively does not use its stack. We will use a single example that suggests a method by which any DFSR could be converted into an equivalent DPDR. The example deterministic FSR is $M_5{}^d$, from Chapter 4, shown in Figure 5.11.

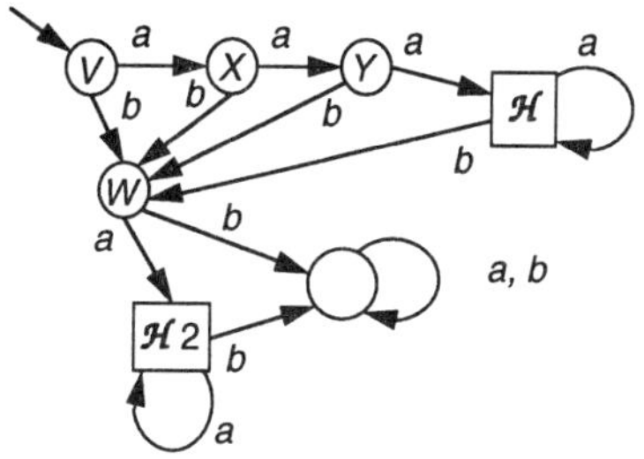

Figure 5.11 The DFSR $M_5{}^d$ from Chapter 4

This produces the DPDR of Figure 5.12.

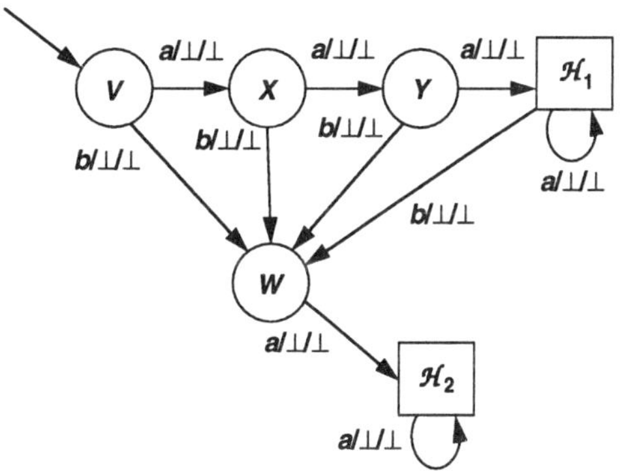

Figure 5.12 The DPDR equivalent to $M_5{}^d$ (Figure 5.11)

The DPDR in Figure 5.12 has two **halt states** (we have hitherto said nothing to prohibit this). We have also ignored the **null state** of the DFSR. We could clearly amend any DFSR to produce an equivalent DPDR as we have done above.

However, for the DPDR, we do need to amend our definition of the acceptance conditions as they applied to the NPDR, which our rules ensure always has only one halt state.

The acceptance conditions for the DPDR, for an input string x, are specified in Table 5.8.

You may notice that the condition 'the stack contains only the stack bottom marker ⊥', that applied to NPDRs (Table 5.5), does not appear in Table 5.8. An exercise asks you to justify that the language $\{a^ib^j : i \geq 1, j = i \text{ or } j = 0\}$ can only be recognized by a deterministic PDR if that machine is *not* required to have an empty stack every time it accepts a string.

Table 5.8 The acceptance conditions for the DPDR

The machine begins in state 1, with the stack containing only the stack bottom marker, ⊥.
If there is a sequence of transitions by which the machine can reach one of its halt states, and on doing so, the input is exhausted, then the string x is said to be acceptable.

So far, we have established the existence of the deterministic context free languages. Moreover, we have also established that this class of languages includes the regular languages. What we have yet to do is establish that there are some CFLs that are *necessarily non deterministic*, in that *they can be accepted by an NPDR but not a DPDR*.

5.5.2 *The non deterministic CFLs*

Consider the following CFG, G_{11}:

$S \rightarrow a \mid b \mid c \mid aSa \mid bSb \mid cSc$

$L(G_{11})$ is the set of every possible *non empty odd length* **palindromic** string of *a*s and/or *b*s and/or *c*s[2]. We could use our procedure from Table 5.4 to produce a **NPDR** to accept $L(G_{11})$. However, could we design a **DPDR** to do the same? We cannot, as we now establish by intuitive argument. General palindromic strings are of the form specified in Figure 5.13.

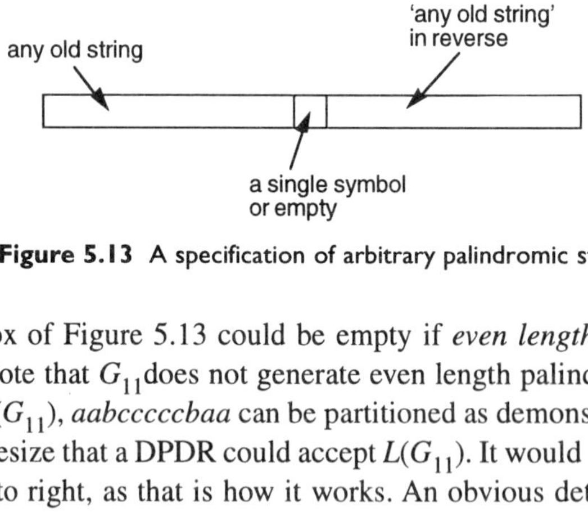

Figure 5.13 A specification of arbitrary palindromic strings

The centre box of Figure 5.13 could be empty if *even length palindromic strings* were allowed. Note that G_{11} does not generate even length palindromes[3]. An example sentence from $L(G_{11})$, *aabccccbaa* can be partitioned as demonstrated in Figure 5.14.

Let us hypothesize that a DPDR could accept $L(G_{11})$. It would have to read the input string from left to right, as that is how it works. An obvious deterministic way to do the task on that basis is as follows:

[2] A palindromic string is the same as the reverse of itself.

[3] It is very simple to amend the grammar so that it generates all (even and odd length) palindromic strings, as you may like to see for yourself.

a	*a*	*b*	*a*	*c*	*c*	*c*	*c*	*c*	*a*	*b*	*a*	*a*

Figure 5.14 A palindrome, partitioned according to Figure 5.13.

1. Read, and PUSH onto the stack, each input symbol encountered until the 'centre' of the string is reached.
2. Read the rest of the string, comparing each symbol to the next symbol on the stack. If the string is valid, the string on the stack following (1) will be the part of the string after the centre in reverse.

The problem with the above is in the statement 'until the 'centre' of the string is reached' in stage (1). How can the DPDR detect the centre of the string? Of course, it cannot. If there is a symbol in the centre it will be one of the symbols – *a*, *b*, or *c* – that can feature anywhere in the input string. The machine must PUSH every input symbol onto the stack, on the assumption that it has not yet reached the centre of the input string. This means that the machine must be allowed to **backtrack**, once it reaches the end of the input, to a situation where it can see if it is possible to empty its stack by comparing the stack contents with the remainder of the input. By similar argument, any such language of arbitrary palindromic strings defined with respect to an alphabet of two or more symbols is necessarily non deterministic.

We have argued that the problem vis-à-vis palindromic strings lies in the PDR's inability to detect the 'centre' of the input. If a language of palindromic strings is such that every string is of the form shown in Figure 5.15 then it can be accepted by a DPDR, and so is *deterministic*.

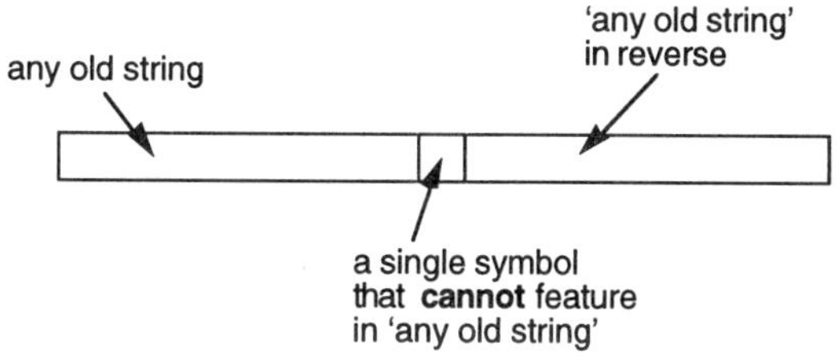

Figure 5.15 Palindromes with a distinct central symbol

As an example of a *deterministic* palindromic language, consider $L(G_{12})$, where G_{12} (a slightly amended G_{11}) is as follows:

$S \rightarrow d \mid aSa \mid bSb \mid cSc$

$L(G_{12})$ is the set of all palindromic strings of a form described in Figure 5.16.

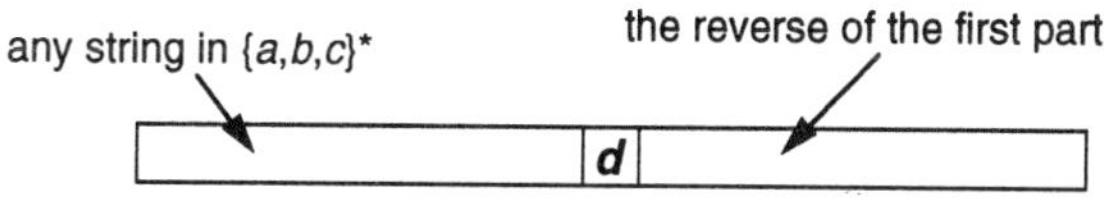

Figure 5.16 Sentences of $L(G_{10})$

$L(G_{12})$ is accepted by the DPDR, M_{12} depicted in Figure 5.17.

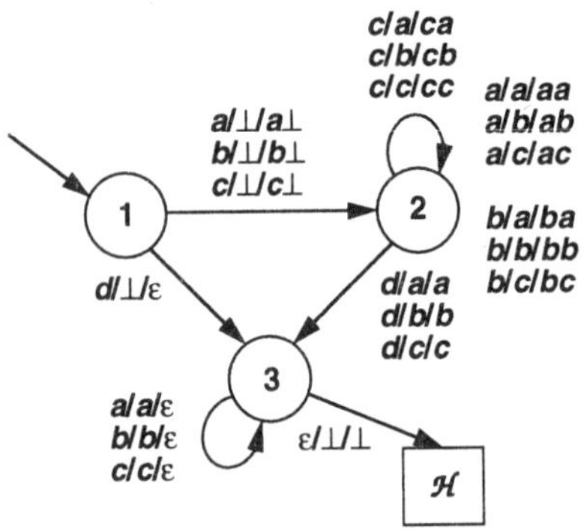

Figure 5.17 The DPDR M_{12}

5.5.3 *A refinement to the Chomsky hierarchy in the case of CFLs*

The existence of **properly** non deterministic CFLs suggests a slight refinement to the **Chomsky hierarchy** with respect to the context free and regular languages, as represented in Figure 5.18.

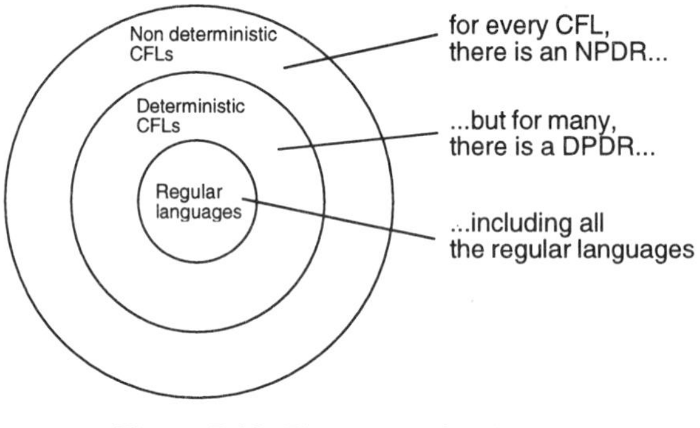

Figure 5.18 The context free languages

5.6 THE EQUIVALENCE OF THE CFLS AND THE PDRS

The situation for FSRs and regular languages, i.e. that any regular grammar can be represented by an **equivalent** FSR, and every FSR can be represented by an equivalent regular grammar, is mirrored in the relationship between PDRs and CFGs. In this chapter, we have seen that for any CFG we can construct an equivalent NPDR. It turns out that for any NPDR we can construct an equivalent CFG. This will not be proved here, as the proof is rather complex, and it was considered more important to investigate the situation pertaining to the PDR as the recognizer for the CFLs, rather than the converse result.

One way of showing that every NPDR has an equivalent CFG is to show that from any NPDR we can create CFG productions that generate exactly the set of strings that enable the NPDR to reach its halt state, leaving its stack empty. The details are not important, but the result is powerful, as it shows us that any language that cannot be generated by a CFG (and we see two such languages in the next chapter) needs a machine that is more powerful than a PDR to recognize it. Later in the book we consider abstract machines as *computers*, rather than language recognizers, and we see the close relationship between computation and language recognition.

Consider the 'multiplication language'

$$\{a^i b^j c^{i \times j} : i, j \geq 1\}$$

introduced in Chapter 2. This is shown to be not a CFL at the end of Chapter 6, a result that means that the language cannot be recognized by a PDR. This leads us to speculate that we need a more powerful machine than the PDR to model many computational tasks. We return to this theme in the second part of the book.

5.7 OBSERVATIONS ON CONTEXT FREE GRAMMARS AND LANGUAGES

The lack of general equivalence between deterministic and non deterministic context free languages is problematic for the design of programming languages. Efficient parsers can be designed from deterministic PDRs. As argued in Chapter 4, non determinism is undesirable, as it is computationally expensive. Moreover, unnecessary non determinism is simply wasteful in terms of resources. It turns out that any deterministic context free language can be parsed by a pushdown machine that never has to look ahead more than one symbol in the input to determine the choice of the next transition.

Consider, for example, sentences of the language $\{a^i b^i : i \geq 1\}$. If we look at the next symbol in the input, it will either be an a or a b, and, like our deterministic machine M_3, above, we know exactly what to do in either case. Now consider strings of arbitrary palindromes, with no distinct central 'marker' symbol. In this case, for any machine that could look ahead a *fixed* number of symbols, we could simply *present that machine with a palindromic string long enough to ensure that the machine could not tell when it moved from the first to the second 'half' of the input.* Languages that can be parsed by a PDR (and are therefore context free) that never has to look ahead more than a fixed number, say k, of symbols in the input are called **LR(k) languages** (**LR** stands for **L**ook ahead **R**ight). The **LR(k)** languages *are* the deterministic context free languages. In fact, the deterministic languages are all **LR(1) languages**.

Languages of arbitrary length palindromic strings with no distinguishable central marker are clearly not **LR(k)** languages, for any fixed k.

The preceding chapter closed with the observation that the language $\{a^ib^i : i \geq 1\}$ is not regular. It was promised that this would be proved in Chapter 6. Now we make a similar observation with respect to the context free languages, in that we argue that there are languages that are not context free, and cannot therefore be generated by a context free grammar, or recognized by an NPDR. They therefore must be either **type 1** (**context sensitive**) or **type 0** (**unrestricted**) languages (or perhaps *neither*).

In Chapter 6, we will see that both the 'multiplication language' and the language:

$$\{a^ib^ic^i : i \geq 1\}$$

i.e. the set of all strings of the form *as* followed by *bs* followed by *cs*, where the number of *as* = the number of *bs* = the number of *cs*, are not context free. Given that the language $\{a^ib^i : i \geq 1\}$ *is* context free, it may at first seem strange that $\{a^ib^ic^i : i \geq 1\}$ is not. However, this is indeed the case. Part of the next chapter is concerned with demonstrating this.

EXERCISES

1 Given the following grammar:

$S \rightarrow ABCA$
$A \rightarrow aA \mid XY$
$B \rightarrow bbB \mid C$
$X \rightarrow cX \mid \varepsilon$
$Y \rightarrow dY \mid \varepsilon$
$C \rightarrow cCd \mid \varepsilon$

produce an equivalent **Chomsky normal form** grammar.
Note: remember that you first need to apply the rules for removing the empty string.

2† $\{a^ib^j : i \geq 1, j = i \text{ or } j = 0\}$ is a **deterministic CFL**. However, as mentioned earlier in this chapter, it can only be accepted by a **deterministic PDR** that does not always clear its **stack**. Provide a DPDR to **accept** the language, and justify the preceding statement.

3 Argue that we can always ensure that an NPDR clears its stack, and that NPDRs need have only one **halt state**.

4 Amend $M_3{}^d$ from earlier in the chapter, to produce DPDRs for the languages $\{a^ib^ic^j : i, j \geq 1\}$ and $\{a^ib^jc^j : i, j \geq 1\}$.
Note: in Chapter 6 it is assumed that the above two languages are deterministic.

5† Justify by intuitive argument that $\{a^ib^jc^k : i, j \geq 1, i = j \text{ or } j = k\}$ (from exercise 1 in Chapter 3) is a non deterministic CFL.

6† Design a program to simulate the behaviour of a DPDR. Investigate what amendments would have to be made to your program so that it could model the behaviour of an NPDR.

7 Design DPDRs to accept the languages $\{a^i b^j c^{i+j} : i, j \geq 1\}$ and $\{a^i b^j c^{i-j} : i, j \geq 1\}$. Note: consider the implications of these machines in the light of the remarks about the *computational power of the PDR*, above.

6 Important features of regular and context free languages

AIMS

To learn about

- closure, which means seeing if operations applied to languages of a given class always result in a language of the same class
- two theorems relating to the Chomsky hierarchy: the repeat state theorem for finite state recognizers and the *uvwxy* theorem for context free languages
- how to use the two theorems in relation to context free, context sensitive and unrestricted languages

6.1 CLOSURE PROPERTIES OF LANGUAGES

In terms of the **Chomsky hierarchy**, the notion of **closure** applies as follows:

1. Choose a given type from the Chomsky hierarchy.
2. Choose some operation that can be applied to any language (or pairs of languages) of that type, and which yields a language as a result.
3. If it can be demonstrated that when applied to each and every language or pair of languages of the chosen type, the operation yields a resulting language which is also of the chosen type, then the languages of the chosen type are said to be **closed under** the operation.

For example, take the **set union** operator, $\cup$, and the regular languages. If for every pair L_1, L_2, of **regular languages** the set $L_1 \cup L_2$ was also a regular language, then the regular languages would be closed under union (in fact they are, as we see, shortly).

In the following two sections, we investigate various closure properties of the regular and **context free languages**, with respect to the following operations: **complement**, **union**, **intersection**, and **concatenation**. As usual, we will be content with intuitive argument.

6.2 CLOSURE PROPERTIES OF THE REGULAR LANGUAGES

6.2.1 *Complement*

As we discovered early on in the book, given some **finite** non empty **alphabet** A, A^* denotes *the infinite set of all possible strings that can be formed using the symbols of that alphabet*. Given this basis, a formal language was defined to be *any subset of such a set*. Take for example the language

$R = \{a^i b^j c^k : i, j, k \geq 1\}$,

which is a **subset** of $\{a, b, c\}^*$.

Now, $\{a, b, c\}^* - R$ denotes the set of all strings that are in $\{a, b, c\}^*$ *but not in* R ('–' is called the *set difference* operator) i.e.

> all possible strings of *a*s and/or *b*s and/or *c*s *except* for those of the form 'one or more *a*s followed by one or more *b*s followed by one or more *c*s'.

$\{a, b, c\}^* - R$ is called the *complement* of R, and is, of course, a formal language, as it is a subset of $\{a, b, c\}^*$.

In general, then, if L is a language in A^*, $A^* - L$ is the complement of L.

We are now going to see that:

If L is a regular language in A^*, then so is $A^* - L$.

In other words, the regular languages are closed under complement. This is best demonstrated in terms of **deterministic finite state recognizers (DFSRs)**. Our argument will be illustrated here by using the DFSR for R, the language described above, as an example.

We start with a DFSR that accepts R, as shown in Figure 6.1.

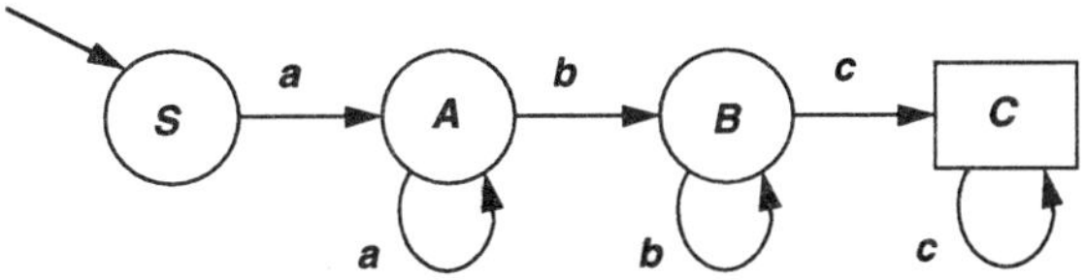

Figure 6.1 A DFSR for the language, *R*

To the machine in Figure 6.1 we add a **null state** to make the machine completely deterministic. The resulting machine can be seen in Figure 6.2.

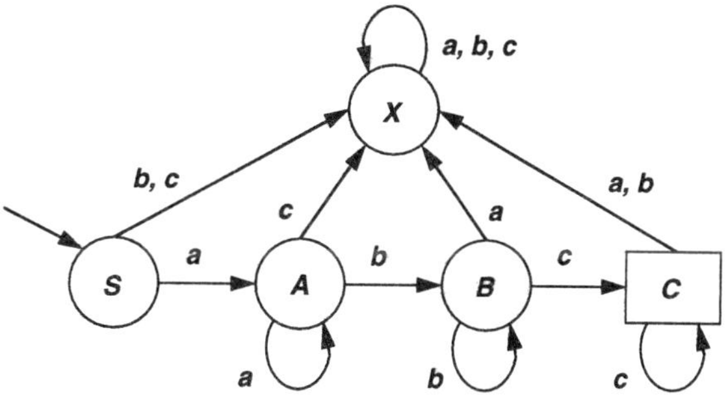

Figure 6.2 The FSR of Figure 6.1 with a null state

We take the machine in Figure 6.2, and make all its non halt states into **halt states**, and all its halt states into non halt states, achieving the machine shown in Figure 6.3.

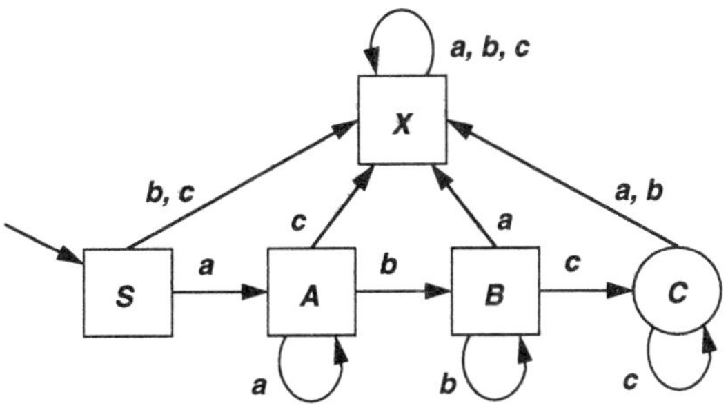

Figure 6.3 The complement of the machines in Figures 6.1 and 6.2

The FSR in Figure 6.3 will reach a halt state *only* for strings in $\{a, b, c\}^*$ for which the original machine (Figure 6.1) *would not*. It thus accepts the *complement* of the language accepted by the original machine. Note that, since *the start state is also a halt state*, the final machine also accepts as a valid input the empty string, as it should, since the original machine did not.

It should be clear that the same method could be applied to *any* DFSR. As we saw in Chapter 4, there is a general equivalence between DFSRs and regular languages. What applies to all DFSRs, then, applies to *all* regular languages.

6.2.2 Union

We now see that:

If L_1 and L_2 are regular languages, then so is $L_1 \cup L_2$.

Consider the DFSR for R, in Figure 6.1 above, and the DFSR for the language

$\{a^i b^{2j} : i \geq 0, j \geq 1\}$,

which is shown in Figure 6.4.

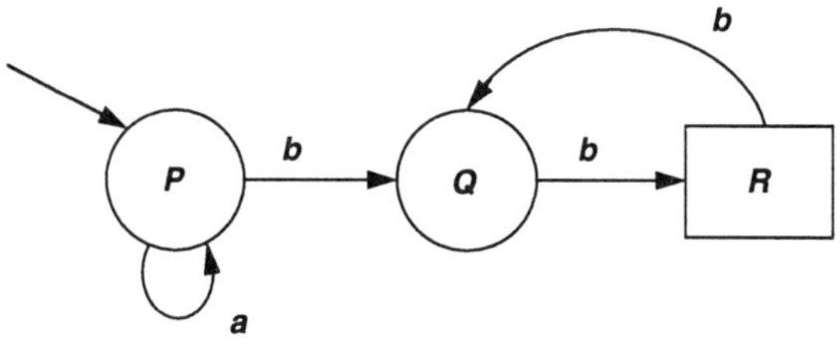

Figure 6.4 A DFSR

We produce a composite machine of the machines from Figures 6.1 and 6.4. As can be seen in Figure 6.5, we have introduced an additional **start state**, I, and for each **outgoing arc** from a start state of either original machine we draw an **arc** from I to the destination state of that arc.

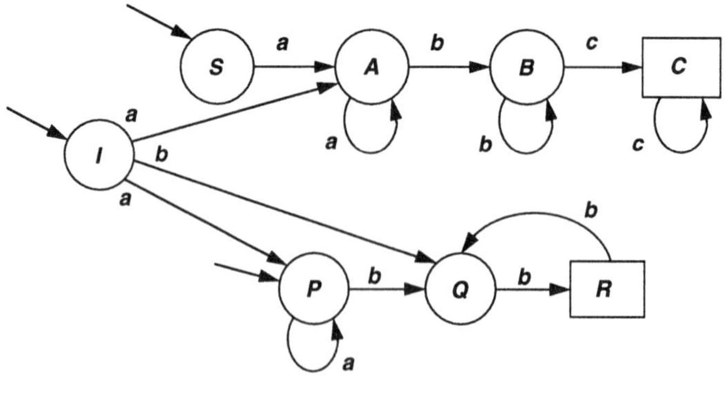

Figure 6.5 The non deterministic union machine for the FSRs in Figures 6.1 and 6.4

The machine in Figure 6.5 has three start states, but if we use our **subset algorithm** from Chapter 4 to make it deterministic, we obtain the FSR in Figure 6.6.

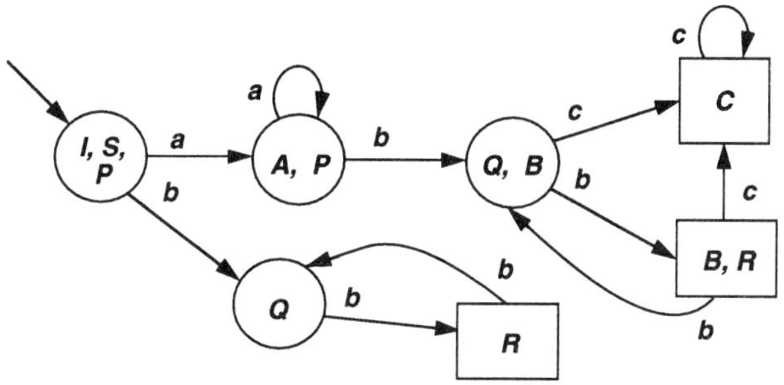

Figure 6.6 A deterministic version of the FSR in Figure 6.5

The machine in Figure 6.6 accepts the language:

$$\{a^i b^j c^k : i, j, k \geq 1\} \cup \{a^i b^{2j} : i \geq 0, j \geq 1\},$$

i.e. all strings accepted by *either, or both,* of the original machines.

You should again satisfy yourself that the suggested method can be applied to any pair of DFSRs.

6.2.3 Intersection

Now we establish that:

If L_1 and L_2 are regular languages, then so is $L_1 \cap L_2$.

A basic law of set theory is one of de Morgan's laws, which states:

$$L_1 \cap L_2 = \overline{\overline{L_1} \cup \overline{L_2}}$$

i.e. the intersection of two sets is the same as the complement of the union of the complements of the two sets. Now, we have to do little to establish that if L_1 and L_2 are regular languages, then so is $L_1 \cap L_2$, since:

- we saw above how to do the complement,

and

- we also saw how to do the union,

so therefore

- if we take the two DFSRs for L_1 and L_2, say M_1 and M_2:
  a. we create the 'complement machines' for each of M_1 and M_2
  b. we create the 'union machine' for the results of (a)
  c. we create the 'complement machine' from the result of (b).

We know that *the complement of a regular language is always regular, and the union of two regular languages is also always regular*. The language recognized by the FSR that results from doing (a) and then (b) and then (c) will therefore also be regular.

6.2.4 Concatenation

As two *strings* can be concatenated together, so can two *languages*. To concatenate two languages A and B together, we simply make a set of all of the strings which result from concatenating each string in A in turn, with each string in B. So, for example, if

$$A = \{a, ab, \varepsilon\}$$

and

$$B = \{bc, c\},$$

then A concatenated to B, which we write AB, or in this case $\{a, ab, \varepsilon\}\{bc, c\}$ would be

$$\{abc, ac, abbc, bc, c\}.$$

Analogously to the way we use the superscript notation for strings, so we can use the superscript notation for languages, so that A^3 represents the language A concatenated *to itself, and the result of that concatenated to A again* (i.e. AAA), or in this case (given the language A as defined above):

$$A^3 =$$
$$\{a, ab, \varepsilon\}\{a, ab, \varepsilon\}\{a, ab, \varepsilon\} =$$
$$\{aa, aab, a, aba, abab, ab, \varepsilon\}\{a, ab, \varepsilon\}, \text{ etc.}$$

The same applies to **infinite languages**. For example, we could write:

$$\{a^i b^j : i, j \geq 1\}\{c^i : i \geq 1\}$$

to mean *the set containing each and every string in the first set concatenated to each and every string in the second*. In this case, the language described is R from earlier in this chapter, i.e.

$$\{a^i b^j c^k : i, j, k \geq 1\}.$$

The next thing we are going to show is:

If L_1 and L_2 are regular languages, then so is L_1L_2.

This is easier to show by using *grammars* than FSRs. Table 6.1 describes the combining of two regular grammars G_{13} and G_{14}, to produce a grammar, G_{15}, such that $L(G_{15}) = L(G_{13})L(G_{14})$.

Table 6.1 Combining two regular grammars to create a regular grammar that generates the concatenated language

G_{13}	G_{14}
$S \to aS \mid a \mid bB$	$S \to aS \mid aA$
$B \to b \mid c \mid bB$	$A \to dA \mid d$
so that:	
$L(G_{13}) =$	$L(G_{14}) =$
$\{a^i b^j x : i \geq 0, j \geq 1, x = b \text{ or } x = c\}$	$\{a^i d^j : i, j \geq 1\}$

To produce a composite grammar which generates $L(G_{13})L(G_{14})$:

Step	Description	Result
1.	Rename the non terminals in the second grammar so that the two grammars have no non terminals in common	G_{14} is now: $X \to aX \mid aA$ $A \to dA \mid d$ with X as the start symbol
2.	In the first grammar, replace each production of the form $x \to y$, where y is a single terminal, by a production $x \to yZ$, where Z is the start symbol of the second grammar	G_{13} is now: $S \to aS \mid aX \mid bB$ $B \to bX \mid cX \mid bB$
3.	Put all the productions together. They now constitute one grammar, the start symbol of which is the start symbol of the first grammar. The resulting grammar generates the language which is the language generated by the first grammar concatenated to the language generated by the second.	Composite grammar, L_{15}: $S \to aS \mid aX \mid bB$ $B \to bX \mid cX \mid bB$ $X \to aX \mid aA$ $A \to dA \mid d$

The composite grammar, G_{15}, shown in Table 6.1 is such that $L(G_{15}) = L(G_{13})$ $L(G_{14})$, i.e.

$$\{a^i b^j x : i \geq 0, j \geq 1, x = b \text{ or } x = c\}\{a^i d^j : i, j \geq 1\}$$
$$= \{a^h b^i x a^j d^k : h \geq 0,\ i, j, k \geq 1,\ x = b \text{ or } x = c\}.$$

It is obvious that the method in Table 6.1 would work for any pair of regular grammars. Note that the method could also be used repeatedly, beginning with a grammar G, to create a grammar that generated $L(G)^{n,}$ for any finite n.

6.3 CLOSURE PROPERTIES OF THE CONTEXT FREE LANGUAGES

In this section, we investigate the closure properties of the **context free languages (CFLs)** in general. We find that the situation is not so straightforward for the CFLs as for the regular languages. We also find that there are differences between the closure properties of the CFLs in general, and the **deterministic CFLs**, the latter being described in Chapter 5 as those CFLs recognized by *deterministic* PDRs. For the CFLs to be closed under an operation means that the language resulting from the application of the operation to any CFL (or pair of CFLs, if the operation applies to two CFLs) is also a CFL. Moreover, for the deterministic CFLs to be closed under an operation means that the result must always be a deterministic CFL.

To support the arguments, we will use the following languages:

$$X = \{a^i b^i c^j : i, j \geq 1\}$$

and

$$\mathrm{Y} = \{a^i b^i c^j : i, j \geq 1\}$$

First of all, let us observe that the two languages are context free. In fact, X and Y are both *deterministic* CFLs, as we could design DPDRs to accept each of them, as you were asked to do in the exercises at the end of Chapter 5.

In any case, they are certainly context free, as we can show by providing CFGs for each of them. The two grammars, G_x and G_y, are shown in Table 6.2.

Table 6.2 Two example grammars, Gx and Gy

G_x, which generates X	G_y, which generates Y
$A \rightarrow BC$ {note: start symbol is A}	$D \rightarrow EF$ {note: start symbol is D}
$B \rightarrow aBb \mid ab$	$E \rightarrow aE \mid a$
$C \rightarrow cC \mid c$	$F \rightarrow bFc \mid bc$

To simplify our constructions, the two grammars in Table 6.2 have no **non terminals** in common.

6.3.1 Union

The first result is that the CFLs are closed under **union**, i.e.

If L_a and L_b are context free languages, then so is $L_a \cup L_b$.

Suppose that for L_a and L_b there are CFGs, G_a and G_b, respectively. Then to produce a grammar that generates the *union* of L_a and L_b, we carry out the process described

Table 6.3 Constructing a CFG to generate the union of two CFLs (G_x and G_y are defined in Table 6.2)

Step	Description	Result
1	arrange it so the two grammars have no non terminals in common	G_x and G_y are already like this
2	collect all the productions of both grammars together	$A \rightarrow BC$ $B \rightarrow aBb \mid ab$ $C \rightarrow cC \mid c$ } G_x $D \rightarrow EF$ $E \rightarrow aE \mid a$ $F \rightarrow bFc \mid bc$ } G_y
3	add the two productions $S \rightarrow P \mid Q$ where S is a new non terminal and P and Q are the start symbols of the two grammars	$S \rightarrow A \mid D$ $A \rightarrow BC$ $B \rightarrow aBb \mid ab$ $C \rightarrow cC \mid c$ $D \rightarrow EF$ $E \rightarrow aE \mid a$ $F \rightarrow bFc \mid bc$

in Table 6.3 (the example on the right of Table 6.3 uses the two grammars G_x and G_y from Table 6.2.).

Referring to Table 6.3, you should be able to see that the grammar resulting from step 3 generates *all the strings that could be generated by one grammar or the other.* Step 1 is necessary so that any derivation uses only productions from one of the original grammars. If G_a and G_b are the original grammars, the resulting grammar generates $L(G_a) \cup L(G_b)$. You can also see that *if the two starting grammars are context free, the resulting grammar will also be context free.*
Therefore,

the context free languages are closed under union.

Now we focus on our particular example. The new grammar that we obtained from G_x and G_y generates $X \cup Y$, where X and Y are the languages above. This set, which will be called Z, is:

$$Z = X \cup Y = \{a^i b^j c^k : i, j, k \geq 1, i = j \text{ or } j = k\}$$

Now, while this is a CFL, and represents the union of two *deterministic* CFLs, it is not itself a deterministic CFL. To appreciate this, think about a PDR to accept it: such a machine could not be deterministic, as when it was reading the *a*s in the input it would have to assume that it was processing a string in which the number of *a*s was equal to the number of *b*s, which may not be the case (it may be processing a string in which the number of *b*s was equal to the number of *c*s). Thus there would be a need for *non* determinism. For a class of languages to be closed under an operation, the result of every application of the operation must also be a language of that class. So our example (and there are many more) shows us that

the deterministic context free languages are not closed under union.

However, as we showed above, in general, the CFLs *are* closed under union.

6.3.2 *Concatenation*

In this section, we see that:

If L_a and L_b are context free languages, then so is L_aL_b.

Remember that, if X and Y are languages, then XY denotes the language resulting from the **concatenation** of each and every string in X with each and every string in Y. Table 6.4 shows a simple method for taking two CFGs, G_a and G_b, and producing from them a new CFG, G, which generates $L(G_a)L(G_b)$. As before, we use our grammars G_x and G_y, from Table 6.2 to illustrate.

The new grammar created in Table 6.4 ensures that *any terminal string that could be derived by the first grammar is immediately followed by any terminal string that the second grammar could produce*. Therefore, the new grammar generates *the language*

Table 6.4 Constructing a CFG to generate the concatenation of two CFLs (G_x and G_y are defined in Table 6.2)

Step	Description	Example
1	arrange it so the two grammars have no non terminals in common	G_x and G_y are already like this
2	for each production in the first grammar with S (the start symbol of the grammar) on its left hand side, put R (the start symbol of the second grammar) at the end of the right hand side of that production.	New production created: $A \rightarrow BCD$ (only one created, since G_x has only one production with A, its start symbol, on the l.h.s.)
3	Add the rest of the first grammar's productions, and all of the second grammar's productions to the productions created in 2. The start symbol of the first grammar is the start symbol of the new grammar.	New grammar: $A \rightarrow BCD$ $B \rightarrow aBb \mid ab$ } rest of G_x $C \rightarrow cC \mid c$ $D \rightarrow EF$ $E \rightarrow aE \mid a$ } rest of G_y $F \rightarrow bFc \mid bc$

generated by the first grammar concatenated to the language generated by the second grammar. For the example in Table 6.4. the new grammar generates the set:

$$XY = \{a^i b^i c^j a^s b^t c^t : i, j, s, t \geq 1\}.$$

The Table 6.4 construction could be applied to any pair of context free grammars, and so **the context free languages are closed under concatenation.**

However, the deterministic CFLs are *not* closed under concatenation. This is not demonstrated by our example, because XY happens to be deterministic in this case. The two deterministic CFLs

$$\{a^i b^j : i \geq 1, j = 0 \text{ or } j = \text{i}\}$$

and

$$\{b^i c^j : i = 0 \text{ or } i = j, j \geq 1\}$$

concatenated together result in a language which is a *non* deterministic CFL. You are asked in the exercises to argue that the concatenation of the above two languages is a non deterministic CFL.

Our concatenation result for the deterministic CFLs is thus:

the deterministic context free languages are not closed under concatenation.

6.3.3 *Intersection*

Thus far, we have seen that the closure situation is the same for the CFLs as for the regular languages, with respect to both union and concatenation. However, in terms of **intersection**, the CFLs differ from the regular languages in that the CFLs are *not* closed under intersection. To appreciate this, consider the two sets we have been using in this section, i.e.

$$X = \{a^i b^i c^j : i, j \geq 1\}$$

and

$$Y = \{a^i b^j c^j : i, j \geq 1\}.$$

What is the intersection ($X \cap Y$) of our two sets? A little thought reveals it to be the set of strings of *a*s followed by *b*s followed by *c*s, in which the number of *a*s equals the number of *b*s and the number of *b*s equals the number of *c*s, i.e.:

$$X \cap Y = \{a^i b^i c^i : i \geq 1\}.$$

This language was stated to be not context free at the end of the last chapter, and this will be demonstrated later in this chapter. Moreover, both X and Y are deterministic CFLs, so this counter example shows us that:

both the deterministic and the non deterministic context free languages are *not* closed under intersection.

6.3.4 Complement

We can argue that it is also the case that the CFLs are not closed under **complement** (i.e. that the complement of a CFL is not necessarily itself a CFL). You may recall that above we used the following law to show that the *regular* languages were closed under intersection:

$$L_1 \cap L_2 = \overline{\overline{L_1} \cup \overline{L_2}}.$$

We can use the same law to show that the CFLs *cannot* be closed under complement. If the CFLs were closed under complement, the above law would tell us that they were closed under intersection (as we showed that they were closed under union earlier on). However, we have already shown that the CFLs are not closed under intersection, so to show that this is the case is absurd. We must therefore reject any assumption that the CFLs are closed under complement.

The above argument is our first example of proof by a technique called ***reductio ad absurdum***. We simply assume the logical negation of the statement we are trying to prove, and on the basis of this assumption follow a number of logically sound arguments that eventually lead to a nonsensical conclusion. Since the steps in our argument are logical, it must be our initial assumption that is false. Our initial assumption is false, but it is actually the negation of the statement we are trying to prove. Therefore, the statement we are trying to prove is indeed true.

In this case, what our reductio ad absurdum proof shows us is that

the context free languages are not closed under complement.

This result is very important, at least with respect to the pushdown recognizer. Imagine you are writing a **parser** for a programming language that you have designed. Suppose you implement your parser to be equivalent in power to a non deterministic pushdown recognizer. It turns out, unknown to you, that your language is one for which the complement is not a context free language. Now, this is not likely to cause problems for your parser if its input consists entirely of syntactically correct programs. This is highly unlikely, as I'm sure you will agree if you have ever done any programming! However, there will be one (or more) syntactically incorrect 'programs' for which your parser will not be able to make any decision at all (it will probably enter an infinite loop).

If for every string we input to the parser, the parser (which remember is no more powerful than a PDR) could output an indication of whether *or not* the program is syntactically legal, the same parser could be used to accept the complement of our original language (i.e. we simply interpret the original parser's 'yes' as a 'no', and vice versa). However, the fact that the CFLs are not closed under complement tells us that for some languages a parser equivalent in power to a PDR will be unable to make the 'no' statement. I suggest you re-examine the **acceptance conditions** for non deterministic PDRs in the previous chapter. Now you can probably see why there is no condition that dictates that the machine must always halt, only that it must *always* halt in the case of **sentences** of the language.

The issue of whether or not abstract machines eventually stop at some time during a computational process is central to computer science. However, we defer consideration of such issues until much later in the book.

All is not lost, however, for two reasons. Firstly, if your programming language is a *deterministic* CFL, its complement will also be a *deterministic* CFL. Remember, at the end of Chapter 5 we saw that a deterministic CFL was as a language for which a pushdown machine did not have to look more than one symbol ahead in the input. We saw that deterministic CFLs are called **LR(1) languages** for that reason. In such cases there are only a finite number of symbols the machine expects to encounter when it looks ahead to the next one. They form two sets at each stage: the symbols the machine expects to see next, and the symbols it does not expect to see next. If at any stage, the machine looks ahead and finds one of the symbols which at that stage it *does not* expect, the machine simply rejects the input as invalid (moves to a *halt state that denotes rejection,* as opposed to a *halt state that denotes acceptance*). We can make sure, then, that our machine always halts with 'yes' or 'no'. We can then simply exchange the acceptance/rejection status of our machine's halt states, and we have a machine that accepts the complement of the original language.

So,

the deterministic context free languages are closed under complement.

6.4 ESTABLISHING THAT CHOMSKY'S HIERARCHY IS A PROPER HIERARCHY

In this section, we sketch out two fundamental theorems of formal languages. One is for the regular languages, though it actually applies to the FSR, and is called the **repeat state theorem**. The other, for the context free languages, is in some ways similar to this, and is called the **uvwxy theorem**. The usefulness of these theorems is that they apply to every language in their class, and can therefore be used to show that a given language is not in the class. To appreciate this point, think about it like this: if every element in a set *must* possess a particular property, and we come across an object that cannot have that property, then the object cannot belong to our set. If it is true that every bird has feathers, and we come across a creature that is featherless, then that creature is certainly not a bird.

So, if we can use the *repeat state theorem* to show that a certain language cannot be regular, but we can show that the same language is context free, then we know that the regular languages are a **proper subset** of the context free languages (since we know that every regular language is context free, we have then also shown that there are context free languages that are not regular). Moreover, if we use the *uvwxy theorem* to show that a given language cannot be context free, and we then show that it is **type 0**, we know that the context free languages are a *proper subset* of the type 0 languages[1]. We have then established that **Chomsky's hierarchy** is a real hierarchy.

Some students experience problems in thinking in terms of *proper* subsets. This is because when you say to them 'all *x*'s are *y*'s', they automatically assume that you also mean 'all *y*'s are *x*'s'. To demonstrate the silliness of this inference, consider *parrots* and *birds*. If I said to you 'all parrots are birds', you would not then think 'all birds are parrots'. The set of all regular languages corresponds to the set of all parrots, and the set of all context free languages corresponds to the set of all birds. One set is *properly contained in the other.*

6.4.1 The 'repeat state theorem'

Any **FSR** that has a **loop** on some path linking its **start** and **halt states** recognizes an **infinite language**.

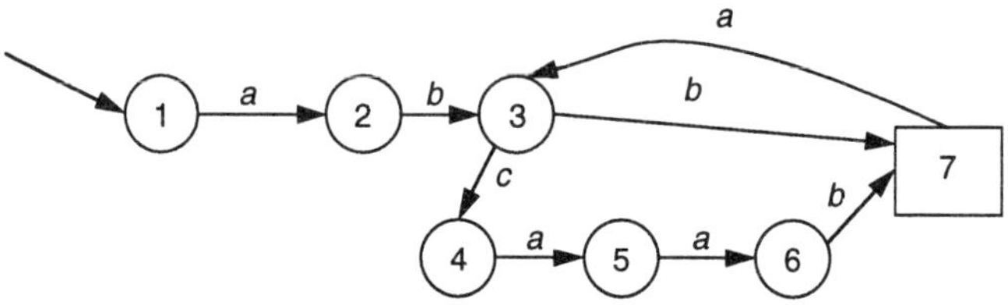

Figure 6.7 The FSR, *M*

Consider the example FSR, *M*, in Figure 6.7.

M of Figure 6.7 has seven states. Consider any string **acceptable** to *M* that is greater than *six* symbols in length. That string must have resulted in the machine passing through one of its states more than once. After all, *M* has only seven states, and it would need *eight* states to accept a string of length 7, if no state was to be visited more than once. Consider, as a suitable example the string *abbacaab*. This string is eight symbols in length, and the sequence of states visited during the acceptance of this string is as shown by the numbers placed next to *M*'s states in Figure 6.8.

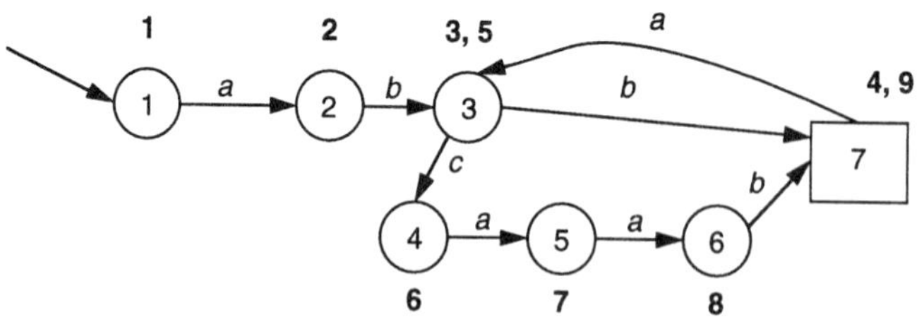

Figure 6.8 The sequence of states visited by *M* for the input *abbacaab*

[1] We omit the **context sensitive** (**type 1**) languages from this discussion. Only the **ε-free CFGs** are context sensitive, as context sensitive grammars are not allowed to have any ε productions.

Let us choose any state that *M* visited more than once in accepting our string, say, state 3. State 3, as the diagram shows, was the third and fifth state visited. Consider the **substring** of *abbacaab* that caused *M* to visit state 3 twice, i.e. *ba*. Where *ba* occurs in *ab**ba**caab*, we could copy it **any** number of times, and we would still obtain a string that *M* would accept. As an example, we will copy it four times: *ab**babababa**caab.* Furthermore, we could omit *ba*, giving *abcaab*, a string that is also accepted by our machine.

The other state that was visited twice in the acceptance of *abbacaab* was state 7 (the halt state). We now choose this as our example repeated state. The substring of *abbacaab* that caused state 7 to be visited twice was *acaab*. As before, our machine *M* would accept the original string with *no* copies of *acaab* in it: *abb*. It would also accept the original string with any number of copies inserted after the first occurrence, for example three copies: *abbacaabacaabacaab*.

To appreciate the generality of the above, consider any FSR that accepts a string of length greater than or equal to the number of states it has. As we said before, one or more of its states was visited twice. We consider any of those 'visited-twice' states. The string that was accepted can be expressed as three **concatenated** strings:

- a possibly empty first part, representing the states visited before the machine got to its 'visited twice' state,
- a non empty second part, representing the part of the string that caused the machine to visit the 'visited-twice' state again. This part of the string can be copied 0 or more times in between the first and third parts, and the resulting string will also be acceptable to the machine,
- a possibly empty third part, representing the states visited after the machine has left the 'visited-twice' state loop.

In our examples for the string *abbacaab*, above, when state 3 was the chosen 'visited-twice' state:

- *first part* was *ab*,
- *second part* was *ba*,
- *third part* was *caab*.

Alternatively, when state 7 was the chosen 'visited-twice' state:

- *first part* was *abb*,
- *second part* was *acaab*,
- *third part* was empty.

For many machines and strings, *first part* may be empty, if the loop began at the start state. In other cases, both *first* and *third parts* may be empty if the loop encompasses every state in the machine.

The repeat state theorem is expressed formally in Table 6.5.

Table 6.5 The repeat state (*vwx*) theorem for regular languages

For any deterministic FSR, *M*: if *M* accepts a string *z*, such that $\mid z \mid \geq n$, where n is the number of states in *M*, then *z* can be represented as three concatenated substrings: $z = vwx$ in such a way that all strings vw^ix, for all $i \geq 0$ are also accepted by *M*.

As was established in Chapter 4, *any language accepted by a DFSR is a regular language*. Therefore, *our theorem applies to any infinite regular language.*

6.4.2 *A language that is context free but not regular*

Now, as promised at the end of Chapter 4, we turn our attention to the language

$\{a^ib^i : i \geq 1\}$.

We know that this language is context free, because it is generated by the context free grammar G_3, of Chapter 2:

$S \rightarrow aSb \mid ab.$

The question is, could it also be a regular language? We shall now use our new theorem to show that it cannot be a regular language, using the technique of ***reductio ad absurdum*** introduced earlier in this chapter.

Our assumption is that $\{a^ib^i : i \geq 1\}$ is a regular language. If it is regular it is accepted by some FSR, *M*. *M* can be assumed to have *k* states. Now, *k* must be a definite number, and clearly our language is infinite, so we can select a sentence from our language of the form a^jb^j, where $j \geq k$. The *repeat state theorem* then applies to this string.

The repeat state theorem applied to our language tells us that our sentence a^jb^j can be split into three parts, so that the middle part can be repeated any number of times within the other two parts, and that this will still yield a string of *a*s followed by an equal number of *b*s. But how can this be true? Consider the following:

> the 'repeatable substring' *cannot* consist of *a*s followed by *b*s, as when we repeated it we would get *a*s followed by *b*s followed by *a*s... Our machine would accept strings that are not in the language $\{a^ib^i: i \geq 1\}$.

This means that the repeatable substring must consist of *a*s alone or *b*s alone. However:

> the repeatable substring *cannot* consist of *a*s alone, or when we repeated it more than once, the *a*s in our string would outnumber the *b*s, and our machine would accept strings not in the language $\{a^ib^i: i \geq 1\}$.

A similar argument obviously applies to a repeatable substring consisting entirely of *b*s.

Something is clearly amiss. Every statement we have made follows logically from our assumption that $\{a^i b^i: i \geq 1\}$ is a regular language. We are therefore forced to go right back and reject the assumption itself. Therefore $\{a^i b^i: i \geq 1\}$ is not a regular language.

Our result tells us that an *FSR could not accept certain strings in a language like* $\{a^i b^i: i \geq 1\}$ *without accepting many more that were not supposed to be acceptable.* We simply could not constrain the FSR to accept *only* those strings in the language. That is why an FSR can accept a language such as $\{a^i b^j : i, j \geq 1\}$, as you will find out if you design an FSR to do so, but the language $\{a^i b^i: i \geq 1\}$, which is a proper subset of $\{a^i b^j : i, j \geq 1\}$ is beyond the computational abilities of the FSR.

One interesting outcome of discovering that $\{a^i b^i: i \geq 1\}$ is not regular is that we can use that fact to argue that a language such as Pascal is not regular. The set of Pascal <compound statement>s is of the form:

$\{\mathbf{begin}^i x \mathbf{end}^i : x$ is a sequence of Pascal <statement>s$\}$.

The repeat state theorem tells us that many strings in this part of the Pascal language cannot be accepted by an FSR unless the FSR accepts many other strings in which the number of **begins** does not equal the number of **ends**. By extension of this argument, *the syntax of Pascal cannot be represented as a regular grammar.* However, as mentioned in Chapter 3, the syntax of Pascal can be expressed as a context free grammar. The same applies to most programming languages, including, for example, Lisp, with its use of arbitrary length strings of balanced parentheses.

You are asked in the exercises to provide similar justifications that certain other context free languages cannot be regular. It is thus clear that *the regular languages are properly contained in the class of context free languages.* In fact, we have shown two things about Chomsky's hierarchy:

1. the regular languages are a proper subset of the CFLs in general,
and, more specifically,
2. the regular languages are a proper subset of the deterministic CFLs.

Point 2 is demonstrated by considering that $\{a^i b^i: i \geq 1\}$ is not regular, but is a CFL, and is also deterministic (as we saw in Chapter 5). So there is at least one language that is a deterministic CFL that is not regular. In fact, none of the deterministic CFLs we considered when establishing the closure results for CFLs in this chapter is regular. You might like to convince yourself of this by using the repeat state theorem.

6.4.3 The uvwxy theorem for context free languages

The theorem described in this section is a context free language counterpart of the repeat state theorem described above. However, we establish our new theorem by using properties of context free grammars and derivations rather than the corresponding abstract machines (PDRs).

Let us assume that we have an ε **free CFG** that is in **Chomsky normal form** (**CNF**). That we can assume that any CFG is so represented was justified in Chapter 5[2]. As an example, we will use a CNF version of G_3 ($S \rightarrow aSb \mid ab$), which we will simply call G:

$S \rightarrow AX \mid AB$
$X \rightarrow SB$
$A \rightarrow a$
$B \rightarrow b.$

G has four non terminal symbols. So if we do a **derivation tree** for a sentence in which there is a path from *S* with more than four non terminals on it, one of the non terminals will appear more than once.

Now, consider the derivation tree for the sentence a^4b^4, shown in Figure 6.9. and labelled DT 1.

In particular, we focus on the path in DT 1 proceeding from the top of the tree to the non terminal marked 'low X', in DT 1. Sure enough, this path features a repeated non terminal. In fact, both *S* – three times – and *X* – also three times – are repeated on this path. We can choose any pair of the repeated non terminals, so we will choose the two instances of the non terminal *X* that have been labelled 'low *X*' and 'high *X*'.

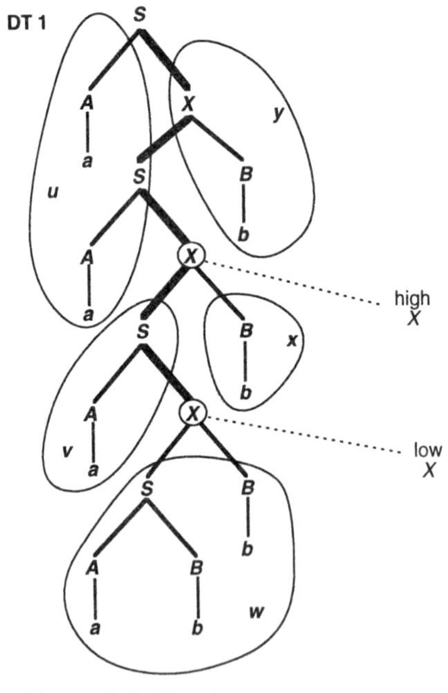

Figure 6.9 The derivation tree, DT 1

[2] We leave out the single ε production, if it exists, and concentrate only on the ε free part of the grammar.

Five substrings, that concatenated together in order make up the sentence have been identified and labelled in Figure 6.9 as follows:

- *u* this is the string derived in the part of the tree from *S* to the left of high *X*, and is the string *aa*
- *v* this is the string derived from high *X* to the left of low *X*, and is the string *a*
- *w* this is the string derived from low *X*, i.e. abb
- *x* this is the string derived from high *X* to the right of low *X*, i.e. *b*
- *y* this is the string derived from *S* to the right of high *X*, and is *b*.

Concatenating all the above strings in order, i.e. *uvwxy*, gives us our sentence a^4b^4.

Careful thought may now be required. The derivation from high *X* in DT 1 is simply the application of a sequence of productions, the first having *X* as its left hand side. *G* is a CFG, so the derivation we did from high *X* in DT 1 could be repeated from low *X*. We would still have a sentence, as the whole derivation begins with *S*, and a terminal string is derived from high *X* in DT 1.

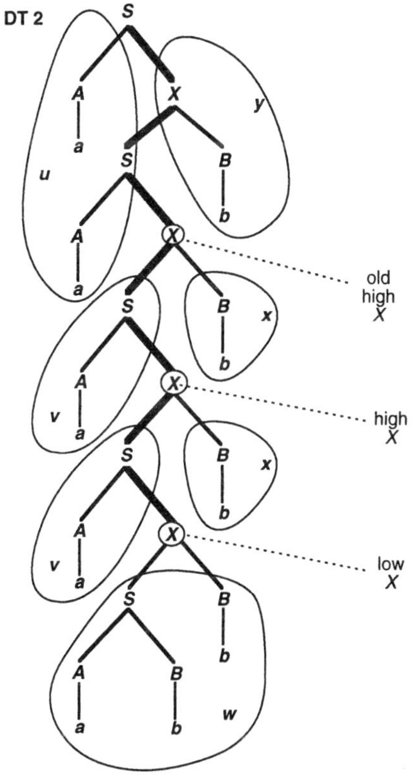

Figure 6.10 The derivation tree, DT 2

Doing the above gives us DT 2, as shown in Figure 6.10. DT 2 is the derivation tree for the sentence a^5b^5. As DT 2 shows, the way we have obtained the new derivation ensures that we now have *two* copies of the substrings v and x, where there was one copy of each, respectively, in the DT 1 sentence. Expressed in an alternative way, we have:

uv^2wx^2y (= a^5b^5).

What we have just done could be repeated, i.e. we could do the high X derivation we did in DT 1 from the new low X near the bottom of DT 2, in Figure 6.10. Then we would have uv^3wx^3y. Moreover, we could repeat this process indefinitely, i.e. we can obtain uv^iwx^iy, for all $i \geq 1$.

Finally, referring back to DT 1 (Figure 6.9), the derivation originally done from low X could have been done from high X instead. If we do this, we obtain DT 3, as shown in Figure 6.11. DT 3 is the derivation tree for the sentence a^3b^3. As can be seen from Figure 6.11, this time there are only *three* of our substrings, namely u, w and y. We have $uwy = a^3b^3$.

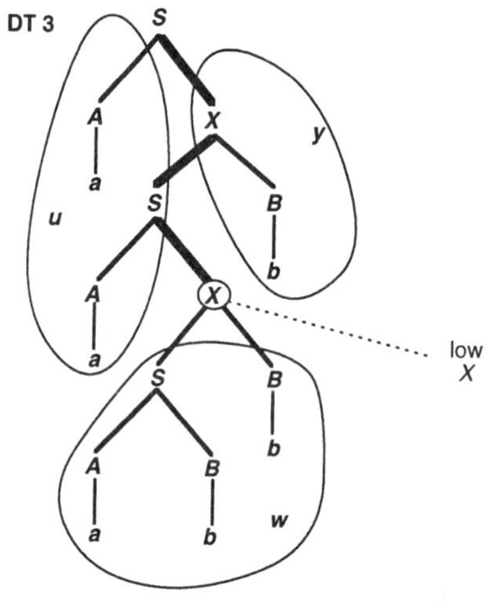

Figure 6.11 The derivation tree, DT 3

As stated in Chapter 2, for any string, s, $s^0 = \varepsilon$, the empty string, and for any string z, $z\varepsilon = z$, and $\varepsilon z = z$. uwy can therefore be represented as uv^0wx^0y.

The constructions used to obtain the three trees, DT 1–3 (Figures 6.9 – 6.11) and our accompanying discussion tell us that, for the language $L(G)$, i.e. $\{a^ib^i : i \geq 1\}$, we have found a string a^4b^4 which is such that:

a^4b^4 can be represented as concatenated substrings u, v, w, x, and y, such that $uvwxy = a^4b^4$, and for all $i \geq 0$, uv^iwx^iy is in $L(G)$.

We initially chose the two Xs called high X and low X in DT 1. However, *any other equal pair of non terminals on the path could have been chosen, and a similar argument could have been made.* For example, we could have chosen two of the repeated S nodes. A possible arrangement in this case is shown in DT 1a (Figure 6.12).

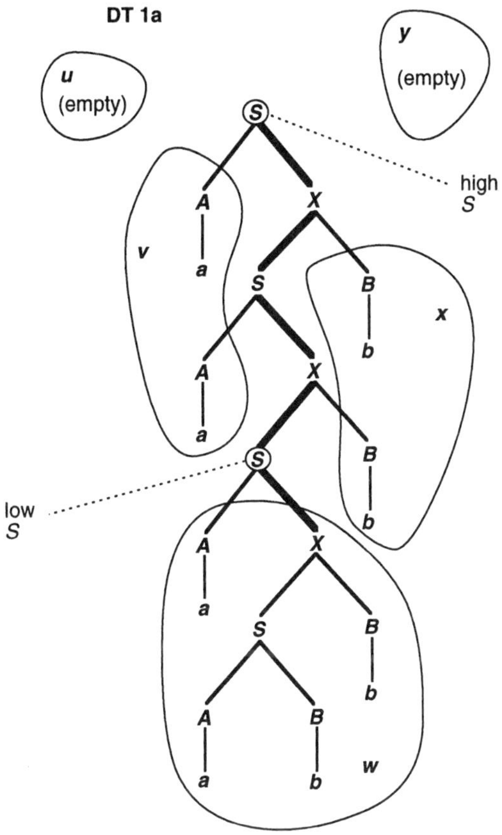

Figure 6.12 The derivation tree, DT 1a

In Figure 6.12 there is no string u to the left of the top S down to high S (as high S *is* the top S), and similarly there is no string y to its right, and both u and y are empty, i.e. $u = y = \varepsilon$. So we now have:

$u = \varepsilon$
$v = aa$
$w = aabb$
$x = bb$
$y = \varepsilon$.

This time, if we duplicated the original high S derivation from low S in Figure 6.12, we would have uv^2wv^2x, i.e., ε concatenated to aa concatenated to aa concatenated to *aabb* concatenated to *bb* concatenated to *bb* concatenated to ε, which is a^6b^6. The next time we repeated it we would obtain uv^3wx^3y, i.e. a^8b^8, and so on. If we duplicated the low *S* derivation from high *S*, we would obtain uv^0wx^0y. Since all the substrings except for *w* is empty, this leaves us with *w*, i.e. *aabb*. So again, our statement above:

> a^4b^4 can be represented as concatenated substrings *u*, *v*, *w*, *x*, and *y*, such that $uvwxy = a^4b^4$, and for all $i \geq 0$, uv^iwx^iy is in $L(G)$,

is true for this case also, as long as we permit *u* and *y* to be empty.

How general is this *uvwxy* type construction? It can be argued to apply to *any* context free grammar that generates a sentence long enough so that its derivation tree contains a path from *S* that contains two (or more) occurrences of one non terminal symbol. Now, any CFG that generates an infinite language must have a path like this. Such a CFG, as we showed in Chapter 5, can have its ε free part converted into CNF. If there are *n* non terminals in a CNF grammar, by the time we generate a sentence that is greater in length than 2^{n-1} (numerically speaking), we know we have a path of the type we need. To appreciate this, suppose that a CNF grammar has three non terminals, i.e. $n = 3$. The shallowest tree for a sentence of length equal to 2^{n-1} (4) is shown in Figure 6.13.

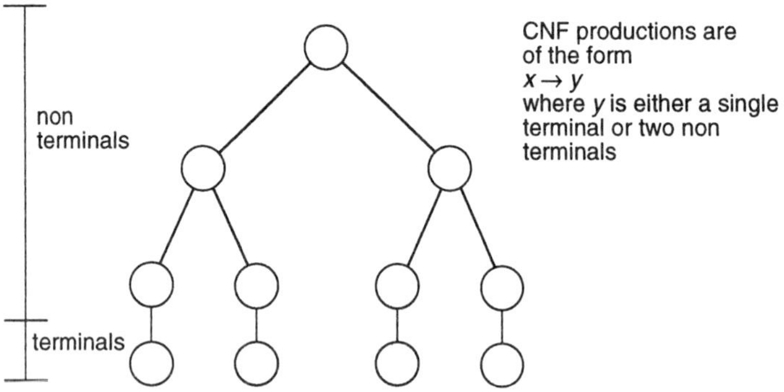

Figure 6.13 The shallowest derivation tree for CNF productions to generate a sentence of length 4

Notice that the longest paths in the tree in Figure 6.13 have length, or number of arcs, 3, and, since the last node on the path would be a terminal, such paths have only three non terminals on them. Such paths are not long enough to ensure that they feature repeated non terminals. Our hypothetical grammar has three non terminals, so to be absolutely sure that our tree contains a path of length greater than 3 we must generate a sentence of length *greater than 4*. You may need to think about this; perhaps drawing some possible extensions to the above tree will convince you: remember, the grammar is assumed to be in CNF. You should also convince yourself that the 2^{n-1} argument applies to any CNF grammar.

Of course, it is not always necessary to generate a long sentence to obtain our 'repeated non terminal path'. Our grammar *G* can be used to create derivation trees for sentences shorter in length than 8 (2^3, since G has four non terminals) that have paths of the type we require. However, here we are interested in defining conditions that apply in general, which requires us to be *sure* that we can obtain a path of the type required.

Let G stand for *any* ε free context free grammar. We now know that if we generate a sentence of sufficient length, the derivation tree for that sentence will have a path, starting from the S at the root of the tree, upon which the same non terminal, say X, appears twice or more. We choose two occurrences of X on that path, and call one high X and one low X. The sentence can be split into five concatenated substrings as before (use the derivation trees DT 1–3 and DT 1a in Figures 6.9 – 6.12 for illustration, if you wish):

- u — the string derived from S at the root and to the left of high X. This string may be empty, either because S = high X (as in DT 1a above), or because our path proceeds directly down the left of the tree.
- v — the string derived from high X to the left of low X. This string may be empty if the path from high X to low X is on the left. However, if this string is empty, x (see below) will not be. As this is a CNF grammar, high X must expand initially to two non terminals. Either (a) one of these is low X, or (b) must eventually expand into two non terminals of which one is low X. The other one expands into part of v or x, depending on the particular tree.
- w — the string derived from low X. This string will not be empty, as the grammar is ε free.
- x — as for v but derived from high X to the right of low X. The same argument as for v applies here. In particular, cannot be empty if v is.
- y — as for u but to the right of high X. This string may also be empty, for analogous reasons to those given above, for u.

As was shown by our example derivation trees DT 1–3, above, we can always repeat the 'deriving what was derived from the high X in the original tree from low X' routine as many times as we wish, thus obtaining the characteristic uv^iwx^iy form, for all $i \geq 1$. Furthermore, we can derive what was derived from low X in the original tree from high X, giving us the uv^0wx^0y case.

Enough has been said to demonstrate the theorem formally stated in Table 6.6.

Table 6.6 The *uvwxy* theorem for context free languages

Any sufficiently long sentence, z, of an infinite context free language, L, can be represented as five concatenated substrings

u, v, w, x, and y, such that $z = uvwxy$,

and uv^iwx^iy is also in L, for all $i \geq 0$.

6.4.4 $\{a^ib^ic^i : i \geq 1\}$ is not context free

As for the **repeat state theorem** for regular languages, we can use our *uvwxy* theorem to show that a given infinite language *cannot* be context free. As promised at the end of Chapter 5, we now demonstrate that the language

$$\{a^ib^ic^i : i \geq 1\}$$

is not context free.

The proof of this is very simple. Again, we use ***reductio ad absurdum*** as our technique. We assume that $\{a^ib^ic^i : i \geq 1\}$ is a CFL. The language is clearly infinite, so the *uvwxy* theorem applies to it. Our sufficiently long sentence is going to be one greater in length than 2^{n-1}, where n is the number of non terminals in a Chomsky normal form grammar that generates our language.

We can assume that our sufficiently long sentence is $a^kb^kc^k$, for some k, where $k > 2^{n-1}$. The theorem tells us that this sentence can be represented as five concatenated substrings *uvwxy*, such that uv^iwx^iy are also in $\{a^ib^ic^i : i \geq 1\}$ for all $i \geq 1$. However, how are substrings of $a^kb^kc^k$ to be allocated to u, v, w, x, and y in this way?

> neither v nor x can be strings of *a*s and *b*s, or *b*s and *c*s, or *a*s, *b*s and *c*s, as this would result in symbols being in the wrong relative order when v and x were repeated.

So this means that the repeatable strings v and x must consist of strings which are either all *a*s, all *b*s or all *c*s. However,

> this would also be inappropriate, as even if, say, v was *aaa* and x was *bbb*, when v and x were repeated, though the number of *a*s would still equal the number of *b*s, the number of each would exceed the number of *c*s. A similar argument can be used to show that no other allocation of substrings to v and x would work.

We must again reject our original assumption that $\{a^ib^ic^i : i \geq 1\}$ is a context free language.

However, $\{a^ib^ic^i : i \geq 1\}$ is a *context sensitive* language, since it is generated by the following **context sensitive grammar**, G_{16}:

$S \to aSBC \mid aBC$
$CB \to BC$
$aB \to ab$
$bB \to bb$
$bC \to bc$
$cC \to cc$

as you might like to justify for yourself.

The arguments in the following section may require some effort to appreciate. The section can be omitted, if required, though the result, as stated in the section's title, should be appreciated.

6.4.5 The 'multiplication language' is not context free

Now we consider one final refinement to our *uvwxy* theorem. We focus on a derivation tree for a sentence of length greater than 2^{n-1}, as described above. We choose the longest path (or one of them, if there are several). Now, as our high X and low X, we pick the lowest two repeated nodes on this path, a constraint that was not enforced in our earlier examples. The string derived from high X (i.e. the one we call *vwx*) is derived by a tree with high X as its root in which the path that passes through low X is the longest path. We selected the two Xs because they were the lowest repeated nodes on our longest path, therefore high X and low X are the only repeated nodes on our 'sub-path'. Therefore, the path must have maximum length $n + 1$, with the last node on the path being a terminal. Furthermore, the longest string that could be generated from high X (the one we call *vwx*) must be such that its length is less than or equal to 2^n (formally, $|vwx| \leq 2^n$).

We have established that for any sentence, z, such that $|z| > 2^{n-1}$, where there are n non terminal symbols in a Chomsky normal form grammar that generated z, we can define the *uvwxy* substrings so that $|vwx| \leq 2^n$. To see why this can be useful, we consider a language introduced at the end of Chapter 2, i.e.

$$\{a^i b^j c^{i \times j} : i, j \geq 1\},$$

which was generated by our **type 0 grammar**, G_4.

It was stated at the close of Chapter 5 that the above language is not context free. We now use the *uvwxy* theorem, along with our newly established result obtained immediately above, to demonstrate this.

Again, we use *reductio ad absurdum*. We assume that $\{a^i b^j c^{i \times j} : i, j \geq 1\}$ is a context free language. This means that the *uvwxy* theorem applies to a sufficiently long string. Consider the following string, z, in our language: $a^{2^n} b^{2^n} c^{(2^n)^2}$, where n is the number of non terminals in a Chomsky normal form grammar for the language. Obviously, the length of z is greater than 2^{n-1}. We can then, as shown in the preceding paragraph, establish a *uvwxy* form for this sentence, such that $|vwx| \leq 2^n$ (n being the number of non terminals). Now, by a similar argument to that applied in the case of the language $\{a^i b^i c^i : i \geq 1\}$ above, we can certainly justify that v and x *cannot be mixtures of different terminals*. This means that v must consist of either all as or all bs, and x must be all cs (otherwise when we increase the number of as or bs for v^i, the cs would not increase accordingly). Therefore,

suppose v is a string of as. Then, since x must consist of cs only, w must include all of the bs. This cannot be so, as both v and x are non empty, so $|vwx|$

exceeds 2^n (since there are 2^n *b*s in w alone).

v cannot be a string of *a*s then, so:

v must be a string of *b*s. Now, suppose $v = b^k$, for some $k \geq 1$. Then x must be $c^{2^n \times k}$. This is because each time uv^iwx^iy inserts a new copy of v (b^k) into the *b*s, it inserts a new copy of x into the *c*s. To ensure that the number of *c*s is still the same as the number of *a*s times the number of *b*s, we must insert 2^n *c*s (2^n being the number of *a*s) for each of the k *b*s. However, again this cannot be so, because if $|x| = 2^n \times k$, then $|vwx|$ is certainly $> 2^n$.

If the language had been context free, we could, for our sufficiently long sentence, have found a *uvwxy* form such that $|vwx| \leq 2^n$. By assuming the existence of this form, we are led to a contradiction. We are therefore forced, once more, to reject our original assumption, and therefore conclude that $\{a^ib^jc^{i \times j} : i, j \geq 1\}$ is not a context free language.

Note that the addition of the length constraint to the *uvwxy* theorem makes it especially powerful. It would have been difficult to establish that $\{a^ib^jc^{i \times j} : i, j \geq 1\}$ is not a context free language by arguing simply in terms of *uvwxy* patterns alone. You may wish to try this to appreciate the point.

6.5 PRELIMINARY OBSERVATIONS ON THE SCOPE OF THE CHOMSKY HIERARCHY

The fact that $\{a^ib^jc^{i \times j} : i, j \geq 1\}$ is not context free suggests that we need more powerful machines than pushdown recognizers to perform computations such as multiplication. This is indeed the case. However, the **abstract machine** that is capable of multiplication (of arbitrary length numbers), is not that far removed from the pushdown machine. The study of the machine, the **Turing machine**, will be a major part of the remainder of this book. It also turns out that the Turing machine is the recognizer for the context sensitive (type 1) and unrestricted (type 0) languages, which is how we introduce it in the next chapter.

In the preceding sections we have seen that there is indeed a hierarchy of formal languages, with each class being properly contained within the class immediately above it. The question arises: *are the type 0 languages a proper subset of the set of all formal languages?* Remember, a **formal language** is simply any set of strings. In Chapter 11, we see that there are indeed formal languages that are outside the class of type 0 languages, and thus cannot be generated by any grammar specified by the **Chomsky hierarchy**.

EXERCISES

1 Produce a **DFSR** to **accept** the language $\{a^{4i} : i \geq 1\}$, then use the **complement** construction described earlier in the chapter to produce a machine that accepts the language $\{a^{4i+j} : i \geq 0, 1 \leq j \leq 3\}$.

2 As mentioned in the text above, if $L_1 = \{a^i b^j : i \geq 1, j = 0 \text{ or } j = i\}$ and $L_2 = \{b^i c^j : i = 0 \text{ or } i = j, j \geq 1\}$, both L_1 and L_2 are **deterministic CFLs**, but the language L_1L_2 is not. Justify this.

3† As expressed above, the first sentence of the section on the **repeat state theorem** (section 6.4.1) is not generally true. Rewrite the sentence so that it is.

4† Use the *repeat state theorem* to show that $\{a^i b^j c^{i+j} : i, j \geq 1\}$ and $\{a^i b^j c^{i-j} : i, j \geq 1\}$, both shown to be deterministic by exercise 7 of Chapter 5, are not **regular languages**.

5† Use the ***uvwxy* theorem** to show that $\{xx : x \in \{a, b\}^*\}$ is not **context free**.

7 Phrase structure languages and Turing machines

AIMS

To introduce the Turing machine (TM) and to look at TMs as language recognizers, learning that

- TMs can do anything that Finite State Recognizers (FSRs) and Pushdown Recognizers (PDRs) can do
- TMs are more powerful than non deterministic PDRs
- TMs are the recognizers for the phrase structure (type 0) languages in general

7.1 THE ARCHITECTURE OF THE TURING MACHINE

The **abstract machine** we consider in this chapter, and for much of the remainder of this book, is called the **Turing machine** (**TM**). Turing was the name of the English mathematician who first described such a machine in 1936. A TM is essentially a finite state machine, like a **finite state recognizer**, but with some very simple additional facilities for input and output, and a slightly different way of representing the **input sequences**.

7.1.1 'Tapes' and the 'read/write head'

The *input* to a TM is regarded as being contained on a '**tape**'. The tape is divided into '**tape squares**', so that each symbol of the input sequence occupies one square of the tape. We assume that the tape is not restricted to any particular length, so that we can place an input sequence of any length we like on the tape (we assume that any unused part of the tape consists of **blank** tape squares). For example, the input sequence *aabbaa* may occupy part of a tape such as that depicted in Figure 7.1.

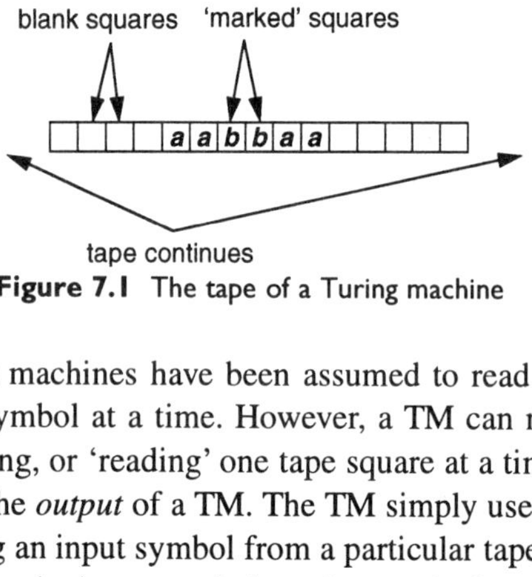

Figure 7.1 The tape of a Turing machine

Hitherto, our abstract machines have been assumed to read their input sequences from left to right, one symbol at a time. However, a TM can move along its tape in either direction, examining, or 'reading' one tape square at a time.

Let us now consider the *output* of a TM. The TM simply uses its tape for output as well as input. On reading an input symbol from a particular tape square in a particular state, the TM can replace the input symbol on that particular square with any designated symbol. As a simple example, consider a tape containing a sequence of *as* and/or *bs*, where we require as output a sequence representing the input sequence, but with all *bs* replaced by *as*, and vice versa.

An example tape is shown in Figure 7.2, as the hypothetical TM described immediately above has completed its processing of the first three symbols (assume that the tape is being processed from left to right).

In order to clarify the notion of a TM 'examining' one square of a tape, and placing a symbol on a tape, we say the TM possesses a **read/write head** (we sometimes simply say **r/w head** , or even just **head**). The r/w head is at any time located on one

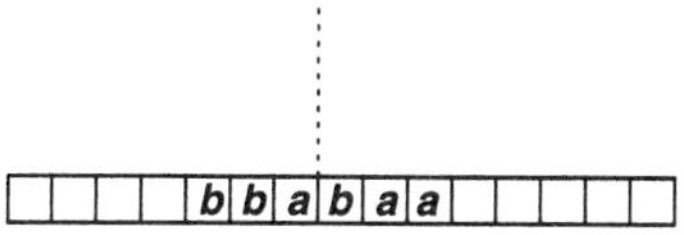

Figure 7.2 A partly processed TM tape

of the tape squares, and is assumed to be able to 'sense' which symbol of some finite alphabet occupies that square. The head also has the ability to 'write' a symbol from the same finite alphabet onto a tape square. When this happens, the symbol written replaces the symbol that previously occupied the given tape square. The read/write head can be moved along the tape, one square at a time, in ways we discuss later.

7.1.2 Blank squares

In Figure 7.2, we examined the state of the tape of an imaginary TM that replaced *b*s by *a*s (and vice versa), when the machine had dealt with only some of the input symbols on its tape. Let us now consider the example tape for Figure 7.2 when the machine has processed the last symbol (the *a* at the right hand end) of the marked portion of the tape, at which point, since the machine is replacing *a*s by *b*s, and vice versa, the tape will be as shown in Figure 7.3.

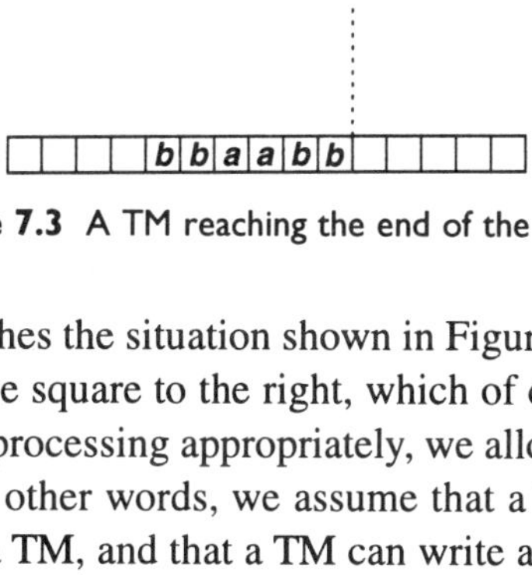

Figure 7.3 A TM reaching the end of the symbols

When our machine reaches the situation shown in Figure 7.3, it will attempt to read the symbol on the next tape square to the right, which of course is **blank**. So that our machine can terminate its processing appropriately, we allow it to make a transition on reading a blank square. In other words, we assume that a blank square can be sensed by the read/write head of a TM, and that a TM can write a symbol into a blank square and even 'blank out' an occupied tape square.

We denote the blank symbol by an empty box[1] (suggesting that it is represented as a *blank tape square*), thus: □

7.1.3 TM 'instructions'

Like FSRs (Chapter 4) and PDRs (Chapter 5), TMs can be represented as drawings, featuring states and labelled arcs. An **arc** in a TM is, like the arc between two **states** of a **PDR**, labelled with three symbols.

[1] It is sometimes represented as a 0, or a β (Greek letter *beta*).

By way of illustration, Figure 7.4 shows part of a TM. Assume that the machine is in state *A*, and that the tape and position of the read/write head are as shown on the right of Figure 7.4.

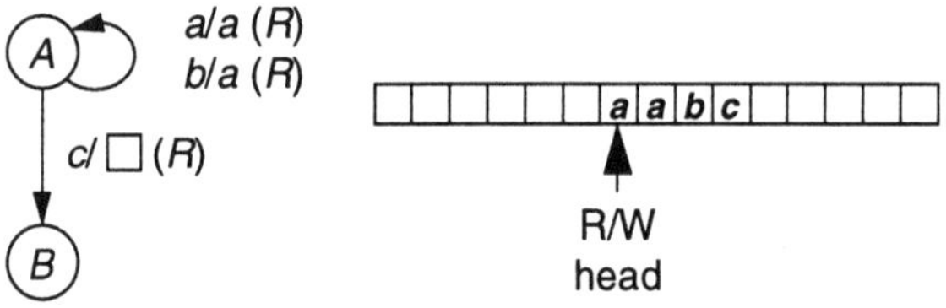

Figure 7.4 Part of a TM, and an appropriate tape set up

The TM represented in Figure 7.4 would carry out the activities described in Table 7.1.

Table 7.1 A trace of the behaviour of a simple Turing machine

Action	State of tape immediately following action
read an *a*, write an *a*, move right (R), stay in state	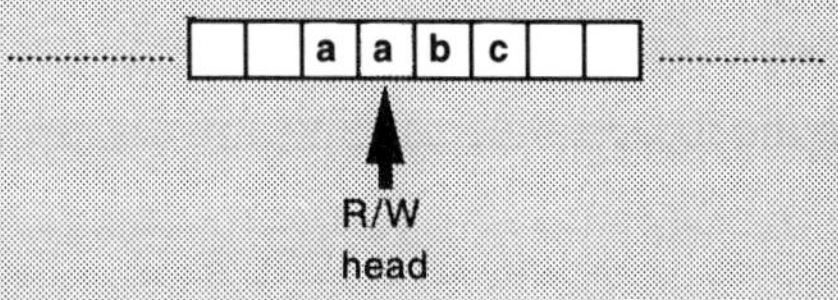
read an *a*, write an *a*, move right (R), stay in state *A*	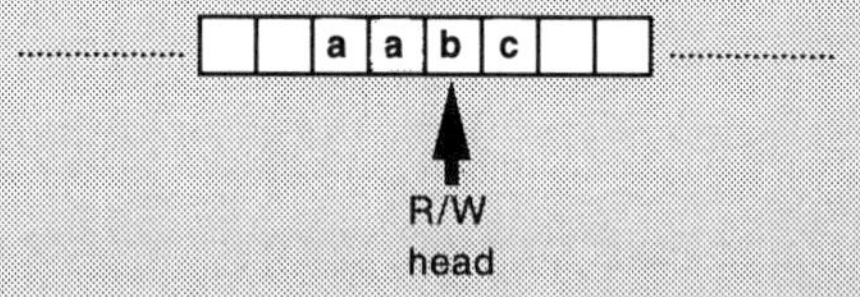
read a *b* write an *a*, move right (R), stay in state *A*	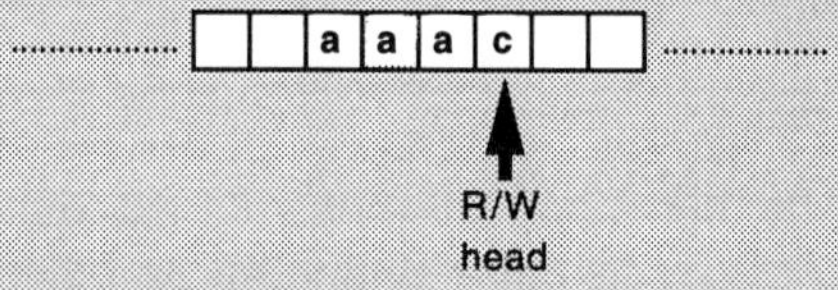
read a *c*, write a blank, move right (R), move to state *B*	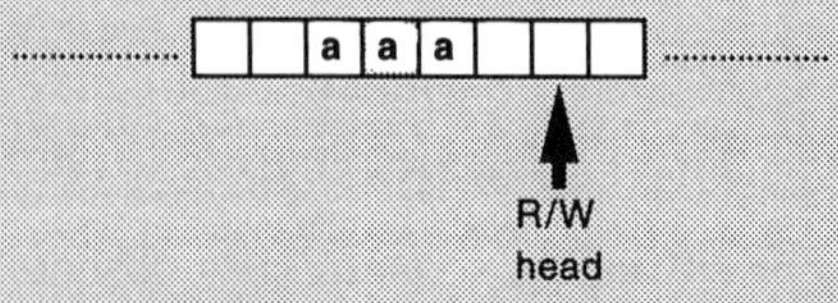

We now use the conceptual framework provided above as the basis of a more rigorous definition of TMs.

7.1.4 Turing machines defined

A TM has essentially the same pictorial formulation as the FSR, except that each arc of a TM is labelled with three instructions:

1. an *input symbol*, which is either □ or a symbol from a finite **alphabet**;
2. an *output symbol*, either □ or a symbol from the same alphabet as for (1);
3. a *direction designator*, specifying whether the read/write head is to move one square left (L), right (R), or not at all (N).

The TM can make a **transition** between states if (1) is the current tape symbol, in which case the TM replaces (1) by (2), and moves one tape square in the direction specified by (3), before moving to the state pointed at by the relevant arc.

Next, we consider a simple example TM, which is discussed in some detail. Much of the remainder of the chapter is devoted to demonstrating that TMs can perform all the tasks that can be performed by the other abstract machines we have hitherto considered, and many tasks that they could not.

7.2 THE BEHAVIOUR OF A TM

Figure 7.5 shows our first full TM, T_1.

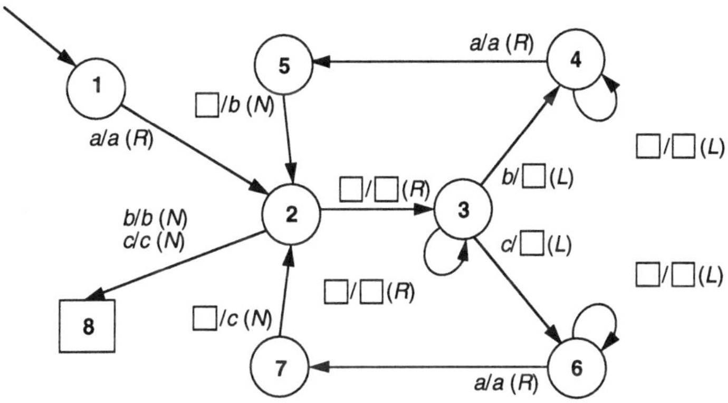

Figure 7.5 The TM, T_1

T_1 processes input tapes of the form shown in Figure 7.6.

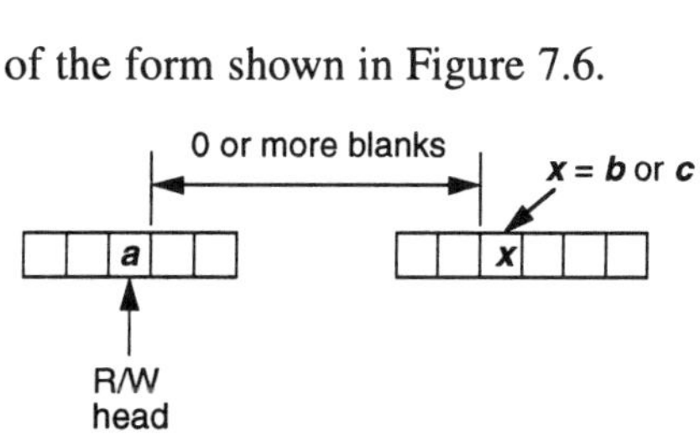

Figure 7.6 The tape set up for T_1

As shown in Figure 7.6, T_1 (Figure 7.5) expects the marked portion of its input tapes to consist of an a followed by zero or more blank squares, followed by either a b or a c. T_1 has its head initially positioned at the a, and produces as its output a tape of the form depicted in Figure 7.7.

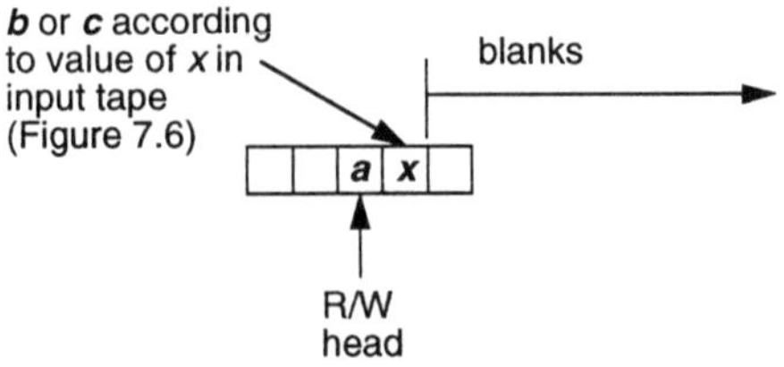

Figure 7.7 The tape when T_1 halts

As Figure 7.7 shows, the b or c of the input tape (Figure 7.6) has been 'erased' from its initial position – replaced by a blank – and placed in the tape square immediately to the right of the a, with T_1's head finally left positioned at that square. We will call this moving of a symbol from one part of a tape to another '**shuffling**' the symbol. We can talk of *right shuffling* and *left shuffling*. T_1 does a *left shuffle* of the symbol denoted by x in Figure 7.6.

We will not trace the behaviour of T_1 in detail here. Table 7.1 showed how a trace of a TM's behaviour is done; you can perform a similar analysis of T_1's behaviour if you wish. However, we will spend a short time examining the function of the states in the machine:

State 1

The start state. Assumes that the head is positioned at a square containing an a. If there is no a, or another symbol occupies the square, no transition is possible.

States 2–5 & 2–7

When state 2 is entered from state 1, a right move of the head has been made. Since there are expected to be 0 or more blanks between the a and the b or c, the head could at this point be pointing at a b or a c (in which case the machine has nothing else to do, so moves to its halt state leaving the head where it is). Otherwise, there are one or more blanks after a, and the machine moves into State 3, where it 'skips over' (to the right) any more blanks, until the head reaches the b or c. State 3 also 'erases' the b or c before moving to state 4 (for a b) or state 6 (for a c). State 4 skips back over any blanks (left) until the head reaches the a, at which point the head moves back to the blank square to the right of a, then state 5 ensures that the blank to the right of a is overwritten by a b, as the transition back to state 2 is made (note that no movement of the head is specified by this transition). States 6 and 7 perform an analogous function to states 4 and 5, but where the symbol after the blanks is c rather than b).

State 8
This state, the **halt state**, is reached only from state 2, when the head points at a *b* or a *c* (which could be either because a *b* or a *c* was initially next to the *a*, or because a *b* or a *c* had been moved there by states 3–5 or states 3–7 (see above). Note that the arcs leaving states 5 and 7 could have been drawn directly to state 8 if wished.

T_1 will reach its halt state, producing an output tape as described in Figure 7.7, when it is given an **input configuration** as specified in Figure 7.6. If the input configuration is not set up correctly, then T_1 may:

(a) *halt in a non halt state*, as would result from the input tape configuration shown in Figure 7.8.
(b) *never halt*, which would be the result of the input tape configuration shown in Figure 7.9.

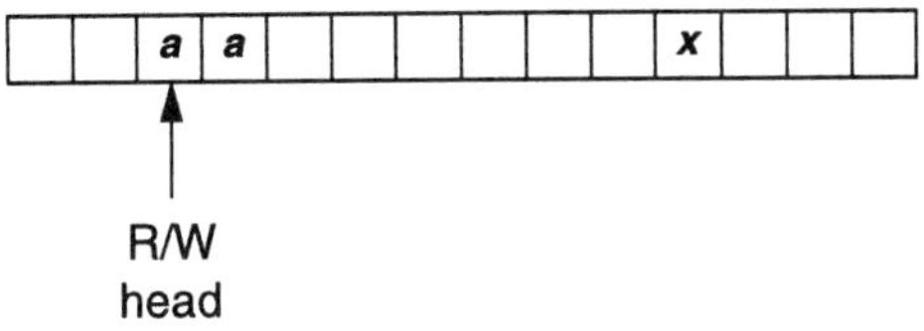

Figure 7.8 A tape that causes problems for T_1

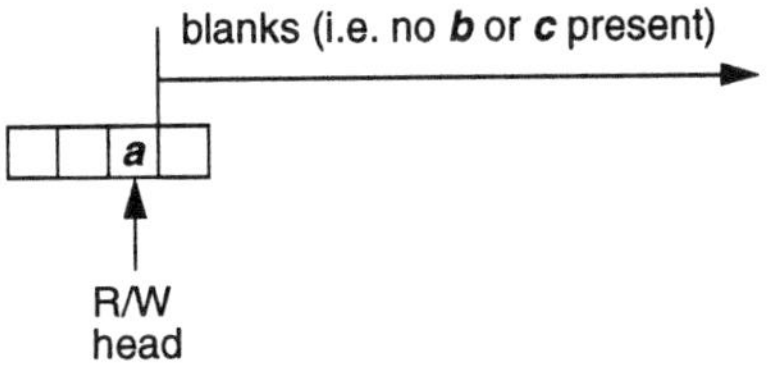

Figure 7.9 A tape that would cause even bigger problems for T_1

You may like to satisfy yourself that (a) and (b) are true for the input configurations of Figures 7.8 and 7.9, respectively. You should also observe that a third general possibility for a Turing machine's halting situation:

(c) *reaches halt state, but produces output not conforming to specification,*

is not possible in the case of T_1, if only blanks lie to the right of the *b* or *c*. The latter comment relates to the fact that *the output specification requires a totally blank tape to the right of the head when T_1 halts.*

The immediately preceding discussion indicates the need for care in describing a TM's expected input configuration (i.e. the marked portion of its tape, and initial location of the read/write head). If we carefully specify the input conditions, then we need not consider what happens when an input situation that does not meet our specification is presented to the machine. Of course, we should also specify how the **output configuration** (the state in which the machine halts, the contents of its tape, and the final location of its read/write head) is to represent the 'result'.

The remainder of this chapter is devoted to demonstrating that for language recognition, TMs are indeed more powerful than the other abstract machines we have studied thus far.

7.3 TURING MACHINES AS LANGUAGE RECOGNIZERS

7.3.1 *Regular languages*

We do not have to expend much effort to demonstrate that TMs are at least as powerful as **finite state recognizers (FSRs)**. Recall from Chapter 4 that for each **regular language**, there exists a **deterministic** FSR (DFSR) to recognize that language. A DFSR is simply *a TM that always moves its read/write head to the right, replacing each symbol it reads by that same symbol, on each transition.*

Thus, the DFSR, $M_5{}^d$, from Chapter 4, shown here in Figure 7.10, becomes the TM, T_2, shown in Figure 7.11.

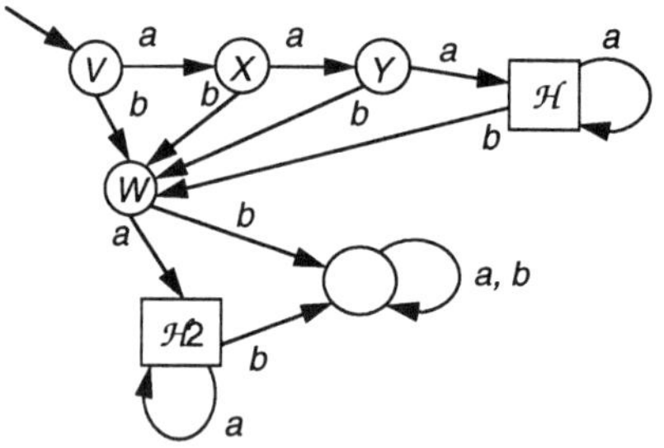

Figure 7.10 The DFSR $M_5{}^d$ from Chapter 4

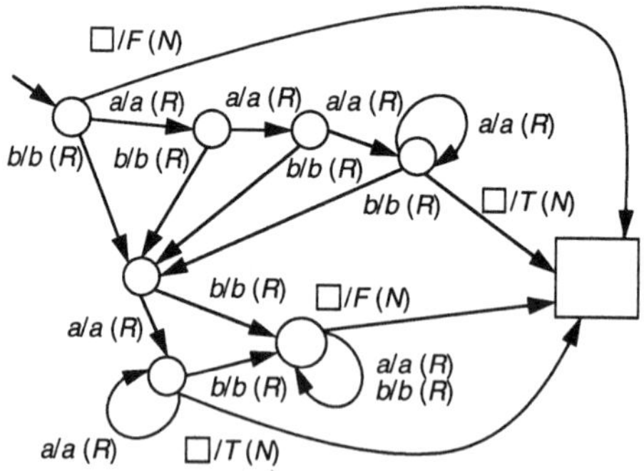

Figure 7.11 The TM, T_2

We have taken advantage of the TM's ability to write, as well as read, symbols, and its ability to detect the end of the input string when reaching a blank square, to ensure that T_2 has two useful features.

1. It prints T for any *valid* string, and F for any *invalid* string.
2. It has *only one halt state*.

We henceforth assume that all our TMs have only one halt state. An exercise asks you to convince yourself that this is a reasonable assumption.

An important point should be noted. T_2 prints F and goes directly to its halt state if the head is initially located on a blank square. In a sense, this reflects an assumption that *if the head is initially at a blank square then the tape is entirely blank*. We will call this assumption the **blank tape assumption**. We will further assume that a blank tape represents the **empty string**, ε.

For our example machine T_2, of Figure 7.11, as ε is not in the language accepted by M_5^d, T_2 prints an F if its head is initially on a blank square. Of course, T_2 can never be *sure* that the tape is empty. No TM can ever establish beyond doubt that its tape is unmarked. In view of the fact that we assume that a tape has no definite ends in either direction, i.e. the blank squares at either end of the marked portion extend indefinitely, it should be clear by now why we have not designed T_2 so that when its head points initially at a blank square, it searches its tape to see if the input string is located somewhere else on the tape.

You will appreciate that we could do the same type of DFSR-to-TM conversion for any DFSR.

7.3.2 *Context free languages*

Recall from Chapter 5 that the abstract machine associated with the **context free languages** is the **non deterministic pushdown recognizer** (**NPDR**). Recall also that some of the context free languages are **deterministic** (can be recognized by a DPDR) while some are not (can be recognized by an NPDR, but *not* a DPDR).

It can be shown that any DPDR can be converted into a TM. We will not consider this here, but merely point out that the basic method is for the TM to use part of its tape to represent the **stack** of the PDR, thus working with two parts of the tape, one representing the input string, the other representing the stack. However, one usually finds that a TM which must do the job done by a DPDR is better designed from scratch. Here, we consider T_3, which is equivalent to M_3^d of Chapter 5, the DPDR that accepts the language

$$\{a^i b^i : i \geq 1\},$$

which we know from Chapter 6 to be **properly** context free, i.e. context free but not regular. T_3 is shown in Figure 7.12.

T_3 expects on its tape an arbitrary string of as and/or bs (using the notation of Chapter 2, a string in $\{a,b\}^*$), finally printing T if the string is in the language $\{a^i b^i : i \geq 1\}$, and F if it is not. Note that, like T_2, T_3's read/write head begins on the leftmost symbol of the input. Moreover, T_3 makes the same *blank tape assumption* as did T_2. T_3

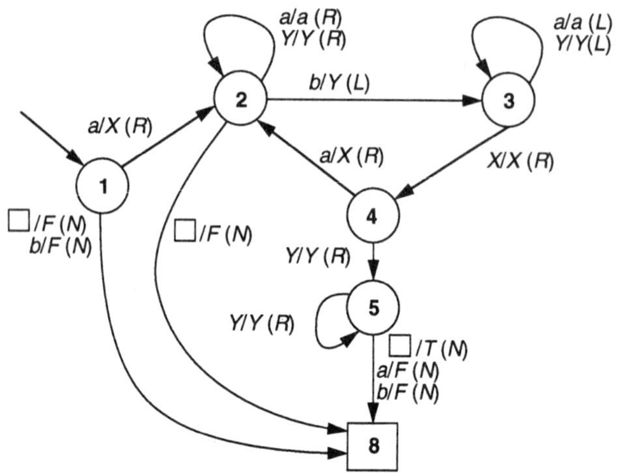

Figure 7.12 The TM, T_3

uses the symbols X and Y to 'tick off' the *as* and corresponding *bs*, respectively. You should trace T_3's behaviour on example **sentences** and non sentences. Such a trace is shown in Table 7.1.

Now for the *non deterministic* context free languages. Recall from Chapter 5 that some context free languages can be accepted by a non deterministic PDR (NPDR), but not a deterministic PDR. Later, in Chapter 11, we briefly consider the conversion of NPDRs into TMs. However, to demonstrate that TMs are more powerful than NPDRs, we see in Figure 7.13 a TM, T_4, that recognizes the language of possibly empty **palindromic strings** of *as* and *bs*. Recall that in Chapter 5 such languages were shown to be non deterministic CFLs, and therefore beyond the processing power of the DPDR.

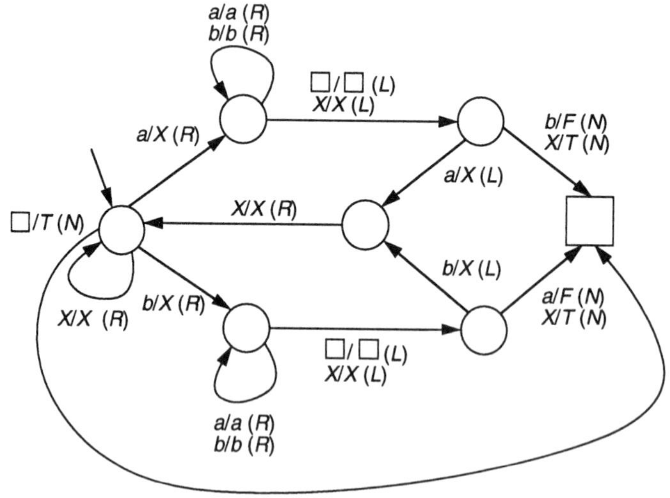

Figure 7.13 The TM, T_4

T_4 accepts only those strings in $\{a, b\}^*$ that are palindromic, and, what is more, does the job deterministically.

T_4 uses only one marker, X, and works from the outside in, 'ticking off' matching symbols at the extreme right and left ends of the string. This time, the *blank tape assumption* results in a T being printed if the read/write head of T_4 starts on a blank, as the empty string is in $\{a, b\}^*$, and is palindromic. Again, you should make sure you understand how the machine works, since more complex TMs follow.

7.3.3 Turing machines are more powerful than PDRs

The above implies that Turing machines are as powerful, in terms of language processing, as FSRs and (deterministic *and* non deterministic) PDRs. This claim is justified later in this chapter. However, by using a single example we can show that TMs are actually *more* powerful than PDRs. Consider the Turing machine, T_5, shown in Figure 7.14, which processes the language

$$\{a^ib^ic^i : i \geq 1\},$$

demonstrated in Chapter 6 to be properly **context sensitive** (i.e. context sensitive but not context free).

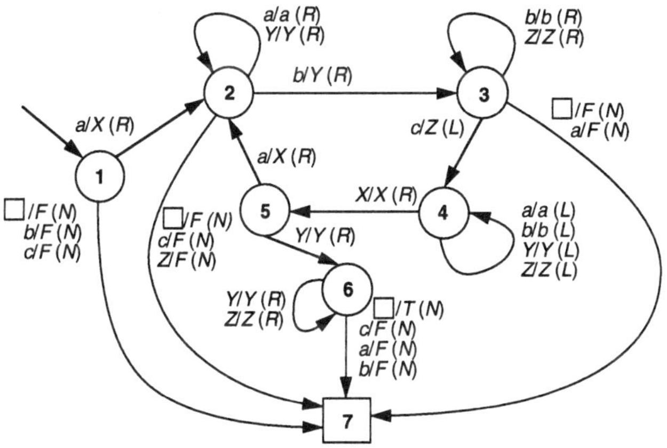

Figure 7.14 The TM, T_5

T_5 requires **input configurations** of the form shown in Figure 7.15.

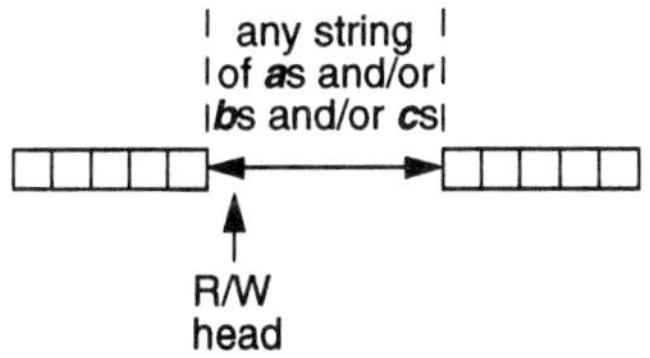

Figure 7.15 An initial tape set up for T_5

It reaches its halt state for valid or invalid strings. For valid strings (i.e. strings of one or more *as* followed by the same number of *bs* followed by the same number of *cs*), the output configuration is as specified in Figure 7.16.

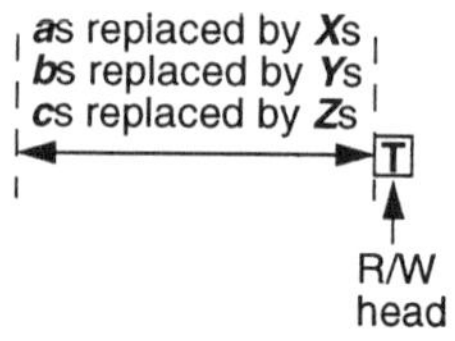

Figure 7.16 The tape after a valid string has been processed by T_5

The input sequence of Figure 7.15 is altered by T_5 to produce a tape of the form described in Figure 7.16 (the symbols X, Y, and Z are used as auxiliary *markers*). Again, T indicates a sentence.

For invalid strings (i.e. any string in $\{a, b, c\}^*$ which is not in $\{a^ib^ic^i : i \geq 1\}$), however, when the halt state is reached, the configuration will be as shown in Figure 7.17.

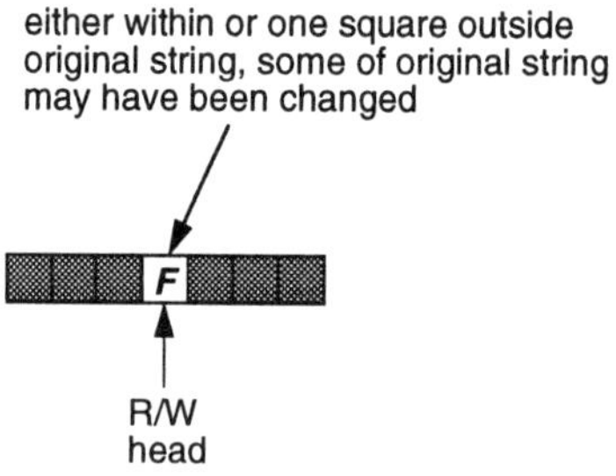

Figure 7.17 The tape after an invalid string has been processed by T_5

In the case of invalid strings, the read head will be left pointing at an F, as shown in Figure 7.17.

When students design T_5 and similar machines, their machines often fail to check for the possible occurrence of extra symbols at the end of an otherwise valid string. For the language $\{a^ib^ic^i : i \geq 1\}$, such machines will indicate that a valid string immediately followed by another string in $\{a, b\}^+$ is valid, when, of course, it is not.[2]

However, students are not the only guilty parties when it comes to failing to check for invalid symbols at the end of an otherwise valid input. I have encountered a Pascal compiler that simply ignores all the source file text that occurs after an end followed by a full stop (in Pascal, the only **end** terminated by a full stop is the last one in the program, and corresponds to a **begin** before the first statement). This caused severe difficulties to a novice who had accidentally put a full stop after an **end** halfway down their program, and happened to have an extra **begin** near the beginning. The program

[2] Recall from Chapter 2 that $\{a, b\}^+$ is the set of all non empty strings of *as* and/or *bs*.

compiled perfectly, but when run only carried out the first part of what was expected by the programmer! The Pascal compiler in question was *accepting an invalid input string*.

7.4 INTRODUCTION TO (TURING MACHINE) COMPUTABLE LANGUAGES

We have seen that TMs are more powerful language recognizers than finite state and pushdown recognizers. Regular languages are associated with finite state recognizers in the same way as context free languages are associated with pushdown recognizers. It seems reasonable to ask, then, if there is a class of languages that are associated with TMs in a similar way. In other words, *is there a class of languages, as defined by a type of grammar in the* **Chomsky hierarchy**, *so that for any language in that class, there is some TM that can recognize that language, and for any TM that recognizes a language, we can be sure that the language is in the class?* In fact, there is such a class of languages, and it turns out that this class is exactly that defined by the most general Chomsky classification, i.e. the general **phrase structure languages** themselves, these being those generated by the **type 0**, or **unrestricted grammars**. Type 0 grammars were defined in Chapter 2 as being those with productions of the form:

$$x \to y, x \in (N \cup T)^+, y \in (N \cup T)^*$$

i.e. a non empty arbitrary string of terminals and non terminals on the left hand side of each production, possibly empty arbitrary string of terminals and non terminals on the right hand sides.

Let us call the languages that can be recognized by a TM the Turing Machine **Computable languages.** For convenience, and with some justification, as we see later in the book, we will refer to them as computable languages. We eventually discover that the computable languages include, *but are not restricted to*, all the regular languages, all the context free languages, and all of the context sensitive languages.

In Chapter 4, the correspondence between regular languages and finite state recognizers was specified. We saw how we can take any regular grammar and construct an FSR to accept exactly the same set of strings as that generated by the grammar. We also showed that we could take any FSR and represent it by a regular grammar that generated the same set of strings as that accepted by the FSR (we did a similar thing with respect to NPDRs and the context free languages in Chapter 5). Analogously, to show the correspondence between TMs and unrestricted languages we would have to show how to create a type 0 grammar from any TM, and vice versa. However, this is rather more complicated than is the case for the more restricted grammars and machines, so the result will merely be sketched here.

We first consider the context sensitive languages, as their defining grammars, the **context sensitive** grammars, do not have the empty string on the right hand side of productions. We then generalise our method to deal with the type 0 grammars in general. The definition of context sensitive productions is as for type 0 productions given above, with the additional restriction that the left hand sides of context sensitive productions are not allowed to be shorter in length than the right hand sides.

7.5 THE TM AS THE RECOGNIZER FOR THE CONTEXT SENSITIVE LANGUAGES

The machine T_5, shown in Figure 7.14, recognizes the language

$\{a^i b^i c^i : i \geq 1\}$.

In Chapter 6 we established that this language is not context free. We also saw that it is, in fact, a context sensitive language, as it is generated by the following grammar, G_{16}:

$S \rightarrow aSBC \mid aBC$
$CB \rightarrow BC$
$aB \rightarrow ab$
$bB \rightarrow bb$
$bC \rightarrow bc$
$cC \rightarrow cc$

We wish to establish that for any context sensitive language we can provide an equivalent TM. T_5 itself is not enough to convince us of this, as it was designed for a specific language, and not constructed by a method for creating TMs from the productions of the corresponding grammar. We therefore require *a method for constructing TMs for context sensitive grammars that we could apply to any such grammar.* Here, we will consider the application of such a method to the grammar G_{16}. I then leave it to you to convince yourself that the method could be applied to any context sensitive grammar.

7.5.1 *Constructing a non deterministic TM for reduction parsing of a context sensitive language*

The TM, T_6, that has been constructed from the productions of G_{16}, is partly depicted in Figure 7.18.

You will note that T_6 is in three sections, namely sections A, B, and C, all of which have state 1 in common. Sections A and B are shown in full, while section C is only partly specified. The machine is far more complex than T_5 (Figure 7.14), a TM that

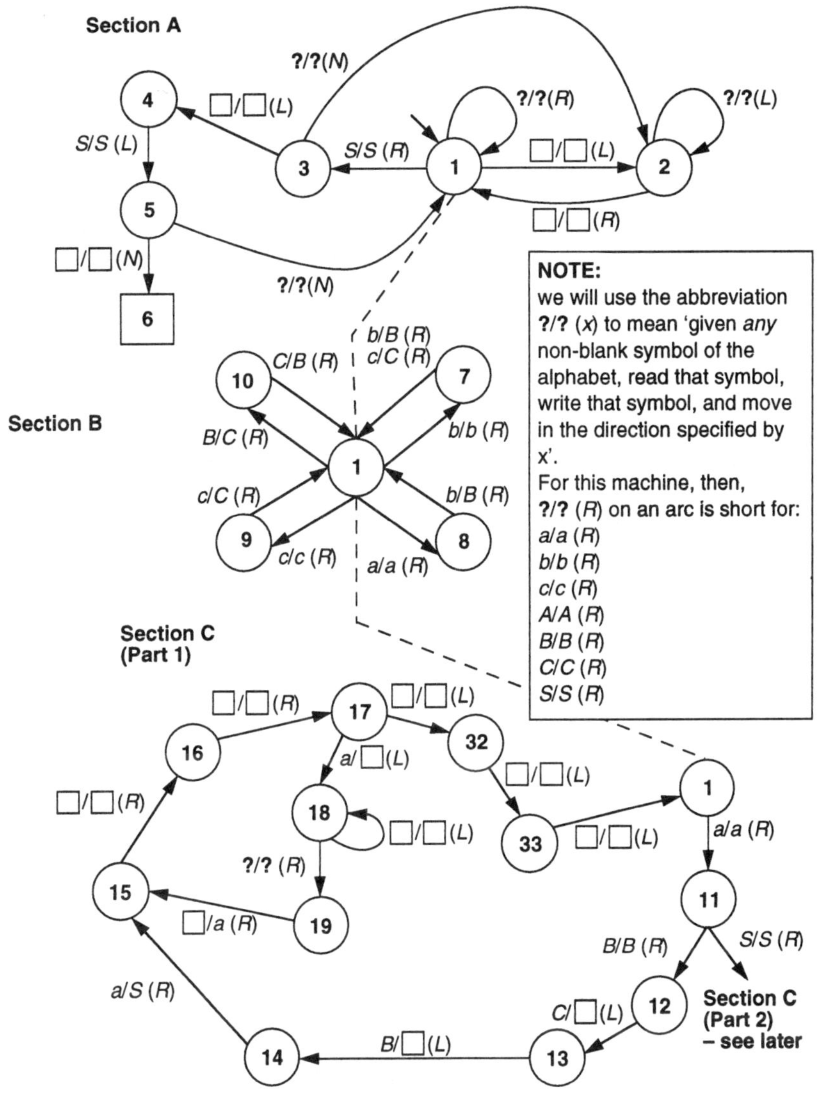

Figure 7.18 The TM, T_6. Part of sections A, B, and C

was designed to recognize the same language. T_6 was constructed from the productions of a grammar (G_{16}), so its purpose is only to demonstrate a general method for constructing such TMs.

The first thing to note is that T_6 is **non deterministic**. Its overall process is to model the **reduction** method of **parsing** introduced in Chapter 3. Beginning with a **terminal string**, we repeatedly substitute **substrings** within that string that are found on the **right hand sides** of productions with the **left hand sides** of the productions. The process is complete if we manage to reduce the string to the **start symbol** S alone, i.e., we finish up with a tape containing only S.

T_6 carries out *reduction parsing* using the grammar G_{16}, by effectively 'scanning' the input string repeatedly from left to right, then right to left, attempting to find a sequence of reductions that will leave only the symbol S on the tape. The process is non deterministic since many reductions may apply at any one time, and thus we may often have to **backtrack** to find alternative reduction sequences. As for all of the other non deterministic machines we have studied in this book, we assume that *the string is accepted if some sequence of* **transitions** *will lead to the machine's* **halt state** (in the case of T_6, this is state 6). T_6 reaches its halt state when only S, the start symbol of the grammar, remains on its tape, i.e. if it finds a sequence of reduction applications that enable the input string to be reduced to S. You may like to convince yourself that T_6's halting conditions will only be met if its input tape initially contains a string from $\{a^i b^i c^i : i \geq 1\}$.

To establish that we could produce a 'T_6-like' TM from any context sensitive grammar, we briefly consider the functions of the three sections shown in the diagram of T_6, in Figure 7.18, and also the correspondence between parts of the machine and the productions of the grammar.

Section A

This section of the machine repeatedly scans the input string (state 1 scans from left to right, while state 2 scans from right to left). States 3 – 5 test if the symbol S alone remains on the tape (in which case the machine can halt in state 6).

Section B

This section contains a state *for each production in* G_{16} *that has a left hand side of the same length as its right hand side* (e.g. $CB \rightarrow BC$). For example, state 1 and state 10 replace BC by CB, i.e. carrying out the reduction based on the production $CB \rightarrow BC$, while state 1 and state 7 perform an analogous function for the productions $bB \rightarrow bb$ and $bC \rightarrow bc$, respectively.

Section C

This section also carries out reduction substitutions, but *for productions whose right hand sides are greater in length than their left hand sides* (in G_{16}, these are $S \rightarrow aSBC$ and $S \rightarrow aBC$). In such cases, a substitution uses up less tape than the sequence of symbols being replaced, so the extra squares of tape are replaced by **blanks**, then any other symbols to the right of the new blanks are **shuffled** up one by one until the occupied part of the tape is packed. Figure 7.18 shows only Part 1 of section C. We first discuss this part, before examining Part 2 (Figure 7.21) below.

Part 1

This section of T_6 deals with the production $S \rightarrow aBC$, i.e. 'reduces' aBC to S.

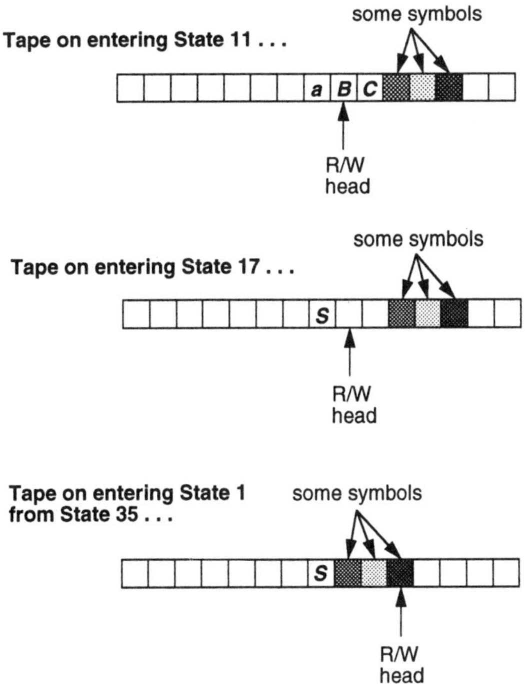

Figure 7.19 Reducing *aBC* to *S* (for states refer to Figure 7.18)

To illustrate, Figure 7.19 shows what happens when we are in state 11 with the tape configuration as shown.

Note that, for simplicity, Figure 7.18 shows only the **loop** of states (states 17, 18, 19, 15, 16) that shuffle an *a* left so that it goes immediately to the right of the next non blank symbol to its left. We have omitted the 12 states that would be needed to shuffle any other symbols of the alphabet (i.e. *b*, *c*, *A*, *B*, *C*, *S*) that may be required. To consider why two states are needed to deal with each symbol, consider the part of T_6 that does the shuffling job for *a*, depicted in Figure 7.20.

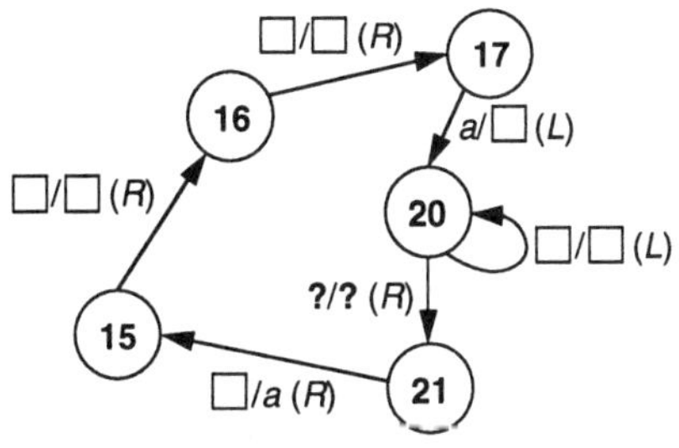

Figure 7.20 Shuffling an '*a*' along

So, states 15, 16, and 17 are common to the shuffling loop for each symbol in the alphabet. We need, say, states 22 and 23 to shuffle any *c*s, states 24 and 25 to shuffle any *A*s, states 26 and 27 to shuffle any *b*s, states 28 and 29 to shuffle any *C*s, and states 30 and 31 to shuffle any *S*s. That is why the state in Figure 7.20 to the right of state 17 is named state 32.

Part 2

This second part of Section C of T_6, which is depicted in Figure 7.21, deals with the production $S \rightarrow aSBC$, i.e. 'reduces' $aSBC$ to S. It is very similar to Part 1 (Figure 7.18), which deals with $S \rightarrow aBC$, and was discussed immediately above.

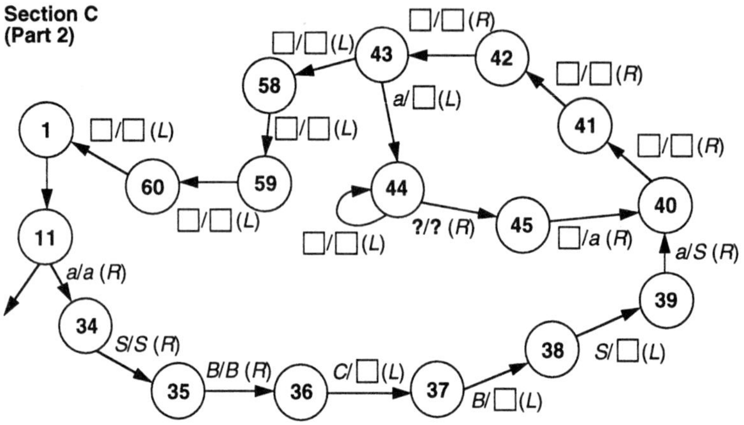

Figure 7.21 Reducing *aSBC* to *S* (for Part 1 see Figure 7.18)

As for Section C Part 1, we have only included the pair of states (state 43 and state 45) between states 43 and 40 that shuffle the *a* to the left (note that in this case, shuffling involves *three* blanks, as the right hand side of $S \rightarrow aSBC$ has *four* symbols). As for Part 1, we assume that there is a similar pair of states linking states 43 and 40 for each of the other alphabet symbols (b, c, S, A, B, C). Thus we need 12 more states (assumed to be numbered 46-57), which is why the state leaving the loop has been labelled 58. We have taken advantage of the fact that both productions dealt with by Section C have *a* as the leftmost symbol of the right hand side. This was not necessary (as our machine is non deterministic), but was done for convenience.

7.5.2 *The generality of the construction*

To see the generality of the construction that enabled us to produce T_6 from G_{16}, consider that, from the definition of context sensitive productions, *the left hand side of each production does not exceed, in length, the right hand side* (i.e. productions are of the form $x \rightarrow y$, where $|x| \leq |y|$). Therefore we can represent any context sensitive grammar by a Turing machine with:

a section A part
To scan back and forth over the input between the start state and another state, enabling the halt state to be reached only when the start symbol, S, appears alone on the tape.

a section B part
That consists of a distinct path *for each production in the grammar with equal length left and right hand sides*, each path leaving and re-entering the start state. The path for each production performs the reduction associated with that production, i.e. when the right hand side of a production appears anywhere on the input tape, it can be replaced by the left hand side of that production.

a section C part
That consists of a distinct path *for each production in the grammar with left hand side shorter in length than the right hand side*, each path leaving and re-entering the start state. As in Section B, the path for each production performs the reduction associated with that production. However, in section C cases the newly placed symbols occupy less tape space than the symbols replaced, so each path has a 'shuffling routine' to ensure that the tape remains in packed form. In G_{16}, only the productions $S \rightarrow aSBC$ and $S \rightarrow aBC$ are of Section C type, and both represent reductions where the replacement string is a single symbol. In general, of course, a context sensitive production could have several symbols on the left hand side. This represents no real problems however, as demonstrated by the sketch of part of a TM that does the reduction for the context sensitive production $XY \rightarrow PQR$, shown in Figure 7.22.

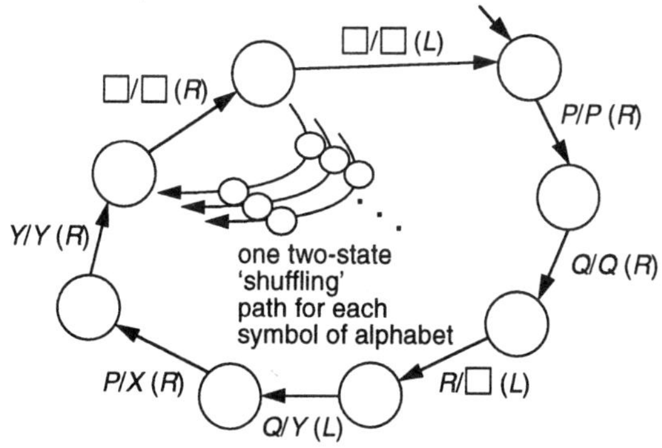

Figure 7.22 Reducing *PQR* to *XY*

As you can see from Figure 7.22, in this example we need only to **skip** over one tape square to the right of the newly written XY. This is because the right hand side of the production $XY \rightarrow PQR$ is one symbol longer than the left. We thus replace the PQ with XY, and the R with a blank. We then need to move over that blank to see if there is a symbol there to be shuffled up, and so on.

In Chapter 5, the non deterministic pushdown recognizers (NPDRs) that we created from the productions of context free grammars recognized the language generated by the grammar by being able to model any derivation that the grammar could carry out. Our non deterministic Turing machines operate by modelling every possible sequence of reductions for the corresponding context sensitive grammar. Such TMs reach their halt state only if the string on the input tape can be reduced to S. The construction sketched out above ensures that this would happen only for inputs that were sentences of the language generated by the original grammar.

Enough has been said to establish the following:

The recognizer for the context sensitive languages is the Turing Machine. Context sensitive languages are computable languages.

You may be wondering why the statement immediately above does not say 'non deterministic Turing machine'. In Chapter 10 we see that *any non deterministic TM can be simulated by a deterministic TM*. Hence, the non deterministic TMs of this chapter could be replaced by equivalent deterministic TMs.

7.6 THE TM AS THE RECOGNIZER FOR THE TYPE 0 LANGUAGES

Now, the sole difference between **context sensitive** productions and **unrestricted**, or **type 0**, productions is that the latter are *not* restricted to having right hand sides that are greater than or equal in length to the left hand sides. This means that, say, a production such as $WXYZ \rightarrow Pa$, which is *not* a valid context sensitive production, is a perfectly reasonable type 0 production. Moreover, type 0 grammars can contain ε **productions**. Productions like $WXYZ \rightarrow Pa$ do not present a severe problem; we simply add another section to our TMs to deal with these types of production, as discussed next (we return to ε productions shortly).

7.6.1 Amending the reduction parsing TM to deal with type 0 productions

We assume that we already have sections A, B and C as defined for our TMs derived from context sensitive grammars (for example, Figure 7.18). We add to such a construction a new section, as follows:

Section D

Consists of *a distinct path for each production in the grammar with left hand side longer in length than the right hand side*, each path leaving and re-entering the start state. As in sections *B* and *C*, the path for each production performs the reduction associated with that production. However, in such cases the newly placed symbols occupy more tape space than the symbols replaced, so each path has a '**shuffling** routine' to ensure that all symbols in the way are each moved to the right an appropriate number of spaces.

Figure 7.23 shows part of the section D component of a TM, in this case the part dealing with the type 0 example production *WXYZ* → *Pa*.

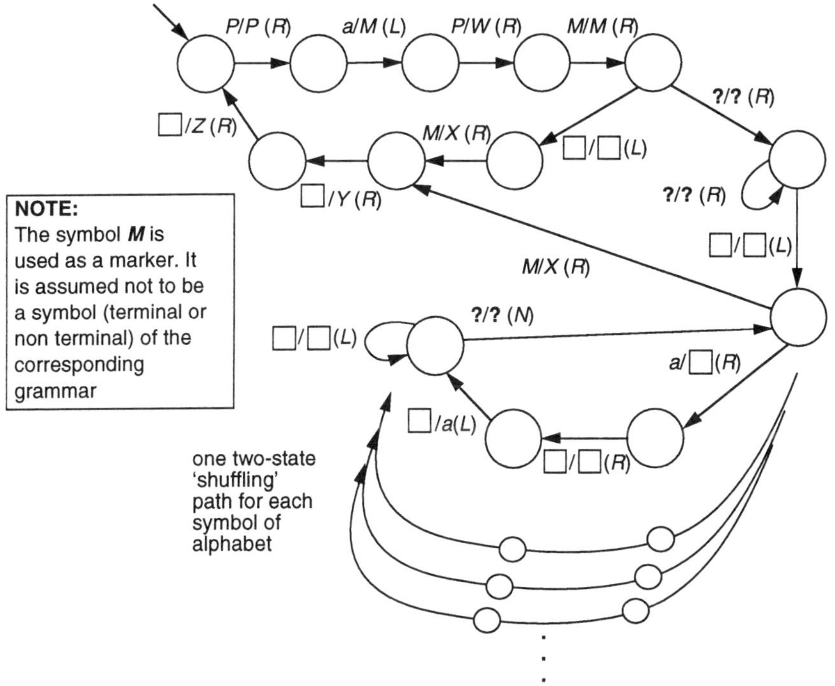

Figure 7.23 Replacing *Pa* by *WXYZ*

For our example production, there are two extra symbols to insert when performing the associated reduction, as the right hand side of our production – *Pa* – has two fewer symbols than the left hand side – *WXYZ*. A machine of the type illustrated in Figure 7.23 therefore has to shuffle all symbols (if any) that were to the right of the *Pa* in question two tape squares to the right, leaving two blanks immediately to the right of *Pa* (which is eventually changed to *WX*), so that *YZ* can be inserted. The symbol *M* is used as a marker, so that the machine can detect when to stop shuffling (when the *M* has a blank next to it, either there are no symbols to its right, or we have shuffled the symbol next to it to the right, and so no more symbols need shuffling). You should convince yourself that a Section D-type construction of the type shown in the example could be carried out for any production where the right hand side is non-empty and of smaller length than the left hand side.

7.6.2 *Dealing with the empty string*

As promised above, we now consider *ε productions.* In fact, we can treat these as a special case of the section D-type construction. We simply allow for the fact that *on either side of any non-blank symbol on the tape, we can imagine there to be as many εs as we like.* This means we can insert the left hand side (i.e. after shuffling to make sufficient room, in a section D-type way) of a type 0 ε production *anywhere we like on the marked portion of the tape.* As you may recall, in earlier chapters we noted that this was a cause of problems in **parsing**. Our machine should only be able to reach its halt state if it inserts the left hand sides of ε productions in the appropriate places, i.e. in terms of a correct reduction parse of the input string being processed. So, we complete our specification of the TM to represent any type 0 grammar by introducing the following, where necessary, to the machine sketched out in Figure 7.18:

Section E
Consists of *a distinct path for each production in the grammar with ε on the right hand side*, each path leaving and re-entering the start state. As in sections *B*, *C*, and *D*, the path for each production performs the reduction associated with that production. Figure 7.24 shows a sketch of a Section E construction for the type 0 production *XYZ* → ε.

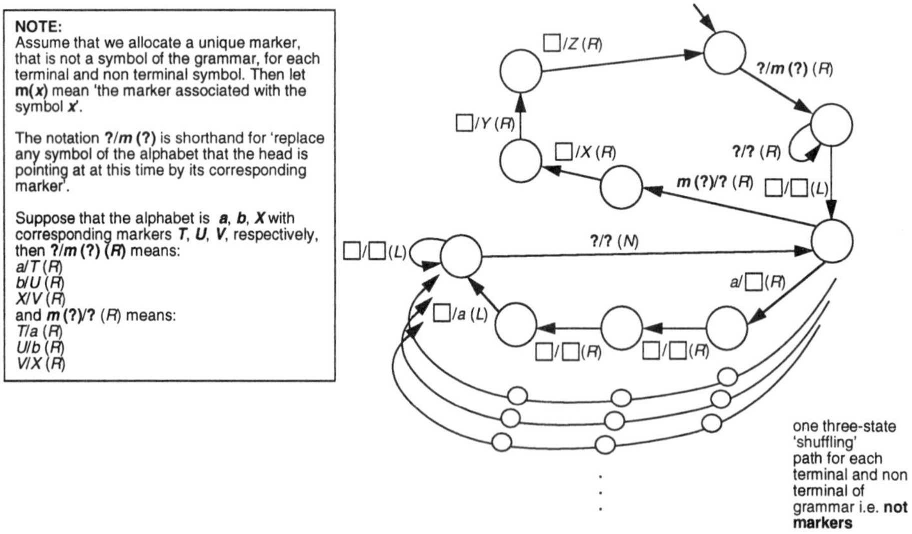

Figure 7.24 Placing *XYZ* into the tape (the reduction associated with the type 0 production *XYZ* → ε)

The section E construction, as illustrated in Figure 7.24, inserts the left hand side of an ε production after any symbol on the tape. There are two problems remaining. Firstly, we must deal with an insertion *before* the leftmost symbol. Secondly, we need to cater for an insertion on a blank tape. Considering the second case first, if ε is in the language generated by the grammar, the corresponding machine should be able to reach its halt state appropriately. Our **blank tape assumption** dictates that we represent ε as the input string by setting up our machine so that its head points initially to a blank square. We can solve both problems with very similar constructions to Section E, though there are a few differences. I leave you to sketch the construction yourself.

7.6.3 The TM as the recognizer for all types in the Chomsky hierarchy

Enough has now been said to support the following claim[3]:

The recognizer for the phrase structure languages in general is the Turing Machine. Phrase structure languages are computable languages.

We argued above that any DFSR can be converted into an equivalent TM. It was then implied that TMs could recognize any of the context free languages. However, by showing that any type 0 grammar can be represented by a TM that accepts the same language, we have also shown that the same applies to the other types of language in Chomsky's hierarchy. This is because *any production of any grammar of type 0, type 1, type 2 and type 3 is catered for in one of the sections of our construction.*

However, if we were to implement the non deterministic TMs that are produced by our construction, we would have very inefficient parsers indeed! That is the whole point of defining restricted types of machine to deal with restricted types of language.

7.7 DECIDABILITY: A PRELIMINARY DISCUSSION

We close this chapter by briefly discussing one of the most important concepts related to language processing, i.e. **decidability**. In doing this, we anticipate a more thorough treatment of the topic in Chapter 11.

7.7.1 Deciding a language

Consider the TMs T_2, T_3, T_4 and T_5 in this chapter. Each accepts an input tape containing a **terminal string** from the appropriate **alphabet**. If each of these machines is

[3] Remember that in Chapter 10 we are going to see why we can omit 'non deterministic' from the statement.

started with a valid **input configuration**, it will halt in a **halt state**, and as it reaches its halt state it will:

print T if the input sequence was a **sentence** of the language, otherwise print F.

A language-recognizing TM that conforms to the above behaviour is said to **decide** the corresponding language (because given any string of the appropriate terminals it can say 'yes' if the string is a sentence *and* 'no' if the string is *not* a sentence).

For example, consider some of the decisions made by T_5, which decides the language $\{a^i b^i c^i : i \geq 1\}$, as shown in Table 7.2.

Table 7.2 T_5's output on accepting and rejecting various input sequences

Input string	**T_5 input and output**	
aabbcc (valid string)	initial configuration:	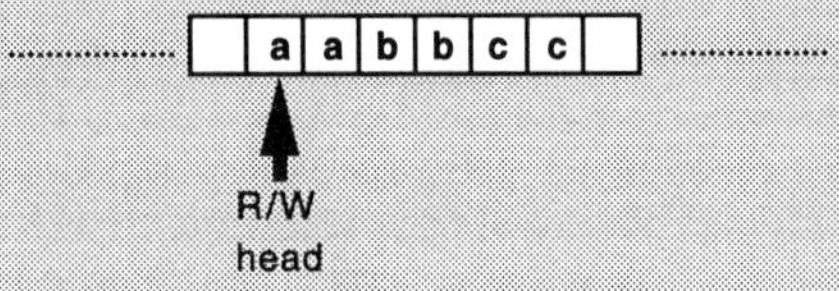
	final configuration:	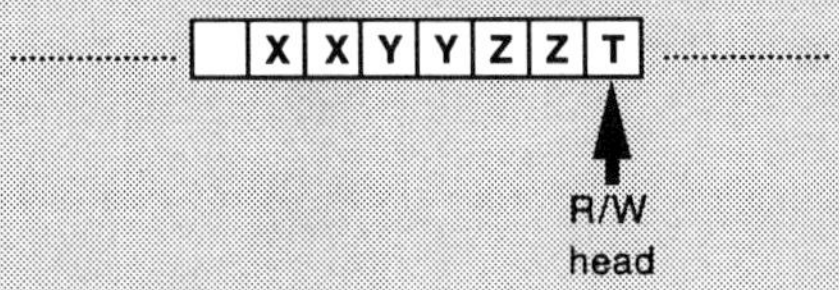
aaabbcc (invalid string – too many *a*s)	initial configuration:	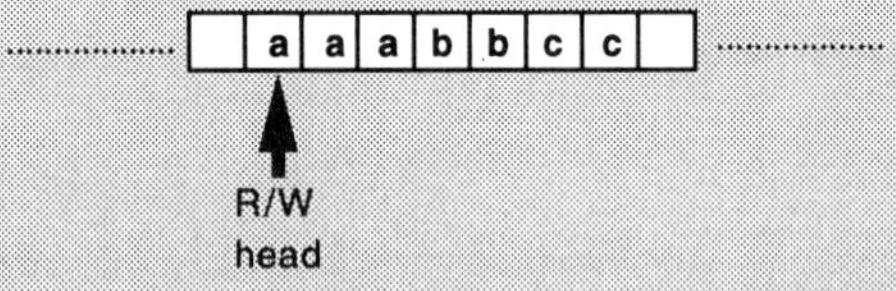
	final configuration:	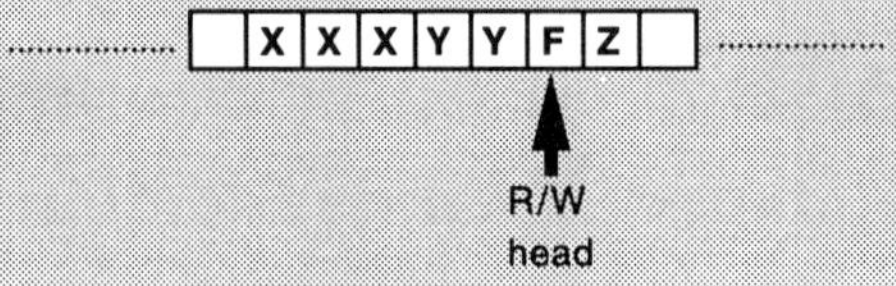
caaaa (invalid string – starts with *c*)	initial configuration:	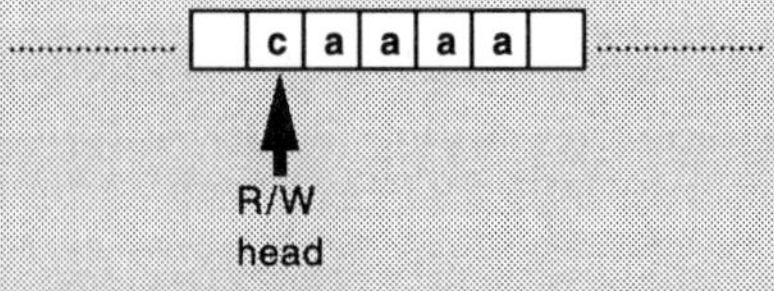
	final configuration:	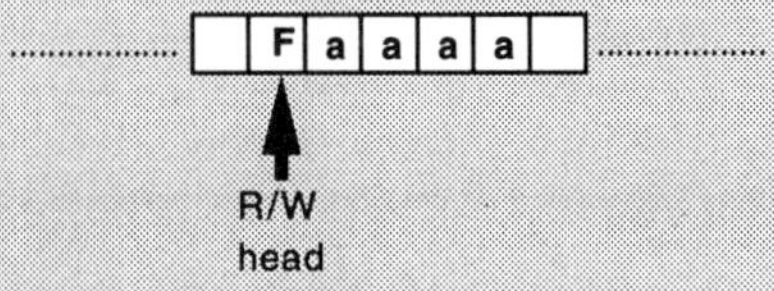

The formal definition of deciding a language is given in Table 7.3.

Table 7.3 Deciding a language

Given some language L, with alphabet A, a TM decides that language if for any string, x, such that $x \in A^*$: if $x \in L$ the machine indicates its acceptance, and if $x \notin L$ the machine indicates its rejection of that string. A language for which there is a TM that decides that language is called a decidable language.

7.7.2 Accepting a language

Suppose we amend T_5 (of Figure 7.14) to produce the machine T_7, depicted in Figure 7.25.

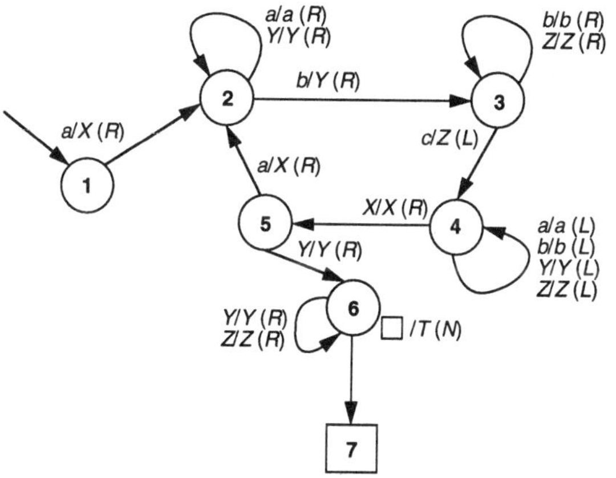

Figure 7.25 The TM, T_7

We have simply removed from T_5 all arcs entering the halt state which result in writing the symbol F, and removed the instructions that write an F from the arc between states 6 and 7. Like T_5, T_7 will now reach its halt state and write a T for valid input strings. However, unlike T_5, for invalid strings T_7 will eventually stop in one of its non halt states, and make no F indication at all. For example, given the input *aaabbcc*, (the second example used for T_5 in Table 7.2), T_7 would eventually come to a stop in state 2, being unable to make any move from that state in the way that T_5 could.

A machine that can output T for each and every valid string of a language (and never outputs T for any *in*valid strings) is said to **accept** that language. Compare this carefully with the definition of *deciding*, from Table 7.3. Clearly, *a machine that decides* *a language also accepts it,* but the converse is not necessarily true. T_5, T_6, and T_7 all *accept* the language $\{a^ib^ic^i : i \geq 1\}$, but *only* T_5 *decides* it.

The formal definition of accepting a language is given in Table 7.4.

Table 7.4 Accepting a language

Given some language L, with alphabet A, a machine accepts that language if for any string, x, such that $x \in A^*$,

if $x \in L$ the machine indicates its acceptance of that string.

A language for which there is a TM that accepts that language is called an acceptable language.

7.8 CONCLUSION

In this chapter, we have encountered *computable* languages, *decidable* languages, and now *acceptable* languages. From the way in which the construction of TMs from type 0 grammars was developed, it can be seen that such TMs would **accept**, rather than **decide**, the language generated by the grammar from which the machine was constructed. In other words, computable languages are acceptable languages. However, we have also seen that some computable languages are decidable (since TMs T_2, T_3, T_4 and T_5 all *decide* their respective languages). A question addressed in Chapter 11 asks whether all computable languages are also decidable. We find that in general they are not, though the more restricted languages of the **Chomsky hierarchy** are.

In Chapters 2 and 6, we saw the type 0 grammar, G_4, that generates what we call the multiplication language:

$$\{a^ib^jc^{i\times j} : i, j \geq 1\}.$$

In discussing this language in Chapters 2 and 5, it was remarked that we could regard **phrase structure grammars** as *computational*, as well as *linguistic*, devices. Subsequently, in Chapter 6, we saw that the multiplication language could not be generated by a context free grammar, which tells us that a pushdown recognizer is insufficiently powerful to accept the language. From the present chapter we know that we could define a TM, from the productions of G_4, that would accept this language. This seems to imply that the TM has a certain computational ability that is worthy of clearer definition and exploration. Such an enterprise has played a central part in computer science, and it is a major aim of the second part of this book to discuss this.

However, this does not mean that we have finished with languages. Far from it. It can in fact be shown that *the computation of any TM can be modelled by some type 0 grammar*. The proof of this is complex, and we will not consider it in this book, but the result is very important, since again it establishes a general **equivalence** between a class of languages and a class of abstract machines. More than this, since the TM is the acceptor for the type 0 languages, and thus for all the subordinate language types, such a result establishes a general equivalence between TMs and the entire Chomsky hierarchy.

The TM is the first machine we have seen in this book that is capable of producing a string of symbols (on its tape) as a *result*, when given a string of symbols as its *input*. This means that the TM can carry out forms of computation that are not restricted to expecting 'yes/no' answers. The second part of this book investigates the nature of the computational power of the TM. In the process of this, we discover that the TM is more powerful than any digital computer. In fact, the TM is the most powerful computational model we can define. Eventually, our investigations bring us full circle, and enable us to precisely specify the relationship between formal languages, computable languages, and abstract machines. In doing so, we are able to answer a question that was asked at the end of Chapter 6: are there formal languages that are a **proper superset** of the type 0 languages?

EXERCISES

1† Sketch out a general argument to demonstrate that any **Turing machine** needs only one **halt state**, and also that that halt state needs have no **outgoing arcs.**

2 Design Turing machines to **decide** the following languages:

(a) $\{a^{2i+1}c^jb^{2i+1} : i, j \geq 1\}$
(b) $\{xx : x \in \{a, b\}^*\}$
(c) $\{a^ib^jc^{i+j} : i, j \geq 1\}$
(d) $\{a^ib^jc^{i-j} : i, j \geq 1\}$
(e) $\{a^ib^jc^{i \times j} : i, j \geq 1\}$
(f) $\{a^ib^jc^{i \text{ div } j} : i, j \geq 1\}$ (div is integer division)

Hint: in all cases, first design the machine so that it deals only with **acceptable** strings, then add additional arcs so that it deals appropriately with non acceptable strings.

3 The following is a *recursive definition* of 'well formed parenthesis' strings (WPEs):

() is a WPE
if X is a WPE, then so is (X)
if X and Y are WPEs, then so is XY

(a) Define a TM to decide the language of all WPEs.
(b) The language of all WPEs is **context free**. Show this by defining a **context free grammar** to generate it.

Hint: the recursive definition above converts almost directly into a CFG.

PART 2

From computation to languages

8 Finite state transducers

AIMS

To learn about

- the types of computation that can be carried out by finite state transducers
- the various limited tasks involving memory of input sequences carried out by FSTs
- the addition and subtraction of arbitrary length numbers by FSTs
- the restricted multiplication and modular division performed by FSTs
- the inability of FSTs to do multiplication of arbitrary length numbers
- FSTs as poor models of real computers

8.1 FINITE STATE TRANSDUCERS

A **finite state transducer (FST)** is a **deterministic finite state recognizer** (DFSR) with the ability to output symbols. Alternatively, it can be viewed as a **Turing machine** (TM) with two **tapes** (one for *input*, one for *output*) that

- always moves its head to the right
- cannot recognize **blank** squares on its tape.

As the machine makes a **transition** between two **states** (according to the input symbol it is reading, of course), it outputs one symbol. In addition to performing recognition tasks, such a machine can also carry out *computations*. The purpose of this chapter is to investigate the scope of the FST's computational abilities. We shall see that we need a more powerful type of machine to carry out all the computations we usually expect machines (i.e. computers) to be able to do. As we will see, this more powerful machine is the one we encountered in Chapter 7. It is the TM.

8.2 FINITE STATE TRANSDUCERS AND LANGUAGE RECOGNITION

First of all, you should appreciate that the FSRs used for regular language recognition in Chapter 4 are simply a special case of FSTs. We could have defined FSRs so that on each transition they produce an output symbol, and we could have defined these output symbols to be significant in some way. In the following example machine, we assume that, when the input is **exhausted**, if the last symbol the machine outputs is a 1, then the input string is **accepted**, and if the last symbol output is a 0, then the string is rejected. Figure 8.1 shows an example of such a machine.

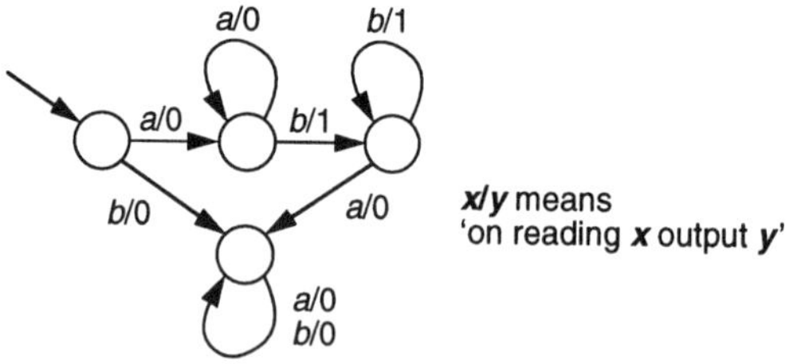

Figure 8.1 A finite state transducer for recognizing a regular language

The FST in Figure 8.1 accepts the language $\{a^i b^j : i, j \geq 1\}$. It indicates acceptance or rejection of an input string by the last symbol it outputs as the last symbol of the input is read (1 = accept, 0 = reject). Some examples of the machine's output are shown in Table 8.1. The significant symbol of the output (the last) is underlined in each case.

Table 8.1 Outputs from the finite state transducer of Figure 8.1

input string	output string	ACCEPT or REJECT
aaab	0001	ACCEPT
aa	00	REJECT
aabba	00110	REJECT
aabbb	00111	ACCEPT

As you can see, the machine in Figure 8.1 has no state designated as a **halt state** or accept state. This is because *the output is now used to tell us whether or not a string is accepted.*

8.3 FINITE STATE TRANSDUCERS AND MEMORY

An interesting application of FSTs is as 'memory' devices. For example, FST_1, in Figure 8.2 processes inputs that are strings of binary digits. As output, the machine produces strings of binary digits, representing the input string 'shifted' two digits to the right.

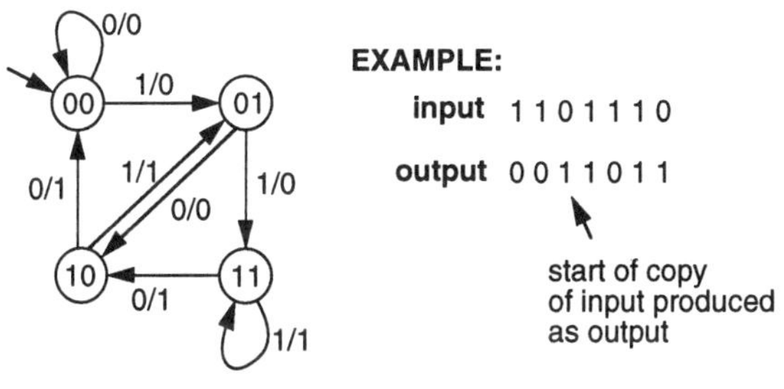

Figure 8.2 A binary two digit 'shift' FST, FST_1

You may think that the names of FST_1's states look strange. Of course, the state names do not affect the operation of the machine, but they have been chosen for symbolic reasons, which should become apparent as the chapter continues.

The next machine, FST_2, does a similar task, but with a right shift of three digits. FST_2 is shown in Figure 8.3.

Now consider FST_3, shown in Figure 8.4, which does a 'shift two to the right' operation for inputs consisting of strings in $\{0, 1, 2\}^+$ (remember from Chapter 2 that A^+ denotes the set of all *non empty* strings that can be taken from the **alphabet** A).

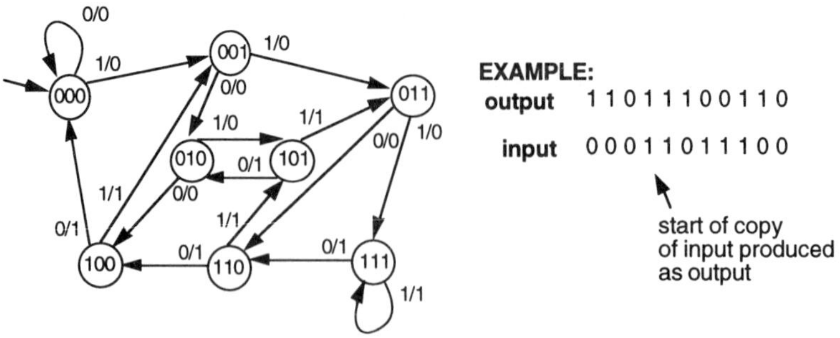

Figure 8.3 A binary three digit 'shift' FST, FST_2

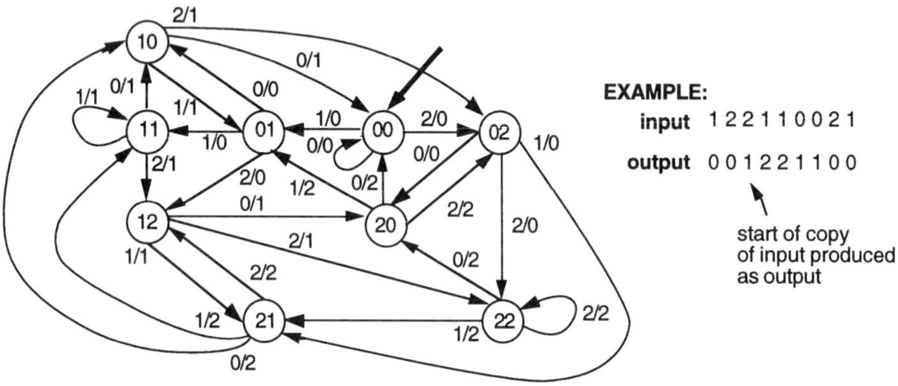

Figure 8.4 A 'trinary' two digit 'shift' FST, FST_3

Machines like $FST_{1,\ 2}$ and $_3$ are sometimes called 'memory machines' as they perform a simple memory task. Imagine that a 'clock' governs the processing of the input, a concept we return to in Chapter 10. At each 'tick' of the **clock**, the next symbol is read, and the appropriate symbol is output. Then:

FST_1 stores a symbol of a two symbol alphabet for two 'ticks' and then outputs it;

FST_2 stores a symbol of a two symbol alphabet for three 'ticks' and then outputs it;

FST_3 stores a symbol of a three symbol alphabet for two 'ticks' and then outputs it.

You should be able to see that we could design memory machines for an alphabet of any number, s, of symbols, and for any number, t, of clock ticks, as long as we know in advance the values of s and t. You should also be able to see that we need to increase the number of states as the values of s and t increase.

In fact, and this is where the names of the states in our three machines are significant, there is a simple numeric relationship between the number of symbols, s, in the alphabet, the number of ticks, t, that each input symbol has to be 'remembered' for, and the minimum number of states required to do the job. Since there are s^t (numerically speaking) distinct sequences of length t when the alphabet has s symbols, and the only way the FST can remember which of the s^t sequences it has just read is to have a state for each one, the FST needs a minimum of s^t states. As you can see, the state names in the machines in this section represent, for each machine, the s^t sequences of length t we can have for the s-symbol alphabet in question.

So,

FST_1 where $t = 2$ and $s = 2$, has $s^t = 2^2 = 4$ states;
FST_2 where $t = 3$ and $s = 2$, has $s^t = 2^3 = 8$ states;
and
FST_3 where $t = 2$ and $s = 3$, has $s^t = 3^2 = 9$ states.

8.4 FINITE STATE TRANSDUCERS AND COMPUTATION

In this section, we shall see that FSTs are capable of some reasonably sophisticated computation (subject to some creativity in defining the way in which the input and/or output sequences are interpreted). As an example of such 'creativity', we will first look in a new way at the tasks carried out by our machines FST_{1-3} (Figures 8.2–4), in the preceding section.

It should be pointed out that there is no trickery in the way we are going to interpret the input and output of our machines. We are simply defining the type of input expected by a particular machine, and the form which the output will take. This, of course, is a crucial part of problem solving, whether we perform it with formal machines or real programs.

8.4.1 *Simple multiplication*

Beginning with FST_1, the machine that shifts a binary sequence two digits to the right, let us consider that the sequence of 1s and 0s presented to the machine is first subjected to the following (using 1011 as an example):

1. The string 00 is appended to the rightmost end (giving 101100, for the example).
2. The resulting sequence is interpreted as a binary number *in reverse* (for the example we would then have 001101, which is 13 in *decimal* (base 10).

The output sequence is then also interpreted as a binary number in reverse.

For the example sequence 101100, FST_1 would produce as output 001011, which in reverse (110100) and interpreted as a binary number is decimal 52.

You can convince yourselves that under the conditions defined above, FST_1 performs multiplication by 4.

For FST_2, if we apply similar conditions to the input, except that for condition (1) we place three 0s at the rightmost end of the input sequence, FST_2 then performs multiplication by 8.

For FST_3, the same conditions apply as those for FST_1, except that the input and output number are interpreted as being in base 3, in which case FST_3 performs multiplication by 9. Thus, given the input 121100 (i.e. 001121, or 43 decimal), FST_3 would produce as output 001211 (i.e. 112100) which, according to our specification, represents 387 (i.e. 43×9).

So, we have seen that FSTs can carry out certain restricted multiplication tasks. Later in this chapter we see that there are limitations to the abilities of FSTs with respect to multiplication in general.

8.4.2 *Addition and subtraction*

FSTs are capable of adding or subtracting binary numbers of any size. However, before we see how this is done, we need to define the form of our input and output sequences.

The input

When we add or subtract two numbers (assuming that the numbers are too long for us to mentally perform the calculation), we usually work from right to left (least significant digits first). It seems reasonable, then, in view of the need to deal with any 'carry' situations that may arise, that our machines could do likewise. In the previous section we came across the notion of the input being in reverse. Clearly, this method can also be used here, and will then represent the machine processing the pairs of corresponding digits in the way that we usually do.

Apart from some minor problems which will be addressed shortly, the remaining major problem is that we have *two* numbers to add or subtract, whereas *our machines only accept one sequence as input*. Our solution to this problem is to present the two binary numbers (to be added or subtracted) as one sequence, in which the digits of one of the numbers are interleaved with the digits of the other. This, of course, means that the numbers must be of the same length. However, we can ensure that this is the case by placing sufficient 0s at the leftmost end of the shorter of the two numbers before we present the numbers to our machines.

Table 8.2 summarizes the preparation of input for the FSTs for addition and subtraction which we will define shortly.

We now turn to the output.

Table 8.2 Data preparation for binary adding and subtracting FSTs

To prepare two binary numbers for input to the addition or subtraction FSTs:	
1 Ensure numbers are the same length by padding the shorter number with leading 0s	first number: 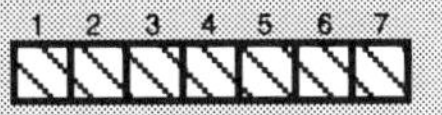 second number: 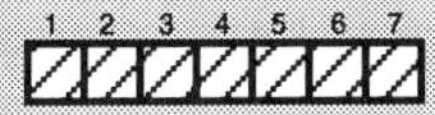
1a. (For addition only) Place an extra leading 0 on each number, to accommodate possible final carry	
2 Reverse both numbers	reverse of first number: 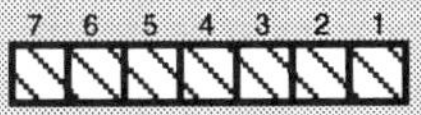 reverse of second number: 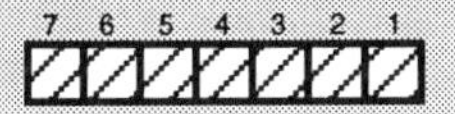
3 Make one sequence by interleaving the corresponding digits of each reversed number (Note: for subtraction FST, begin with second number)	interleaved digits of reversed numbers: 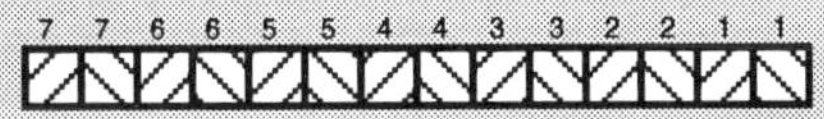

The output

For our addition and subtraction FSTs to model our behaviour, they must process the two numbers by examining pairs of corresponding digits, in least to most significant digit order of the original numbers. However, as an FST can only read one digit at a time, it will not be able to output a 0 or 1 representing a digit of the answer until it has examined the second digit of each pair of corresponding digits. Moreover, our FSTs *must output a symbol for each input symbol encountered.* For the first digit in each corresponding pair then, our FSTs will output the symbol *. Note that there is no special significance to this symbol, it is simply being used as a separator.

Thus, given input of the form indicated by the diagram accompanying step 3 in Table 8.2, our FSTs will produce output as represented in Figure 8.5.

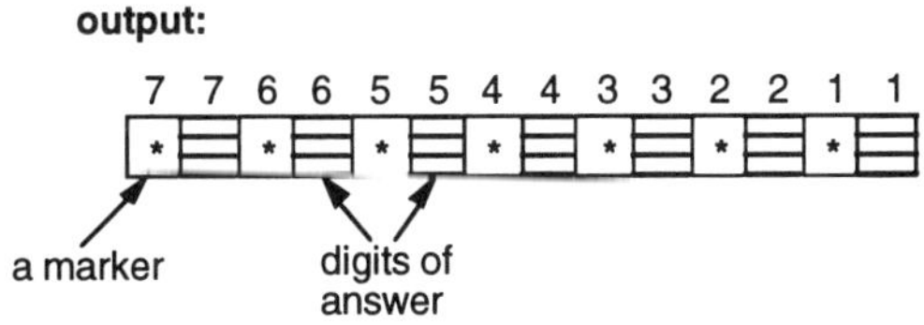

Figure 8.5 Specification of output for arithmetic FSTs

The output shown in Figure 8.5 represents the digits of the answer in reverse, with each digit preceded by *. The *s are not part of the answer, of course, and so we read the answer as specified in Figure 8.6.

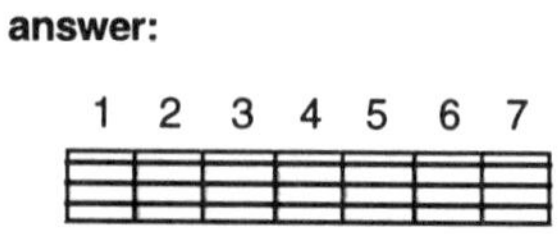

Figure 8.6 How we read the answer from the output specified in Figure 8.5

The machines

We are now ready to present the two machines, FST_4, the binary adding FST (Figure 8.7), and FST_5, the binary subtractor (Figure 8.8). Each machine is accompanied by an example showing an input and the resulting output. I leave it to you to convince yourself that the machines operate as claimed.

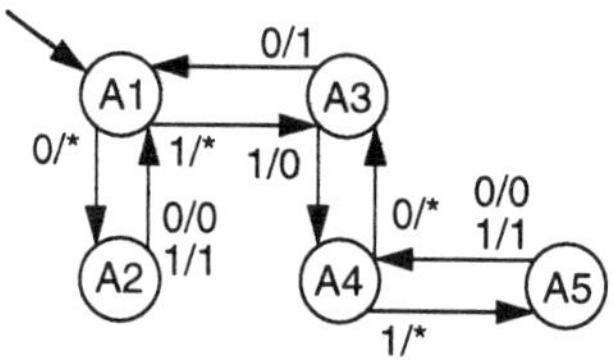

EXAMPLE:
0 1 1 0 1 + 0 0 1 1 0
(i.e. 13 + 6)
is presented to the machine as:
0 1 1 0 1 1 0 1 0 0
(i.e. numbers in reverse, one digit of each number in turn, doesn't matter which one first)
This results in the output:
*** 1 * 1 * 0 * 0 * 1**
which is also in reverse, so it represents
1 0 0 1 1 (i.e. 19)

Figure 8.7 A binary adder FST, FST_4

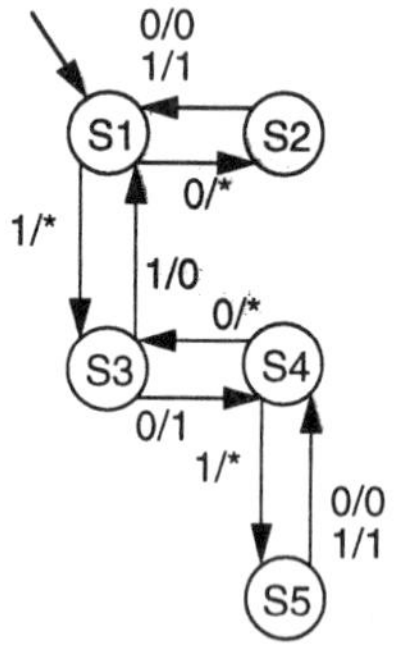

EXAMPLE:
1 1 0 1 – 0 1 1 0
(i.e. 13 – 6)
is presented to the machine as:
0 1 1 0 1 1 0 1
(i.e. numbers in reverse, one digit of each number in turn, beginning with second number)
This results in the output:
*** 1 * 1 * 1 * 0**
which is also in reverse, so it represents
0 1 1 1 (i.e. 7)

Figure 8.8 A binary subtractor FST, FST_5

It is important to note that *for both machines there is no limit to the length of the input numbers*. Pairs of binary numbers of any length could be processed. It is clear, therefore, that *the FST is capable of adding and subtracting arbitrary length binary numbers.*

8.4.3 Simple division and modular arithmetic

Certain restricted forms of division are also within the capabilities of the FST. For example, FST_6, in Figure 8.9, performs integer division of a binary number by 3, returning the result as a binary number. In some programming languages integer division is represented by the *infix* operator **div**, so FST_6 actually does x **div** 3, where x is the input number[1]. However, FST_6 does not require the input sequence in reverse. We usually perform long division from the most significant end of the number, and so does FST_6. The machine also outputs the result in the correct order. Figure 8.9 includes an example input sequence, and its corresponding output sequence.

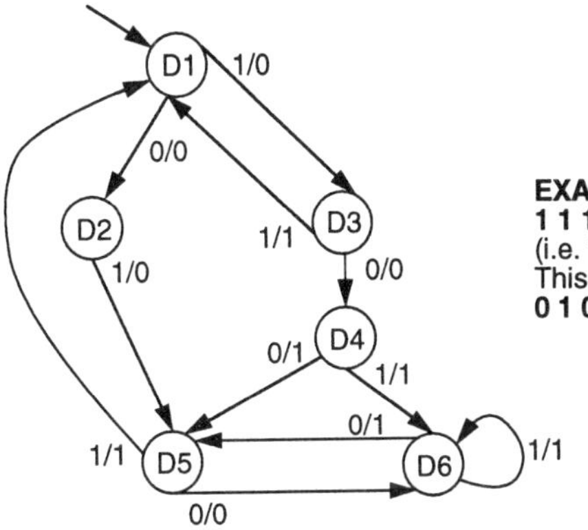

Figure 8.9 A binary 'div 3' FST, FST_6

We can quite easily use FST_6 as the basis of a machine that computes the quotient *and* the remainder by making the following observations about states of FST_6 :

D5 represents a remainder of 1 (i.e. a carry of 1);
D6 represents a remainder of 2 (i.e. a carry of 2);
D1–4 represent a remainder of 0 (i.e. no carry).

Now, the remainder resulting from a division by 3 requires a maximum of two binary digits, as it can be 0, 1, or 10. We could make sufficient space for the remainder by placing *** (three asterisks) after the input sequence. I leave it to you to decide how to amend the machine to ensure that the quotient is followed by the binary representation of the remainder. The first of the three asterisks should be left unchanged by the machine, to provide a separator between quotient and remainder.

We could also amend our machine to provide the remainder *only*. For this we would ensure that all the outputs of FST_6 were changed to '*', and then carry out the amendments discussed in the preceding paragraph. Then our machine would carry out an operation similar to that called **mod** in programming languages, except it would be restricted to **mod** 3.

[1] An *infix* operator is written in between its operands. For example, '+' is thus an infix operator.

8.5 THE LIMITATIONS OF THE FINITE STATE TRANSDUCER

We have seen that FSTs can be defined to do restricted forms of multiplication and division, and also that FSTs are capable of unrestricted addition and subtraction. You will note that the preceding sentence does not include the word 'binary'. This is because we could define adders and subtractors for *any* number base (including base 10), since there are only a finite number of 'carry' cases for addition and subtraction in any number system. Similarly, we can define FSTs to do multiplication or division by any fixed multiplicand or divisor, in any number base. However, the binary machine is much simpler than would be the corresponding FST for, say, operations on base 10 numbers. Compare the complexity of FST_1 (Figure 8.2) and FST_3 (Figure 8.4), for example. I will leave it to you to consider the design of FSTs for number bases from three upwards.

In fact, our intuition tells us that the binary number system is sufficient; after all, we deal every day with a machine that performs all its operations on representations that are essentially binary numbers, and we never use that as the basis of an argument that the machine is insufficiently powerful! We return to the issue of the universality of binary representations several times in subsequent chapters.

For now, our purpose is to establish that the FSTs are not a sufficiently powerful formalism for modelling all computational tasks that we may wish an abstract machine to model. We have seen that the FST can carry out unrestricted addition and subtraction. The question arises, *can we design an FST to do unrestricted multiplication*? We shall eventually demonstrate that the answer to this last question is 'no'. This is obviously a critical limitation, since the ability to perform multiplication is surely one of the basic requirements of useful computing systems. First, however, we show that there are some multiplication operations we *can* perform with FSTs.

8.5.1 *Restricted FST multiplication*

Earlier in this chapter, we saw that FSTs are capable of multiplying a base n number by some constant c, where c is a power of n (for example, FST_1 was used to multiply a binary – base 2 – number by 4, i.e. 2^2). Suppose we wished to multiply a number, say a binary number, by a number that cannot be expressed as an integral power of 2, say 3? One way to achieve such tasks is to effectively 'hardwire' the multiplicand 3 into the machine, in a similar way that the divisor 3 was represented in the **div** 3 machine, FST_6 (Figure 8.9).

FST_7, shown in Figure 8.10, multiplies an arbitrary length binary number by 3.

To see how FST_7 works, consider its operation in terms of writing down a binary number three times, and adding the three copies together. Figure 8.11 represents the manual version of the same example shown in Figure 8.10.

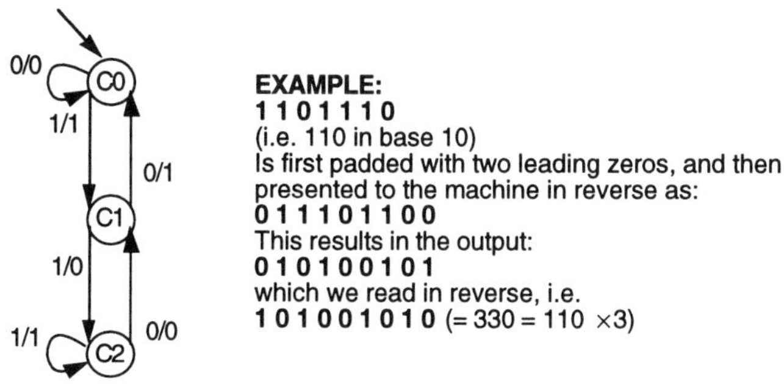

Figure 8.10 A binary '× 3' FST, FST_7

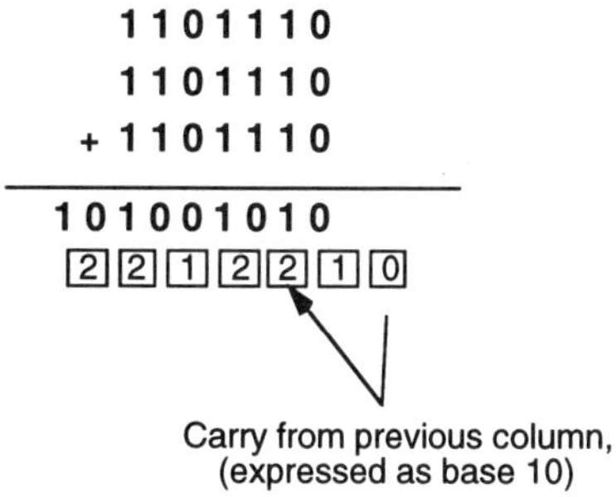

Figure 8.11 Adding in binary, with carry in decimal, to achieve multiplication by 3

In adding together three identical binary numbers, beginning from the rightmost column, we can either have three 1s (i.e. 1 + 1 + 1) = 11, i.e. 1 carry 1, or three zeros (0 carry 0), i.e. a carry of 1 or 0. If there is a carry of 0, we continue as in the previous sentence. Otherwise, we have a carry of 1 and the next column could be three 1s (i.e. 1 + 1 + 1 + 1 – adding in the carry) so we write down a 0 and carry 2 (decimal). If the next column is three 0s, we have 0 + 0 + 0 + 10 = 10, i.e. 0 carry 1 – back to carry 1, which has been discussed already. Otherwise, we have three 1s and a carry of 10, i.e. 1 + 1 + 1 + 10 = 101 = 1 carry 2 – back to carry 2, which, again, we have already considered. The whole situation is summarized in Table 8.3.

Table 8.3 Carry situations, expressed in base 10, for multiplication by 3 by adding three copies of a binary number

		Column			
		1		0	
Carry	0	1	0	0	0
	1	0	2	1	0
	2	1	2	0	1
		result	new carry	result	new carry

The states in Figure 8.10 were labelled $C0-2$ to represent the three carry situations found in Table 8.3. From Table 8.3, you should be able to see why only three states are required for FST_7, but why *we could not define a machine of fewer than three states to carry out the same task.*

A similar method can be used to create a machine, FST_8 that multiplies a binary number by 5. The machine is shown in Figure 8.12, and as you can see, requires 5 states.

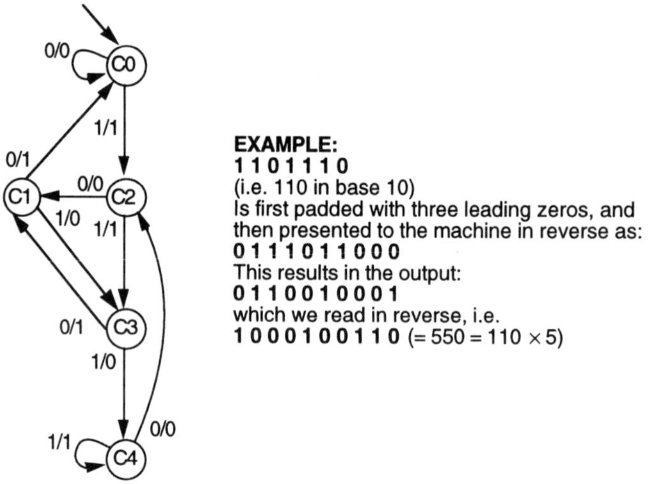

Figure 8.12 FST_8 does binary multiplication by 5

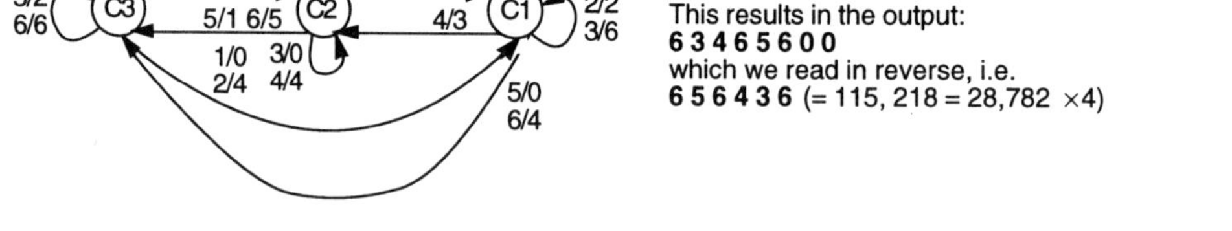

Figure 8.13 FST_9 multiplies a base 7 number by 4

Finally, we consider in Figure 8.13 the rather unusual FST_9, which multiplies a base 7 number by 4 (!).

I leave it to you to justify to yourself that the above machines, FST_{7-9}, operate as claimed.

The above multipliers, FST_{7-9}, reflect a construction suggesting that a machine to multiply a number in any base by a constant c needs no more states than c (i.e. one for each of the possible base 10 carry values). As we saw above:

FST_7, where $c = 3$ had 3 states;
FST_8, where $c = 5$, had 5 states;
FST_9, where $c = 4$, had 4 states.

However, you may like to consider what happens to our construction when the numbers to be multiplied are in bases greater than 10.

8.5.2 FSTs and unlimited multiplication

In this section we see that FSTs are incapable of multiplication of arbitrary length numbers. The argument used is essentially an informal application of the **repeat state theorem** introduced in Chapter 6. Again, the method of 'proof' used is ***reductio ad absurdum***.

I will assume, for sound reasons that are discussed in later chapters, and hinted at earlier in this chapter, that it is sufficient to focus on the task of multiplying arbitrary length binary numbers. Our assumption is that *we have an FST, M, that can multiply arbitrary length pairs of binary numbers, and print out the result.* Now, we can assume that M has a fixed number of states. Say it has k states. We ask M to multiply the number 2^k by itself:

- 2^k is a 1 followed by k 0s;
- $2^k \times 2^k$ is a 1 followed by $2k$ 0s
  (example: $2^3 = 1000$, $2^3 \times 2^3 = 2^6 = 1000000$, i.e. $8 \times 8 = 64$).

Suppose M reads the corresponding digits of its input numbers simultaneously. M has only k states, and it must use at least one of them to process the input digits. However, after it has processed the input digits it still has to print out the rest of the 0s in the answer. Assuming it only uses one of its states to do the multiplication (an extremely conservative estimate!) and print out the 1 followed by the first k 0s of the answer (one digit for each of the k pairs of input digits it encounters), M has only $k - 1$ states left with which to print out the remaining k 0s of the answer.

M must therefore loop when it prints out the rest of the 0s. It is printing out the 0s without any further input of digits, so there is no way of controlling the number of 0s that M prints. The *only* way to make an FST generate a fixed number, k, of symbols without input is to have a sequence of $k + 1$ states to do it, a notion that was discussed in the context of **finite state recognizers** in Chapter 4.

We are forced to reject our initial assumption: the machine M cannot exist. *Multiplication of arbitrary length binary numbers is beyond the power of the FST*. By extension of this argument, multiplication of arbitrary length numbers in any number base is also beyond its power.

8.6 FSTs AS UNSUITABLE MODELS FOR REAL COMPUTERS

It is unfortunate that FSTs are not powerful enough to perform all the operations that we expect computers to be able to carry out. As you can probably guess from considering the parsing routine for the FSR in Chapter 4, FSTs also lend themselves to conversion into very simple programs. However, at the very least, we expect any reasonable model of computation to be able to deal with arbitrary multiplication and division. You have seen that such basic requirements are beyond the capabilities of FSTs.

You may think you detect a flaw in an argument that assumes that real computers can perform operations on arbitrarily large data. Most of us who have ever written any non trivial programs have experienced having to deal with the fact that the computer we use is *limited,* not limit*less*, in terms of its storage and memory capacity. Since a computer is, in terms of available storage at any given point in time, finite, it could be regarded as a (huge) FST. As such, for any given computer, there is, even for basic operations such as multiplication, a limit to the size of the numbers that can be dealt with. In this sense, then, a computer is an FST.

It turns out, however, that treating a digital computer as if it were an FST is not, in general, a useful position to adopt, either theoretically or practically[2]. Let us look at the practical issues first. When a deterministic FST enters the same state (say q) twice during a computation, it is looping. Moreover, once the machine reaches state q, repeating the input sequence that took it from q back to q (perhaps via several other states) will result in the same behaviour being exhibited again. This was the basis of the *repeat state theorem* for FSRs in Chapter 6.

Suppose a program is performing some calculations, subsequently to print some output at the terminal, and receives no output from external sources once it has begun (i.e. it operates on data stored internally). The *state* of the computer running the program *is its entire internal configuration*, including the *contents of its memory*, its *registers*, its *variables*, its *program counter*, and so on. Viewed in this way, if such a state of the computer is ever repeated during the execution of the program, the program will repeat the whole cycle of events that led from the first to the second occurrence of that configuration over and over again, *ad infinitum.* If this happens we have obviously made a (fairly common) mistake in our coding, resulting in what is often called an *infinite loop*.

It would be useful if, before we marketed our programs, we could test them to make sure that such infinite loops could never occur. Let us suppose that we have some way of examining the internal state of the machine each time it changes, and some way of deciding that we have reached a state that has occurred before. In theory, this is

[2] This is not altogether true. The FST is used, for example, to model aspects of computer networks (see Tanenbaum, 1988, in the *Further Reading* section). Here, I am referring to its ability to model *arbitrary computations*.

possible because, as stated above, a computer at a given point in time is a finite state machine.

Suppose that our computer possesses 32 kilobytes of total computer storage, including data, registers, primary memory, and so on. Each individual bit of the 32K can be either 1 or 0. Thus we have a total of 262,144 bits, each of which can be either 1 or 0. This means that our machine can, at any point, be in one of $2^{262,144}$ states, $2^{262,144}$ being about $10^{79,000}$. This is an *incredibly* large number. In Chapter 10 we come across a really fast (over three million million instructions per second) hypothetical machine that would take 10^{80} *years* (a 1 followed by eighty 0s) to solve a problem involving passing through 10^{100} states. Our computer may thus have to go through a huge number of internal states before one of these states is repeated. Waiting for even a tiny computer, like our 32K model here, to repeat a state because it happens to be an FST is thus a rather silly thing to do!

In the remainder of this book, we study the deceptively simple abstract machine that was introduced in Chapter 7, i.e. the **Turing machine** (**TM**). The TM is essentially an FST with the ability to move left *and* right along a single input tape. This means that the TM can overwrite symbols on its tape with other symbols, and can thus take action on the basis of symbols placed there earlier in its activities. We find in Chapters 9 and 10 that this simple machine is actually more powerful than any digital computer. In fact, in some senses the Turing machine is the most powerful computational device of all. In Chapter 11, however, we find that there is something about the problem of whether or not a certain computation will eventually stop; discussed in terms of the FST above, that puts its general solution beyond *any* computational device.

EXERCISES

1 **FSTs** can be used in logic design[3]. Design FSTs to perform bitwise manipulation of their binary number inputs. For machines needing two input values, assume an input set up similar to that defined for FST_4 and FST_5, the addition and subtraction machines of Figures 8.7 and 8.8, respectively. The operations you may wish to consider are:

- and
- or†
- not
- nand
- nor

[3] See Hutchison and Silvester (1987), in the *Further Reading* section.

9 Turing machines as computers

AIMS

To learn

- how TMs can perform computational tasks such as multiplication and division
- how TMs can perform computer operations such as logical operations, memory accessing operations and control operations
- about Turing's thesis

9.1 TURING MACHINES AND COMPUTATION

In Chapter 7, **Turing machines** (**TMs**) for language recognition were introduced. We saw that the TM is the **recognizer** for *all* the languages in the Chomsky hierarchy. Chapter 8 demonstrated that the **finite state transducer** (**FST**), which is essentially a TM that can move only to the right on its **tape**, is capable of some fairly sophisticated computational tasks, including certain restricted types of multiplication and division.

Coupled with the fact that any given digital computer is essentially finite in terms of storage capacity at any moment in time, this seemed to suggest that seeing the computer as an FST might be a useful perspective to take, especially since the FST lends itself to conversion into very simple programs. However, we saw that the huge number of internal states possible in even a smallish computer meant that notions typically applied to FSTs, such as the **repeat state theorem**, were of limited practical use in this context.

In this chapter, we are going to see that, in terms of computation, the Turing machine is a much better counterpart of the computer than is the FST. Simple as it is, and resulting as it does from addition of a few limited facilities to the FST, *the TM actually exceeds the computational power of any single computer, of any size*. In this sense, the TM is an abstraction over all computers, and the theoretical limitations to the power of the TM are often the practical limitations to the digital computer, not only at the present time, but at any time in the future. However, we shall descend from these heady philosophical heights until the next chapter. For now, we concentrate on demonstrating that the TM is capable of the basic computational tasks we expect from any *real* computer.

9.2 TURING MACHINES AND ARBITRARY BINARY MULTIPLICATION

Chapter 8 established that FSTs are not capable of multiplication of arbitrary length numbers in any number base. In this section, we sketch out a TM to perform multiplication of two binary numbers of any length. I will leave it to you to realize that similar TMs could be defined for any number base (cf. the treatment of differing number bases in Chapter 8). However, here we choose the binary number system, for obvious reasons.

9.2.1 Some basic TM operations

A side effect of defining a TM for multiplication is that we will appreciate a notion actually formulated by Turing himself in conjunction with his machines, and one which occurs in some form in many programming languages and computer environments. Essentially, we shall build up our binary multiplier by creating a 'library' of TM 'subroutines'. These subroutines, like subroutines in typical programming languages ('procedures' in Pascal), represent operations that we wish to carry out many times in a machine. However, since there are no straightforward mechanisms for *parameter passing* in TMs, our subroutines are more of an analogy to *macros*, i.e. we have to imagine that the 'sub-machine' that constitutes the macro is actually inserted into the appropriate place in the overall machine. This means that we have to 'call' our sub-machine by ensuring that the 'calling' machine configures the tape and r/w head appropriately.

Some operations needed by our multiplier Turing machine are now specified.

Our multiplication routine will work by repeated addition, based on the common 'shift and add' long multiplication method (we examine this in more detail in the next section). Clearly, then, we need an ADD routine. Our ADD routine will make use of two sub-machines, WRITE-A-ZERO and WRITE-A-ONE, as specified in Figure 9.1.

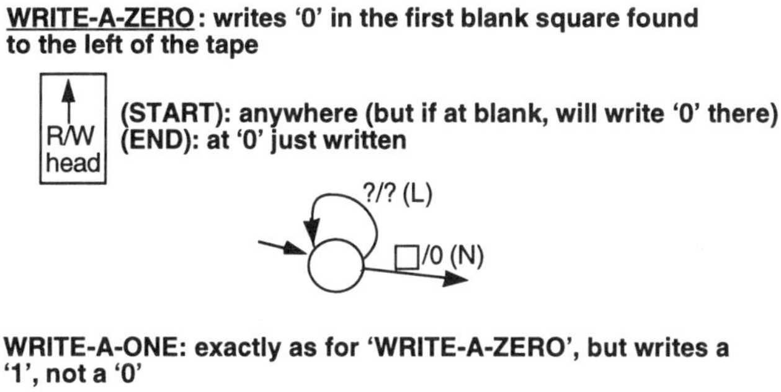

Figure 9.1 'WRITE-A-ZERO' and 'WRITE-A-ONE'

Referring to Figure 9.1, recall from Chapter 7 that we use ?/? to mean 'replace any non **blank** symbol of the alphabet for the machine by the same symbol'.

Our ADD routine adds two arbitrary length binary numbers, adding pairs of digits in least to most significant order (as we usually do). The machine assumes that the two numbers are initially represented on a tape as specified in Figure 9.2.

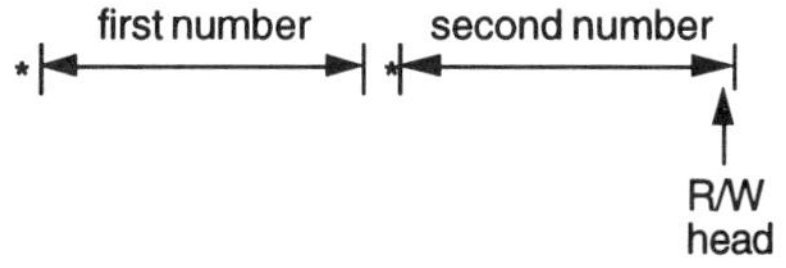

Figure 9.2 The tape set-up for the ADD TM

So, ADD expects on its tape a * followed by the first number, followed by a * followed by the second number. Its **head** is initially located on the least significant digit of the second number. ADD will not be concerned with what is to the left of the relevant part of the input tape, but will assume a blank to the right of the second number. The left asterisk will be used by ADD to indicate the current carry situation during the computation (* = no carry, C = carry). The machine will write the result of the addition to the left of the currently occupied part of the input tape (and thus assumes that the first blank found to the left of the left * is the start of the unoccupied part of the tape, i.e. ADD assumes a **packed** tape).

The description of ADD will be supported by an example input tape, and we will examine the effects of each major part of ADD on the contents of this tape. The example input tape we will use is shown in Figure 9.3.

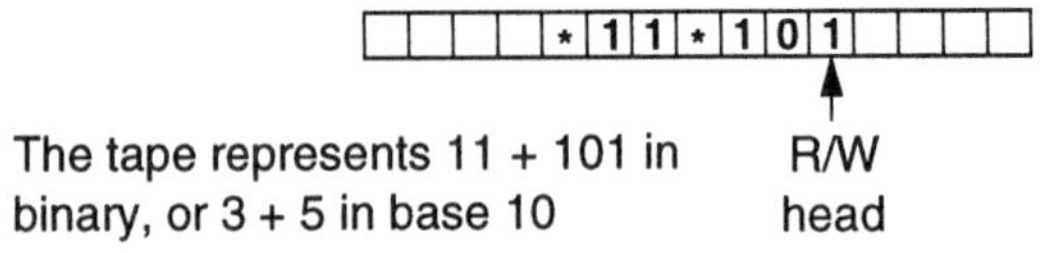

Figure 9.3 An example input configuration for the ADD TM.

9.2.2 The 'ADD' TM

Figure 9.4 shows Part 1 of the ADD TM.

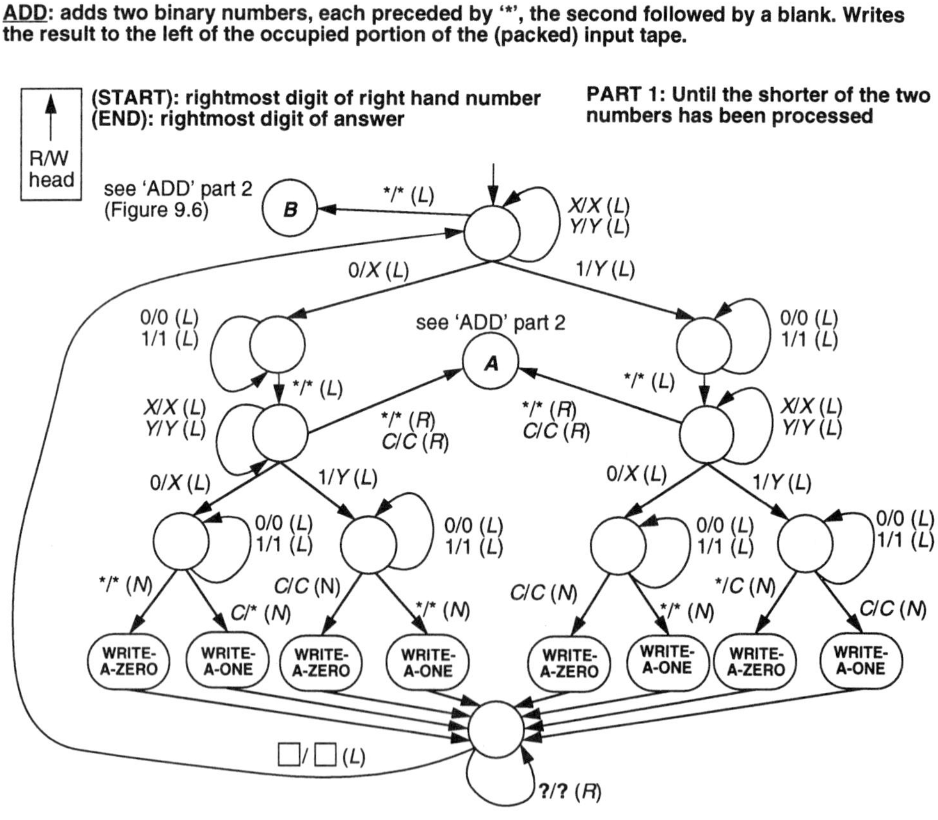

Figure 9.4 The ADD TM, Part 1

Part 1 of ADD, shown in Figure 9.4, deals with *the adding of corresponding digits of the two numbers until the digits of one or both of the numbers have been used up.* Note that *X* and *Y* are used as markers for 0 and 1, respectively, so that ADD can detect how far along each number it has reached, at any stage, and thus avoid processing the same digit more than once. When the final digit of one or both of the numbers has been reached, Part 2 of ADD (shown in Figure 9.6.) takes over. When we are ready to enter ADD Part 2, our example tape is configured as shown in Figure 9.5.

As can be seen in Figure 9.6, there are two entry points *A* and *B*, to ADD Part 2.

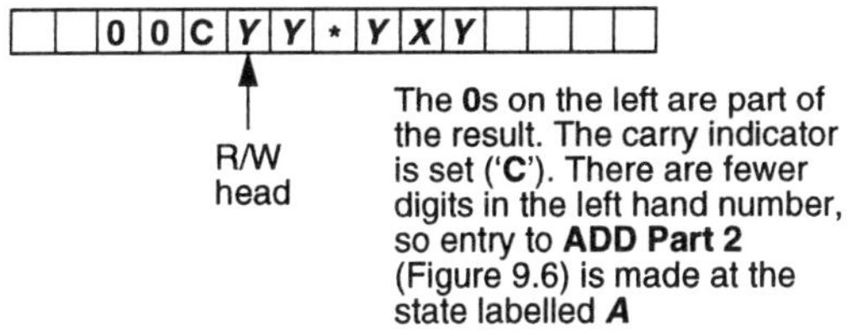

Figure 9.5 Output from ADD Part I (Figure 9.4) for the example input in Figure 9.3

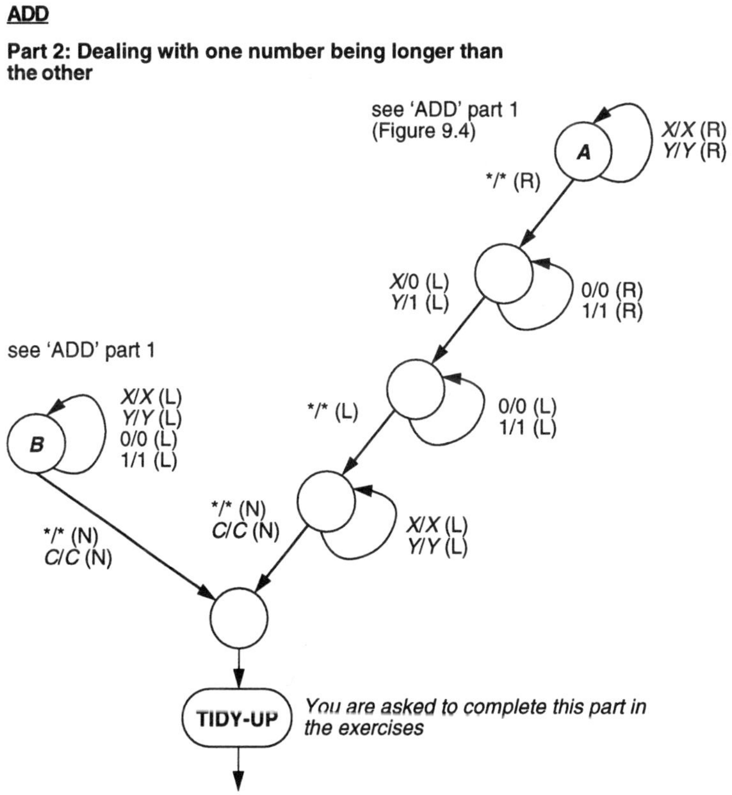

Figure 9.6 ADD, Part 2

Entry point *A*
is entered from ADD (Part 1) when *there are no digits remaining in the left hand number, but a digit was read from the right number*. Since ADD has just overwritten either a 0 (by *X*) or a 1 in the right hand number (there must have been at least one more digit in the right number than in the left number or we would not have reached entry point *A*), this digit (represented by the leftmost *X* or *Y* in the right number) is set back to its original value, so that it can be processed as an extra digit by the sub-machine TIDY-UP, the definition of which is left as an exercise.

Entry point *B*
is entered from ADD (Part 1) *when there are no digits remaining in the right number.* This case is simpler than that for entry point *A*, as no extra digits have been marked off (ADD always looks at the digit in the *right* number first, before it attempts to find the corresponding digit in the left number).

Entry points *A* and *B* both ensure that the head is located at the square of the tape representing the *carry* situation. Remember that this is the square immediately to the left of the left number, and is occupied with a * for no carry, and a *C* for carry.

Our example tape would have resulted in entering add at entry point *A*, since the right hand number ran out first. Immediately before the machine enters the component labelled TIDY-UP, which you are invited to complete as an exercise, our example tape from Figure 9.3 would be as described in Figure 9.7.

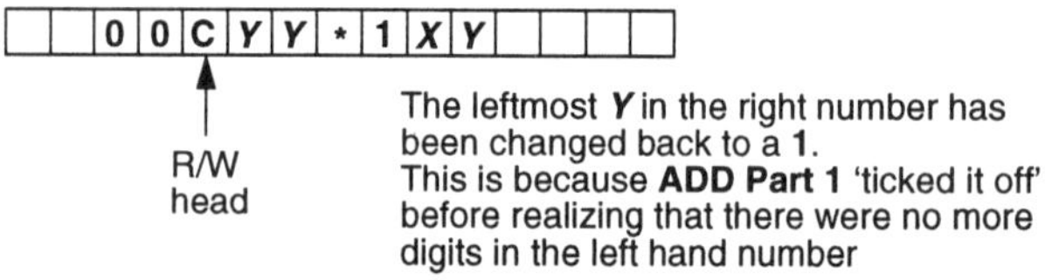

Figure 9.7 The input from Figure 9.3 on entry to TIDY-UP in ADD Part 2 (Figure 9.6)

ADD should now complete its computation, the result being the binary number at the left of the occupied portion of the tape. For our example tape, Figure 9.8 shows an appropriate outcome from TIDY-UP, and thus an appropriate representation of the result of ADD, given the input tape of Figure 9.3.

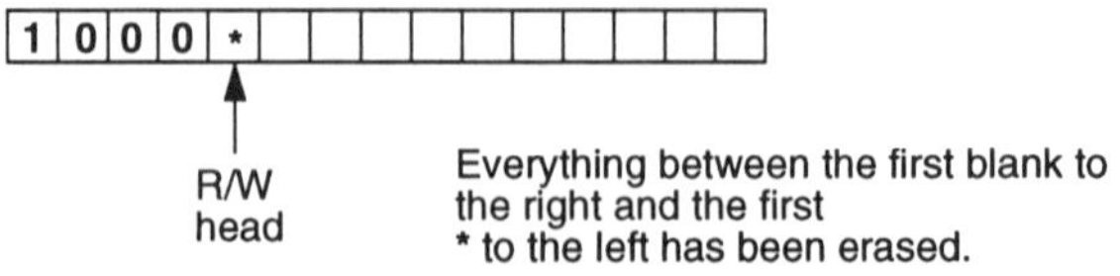

Figure 9.8 The tape of Figure 9.7 after processing by TIDY-UP of ADD Part 2 (Figure 9.6)

9.2.3 *The 'MULT' TM*

We are now ready to sketch out the description of a TM, MULT, to multiply two arbitrary length binary numbers. As mentioned earlier, our machine uses the 'shift and add' method. For example, suppose we wish to compute 1110 × 101. This would be carried out as shown in Figure 9.9.

```
   1110
   ×101
-------
 111000
  +1110
-------
1000110
```

Figure 9.9 The 'shift and add' multiplication method: binary version

An example of the same method being employed for the multiplication of two base 10 numbers may illustrate the method in more familiar terms. Figure 10 shows the method being used for the base 10 computation 345 × 23.

```
  345
  ×23
-----
 6900
+1035
-----
 7935
```

Figure 9.10 The 'shift and add' multiplication method: decimal version

The 'shift and add' process is simpler for binary numbers, since the same rule applies for placing zeros at the end of each stage, but we only ever have to multiply at intermediate stages by either 1 or 0. Multiplying by 1 involves simply copying the number out exactly, while multiplying by zero can, of course, be ignored. An algorithm to do 'shift and add' binary multiplication is given in Table 9.1.

Table 9.1 An algorithm to perform 'shift and add' multiplication of binary numbers

```
{n1 and n2 are the two numbers to be multiplied}
{let d_i be the ith digit from the right of n2}
if d_1 = 1
then ans := n1
else ans := 0
endif;
for each digit d_i, where i ≥ 2 in n2 do
     if d_i ≠ 0
     then ans:= ans + (n1 with i – 1 0s appended to its rightmost end)
     endif
endfor
```

Our MULT machine will be based on the 'shift and add' algorithm shown in Table 9.1. The detailed implementation has been left to the exercises. The MULT machine will expect its input to be configured exactly as that for the ADD TM, as specified in Figure 9.2.

An example input configuration for MULT is shown in Figure 9.11. Note that we have decided that the read/write head should be positioned initially on the rightmost digit of the right hand number, this number being called $n2$ in the algorithm of Table 9.1.

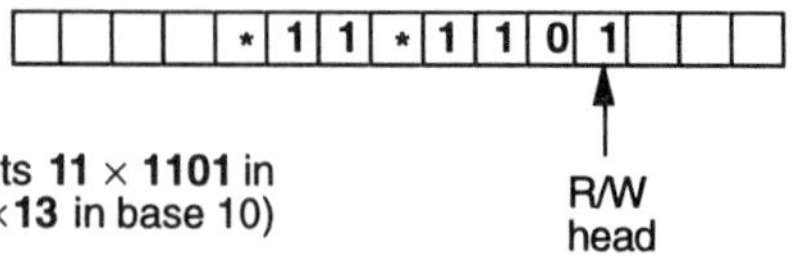

Figure 9.11 An example input tape for the MULT TM

We will now sketch out the actions to be carried out by MULT, in terms of the algorithm of Table 9.1. The first part of the algorithm is the 'if' statement.

if $d_1 = 1$
then ans := $n1$
else ans := 0

The head is currently over the first (rightmost) digit of n_2, which in the algorithm is called d_1. If d_1 is a 0, MULT initializes the answer to 0, otherwise the answer is initialized to $n1$. MULT will use the area to the left of $n1$ as the 'work area' of its tape, and leave the answer there when it terminates, separated by a single blank from the * preceding $n1$. ans := $n1$ thus means 'copy $n1$ into the answer area'. For this we need a copy routine, which we will call COPY-L. COPY-L is defined in Figure 9.12.

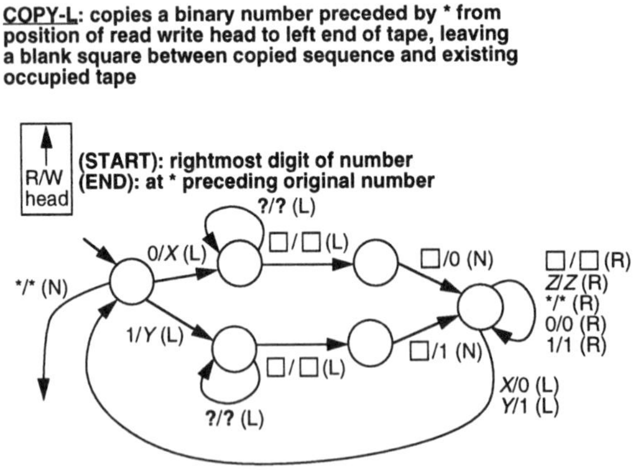

Figure 9.12 The TM, COPY-L for copying a binary number to the left hand end of the marked tape

COPY-L needs little explanation. The symbols X and Y are again used as temporary markers for 0 and 1, respectively. The machine leaves the copied sequence exactly as it finds it. Clearly, the machine is designed to expect an alphabet of (at least) $\{*, Z, X, Y, 0, 1\}$, which is due to the requirements of the multiplier[1]. The machine could easily be amended to deal with other alphabets. It would also be a simple matter to create a corresponding COPY-R ('copy right') machine, if required. If $d_1 = 0$, then MULT simply writes a 0 in the answer area. In our example here, $d_1 = 1$, so MULT must move its head to the rightmost digit of $n1$, then enter COPY-L. At this point, MULT could also place a * at the left hand end of the newly written answer sequence. The example tape would then be as shown in Figure 9.13.

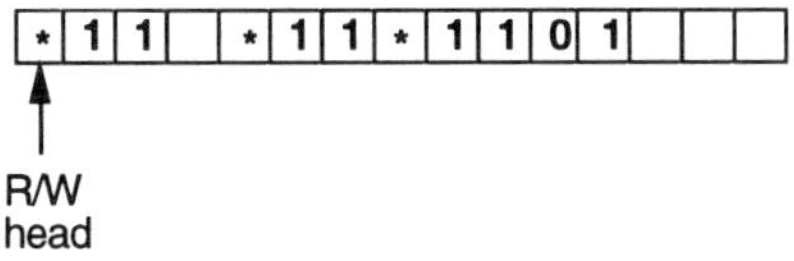

Figure 9.13 The state of the input tape from Figure 9.11 after the statement ans: = $n1$ (Table 9.1)

MULT will now deal with the next part of the algorithm, i.e. the 'for loop'.

for each digit d_1, where $i \geq 2$ in $n2$ do
  if $d_i \neq 0$
  then ans := ans + ($n1$ with $i - 1$ 0s appended to its rightmost end)
  endif
endfor

Now that d_1 has been processed, MULT turns its attention to the remaining digits of n_2. We have seen examples of the type of processing involved here earlier in this book; TMs use auxiliary symbols to 'tick off' each symbol (i.e. temporarily replace it by another symbol) so that they can return to that symbol, thus being able to locate the next in the sequence, and so on. For the algorithm above, MULT must examine all the digits, d_i, of n_2 (for $i \geq 2$). If a d_i is 0, MULT simply proceeds to the next digit (if there is one), else (d_i being a 1), MULT must write 0 at the left hand end of its tape for each digit in n_2 to the right of d_i (this corresponds to us placing zeros at the end of a number in the 'shift and add' method), and then it must do a COPY-L to copy n_1 immediately to the left of the leftmost 0 just written. If MULT then places a * to the left of the copied n_1 and moves the head right until it reaches a blank, the tape is now set up so that our ADD TM can take over. Via ADD, MULT is now carrying out the

ans:= ans + ($n1$ with $i-1$ 0s appended to its rightmost end)

part of the algorithm.

[1] Since MULT is going to use ADD, the sub-machines we define for MULT may need to take account of symbols used by ADD, such as C, the *carry indicator*, and so on.

For our example tape, $d_2 = 0$, but d_3, the leftmost digit of $n2$, is 1. MULT must then place two zeros to the left of the answer field, then copy $n1$ to the left of those zeros, meaning that the tape on input to ADD would be as shown in Figure 9.14.

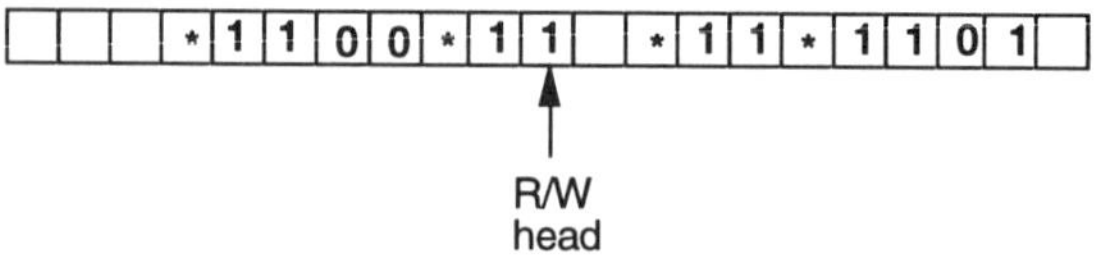

Figure 9.14 The example input tape from Figure 9.11, immediately before 'ans := ans + (n1 and two zeros appended to its rightmost end)' (Table 9.1)

ADD was designed so that it erases its tape from the right of the answer as far as the first blank to the right. This means that ADD would not erase MULT's input numbers, since a blank separates the input to MULT from the answer. MULT would then need to prepare the tape for the next digit of $n2$ (d_4 in our example) to be processed. This could involve simply '**shuffling**' the answer sequence up so that only one blank separates it from MULT's input sequence. Our example tape would now be as displayed in Figure 9.15 (subject to some slight repositioning of the *).

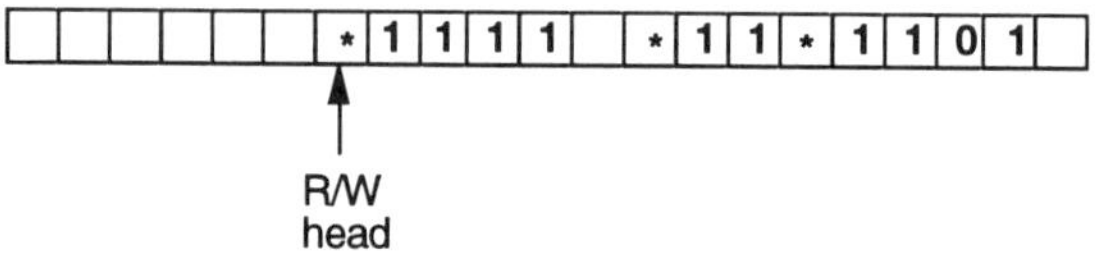

Figure 9.15 The example input tape from Figure 9.11, immediately after 'ans := ans + (n1 with two zeros appended to its rightmost end)' (Table 9.1)

MULT would now deal with d_4 of $n2$ in an analogous way to its treatment of d_3, described above. This time, three zeros would be needed, so the tape on input to ADD would be as shown in Figure 9.16.

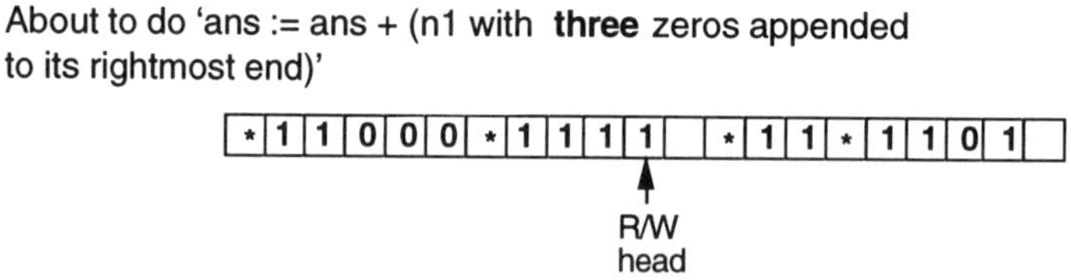

Figure 9.16 The example input tape from Figure 9.11, immediately before 'ans := ans + (n1 with three zeros appended to its rightmost end)' (Table 9.1)

Figure 9.17 shows a suitably tidied up form of the final result.

Sufficient detail has been presented to demonstrate that such a MULT machine could be implemented. The exercises ask you to do this. It is clear that such a MULT machine would operate on binary numbers of any length. We established in the preceding chapter that multiplication of arbitrary length numbers is beyond the capabili-

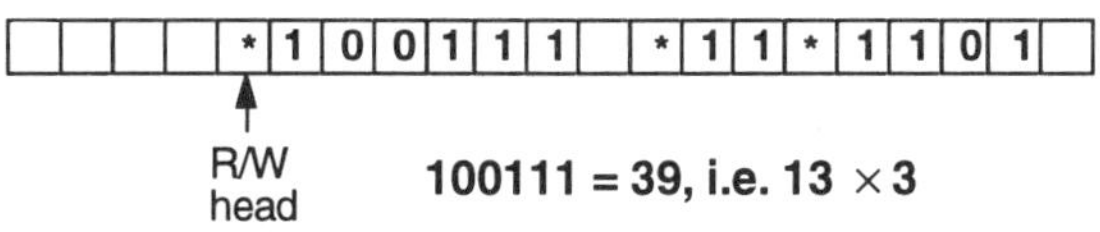

Figure 9.17 The example input tape from Figure 9.11, after the algorithm of Table 9.1 has been carried out by the MULT TM

ties of the FST. We now know, therefore, that *the TM possesses greater computational power than does the FST.*

9.3 TURING MACHINES AND ARBITRARY INTEGER DIVISION

As we can do *multiplication by repeated addition*, so we can do *division by repeated subtraction*: we keep subtracting one number from the other until we obtain zero or a negative result. We keep a count of how many subtractions have been carried out, and this count is our answer. In this section, we sketch a TM that does arbitrary integer division. The actual construction is left as an exercise.

Our machine, DIV, will perform division by repeated subtraction. We therefore require a SUBTRACT sub-machine for our DIV machine (as we needed an ADD machine for MULT).

9.3.1 The 'SUBTRACT' TM

It turns out that we can do subtraction in terms of addition, and you may be familiar with the approach considered here. For example, 8 – 5 is really the same as saying 8 + (–5). If we have a way of representing the negation of the second number, we can then simply add that negation to the first number. The usefulness of this method for binary numbers relates to the fact that the negation of a number is simple to achieve, using a representation called the *twos complement* of a binary number.

The process of obtaining the twos complement of a binary number is described in Figure 9.18.

To compute $x - y$, for binary numbers x and y, we compute the twos complement of y and add it to the first number.

Referring to the example of 8 – 5 mentioned above, we can represent this in binary as 1000 – 101. The twos complement of 101 is 011 (the inverse is 010, and 010 + 1 = 011). 1000 + 011 = 1011. Now, this result appears to be 11 (eleven) in base 10. However, after the addition we ignore the leftmost digit of the result, and thus our answer is 011 in binary (i.e. 3 in base 10), which is the correct result.

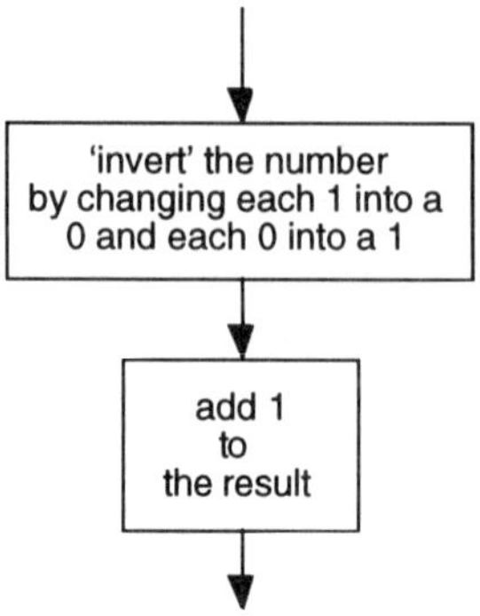

Figure 9.18 Obtaining the twos complement of a binary number

If you have not come across the method before, you should convince yourself that twos complement arithmetic works, and also discover for yourself why the leftmost digit of the result is ignored.

In terms of the development of the SUBTRACT machine, the subtraction method we have just described can be done in terms of the ADD TM described earlier in the chapter. We can even use ADD in the sub-machine that computes the twos complement, since once we have inverted a binary number, we then need to add 1 to the result. A TM, TWOS-COMP that embodies such an approach is described in Figure 9.19.

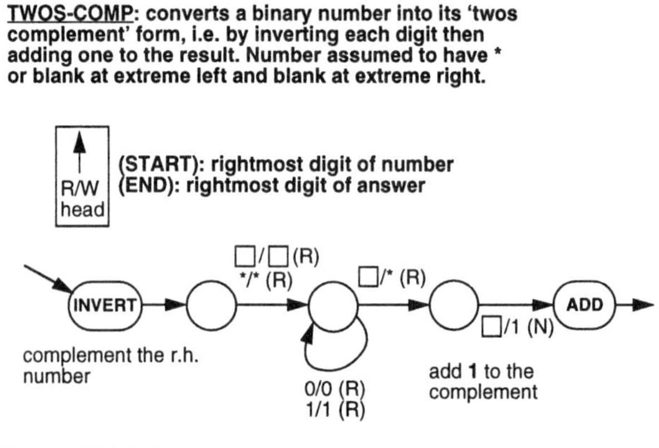

Figure 9.19 The TWOS-COMP TM, to compute the twos complement representation of a binary number

As you can see from Figure 9.19, TWOS-COMP makes use of the TM INVERT, which is defined in Figure 9.20.

You can study the behaviour of TWOS-COMP for yourself, if you wish.

We could set up our SUBTRACT TM so that it uses the same input format as that used for ADD, and shown in Figure 9.21.

We assume that the 'second number' of Figure 9.21 is to be subtracted from the 'first number'.

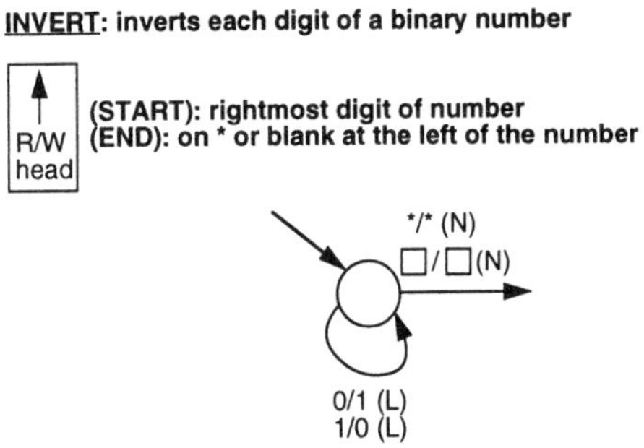

Figure 9.20 The INVERT TM, used by TWOS-COMP (Figure 9.19)

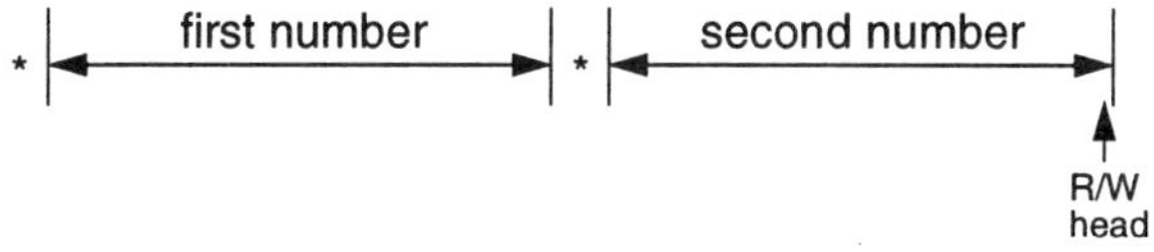

Figure 9.21 The tape set-up for the SUBTRACT TM

The exercises ask you to complete the SUBTRACT machine. This simply involves using the ADD machine to add the twos complement of one number to the other number. The main problems, as for the MULT machine, concern shuffling the various intermediate sequences around to ensure that essential information is not corrupted; but it is not too difficult to achieve this.

9.3.2 The 'DIV' TM

We now sketch a TM for performing integer division by repeated subtraction. Again, its implementation is left as an exercise. An algorithm to carry out the task is specified in Table 9.2.

Table 9.2 A 'repeated subtraction' algorithm for division, that makes use of TMs defined earlier

```
count := 0;
temp := n1;
while n2 ≤ temp do
    temp := SUBTRACT(temp,n2);     { T(x,y) is a functional representation of the
                                     statement: 'apply the TM, T, to the tape
                                     appropriately configured with the numbers x
                                     and y' }
    count := ADD(count,1)
endwhile;
count is the result
```

As for the MULT and SUBTRACT TMs, the main difficulty in implementing the DIV TM is in ensuring that the sub-machines are 'called' properly, and do not accidentally access inappropriate parts of the marked tapes. This needs careful consideration of where each sub-machine expects asterisks or blanks as delimiters, and which parts of the tape a sub-machine erases after completing its computation. One way is to use different areas of the tape (separated by one or more blanks) for different purposes. For example, you might represent the *count* variable from the algorithm in one place, the original $n1$ and $n2$ in another place. Sometimes, you may have to shuffle up one marked area to make room for the result from another marked area. However, as the main operations that increase the tape squares used are *copying* and *adding*, your machine can always be sure to create enough room between marked areas to accommodate any results (for example, if we add two binary numbers we know that the length of the result cannot exceed the length of the longer of the two numbers by more than one digit). All this *shuffling* can be quite tricky, and it is more important to convince yourself that it can be done, rather than to actually do it.

You will notice that the division algorithm in Table 9.2 includes the ≤ test. As yet we have not designed a TM to perform such logical comparisons. Therefore, in the next section we develop a generalized COMPARE TM. COMPARE may also be of use to the SUBTRACT machine (to detect if the number being subtracted is larger than the number from which it is being subtracted).

9.4 LOGICAL OPERATIONS

The generalized comparison TM, COMPARE tells us whether two arbitrary length binary numbers are *equal*, or whether one number is *greater than*, or *less than* the first number. COMPARE's **input configuration** will follow that for ADD, MULT and SUBTRACT, and is shown in Figure 9.22.

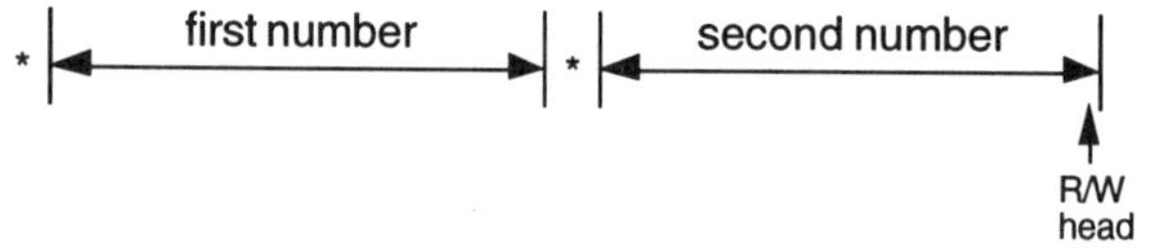

Figure 9.22 The tape set-up for the COMPARE TM

COMPARE will write the symbol =, <, or > in place of the * between the two numbers in Figure 9.22 according to whether the 'second number' is equal to, less than, or greater than the 'first number', respectively. Thus, for example, given the example input tape configuration shown in Figure 9.23, COMPARE will produce an **output configuration** as shown in Figure 9.24.

The COMPARE TM is shown in Figures 9.25 (Part 1) and 9.26 (Part 2). Part 1 deals with the comparison until all the digits of one number have been processed.

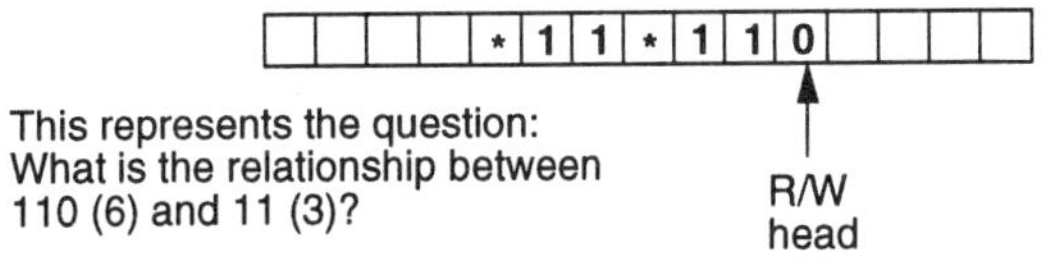

Figure 9.23 An example input tape for the COMPARE TM

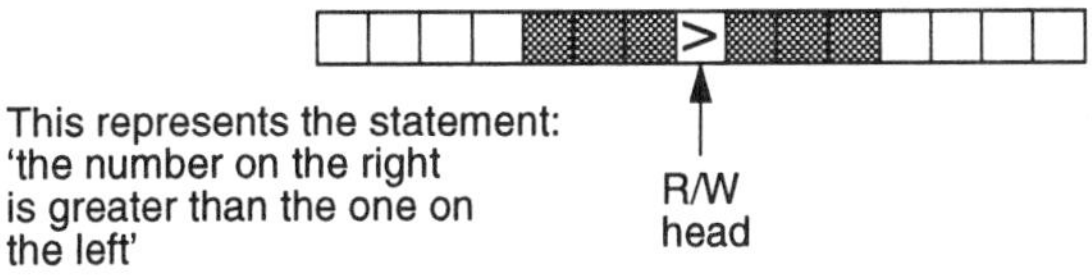

Figure 9.24 Suitable output from COMPARE, for the input tape from Figure 9.23

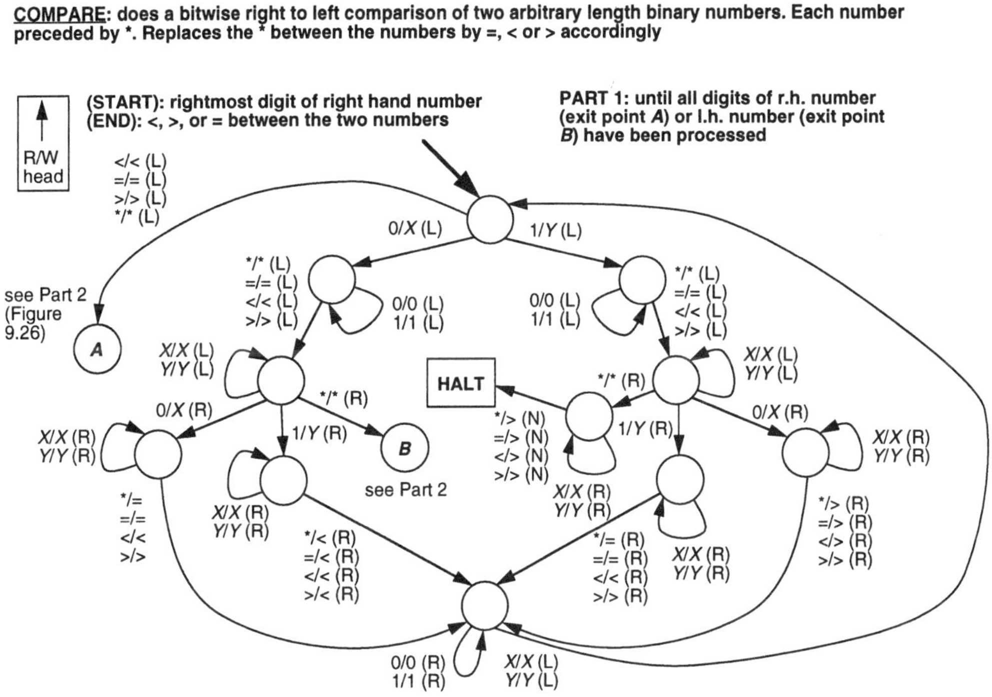

Figure 9.25 The COMPARE TM (Part 1)

When all the digits of one of the numbers have been processed, Part 2 of COMPARE (Figure 9.26) takes over.

I leave it to you to follow the behaviour of COMPARE on some examples, and to convince yourself that it operates as claimed. As part of the DIV machine (see the exercises), you could use COMPARE to carry out the test to determine when the repeated subtractions should stop.

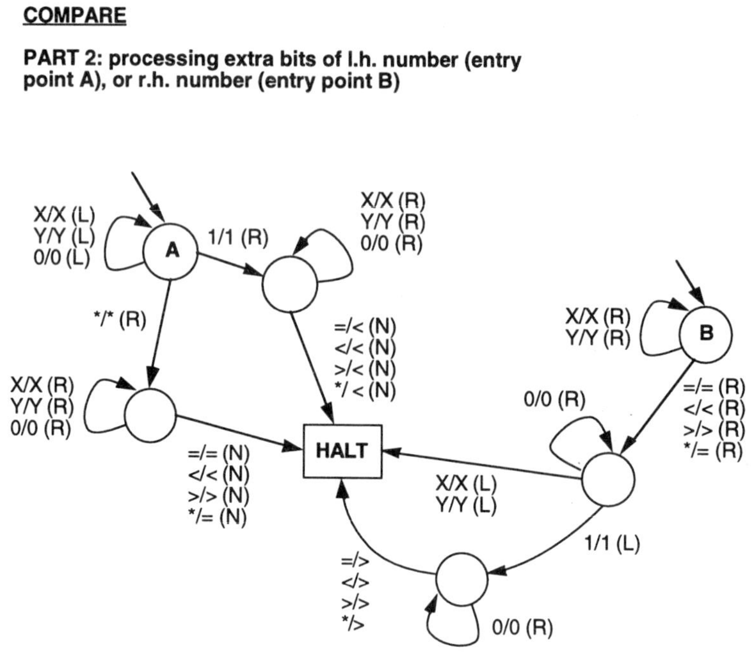

Figure 9.26 The COMPARE TM (Part 2), dealing with the rest of the longer of the two input numbers

9.5 TMS AND THE SIMULATION OF COMPUTER OPERATIONS

TMs are extremely primitive machines, with a one-dimensional data storage device. It thus may seem strange to claim, as we did at the beginning of this chapter, that TMs are actually as powerful as, and in some senses more powerful than, *any* digital computer can be. To provide evidence for this claim, we have seen TMs that do *multiplication* and *division* of *arbitrary length binary numbers*. Such operations are beyond the capabilities of any machine with a fixed amount of storage, such as any real computer at a given point in time. We have also seen how *logical operations* such as comparison of (again, arbitrarily large) numbers can be carried out by our TMs.

In this chapter, we considered only the *binary* number system. You should not see this as a limitation, however, as your experience with computers tells you that ultimately, everything that is dealt with by the computer, including the most complex program, and the most convoluted data structure, is represented as binary codes. Even the syntactic rules (i.e. grammar) of our most extensive programming languages are also ultimately represented (in the compiler) as binary codes, as is the compiler itself.

In the next section, we take our first look at **Turing's thesis**, concerning the computational power of TMs. Before this, we consider more evidence supporting the claim that TMs are as powerful as any computers by briefly mapping out how many internal functions performed by, and many representations contained within, the digital computer can be modelled by a TM. This is not an exhaustive map, but a sketch of the forms which the TM implementation of computer operations could take. I leave it to you to convince yourself of the general applicability of TMs to the modelling of any other operations found in the modern computer.

Tables 9.3–9.6 show, for each type of internal operation, a number of examples, and for each example, either a TM from this chapter that can model that operation, or a suggestion as to how that operation may be modelled by a TM. In each case, certain limitations are given that would apply to any digital computer at any given moment, but do not apply to TMs.

Table 9.3 suggests how *arithmetic operations* can be modelled by TMs. In Table 9.4, logical operations are considered. *Memory and array representation and accessing* feature in Table 9.5, while Table 9.6 briefly considers the TM *simulation of program execution* (a subject which is given much more attention in Chapters 10 and 11).

It is worth focusing briefly on memory and array operations (Table 9.5), as these did not feature earlier in this chapter. In the examples given in Table 9.5 we have used memory structures where each element was a single binary number. This is essentially the memory organization of the modern digital computer. I leave it to you to appreciate how complex data items (such as *records*, etc.) could also be incorporated into the scheme.

9.6 TURING'S THESIS

We close this chapter by briefly looking at what has been called **Turing's thesis**. What you have to appreciate about a *thesis* is that it is not a *theorem*. A *theorem* is a statement that can be proved to be true by a step by step argument that follows valid logical rules, just as the **repeat state theorem** for finite state recognizers was 'proved' in Chapter 6. A *thesis*, on the other hand, is something that somebody asserts, for some reason, as being true. In other words, anybody can state any assertion is a thesis, but it serves little use as a thesis if someone else immediately shows that it cannot be true.

However, Turing's thesis, which was initially posited in the 1930s, has yet to be disproved. In fact, not only has it not been disproved, but related work carried out by other mathematicians has led to essentially the same conclusions as those reached by Turing himself[2]. For example, an American mathematician, Alonzo Church, working at around the same time as Turing, described the theory of recursive functions. Similarly, Emile Post, also a contemporary of Turing and Church, and like Church, an

[2] References to the research in this section can be found in the *Further Reading* section.

Table 9.3 TM simulation of arithmetic operations

Example operations	TM implementation	Computer limitations
Division	DIV	Size of operands/ size of result
Multiplication	MULT	"
Addition	ADD	"
Subtraction	SUBTRACT	"
Power (x^y)	result := 1 {write a 1 in the result area of tape} while $y \neq 0$ {COMPARE(y,0) in another area of the tape} result := result × x {MULT(result,x) in another area of tape} $y := y - 1$ {SUB(y,1) in another area of tape} endwhile;	"

Table 9.4 TM simulation of logical operations

Example operations	TM implementation	Computer limitations
<, >, =	COMPARE	length of operands
≥, ≤, ≠	e.g. ≠ 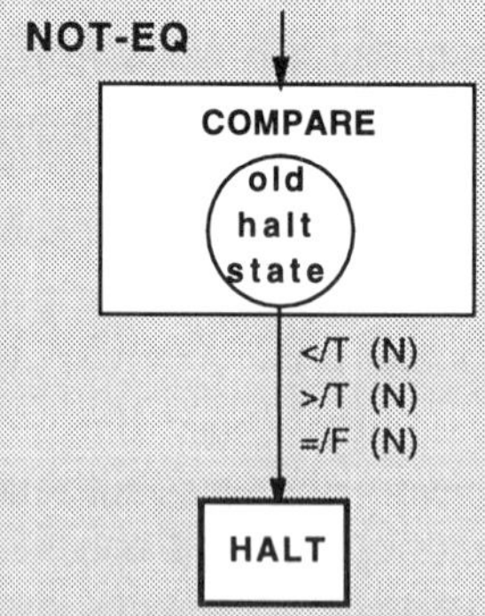 	"
bitwise not	INVERT	length of operand

Table 9.5 TM simulation of memory/array structure and access operations

Example operation	TM implementation	Computer limitations
1-D ARRAY	ACCESSING THE MEMORY LOCATION 'address' 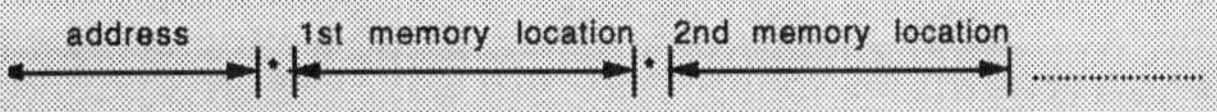 Start: Proceed right along tape, until reach a * or a blank: if a * was found, change it to X, go back and ADD 1 to a count (initially set to zero, and somewhere to the left of address); if a blank was reached address was too high, so halt. COMPARE count to address: if they are equal, go right to the first * at the right of address and copy the number that is to the left to the leftmost end of the marked tape, set all Xs back to *s, and halt; else find rightmost X, and goto Start	word length address space memory/ array size
INDIRECT ADDRESS	As above, but use found value to replace address then start again.	
MULTI-DIMENS-IONAL ARRAYS	EXAMPLE: THREE DIMENSIONAL ARRAY STRUCTURE 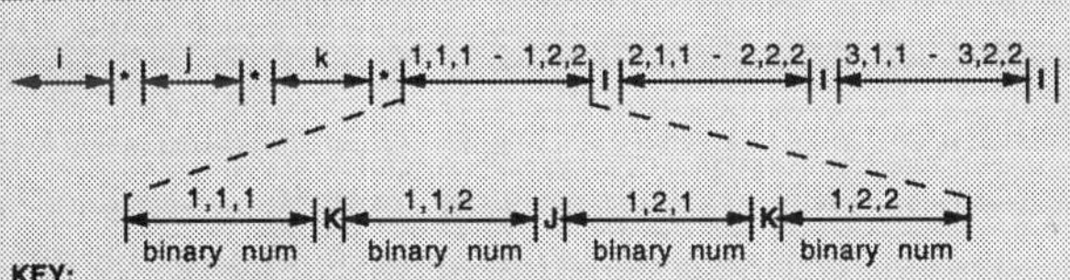 KEY: i, j, k: ADDRESS – 'access the kth element of the jth array in the array' K: marker for increment of k subscript J: marker for increment of j subscript, and to set k subscript to 1 I: marker for increment of I subscript, and to set both j and k subscripts to 1	as for 1-D array above, plus possible limit to number of dimensions in an array

Table 9.6 TM simulation of program execution

Example operations	TM implementation	Computer limitations
Running a program	Use binary numbers to represent codes of operations such as ADD, MULT, memory access, and so on. Set up data and memory appropriately on the tape. Then a portion of tape can be used to represent a binary coded version of the program, etc.	size of program amount of data number of operations

American, described in 1936 a class of abstract machines consisting of an infinite tape on which an abstract problem-solving mechanism could either place or erase a mark, and also described the result as being the marked portion of the tape on completion of the process. All these formalisms, and later ones such as *Wang's machines* (like TMs but which have only the alphabet blank and *), and the *register machines* of Sheperdson and Sturgis (closely resembling a simple assembler code-based system but with registers that can store arbitrarily large integers), have been shown to be:

(a) equivalent in computational power to Turing machines, and therefore,
(b) more powerful than any machine with limited storage resources.

Turing's thesis concerns the computational power of the primitive machines which he defined, and which we now call Turing machines. Essentially, in its broadest sense, Turing's thesis says this:

> Any well defined information processing task can be carried out by some Turing machine.

However, in a mathematical sense, the thesis says:

> Any computation that can be realized as an **effective procedure** can also be realized by some Turing machine.

This last statement of the thesis is probably not particularly helpful, as we have yet to specify what constitutes an effective procedure. Turing was working in an area of pure mathematics which had, for many years, studied the processes involved in 'doing' mathematics itself, i.e. the procedures that were used by mathematicians to actually carry out the calculations and reasoning that mathematicians do. At the time Turing formulated the notion of TMs, the 'computers' that his machines were intended to emulate were thus *humans engaged in mathematical activity*. An effective procedure, then, is a step by step following of a set of unambiguous instructions to carry out a task, *but specified to such a level of detail that they could be executed by a machine*. In this context, as far as we are concerned, Turing's thesis tells us this:

> There is no machine (either real or abstract) that is more powerful, in terms of what it can compute, than the Turing machine.

Therefore:

> *The computational limitations of the Turing machine are the least limitations of any real computer.*

Turing machines are radically different from the computers with which you and I interact in our everyday lives. These real computers have interfaces; they may display detailed graphics, or even animations and video, or play us music, or enable us to speak to, or play games with them. The computer may run an artificial intelligence program, such as an expert system that solves problems that even 20 years ago would have been impossible on anything but the largest mainframe. Yet, in a formal sense, everything that happens on the surface, so to speak, of the computer system, is merely a re-presentation, an alternative encoding, of the results of symbol manipulation procedures that can be modelled by a simple machine that merely repeatedly reads a single symbol, writes a single symbol, and then moves to examine the next symbol to the right or left. Moreover, this simple abstract machine was formulated at a time when 'real computers' were things like mechanical adders and Hollerith card readers.

The Turing machine represents a formalism that allows us to study the nature of computation in a way that is independent of any single manufacturer's architecture, machine languages, high level programming languages or storage characteristics and capacity. TMs are thus a single formalism for application to the study of topics such as the complexity of automated processes and languages.

In terms of languages, we have already seen the close relationship between TMs and the **Chomsky hierarchy**, and we refine this still further in Chapter 11. In the next chapter we study the notion of **complexity** as it applies to TMs. However, an even more exciting prospect is suggested by our statement that the limitations of the TM are the least limitations of any real computer, no matter how powerful that real computer is (and only a real computer to which we could constantly add additional storage as required could approach the power of the TM). A discussion of some of these limitations, and their ramifications in the real world of computing, form a major part of the remaining two chapters of this book.

EXERCISES

1 Define the **TM** TIDY-UP for the ADD machine, above.

2 Complete the definitions of the TMs MULT (using the ADD TM), SUBTRACT and DIV (perhaps using COMPARE).

3 Design a TM that accesses elements of a two dimensional array, following the specification given in Table 9.5.

4† What **function** is computed by the TM in Figure 9.27, assuming that its input tapes are configured as specified in Figure 9.28?

In Figure 9.28, y is an arbitrary string of the form 1^n, $n \geq 1$, representing the integer n, followed by a marker, A. The output is assumed to be the integer represented by m, where m is the number of 1s to the right of the A when the machine halts.

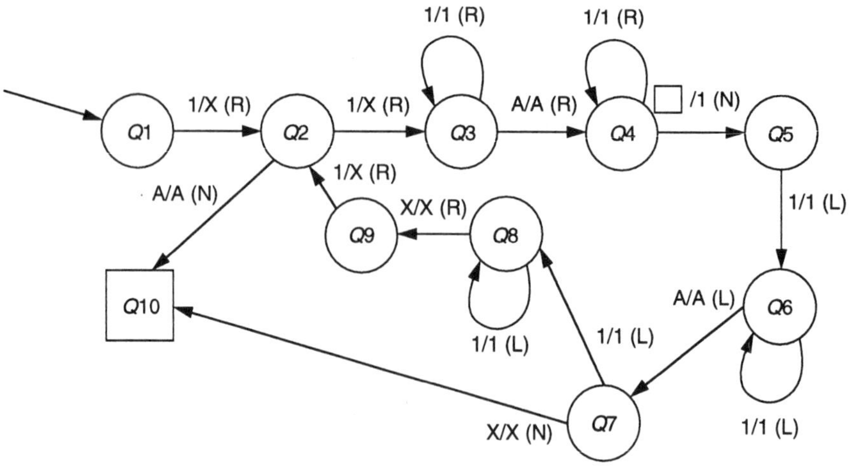

Figure 9.27 What function is computed by this TM?

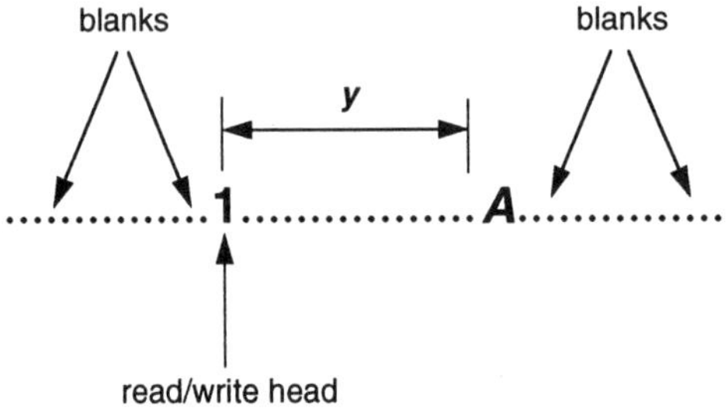

Figure 9.28 An appropriate input configuration for the TM of Figure 9.27

5 The Turing machine, T, is as depicted in Figure 9.29. The Initial tape is of the form shown in Figure 9.30.

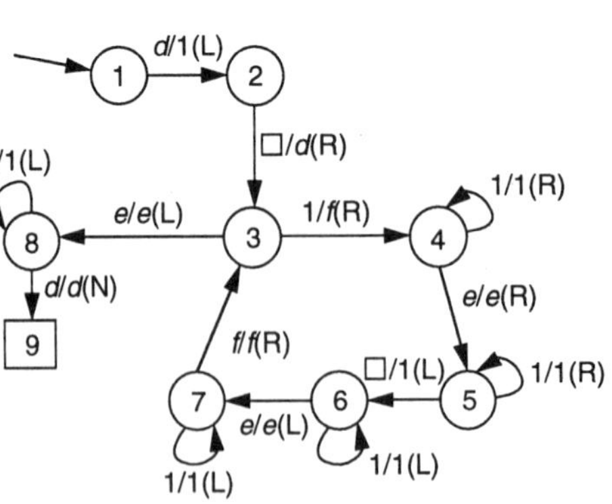

Figure 9.29 A TM for language recognition and computation

Figure 9.30 A specification of the input configuration for the TM of Figure 9.29

Referring to Figure 9.30, note that:

d, *e*, and *f* are alphabet symbols;
x is a (possibly empty) sequence of 1s;
the arrow indicates the initial position of read/write head.

(a)† Briefly describe the relationship between the tape on entering the **loop** of states 3–7, and the tape when all iterations through the loop have been completed.

(b)† If the **arc** between state 3 and state 8 labelled '*e*/*e* (*L*)' was altered to '*e*/1 (*L*)', what function, expressed in terms of *x*, would the amended machine compute, assuming that $|x|$ (i.e., the number of 1s on the initial tape) represented an integer, and that the result was the number of 1s to the right of *d* when the machine halted?

(c) Delete state 1 from *T*, and by amending arcs as necessary, draw a machine, T_1, which **accepts** the language $\{d1^n e1^n \mid n \geq 0\}$. State 2 of *T* should become the start state of T_1 and state 9 of *T* its halt state. Additional alphabet symbols may be required, but you should introduce no additional arcs.

10 Dimensions of computation

AIMS

To learn about

- function (what is computed), space (how much storage computation takes) and time (how long computation takes)
- the addition of facilities and how they do not increase the computational power of the TMs
- the non-deterministic TM as a parallel computer
- whether a non deterministic TM can be replaced by an equivalent deterministic TM that does the job as efficiently

10.1 ASPECTS OF COMPUTATION: SPACE, TIME AND COMPLEXITY

The last chapter ended by arguing that the limitations, in terms of computational power, of the **Turing Machine (TM)** are also the limitations of the modern digital computer. We argued that, simple as it is, the TM is actually more powerful than any real computers unless we allow for an arbitrary amount of storage to be added to the real computer, as required, during the course of its activity. Even then, the computer would not be *more* powerful than the TM. However, claims about the power of the TM must be appreciated in terms of the TM being an **abstract machine**. In Chapter 8, when discussing the **FST**, we presented so called memory machines, that 'remember' an input symbol for a fixed number of state transitions before that symbol is output. In a sense, by doing this we were using an implicit model of *time*, and the basic assumption of that model was that the **transition** between two states of a machine took exactly one unit of this time, which we will now call a **moment**.

Turing's thesis, as discussed in Chapter 9, reflects a functional perspective on computation: it focuses on *what* the TM can perform. However, as users and programmers of computers, we are not only interested in the functions our computer can carry out. At least two other fundamental questions concern us, these being:

- how much *memory* and *storage* will our task require (**space** requirements), and
- *how long will it take* for our task to be completed (**time** requirements)?

In other words, the dimensions of computations that occupy us are **function**, space and time. It is clear then that reference to *computational power*, a term used freely in the last chapter, should be qualified in terms of those dimensions of computational power to which reference is being made.

Now, in terms of space requirements, our binary TMs of Chapter 9 seem to require an amount of memory (i.e. occupied **tape** squares) that does not differ significantly from that required by a computer carrying out a similar task on a similar set of data. For example, consider the descriptions of the memory accessing TMs towards the end of Chapter 9. Apart from the binary numbers being processed, the only extra symbols that our machines required were special markers[1] to separate one number from the next. However, these markers were needed because we had implicitly allowed for variable memory 'word' (or array element) length. If we had introduced a restriction on word length, as is the case in most memory schemes, we could have dispensed with the need for such markers. However, if we had dispensed with the markers between memory items, we would have had to 'program in' the knowledge of where the boundaries between items occurred, which in terms of TMs means we would have had to introduce more states to deal with this.

[1] The use of the word 'marker', as used throughout this chapter, refers to the way in which the TM uses a symbol. Such a 'marker' symbol is simply a symbol of the TM's alphabet.

The discussion above seems to imply that *we can reduce the number of states in a (well-designed) TM at the expense of introducing extra alphabet symbols, and we can reduce the number of alphabet symbols at the expense of introducing extra states.* In fact, this relationship has been quantified, and it has been shown that

> any TM that has more than two states can be replaced by an **equivalent** TM that has only two states.

More importantly, from our point of view, it has been shown by the information theorist Claude Shannon that

> any TM that uses an alphabet of more than two symbols can be replaced by an equivalent TM that uses only two.

The fact that any TM can be replaced by an equivalent TM using only a binary alphabet is of fundamental importance to the practical use of computers as it indicates that any shortfalls in functional power that real computers have is certainly not a consequence of the fact that they only use a two-symbol alphabet.

Due to the reciprocal relationship outlined above between the number of states in a TM and the number of alphabet symbols it needs, the product of the number of states and the number of alphabet symbols is often used as a measure of the **complexity** of a TM. However, there are other aspects of TMs that could be said to relate to their complexity. One of these aspects is **non determinism**, which, with respect to TMs we encountered in Chapter 7. We have already seen that non determinism is computationally expensive, and therefore we would like to do without it, if possible. For the finite state recognizers, it is possible to dispense with non determinism, but for the **pushdown recognizers** it is not always possible to do so. As we will discover, non determinism is not necessary in the case of the Turing machine. However, as we see later in the chapter, there are implications for the *space* and *time* dimensions of computation if we remove it.

10.2 NON DETERMINISTIC, DETERMINISTIC AND MULTI-TAPE TMs

In Chapter 7, we saw that the non deterministic TM was the abstract machine counterpart of the **type 0**, or **unrestricted grammars**, the most general classification of grammars of the **Chomsky hierarchy**. We saw a method for constructing non deterministic TMs from the productions of type 0 grammars. Now we return to the notion of non deterministic TMs to demonstrate that non determinism in TMs provides us with no extra functional power (although we see later in the chapter that things change if we also consider the time dimension of computation). This result has implications for *parallel computation*, to which we return later in this chapter. Only a sketch will be given of the method for converting any non deterministic TM into an equivalent deterministic TM. However, some of the techniques introduced are fundamental to discussions later in the chapter.

10.2.1 Quintuples

Hitherto, this book has used a pictorial representation of TMs. However, many books featuring TMs also use a representation known as **quintuples**, where each quintuple represents one arc in a TM, and is written as a five element list as follows:

(<current state>, <read symbol>, <write symbol>, <move>, <new state>).

Thus, the pictorial TM on the left of Figure 10.1 is represented by the quintuples shown on the right of the figure.

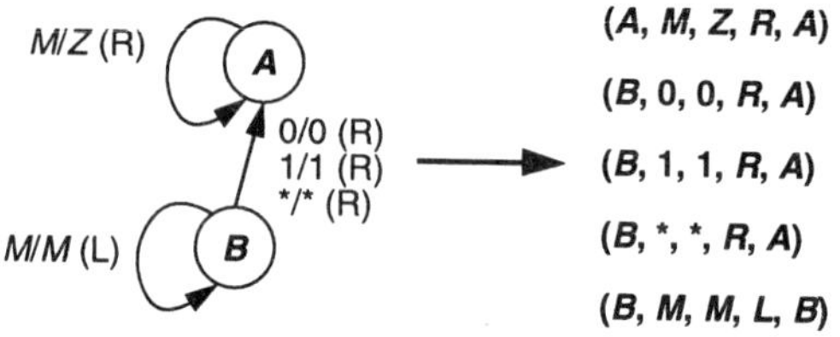

Figure 10.1 Diagrammatic representation as quintuples (right)

10.2.2 The problem solving behaviour of the non deterministic TM

If a TM is non deterministic, and it correctly computes some function (such as **accepting** the strings of a language), that TM will be capable of reaching its **halt state**, leaving some kind of result on the tape. For a non deterministic machine this is alternatively expressed as 'there is some sequence of transitions that would result in the machine reaching its halt state from one of its start states'. In terms of non deterministic TMs the phrase:

'there is some sequence of *transitions*'

can now be stated as:

'there is some sequence of *quintuples*'.

Suppose, then, that we have a non deterministic TM that attempts to solve some problem, or produce some result. If there is a result, and it can try all possible applicable sequences of quintuples *systematically* (we will return to this in a moment), then it will find the result. What we are going to discover is that there is a deterministic method for trying out every possible sequence of quintuples (shorter sequences first), and stopping when (or rather *if*) a sequence of quintuples is found that leads to a halt state of the original machine. Moreover, it will be argued that the method described could be applied by a deterministic TM. The construction described represents an exciting development, because it is our first example where one TM models the behaviour of another TM by executing its quintuples as if they were a 'program'. The possibility of this was briefly alluded to towards the end of Chapter 9.

In order to simplify the description of our deterministic version of a non deterministic TM, we shall assume that we have a special TM with four tapes. Then, in the next section, we shall show that any deterministic TM with more than one tape can be replaced by an equivalent deterministic machine with only one tape!

10.2.3 Multi-tape TMs

A four-tape TM is a special case of the notion of a **multi-tape TM**, this being a TM with more than one tape, and a corresponding **read/write head** for each tape. The tapes of a k-tape TM are numbered 1, 2, .., k. On each of the arcs of a multi-tape TM we find an extra designator (an integer between 1 and k) that specifies the tape on which the next operation is to occur. The machine is assumed to begin its operation on tape 1, and each time processing resumes on a given tape, the read/write head for that tape is assumed to be located where it was when that tape was last used. Multi-tape TMs are represented as **sextuples** rather than quintuples, as demonstrated by the fragment of a two-tape machine shown in Table 10.1. The table shows a diagrammatic representation, the sextuples, and a description of the behaviour specified by the machine fragment. Assume that in Table 10.1 the machine is currently in state A, and using tape 1.

Table 10.1 A k-tape TM fragment: diagram, sextuples, behaviour

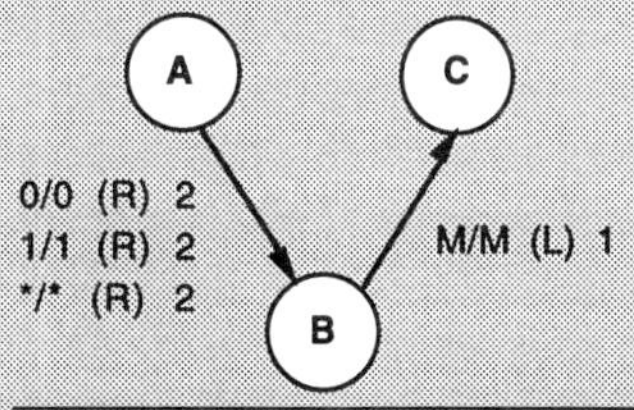

Diagram	Sextuples	Behaviour
	$(A, 0, 0, R, B, 2)$ $(A, 1, 1, R, B, 2)$ $(A, *, *, R, B, 2)$	From state A: if the symbol at the read/write head on tape 1 is a 0, a 1 or a *, replace it by the same symbol, move right on tape 1, then switch to tape 2, and enter state B.
	$(B, M, M, L, C, 1)$	From state B: if the symbol at the read/write head on tape 2 is M, replace it by M, move left on tape 2, then switch to tape 1, and enter state C.

10.3 CONVERTING A NON DETERMINISTIC TM INTO A FOUR-TAPE DETERMINISTIC TM

We now describe the conversion of a non deterministic TM into a four-tape deterministic TM. Let us call the **N**on deterministic TM *N*, and the corresponding **D**eterministic 4-tape machine, *D*.

10.3.1 The four tapes of the deterministic machine, D

We begin by describing the use of *D*'s four tapes, beginning with tape 1, which is shown in Figure 10.2.

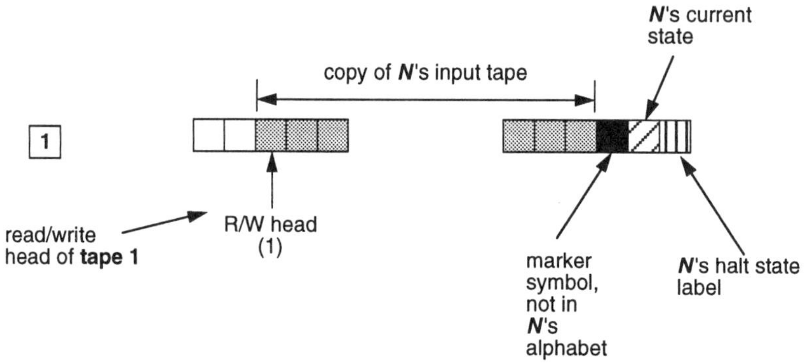

Figure 10.2 Tape 1 of the four-tape deterministic TM, *D*

As shown by Figure 10.2, tape 1 of *D* stores:

- a copy of the *marked portion of the tape that N would have started with* (we can assume for simplicity that *N*'s computation would have begun with its read/write head on the leftmost symbol of its input);
- *the label of N's current state*, initially marked with *N*'s start state label (let us assume that the start state is always labelled *S*);
- *the label of N's halt state* (we can assume that *N* has only one halt state: cf. exercises, Chapter 7), which in Figure 10.2 is *H*.

Note that we are making the assumption that labels such as state names and alphabet symbols each occupy one square of a tape, i.e. are *single symbols*. In the formal world, there is no concept of a 'character set' in which we 'run out' of single symbol labels: there are a potentially infinite number of available single symbol labels. Thus, *a TM of any size can be assumed to require state and alphabet labels each consisting of one symbol.*

Now we can describe tape 2, schematically represented in Figure 10.3.

Figure 10.3 tells us that tape 2 of *D*, the deterministic four-tape TM, contains the quintuples of *N*, each occupying five consecutive tape squares, each preceded by a unique single symbol that is not a symbol of *N*'s alphabet. To illustrate, Figure 10.4 shows a quintuple from the TM fragment in Figure 10.1, along with its corresponding representation according to the scheme specified in Figure 10.3.

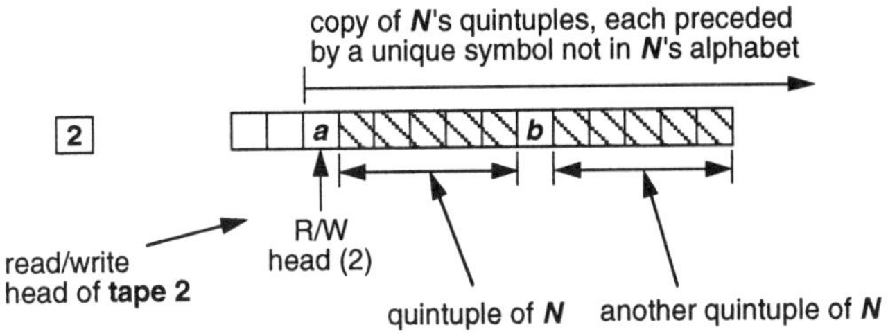

Figure 10.3 Tape 2 of the four-tape deterministic TM, *D*

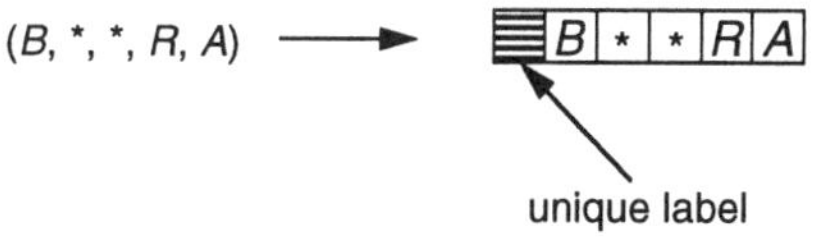

Figure 10.4 The representation of a single quintuple of the non-deterministic TM, *N*, on Tape 2 of *D* (Figure 10.3)

Next, tape 3 of *D*. Tape 3 is where *D* will repeatedly perform the systematic application of *N*'s quintuples, starting from a copy of *N*'s input tape (from tape 1, specified in Figure 10.2). *D*'s first activity, then, is to set up tape 3 as shown in Figure 10.5.

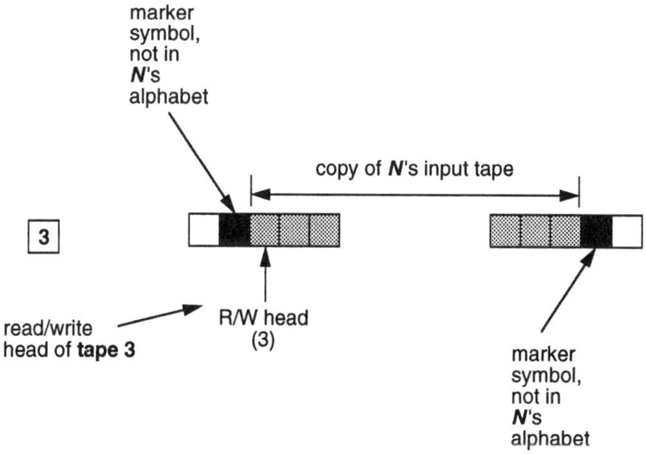

Figure 10.5 Tape 3 of the four-tape deterministic TM, *D*

Note that D places special 'markers' at either end of the copied input. These are necessary, as after the application of a sequence of N's quintuples that leads to a dead end, D will have to erase the marked portion of tape 3, and copy the original input from tape 1 again. The potential problem is that N's computation may result in blank squares in between marked symbols, resulting in a tape that is no longer **packed**, so D needs a way of detecting the extreme ends of the marked portion of the tape.

The existence of the markers causes a slight complication in the operation of D. One of N's quintuples may result in D's tape 3 head moving onto the marker. When this happens D must simply move the marker one square to the right or left (depending on whether the marker was encountered on a right or left move, respectively), i.e. replace the marker by a blank, and then overwrite the blank on the right or left, respectively, with the marker. D must also then move the head back one square to where the marker originally was (this corresponds to the position in the tape expected by the next applicable quintuple of N). Every time D makes a left or right move on tape 3, then, it must check if the next symbol is the marker; if so, it must take the appropriate action before attempting to apply the next quintuple of N.

10.3.2 The systematic generation of the strings of quintuple labels

The whole process hinges on the statement, made more than once in the above, that D *will apply the quintuples of N in a systematic way*. As N can consist of only a finite number of quintuples, the set of symbols used to label the quintuples of N (on tape 2) is an *alphabet*, and a sequence of symbols representing labels for some sequence of quintuples of N is a string **taken from** that alphabet. So, the set of all possible sequences of quintuples that we may have to try starting from the initial tape given to N is denoted by the set of every possible non-empty string formed using symbols of the alphabet of labels.

Let us call the alphabet of quintuple labels Q. Recalling concepts from Chapter 2, the set of every possible non-empty string formed using symbols of the alphabet Q is denoted by Q^+. Now, Q^+, for any alphabet Q, is not only infinite but also enumerable. Q^+ is a **countably infinite** set. Now, by Turing's thesis, if a program can enumerate Q^+, then a TM can do it[2]. That is exactly what we need as part of D:

> a sub-machine that will generate sequences of quintuple labels, one by one, so that the sequence of N's quintuples denoted by the sequence of symbols can be executed by D, and we are sure that every possible sequence is going to be tried, if it proves necessary to do so.

To be prepared to try every possible sequence of quintuples is a rather brute force approach, of course. Many (in fact probably most) of the strings of labels generated

[2] A pseudo-code program was given in Chapter 2 to perform the same task.

will not denote 'legal' sequences of N's quintuples for the given tape, or for any tape at all. Moreover, the method will try any sequence that has a prefix that has already led nowhere (there are likely to be an infinite number of these, also). However, at least we know that if there *is* a solution that N could have found, our machine D will eventually come across the sequence of quintuples that will model such a solution. We should also point out that if there is not a solution, then D will go on forever trying different sequences of quintuples (but then, if a solution does not exist, N would also be unable to find it!).

We finally come to tape 4 of D. Tape 4 is where D is going to repeatedly generate the next sequence of quintuple labels (strings in the set Q^+) that are going to be tried. Only an overview of one method will be given here. You are invited to construct the actual machine as an exercise.

To demonstrate the method, we will assume an alphabet $\{a, b, c\}$. The approach will be:

generate all strings of length 1:
a, b, c
generate all strings of length 2:
aa, ab, ac, ba, bb, bc, ca, cb, cc
generate all strings of length 3:
aaa, aab, aac, aba, abb, abc, aca, acb, acc, baa, bab, bac, bba, bbb, bbc, bca, bcb, bcc, caa, cab, cac, cba, cbb, cbc, cca, ccb, ccc

.
.
.

You may notice from the order in which the strings are written that we obtain all of the strings of length n by copying each of the strings of length $n-1$ three times (as there are three alphabet symbols) and appending a different symbol of the alphabet to each one. For example, from *aa* we generate *aaa*, *aab*, and *aac*.

Let us assume that the machine initially has the three alphabet symbols somewhere on its tape. To generate the three strings of length 1 it simply copies each symbol to the right, each being followed by a blank, with the final blank followed by some marker (say *) as shown in Figure 10.6.

The blanks following each of the strings in Figure 10.6 can be used both to separate the strings and to enable an auxiliary marker to be placed there, thus allowing the machine to detect the next string to be copied.

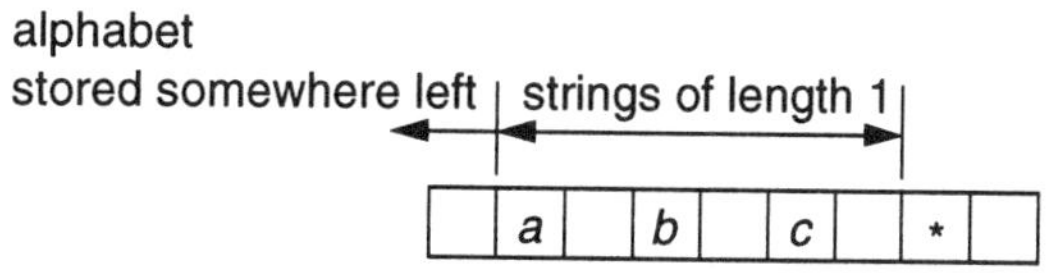

Figure 10.6 Generating all strings in $\{a, b, c\}^+$ of length 1

The next stage, shown in Figure 10.7, involves copying the first string of length 1 (a) three times to the right of the *. The number of times the string is copied can be determined by 'ticking off', one by one, the symbols of the alphabet, which, as shown in Figure 10.6, is stored somewhere to the left of the portion of tape being used to generate the strings.

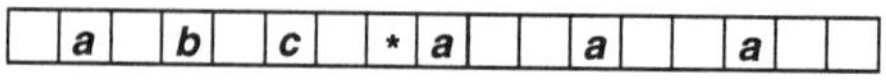

Figure 10.7 The first stage of generating all strings in $\{a, b, c\}^+$ of length 2

From the situation in Figure 10.7, the next stage is to append each symbol of the alphabet in turn to the three copied *a*s, giving the situation in Figure 10.8.

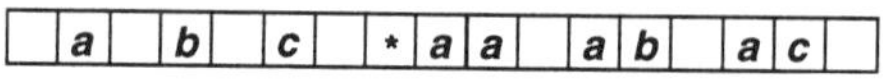

Figure 10.8 The second stage of generating all strings in $\{a, b, c\}^+$ of length 2

The next string of length 1, (b) is then copied three times to the right, as illustrated in Figure 10.9.

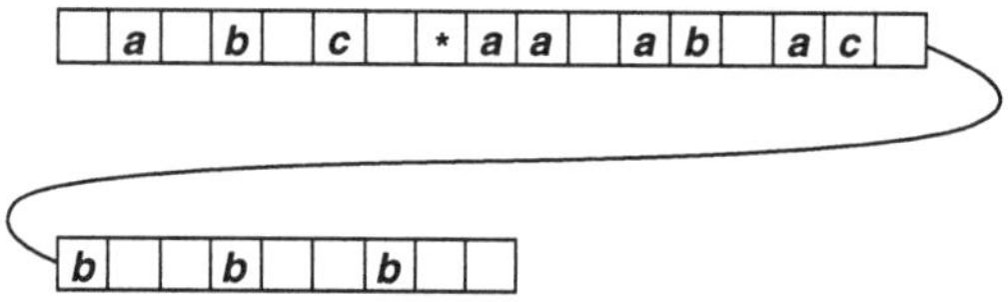

Figure 10.9 The third stage of generating all strings in $\{a, b, c\}^+$ of length 2

From Figure 10.9, each symbol of the alphabet is appended in turn to the strings just copied, yielding the situation in Figure 10.10.

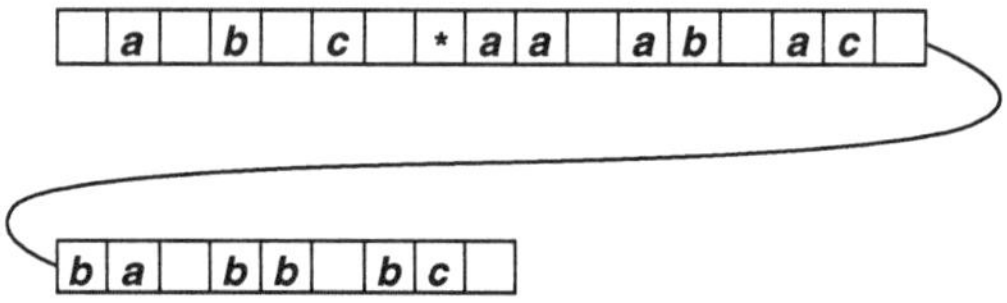

Figure 10.10 The fourth stage of generating all strings in $\{a, b, c\}^+$ of length 2

The next stage from Figure 10.10, is to copy the next string of length 1 (c) three times to the right, leading to the set up shown in Figure 10.11.

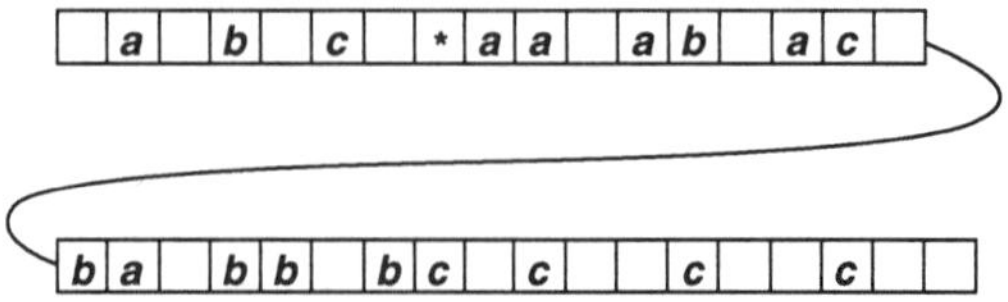

Figure 10.11 The fifth stage of generating all strings in $\{a, b, c\}^+$ of length 2

From Figure 10.11, each symbol of the alphabet is appended to each string that was copied in the previous stage, giving a situation shown in Figure 10.12.

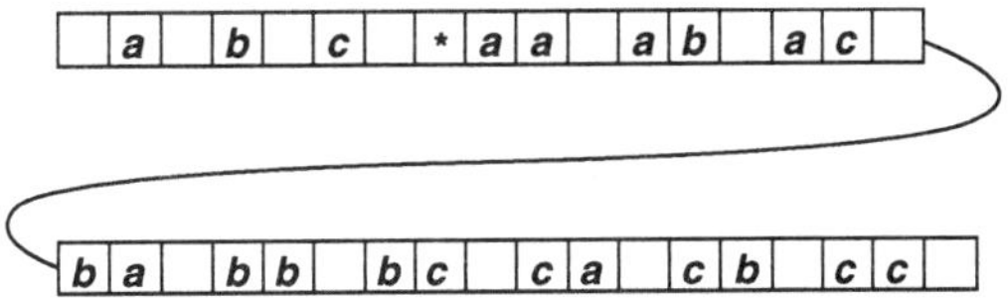

Figure 10.12 The sixth stage of generating all strings in $\{a, b, c\}^+$ of length 2

Now, when the machine returns along the tape, then attempts to copy the next string of length 1, it encounters the *. The machine thus detects that it has finished generating all strings of length 2. The machine can place a * at the end of the strings it created (Figure 10.12), as depicted in Figure 10.13.

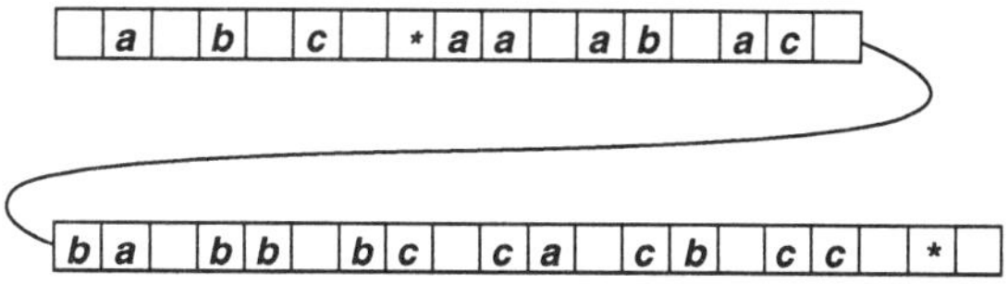

Figure 10.13 The seventh and final stage of generating all strings in $\{a, b, c\}^+$ of length 2

From Figure 10.13, the machine is ready to begin the whole process again, i.e. copying each string between the two *s three times to the right, each time appending each symbol of the alphabet in turn to the newly copied strings, and so on.

Of course, it will be necessary for *D* to try the quintuple sequences each time a certain number of them have been generated (since the generation process will go on forever, otherwise). It could, for example, try each new sequence as it was created, i.e. each time a symbol of the alphabet is appended to a recently copied sequence. Alternatively, it could generate all of the sequences of a given length, and then try each of those sequences in turn.

10.3.3 The operation of D

Here then, is a sketch of the method used by the four-tape TM, *D*, to deterministically model the behaviour of the non deterministic TM, *N*:

D is assumed to be initially configured so:
Tape 1 contains a copy of *N*'s input
Tape 2 contains the labelled quintuples of *N*
Tape 4 contains the quintuple label symbols
} as described above

D operates as shown in Figure 10.14.

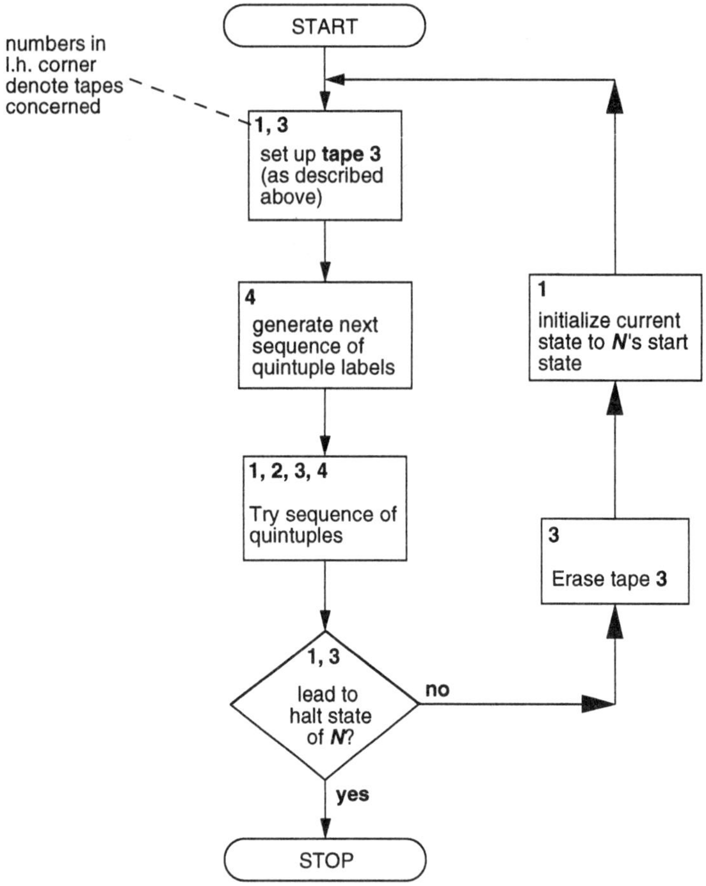

Figure 10.14 The operation of the four-tape deterministic TM, *D*

The most complicated process in the method specified in Figure 10.14 is 'Try sequence of quintuples'. This is expanded in Figure 10.15.

It may not be obvious how the machine *D* carries out the instructions specified by a quintuple of *N*. By way of illustration, suppose the label for the quintuple of *N* (the non deterministic machine) that is next to be tried in the sequence of quintuples is the label for the quintuple.

(*A*, 1, 0, *R*, *B*),

Imagine that *D* has located the quintuple label on tape 2 (the tape on which the quintuples of *N* are represented – see Figure 10.3) as shown in Figure 10.16.

D now has to examine the square on tape 1 that holds the symbol representing the 'current state' of *N* (see Figure 10.2 for the organization of tape 1). The quintuple (*A*, 1, 0, *R*, *B*) will be applicable if the current state symbol on tape 1 is *A*.

Suppose that tape 1 is configured as in Figure 10.17.

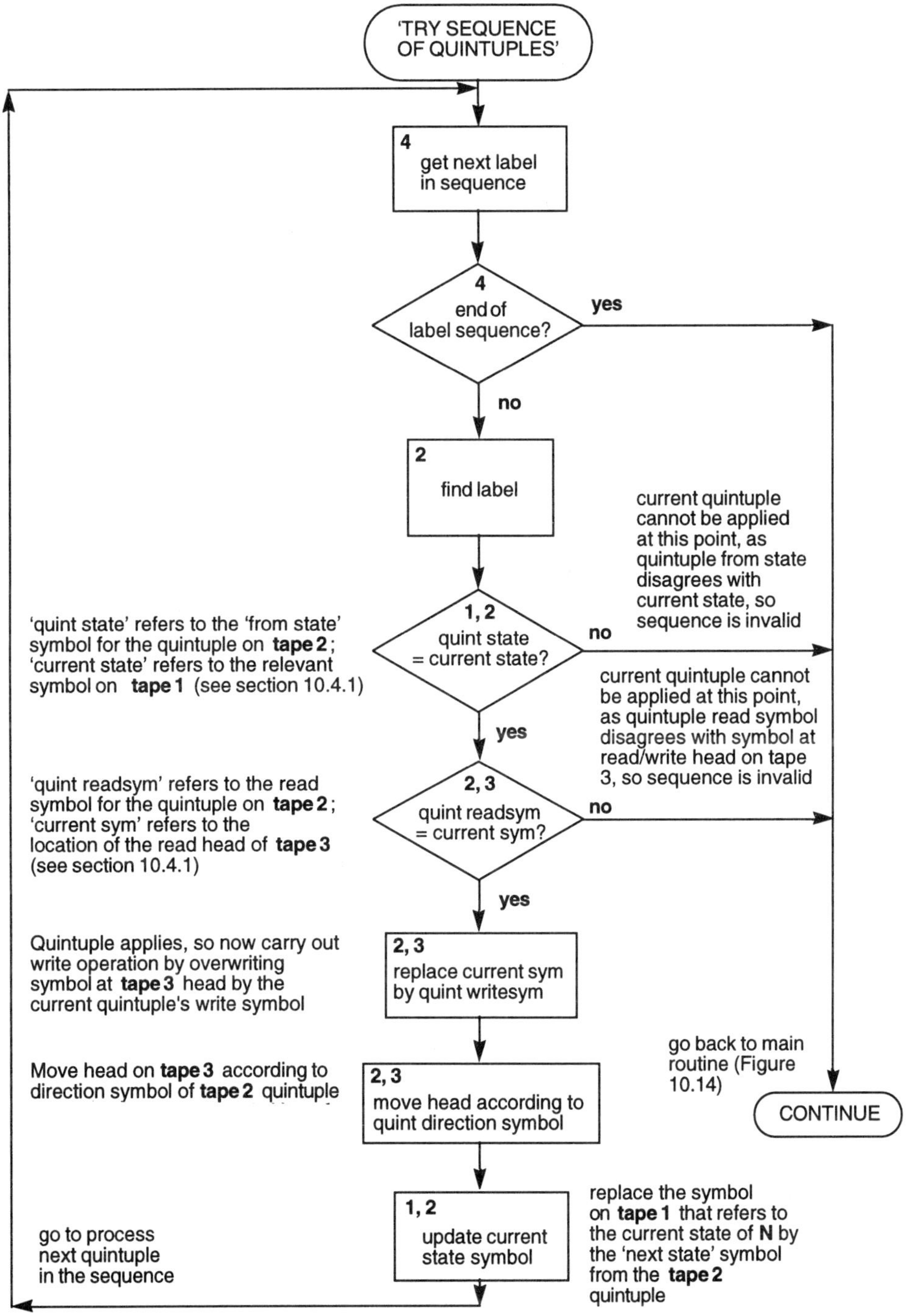

Figure 10.15 How *D* tries the sequence of *N*'s quintuples

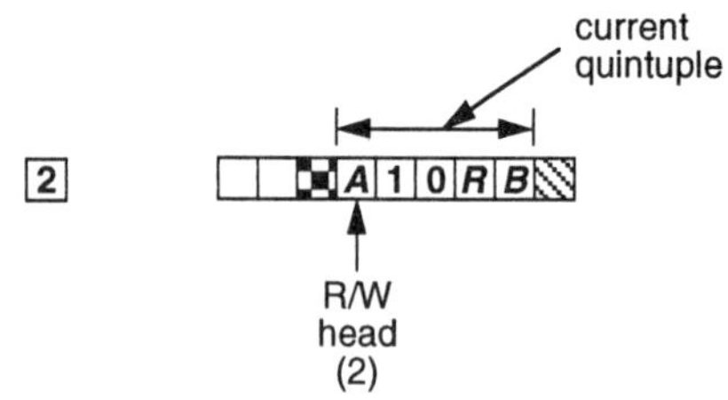

Figure 10.16 Tape 2 of *D* indicating that the current quintuple of *N* is '(*A*, 1, 0, *R*, *B*)'

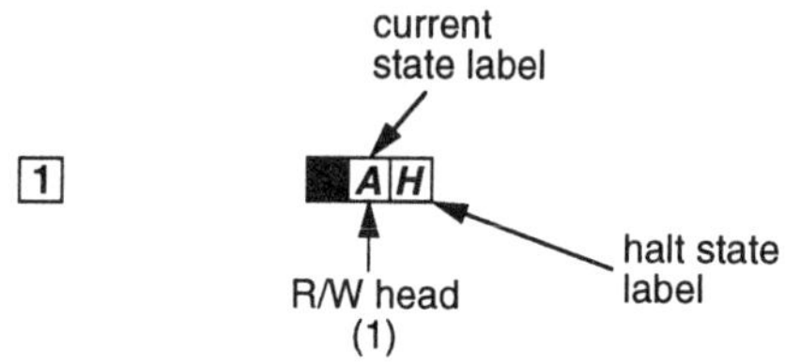

Figure 10.17 Tape 1 of *D* indicating that the current state of *N* is *A*

Figure 10.18 Tape 3 of *D* indicating that the current read symbol of *N* is 1

Now, *D* must examine the symbol at the r/w head of tape 3, since this tape represents the current state of *N*'s tape at the stage in the current sequence of quintuples that *D* is applying (see Figure 10.5).

Let us suppose that tape 3 of *D* is as shown in Figure 10.18.

As the current configuration of tape 3 in Figure 10.18 indicates, the quintuple (*A*, 1, 0, *R*, *B*) is indeed applicable. *D* must therefore:

1. replace the 1 on tape 3 by 0 (Figure 10.18)
2. move the r/w head of tape 3 right (Figure 10.16)
3. overwrite the *A* on tape 1 with a *B*, indicating that the current state of *N* in the simulated computation would be *B* (Figure 10.17)
4. get the next quintuple label symbol, if one exists, find the quintuple associated with that label on tape 2 (Figure 10.16), and repeat the process above for that quintuple, and so on.

The exercises ask you to sketch out a sub-machine that would use the four-tape set up to simulate the application of this quintuple. From the exercise, you should be able to appreciate that the construction could be applied to any similar situation.

10.3.4 The equivalence of non deterministic, and four-tape deterministic, TMs

This section has hopefully convinced you that:

> any non deterministic TM, *N*, can be represented by a four-tape deterministic TM, *D*, in such a way that *D* and *N* are equivalent, in the sense that, given any input tape to *N*, and assuming that *D*'s tapes are initially configured as described above, if *N* could have found a solution then so will *D*, and if *N* would never find a solution then neither will *D*.

However, multi-tape TMs are not the 'standard' TMs that featured in the previous chapter. It would be problematic if, to solve certain problems, or to compute certain functions, we would have to introduce extra tapes. For this would mean we would have to discover which type of problem required, say a three-tape machine, and which other type of problem required, say, only a two-tape machine, and so on. This would not be as useful as having a single, simple formalism which we knew was capable of carrying out any of our computational tasks. However, we see in the next section that the conventional single tape, deterministic TM is that single, simple formalism.

10.4 CONVERTING A MULTI-TAPE TM INTO A SINGLE-TAPE TM

A multi-tape TM, as described above, is a TM with two or more tapes, each of which has its own read/write head. The instructions on the arcs of such TMs contain an extra designator, this being the number of the tape on which the next operation is to take place. Any such machine can be modelled by a single-tape TM, as will now be demonstrated.

Let us call the multi-tape machine *M*, and resulting single-tape machine *S*. The conversion method we consider here consists of representing the symbols from *M*'s many input tapes on *S*'s single tape in such a way that a **sextuple** of *M* can be represented as several quintuples of *S*. We will use an example involving the conversion of a three-tape machine into a single tape machine to demonstrate the method.

10.4.1 Example: representing three tapes as one

Let us suppose we have a three-tape machine, *M*, with its tapes initially set up as in Figure 10.19.

We use a scheme that places the symbols from the three tapes of *M* on the single tape of *S*. From the three tapes above, we present the tape to *S* that is shown in Figure 10.20.

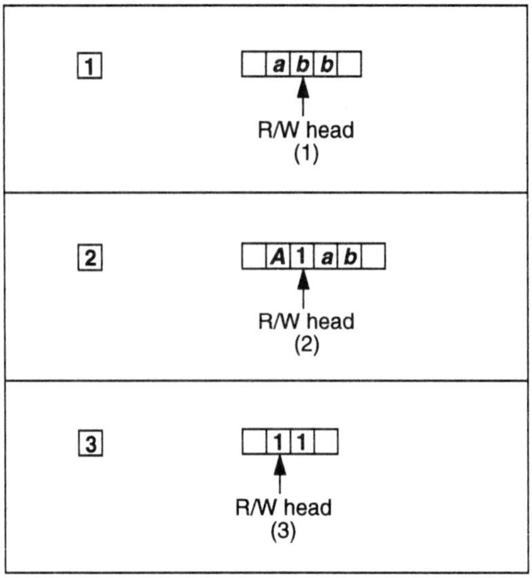

Figure 10.19 The three tapes of a three-tape machine, *M*

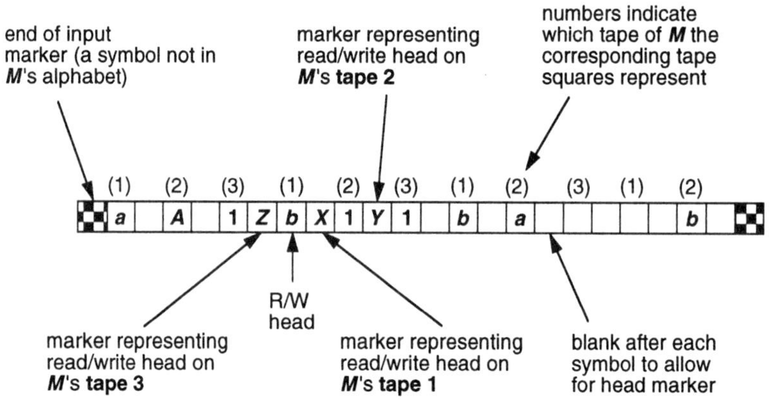

Figure 10.20 How the three tapes of Figure 10.19 could be represented on a single tape

Thus, from left to right, and taking each tape of *M* in turn, we place the leftmost symbol from tape 1, followed by a blank (or a special marker if this symbol was pointed at by the read/write head of tape 1), followed by the leftmost symbol from tape 2, followed by a blank (or a special marker, if necessary, representing the read/write head of tape 2), and so on. It will be noted that tape 3 had the least marked squares, so pairs of blanks are left where tape 3 symbols would have been found on *S*'s tape. Likewise for tape 1, where two blanks were left so that the final symbol of tape 2, the tape with the most marked squares, could be placed on the single tape.

The end of input tape markers, right and left, and the three read/write head markers (X, Y, and Z, for tapes 1 – 3, respectively) are required to be symbols that are *not* in the alphabet of M.

The encoding of the three tapes of M as a single tape of S represented in Figure 10.20 captures all of the information from the original three tapes. For example, consider the second tape square marked (1) from the left. This contains a b, which tells us the second tape square from the left of tape 1 of M should also contain a b (as it does). Moreover, the square to the right of the b in question, on S's tape, contains X, the read/write head marker representing the head position on tape 1 of M. This tells us that the read/write head of M's tape 1 should be pointing at the second symbol from the left, i.e. the the first b from the left (as it is). All other information from the initial three tapes can be similarly recovered from our single tape representation.

10.4.2 The operation of the single-tape machine, S

In the machine S, single instructions (sextuples) of the multi-tape machine, M, become several instructions (quintuples) of the single tape machine, S, that operate on a single tape set-up representing the multiple tapes of M, as specified in Figure 10.20.

Consider as an example the sextuple (1, a, A, R, 2, 2). The meaning of this sextuple is:

> if the symbol at the read/write head of the current tape is a, replace it by A, move right one square on the current tape, switch processing to tape 2 and move into state 2.

Let us assume that the alphabet of tape symbols of S is $\{a, b, A, 1\}$, and that (as in Figure 10.20) the markers used on the single tape to represent the read/write heads on the three tapes, tapes 1, 2, and 3, are X, Y, and Z, respectively. In terms of the corresponding single-tape machine S, and assuming that the read/write head of S is currently located at the tape square representing the appropriate marked square of M's tape 1, the sextuple (1, a, A, R, 2, 2) is interpreted by the single tape machine as explained in Table 10.2.

Every single instruction (i.e. *sextuple*) of the multi-tape machine has to be represented in a similar way to that described above. For a left move instruction a very similar construction could be used, except that the single tape machine would have to move left six squares from the symbol to the left of the current tape's read/write head marker. For a *no* move instruction, no movement of the read/write head marker would be necessary. For a sextuple that specified that the next operation was to take place on the same tape, there would be no need to search for the marker representing the read/write head of another tape.

Like our four-tape deterministic machine D earlier in the chapter, S uses 'marker' symbols to indicate the extremes of the marked portion of its tape. Thus, like D, S has to check for this 'end of tape' marker each time it moves its head to the right or left in the portion of tape representing the tapes of the multi-tape machine (Figure 10.20).

Table 10.2 Overview of the simulation of a sextuple for a three-tape TM, *M*, by a 1-tape TM, *S*

***M* instruction**	***S* interpretation**
if the symbol at the read/write head of tape 1 is *a*, replace it by *A*...	Since we are assuming that *S* is already pointing at the tape square representing the current symbol of *M*'s tape 1 we just test if the current symbol is an *a*, replacing it by *A* if it is.
...move right one square on tape 1...	We have three tapes encoded as one tape for *S*, with each tape square of *M* being represented by two tape squares of *S*'s tape (see tape coding scheme above), so moving 'one square' on a tape of *M*, involves moving six squares on *S*'s tape. *S* also has to move the marker (*X*) representing *M*'s tape 1 read/write head.
...then switch processing to tape 2 and move into state 2	This involves searching for the marker that represents the read/write head of *M*'s tape 2 (in our example, *Y*)

Such situations correspond to where the multi-tape machine would move its head onto a blank square outside of the marked portion of one of its tapes. In such circumstances, *S* must **shuffle** the 'end of tape marker' to the left or right by $2k$ squares, where k is the number of tapes of the simulated machine, *M*. For example, a 'move right' on a single tape representing a 10-tape TM would involve moving 20 squares to the right (shuffling the 'end of tape marker' right appropriately if necessary), and we would of course need 10 distinct read/write head markers, and so on.

You should be able to see how the construction of both the tape configuration (Figure 10.20) and the quintuples of the single-tape machine (Table 10.2) could be adapted for multi-tape machines with any number of tapes. You are asked to add more detail to the construction in an exercise at the end of this chapter.

10.4.3 The equivalence of deterministic multi-tape, and deterministic single-tape TMs

The preceding discussion justifies the following statement:

> Any deterministic multi-tape TM, *M*, can be replaced by a deterministic single-tape TM, *S*, that is equivalent to *M*.

It is worth pointing out some reasons why multi-tape machines are useful. Recall the previous chapter, when we described TMs such as MULT and DIV. These machines featured as 'sub-machines' other TMs we had defined, such as ADD, and SUBTRACT. We were forced to use different areas of the tape to deal with the computations of different sub-machines, which led to some tricky *copying* and *shuffling*.

A multi-tape approach would have enabled us to use certain tapes in a similar way to the 'registers' or 'accumulators' of the CPU, to store temporarily the results of sub-machines that would be subsequently needed.

A second related feature of multi-tape machines is that they permit a modularity of 'memory organization', a memory 'architecture', so to speak, which has more in common with the architecture of the real computer system than the single-tape TM. This can be appreciated by considering TMs such as the deterministic multi-tape machines we specified in the previous section, where the *program* (i.e. the quintuples of another machine) was stored on one tape, and the *data* was stored on another. Moreover, the machine used a further tape as a 'working memory' area, and another tape as a kind of *program counter* (the tape where the sequences of quintuple labels were generated).

The modularity facilitated by a multi-tape TM architecture can be useful for specifying complex processes, enabling what is sometimes called a 'separation of concerns'. For example, there should be no need for MULT to be concerned with the internal workings of ADD. It needs only to gain access to the result of each addition. It would therefore be appropriate if MULT simply copied the two numbers to be added onto a particular tape, then passed control to ADD, which would then leave the result in an agreed format (perhaps on another tape), where it would be collected by MULT ready to set up the next call to ADD, and so on.

That a multi-tape TM can be replaced by an equivalent single-tape construction means that we can design a TM that possesses any number of tapes, in the knowledge that our machine could be converted into a single-tape machine. We take advantage of this when we describe what is probably the most significant TM of all, in the next chapter.

10.5 THE IMPLICATIONS OF THE EQUIVALENCE OF NON DETERMINISTIC AND DETERMINISTIC TMs

We began by showing that *from any non deterministic TM we could construct an equivalent four-tape deterministic TM*. We then showed that *from any multi-tape deterministic machine we could construct an equivalent deterministic TM*. We have thus shown the following.

For any non deterministic TM there is an equivalent deterministic TM.

Moreover, in Chapter 7 we showed that the non deterministic TM is the corresponding abstract machine for the **type 0 languages** (in terms of the ability to accept, but not necessarily to decide those languages, as we see in Chapter 11).

We can now say:

> The deterministic TM is the **recognizer** for the **phrase structure languages**, in general.

This is so because:

> any phrase structure grammar can be converted into a non deterministic TM, which can then be converted into a deterministic TM.

(via the conversion of the non deterministic TM into an equivalent four-tape deterministic TM, and *its* conversion into an equivalent deterministic single-tape TM).

10.5.1 Non deterministic TMs viewed as parallel processors

We saw earlier in this chapter that computation is concerned not only with **function**, but also with **space** and **time**. When we make statements about the **equivalence** of Turing machines, as we have in this chapter, we are usually talking about equivalence of *function*. For example, we say that the result of our 'non deterministic to deterministic TM conversion' is 'equivalent' to the original machine. However, there are different ways of viewing the operation of a non deterministic machine. One is to imagine that the machine attempts to follow a sequence of transitions until it finds a solution or reaches a 'dead end', as none of its available instructions can be applied. In the latter case, we have assumed that it then tries an alternative sequence. When combined with our notion of time as a measure of the number of transitions made by the machine, this perspective adopts a *serial* model of computation. Our earlier discussions regarding **non deterministic finite state recognizers** (Chapter 4) and **pushdown recognizers** (Chapter 5) also reflect this view, when considering concepts such as **backtracking**, for example.

As an alternative to a serial model of execution, we can assume that all possible sequences of transitions to be considered by the non deterministic TM are investigated *in parallel*. When the machine is ready to start, imagine that a signal arises, analogously to the way in which the internal 'clock' governs the state changes of the CPU. On this signal, *each and every applicable transition is carried out simultaneously* (each transition being allowed to take with it its own copy of the input tape, since each sequence of transitions may result in different configurations of the tape). Figure 10.21 shows an example starting situation with three applicable transitions.

Figure 10.21 is intended to represent the situation that arises on the first 'clock tick', which we assume results in the execution of the three applicable transitions in parallel (the result of each being shown by the dashed arrows). Note that the new tape configuration for the three cases includes a small state circle showing which state the machine has reached after making that transition. A description of the marked portion

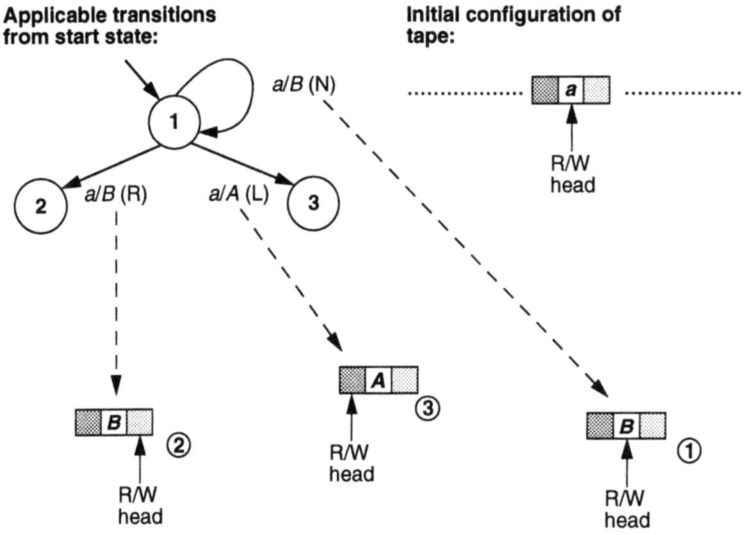

Figure 10.21 The operations of a non deterministic TM viewed as parallel processes

of a tape, the location of the read/write head and the current state of a machine at any stage in a TM's computation is sometimes called an **instantaneous description**.

The next clock tick would result in the simultaneous execution of:

- each applicable transition from state 2 given the tape configuration on the left of Figure 10.21,
- each applicable transition from state 3 given the tape configuration in the centre of Figure 10.21, and,
- each applicable transition from state 1 given the tape configuration on the right of Figure 10.21.

Then the next clock tick would result in the simultaneous execution of each applicable transition from each of the situations created at the previous clock tick.

Clearly, if a solution exists this method will find it. In fact, the first sequence of transitions we find that leads us to a solution will be the shortest such sequence that can be found[3]. Now, note that the equivalent deterministic four-tape machine that we could construct using the method described earlier in this chapter is also guaranteed to find the shortest sequence of transitions the parallel non deterministic machine would have found. This is because the deterministic version first tries all single quintuples, then all length 2 sequences of quintuples, then all sequences of three quintuples, and so on, and will stop as soon as one of the sequences of quintuples results in reaching the non deterministic machine's halt state.

[3] The shortest solution sequence may not be unique. In this case, our parallel machine will find all the shortest solutions simultaneously. It will simplify subsequent discussions if we talk as if there is only one shortest solution.

10.5.2 Parallel computations and time

Now our model of time enters the analysis. If there is a solution that requires the execution of n instructions (i.e. n quintuples), the parallel machine will find it in n moments. In our example above, if any applicable sequence of transitions leads directly to the halt state from any of the resulting configurations shown, our parallel machine would have taken two moments to find the solution. The first transitions would be simultaneously executed in one moment, then all the applicable transitions from the three resulting configurations would be similarly executed in the next moment.

However, consider how long it takes our deterministic version to find a solution requiring the execution of n instructions. The deterministic machine will have tried:

- all single instructions
- all sequences of two instructions

  .

  .
- some or all of the sequences of n instructions.

Now, think back to our earlier discussion of the order in which our deterministic version would generate all possible non empty strings taken from the alphabet of quintuple labels $\{a, b, c\}$. There would be three strings of length 1, nine strings of length 2, 27 strings of length 3, which are:

aaa, *aab*, *aac*, *aba*, *abb*, *abc*, *aca*, *acb*, *acc*, *baa*, *bab*, *bac*, *bba*, *bbb*, *bbc*, *bca*, *bcb*, *bcc*, *caa*, *cab*, *cac*, *cba*, *cbb*, *cbc*, *cca*, *ccb*, *ccc*

At each stage, the strings for the next stage were derived by appending each of the three symbols of the alphabet to each of the strings obtained at the previous stage. Thus, for our example here, there would be 81 (i.e. 27×3) strings of length 4, then 243 (81×3) strings of length 5, and so on.

In general, the number of strings of length n from an alphabet of k symbols is k^n (in the example above, where $n = 4$ and $k = 3$ we had 3^4 or 81 strings).

To return to our main discussion, consider a *three-quintuple non deterministic parallel TM*, N. Suppose the shortest solution that this machine could find, given a certain input configuration, involves *four instructions*. N will take four moments to find it. Now consider the deterministic version, D, constructed using our method described earlier. We will simplify things considerably by considering the execution time of D in terms of the number of quintuples of N it tries. We will assume that it takes one moment to try each quintuple. We will also ignore the fact that a large number of quintuple sequences will be illegal, and thus aborted by D (as specified in Figure 10.15) before the entire sequence has been applied. It is reasonable to do this, as D has to generate each sequence of quintuple labels, even if the corresponding sequence of quintuples subsequently turns out to be inapplicable. This machine first tries:

- three sequences of instructions of length 1 (three moments);
- nine sequences of instructions of length 2 (18 moments);
- 27 of length 3 (81 moments);
- between one and 81 sequences of length four (between four and 324 moments).

Adding all these up, we get 3 + 18 + 81 + 4, or 106 moments in the best case (i.e. when the first four-quintuple sequence tried results in a solution), or 3 + 18 + 81 + 324, or 426 moments in the worst case (when all the four-quintuple sequences have to be tried, the last one resulting in the solution). In general, given k quintuples in the non deterministic machine, and a shortest solution requiring n instructions, the parallel TM, N, will take n moments to find the solution, while the corresponding deterministic machine, D, will take somewhere between:

$$\begin{aligned} & (k \times 1) + (k^2 \times 2) +..+ (k^{n-1} \times n-1) + (k^n \times n) \\ = \; & k + 2k^2 +..+ n-1k^{n-1} + nk^n \text{ moments in the worst case,} \end{aligned}$$

and

$$\begin{aligned} & (k \times 1) + (k^2 \times 2) +..+ (k^{n-1} \times n-1) + n \\ = \; & k + 2k^2 +..+ n-1k^{n-1} + n \text{ moments in the best case.} \end{aligned}$$

Now, as we have already seen, even simple Turing machines such as those we have seen in this book, consist of many more that three quintuples, and the solutions of even the simplest problems require the application of sequences of considerably more than four quintuples. For example, if a 10 quintuple non deterministic parallel TM (a very simple machine) found the solution in 11 moments (a very short solution), the best the corresponding deterministic TM constructed by our method could hope to do (as predicted by the above formula) is find a solution in 109,876,543,221 moments. To consider the extent of the difference in magnitude here, let us suppose a moment is the same as 1 millionth of a second (a reasonably slow speed for a modern machine to carry out an operation as simple as a Turing machine transition). Then:

- the non deterministic machine executes the 11 transitions in slightly over $\frac{1}{100{,}000}$ th of a second, while
- its deterministic counterpart takes around 30.5 hours to achieve the same solution!

This example may seem rather contrived, but consider that a parallel algorithm is, say, updating a complex graphical image, and millions of individual operations are being carried out simultaneously. Such computations would be impossible to carry out in a reasonable time by a serial processor. We would not wish to wait 30.5 hours for an image in an animation to change, for example.

10.6 A BRIEF LOOK AT AN UNSOLVED PROBLEM OF COMPLEXITY

The preceding discussion leads us to an as yet unsolved problem of computer science. You may, on reading the discussion, think that the disparity between the non deterministic TMs and their four-tape deterministic counterparts is entirely due to the rather simple-minded conversion scheme we have applied. You may think that there is a more 'efficient' way to model the behaviour of the non deterministic machine than by attempting to execute every possible sequence of its quintuples. We have shown that for any non deterministic TM we can construct a deterministic TM that does the same job. The question that now arises is: *can we construct one that does the same job as efficiently*? In order to discuss whether this question can be answered, we take a slightly more detailed look at complexity.

10.6.1 A beginner's guide to the 'big O'

As far as we are concerned here, the theory of **complexity** examines the relationship between the *length* (number of symbols) *of the input* to a TM and *the number of instructions it executes to complete its computation.* The same applies to programs, where the relationship concerned is between the *number of input elements* and the *number of program instructions executed.* In considering this relationship, we usually take account only of the components of the program that dominate the computation in terms of time expenditure.

Suppose we are to sum all the elements in a two dimensional array of numbers, then print the result, and we can only access one element of the array at a time. We must visit each and every element of the array to obtain each value to be added in to the running total. The time taken by the program is dominated by this process. If the array is 'square', say, $n \times n$, then we are going to need n^2 accessing operations. The times taken by the other operations (e.g. adding the element to the running total in the loop, and printing out the result) we can ignore, as they do not change significantly whatever the size of n.

In overall terms, our array summing program can be said to take an amount of time *approximately proportional to* $n^2 + c$. Even if we had to compute the array subscripts by adding in an offset value each time, this would not change this situation (the computation of the subscripts would be subsumed into c). Obviously, since c is a constant measure of time, the amount of time our algorithm takes is dominated by n^2 (for large values of n). n^2 is called the *dominant expression* in the equation $n^2 + \text{c}$. In this case, then, we say our array processing program takes time *in the order of* n^2. This is usually written, using what is called big O – 'Oh', not nought or zero – notation, as $O(n^2)$. Similarly, summing the elements of a one-dimensional array of length n would take time $O(n)$. There would be other operations, but they would be assumed to take constant time, and so n would be the dominant expression. In a similar way, summing up the elements of a *three* dimensional $n \times n \times n$ array could be assumed to take time $O(n^3)$.

Programs that take times such as $O(n^2)$ and $O(n^3)$, where n is some measure of the length of the input, are said to take **polynomial time** in terms of the input data. A special case of this, as in our one-dimensional array summing program, is when the time is $O(n)$, and in this case we say the program takes **linear** time. If a program must process all its input, then the closer it comes to taking linear time, the more efficient it must be. In general, the goal is to design programs so that the index x in the dominant expression n^x is as small as possible to solve the given problem.

Now, if the dominant expression in an equation denoting the running time of a program is $O(x^n)$, where, again, n is some measure of the length of the input, the amount of execution time rises dramatically as the input length increases. Programs like this are said to take **exponential time** in their execution. Consider the example of the 4-tape deterministic version of the non deterministic TM in the previous section. Simplifying somewhat, we can regard this as taking time $O(nk^n)$, where k is the number of quintuples in the non deterministic machine, in order to find a solution of length n. We saw the striking difference between the time taken by the non deterministic parallel machine, which was $O(n)$, i.e. of linear relationship to the length of the solution, and that taken by the deterministic version, for even small values of n (3 and 11), and small values of k (3 and 10).

We have considered the difference in the time taken by two machines (a non deterministic TM and its four-tape deterministic counterpart) in terms of the length of a given solution. However, the disparity between the time taken by the two machines becomes even greater if we also consider the relationship between the length of the *input* and the length of the solution. For example, suppose the non deterministic machine solves a problem that has minimum length solution n^3, where n is the length of the input. Then the non deterministic machine will find that solution in time $O(n^3)$. Suppose $n = 11$, then, simplifying things grossly, our deterministic machine will find a solution in the best case in a time $O(k^{n^3-1})$, which represents a time of 10^{1330} moments. The point being made is that when the non deterministic machine requires *polynomial* time to find the shortest solution, the deterministic machine constructed from it by our method requires *exponential time*.

10.6.2 The implications of exponential time processes

If you find big O a little daunting, think about it in this way: for our hypothetical problem, our non deterministic machine, N, has 11 squares marked on its input tape. Since $n = 11$, and we know that the shortest solution is n^3 instructions in length, N is thus searching for a solution of 11^3 instructions. If N is a *parallel* machine, as described above, it will find the solution in 11^3 moments.

Now consider the behaviour of D, the deterministic version of N. To get to the first solution of length 11^3, *D will have to first generate all sequences of quintuple labels of length* $11^3 - 1$. If there are 10 quintuples, there are 10^{11^3-1} distinct sequences of labels of length $11^3 - 1$, i.e. 10^{1330}.

Let us now consider a simpler example, so that we can appreciate the size of the numbers we are dealing with here. Suppose the shortest sequence of instructions that a particular 10-quintuple non deterministic machine can find is 101 instructions, for an input of 10 symbols. Before finding the 101 quintuple sequence that yields the solution, the deterministic version will generate all sequences of quintuples of length 100. There are 10^{100} of these sequences, since there are 10 quintuples. The time taken by our deterministic machine is around 10^{100} moments, by the most gross simplification imaginable (i.e. imagining that the generation of each sequence takes only a moment, and ignoring the fact that our machine will have generated all the sequences of length 99, of length 98, and so on).

At this point we need to buy a faster deterministic machine. We go to the TM store, and purchase a machine that does 10^{20} operations in a year. This machine does in excess of *three million million operations each second.* If we used it to find the solution to the problem above that took our original non deterministic 'one-million-instructions-a-second' model 30.5 hours to find, it would take our new machine about $\frac{3}{100}$ of a second! However, our new machine would still take in the order of 10^{80} *years* to solve our new problem, while our non deterministic machine, at a similar instruction execution rate, would take $\frac{1}{30{,}000{,}000{,}000}$ th *of a second.* Given that, by some estimations, the Earth is at this time around 400 million years old, if we had started off our deterministic machine at the time the Earth was born, it would now be about:

$$\frac{1}{250{,}000}\text{ th}$$

of the way through the time it needs to find the solution.

10.6.3 'IS P EQUAL TO NP?'

From a purely formal point of view, the amount of time taken to solve a problem is not important. The requirements are that a solution be found in a finite number of steps, or, put another way in a finite period of time. A time period like 10^{80} years may be to us an incredibly long period of time, but nevertheless it is finite. The purpose of the construction we used to create our deterministic machine was to show *functional* equivalence, i.e. that whenever there is a solution that the non deterministic machine *could* find, the deterministic machine *will* find it (eventually!).

In a more practical vein, in creating a deterministic machine that models one that is non deterministic, we may also wish to maintain invariance between the two machines in the other dimensions of computational power (*space* and *time*) as well as invariance in *functionality*. Given a non deterministic TM that finds solutions in **polynomial** time, we would ideally like to replace it by a deterministic machine that also takes polynomial time (and not **exponential** time, as is the case for the construction method we have used in this chapter). Clearly, this can be done in many many cases. For example, it would be possible to model an array summing program (of the type discussed earlier) deterministically by a polynomial time TM.

The above discussion leads to a question of formal computer science that is as yet unanswered. The question is:

> For each polynomial time non deterministic TM, can we construct an equivalent polynomial time deterministic TM?

This is known as the 'IS *P* EQUAL TO *NP*?' problem, where *P* is the set of all *polynomial time TMs*, and *NP* is the set of all *non deterministic polynomial time TMs*. As yet, no solution to it has been found. Given our analogy between non deterministic TMs and parallel processing, *the lack of a solution to this problem indicates the possibility that there are parallel processes that run in polynomial time, that can only be modelled by serial processes that run in exponential time*. More generally, it suggests that there may be some problems that can be solved in a reasonable amount of time only if solved non deterministically. True non determinism involves *random* execution of applicable instructions, rather than the systematic execution processes considered above. This means that a truly non deterministic process is not guaranteed to find a solution even if there is one.

There may therefore be problems that are such that:

- a solution may be found in *polynomial time* by a *non deterministic program* (but it may not actually find a solution even if one exists), or
- a solution will be found in *exponential time* by a *deterministic program*, if a solution exists, but it may take a prohibitive amount of time to discover it.

10.7 CONCLUSIONS

We have seen in this chapter that, for both theoretical and practical reasons it can be useful to introduce augmentations to the basic TM. We have also seen that, in a purely functional sense, these augmentations do not lend us any extra power. This is compelling evidence in support of Turing's thesis that the (one-tape, deterministic) TM is indeed capable of computing all **effective procedures**.

A central theme of this chapter has been the notion of one TM executing the quintuples of another as if those quintuples were a program. In the next chapter, we develop this notion in the description of a three-tape deterministic TM that takes as its input the description of any other TM, *T*, and carries out the computation that *T* would have performed on any given input tape. We know that the three-tape machine could then be replaced by an equivalent single-tape machine, and thus we will have implicitly specified a single, standard TM that can compute all effective procedures. This

universal TM is then used as the basis of demonstrating the existence of problems that, unlike the 'IS $P = NP$' problem, are not only still to be solved, but in fact can *never* be solved by algorithmic means.

EXERCISES

1 Define a **TM** to generate $\{a, b, c\}^+$, as outlined earlier. Sketch out a convincing demonstration that for any alphabet A, A^+ is similarly **enumerable** (i.e. we could define a TM to print out its elements in a systematic way).

2† Sketch out a TM to execute the four-tape simulation of **quintuple** $(A, 1, 0, R, B)$ described above.

3† Sketch out the part of the single tape machine, S, that deals with the **sextuple** (1, a, A, R, 2, 2) of the three-tape machine, M, described earlier in this chapter.

4 (cf. Exercise 4 of Chapter 4.) Write a '**big** $\boldsymbol{O}$' expression representing the 'worst case' time for the **subset algorithm** described in Chapter 4. The input, n, is assumed to be the number of states in the **non deterministic FSR** that is input. Find an example FSR for which the subset algorithm takes its 'worst case' time.

11 The limits of computation and the scope of phrase structure languages

AIMS

To learn

- how to code a TM and present these codes to a universal TM (UTM)
- how UTM simulates the computation of the original machine
- about the halting problem and how we can decide whether or not a TM will halt on a particular tape
- how formal languages can be totally undecidable or semi-decidable

11.1 PREVIEW: THE UNIVERSAL TURING MACHINE (UTM)

A major part of this, the final chapter, will be concerned with sketching out the description of what we call a **universal Turing machine** (**UTM**). This machine will accept as its input two things:

1. (a coded version of) the **quintuples** of a TM, M
2. (a coded version of) the marked portion of an input **tape** to M.

UTM will then simulate the behaviour of M on the given input tape. The aim of this section is to describe a coding scheme which will facilitate a definition of UTM as a machine that uses the alphabet $\{0, 1\}$.

The existence of UTM not only provides further evidence in support of **Turing's thesis**, that the Turing machine is the most powerful computational machine, but also plays a part in finally establishing the relationship between *computable languages* and *abstract machines*. In the course of this, UTM also features in the demonstration of an extremely significant result in computer science: the general unsolvability of the **halting problem**.

11.2 CODING A TURING MACHINE AND ITS TAPE AS A BINARY NUMBER

We first consider a simple method of coding any TM, by building up a coding scheme for the **states**, the **alphabet**, the quintuples and the whole machine. We then see how the code devised for the machine's alphabet can be used to code any input tape for the coded machine. The coded machine and the coded input can then be used as input to UTM, introduced above.

11.2.1 Coding any TM

To describe the scheme for coding any TM as a string of 1s and 0s we will use an example TM. As we proceed, you should appreciate that the coding scheme could be applied to any TM, consisting of any number of states and using any size of alphabet.

The example machine, shown in Figure 11.1, accepts the **context free language** $\{a^ib^{2i} : i \geq 1\}$ (i.e. all strings of *a*s followed by *b*s in which there are twice as many *b*s as *a*s).

We begin by associating the *states* of M (Figure 11.1) with strings of 0s as shown in Table 11.1. It should be clear that we could code the states of any TM using the scheme.

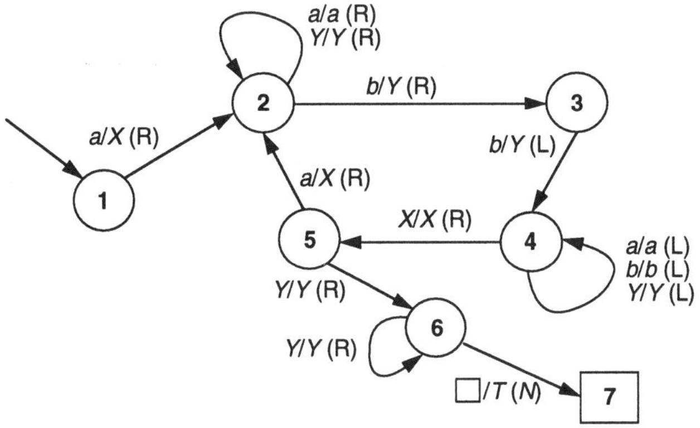

Figure 11.1 A TM, *M*, on which to practise the coding scheme

Table 11.1 Coding the states of a TM

State of *M*	Code	Comments on general case
state 1 (start state)	0	We *always* code the start state of a machine as 0
state 7 (halt state)	00	We *always* code the halt state of a machine as 00
state 2	000	We simply code the other states as sequences of 0s
state 3	0000	We code the states in any order (but we make sure that for each state we use a different length sequence of 0s), and we do not use either the sequence 0 or 00 for any of the states. Since it makes sense to use as few symbols as possible, we have used codes 000, 0000, and so on
state 4	00000	
state 5	000000	
state 6	0000000	

Next, as shown in Table 11.2, we code the *tape symbols* (alphabet) of the machine, which, for our machine *M*, is {*a*, *b*, *X*, *Y*, *T*} and the blank symbol □.

Again, we can see that this scheme could apply to a TM alphabet of any number of symbols.

Table 11.2 Coding the alphabet of a TM

State of *M*	Code	Comments on general case
a	0	
b	00	As for the states, we code the symbols in any order. We can use any number for 0s we like, providing we use a different number for each symbol. Again, we chose here a scheme that enables us to use as few 0s as possible.
X	000	
Y	0000	
T	00000	

We also code the *direction symbols L, R,* and *N,* as shown in Table 11.3.

Table 11.3 Coding the direction symbols of a TM

Symbol	Code	General Case
L	0	Always the same.
R	00	
N	000	

You will note that some of the codes representing the states (Table 11.1) are identical to those used for the alphabet (Table 11.2) and direction symbols (Table 11.3). However, this does not matter; as we will see in a moment, our coding scheme ensures that they do not become mixed up.

We have coded the *states*, the *alphabet*, and the *direction symbols*. We now code the *instructions* (quintuples) themselves. Figure 11.2(a) shows how to code any given quintuple. An example of the coding of a quintuple of the machine *M*, from Figure 11.1, is given in Figure 11.2(b).

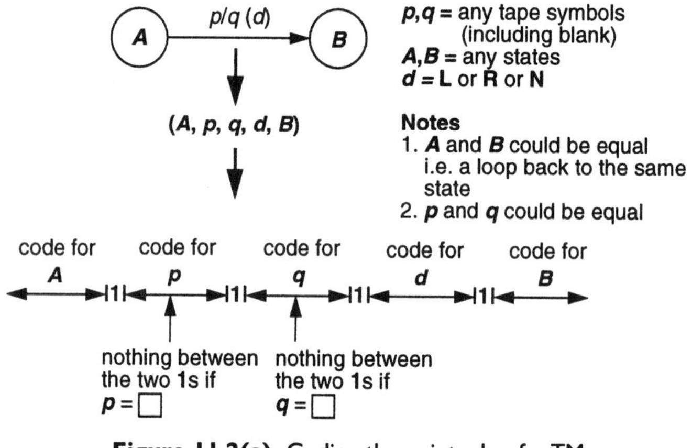

Figure 11.2(a) Coding the quintuple of a TM

Now, we simply code *the whole machine* as a sequence of quintuple codes, each followed by 1, and we place a 1 at the start of the whole code. The scheme is shown in Figure 11.3(a), and a partial encoding of the TM, *M*, from Figure 11.1, is given in Figure 11.3(b).

The above should be sufficient to convince you that we could apply such a coding scheme to *any* TM, since any TM has a finite number of states, tape symbols, and quintuples.

Such a binary code for a Turing machine could be presented as the input to *any* TM that expected arbitrary binary numbers as its input. For example, we could present the

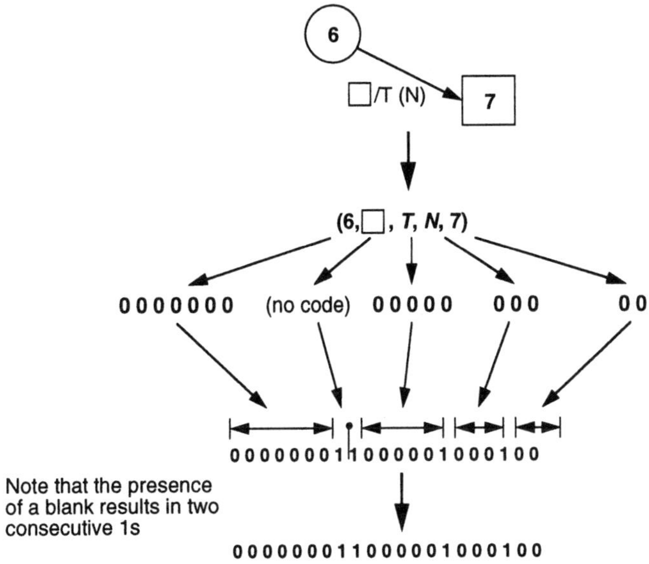

Figure 11.2(b) Coding a quintuple of *M* (Figure 11.1) according to the scheme of Figure 11.2(a)

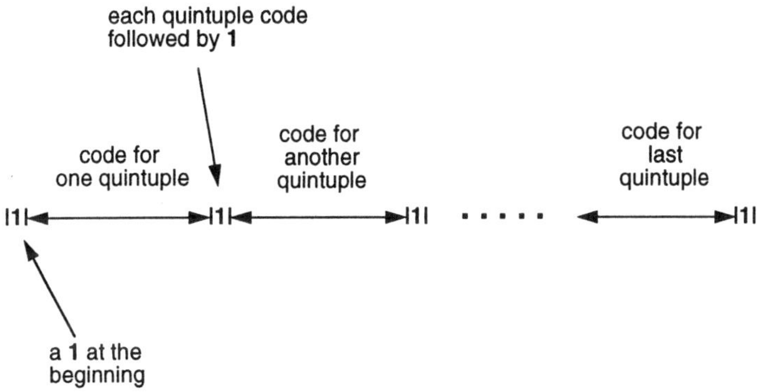

Figure 11.3(a) Coding a whole TM

code for the above machine, *M*, to the MULT TM (described in Chapter 9) as one of the two numbers to be multiplied. We could even present the coded version of MULT to the MULT machine as one of its input numbers, which would mean that MULT *would be multiplying its own code by another number*! All this may seem rather strange, but it does emphasize the point that codes can be viewed at many different levels. The code for *M* can be regarded as another representation of *M* itself (which is how UTM will see it), as a string in $\{0,1\}^+$ (a non empty string of 0s and 1s) or as a binary number. This is essentially no different from seeing Pascal source code as *text* (the *text editor's* view) or as a *program* (the *compiler's* view).

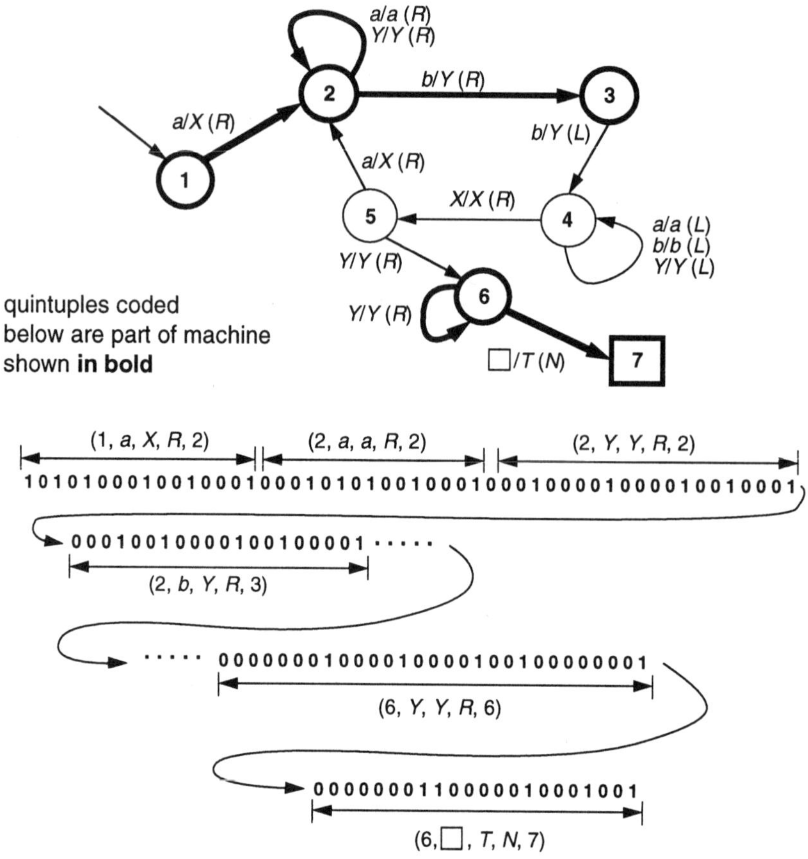

Figure 11.3(b) A partial application of the coding scheme from Figure 11.3(a) to the machine *M* of Figure 11.1

Since our UTM will require not only the coded version of a machine, but also a coded version of an input to that machine, we need to specify a scheme for coding any *marked tape* of the machine we are coding.

11.3.2 Coding the tape

The coding scheme for the input is described in Table 11.4. Note that for a given machine, we use the same codes for the symbols on the input tape as those used to code the machine's alphabet (Table 11.2).

It should be clear that any input tape to any coded machine could be similarly represented using the scheme in Table 11.4.

We have now seen how to take any TM, *M*, and code it, and any of its input tapes, with a coding scheme that requires only the alphabet {0, 1}. In the next section, we

Table 11.4 Coding a TM's input tape

General rule	Application to an example input tape
We represent each symbol using the codes (i.e. sequences of 0s) that we used for the alphabet of the TM (Table 11.2) We make sure that for each symbol of the input, we use the same code that we used when we coded the machine. As for the quintuples, we follow each code by 1, and precede the whole sequence by a 1: Note: The presence of a blank within the marked portion of *M*'s input tape would be represented by two consecutive 1s (as was the case in the quintuple codes of Figure 11.2).	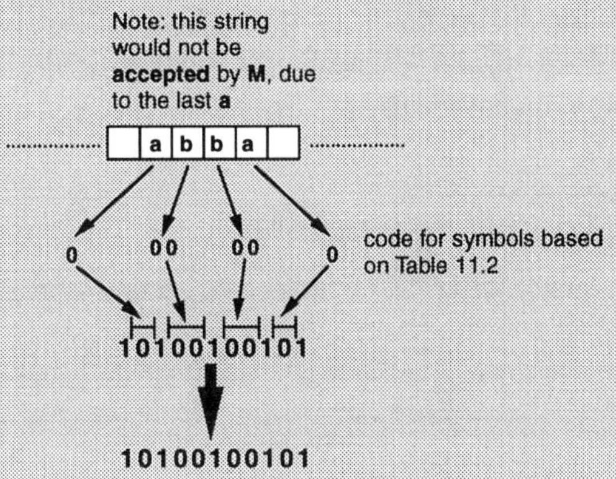

use our coding scheme as an integral component in sketching out the description of our universal Turing machine, UTM.

11.3 THE UNIVERSAL TURING MACHINE

UTM is described here as a three-tape **deterministic TM** that takes as its input a coded version of a TM, and essentially simulates the behaviour of the coded machine on a coded version of input to that machine. UTM therefore models the behaviour of the original machine on the original input, producing as its output a coded version of the output that would be produced by the original machine, which can then be decoded. We know, from the preceding chapter, that our three-tape UTM could be converted into a single-tape TM. The beauty of knowing that this can be done is that we need not actually do it.

You may at this point be concerned that there is some 'trickery' going on here. You might say that everything that UTM does is in terms of manipulating codes, not the 'real' thing. If you do think that it's trickery, then it can be pointed out that every single program you have ever written is part of the same type of 'trickery', as

- the *source file*,
- the *input*, and
- the *output*

are all similarly coded and subsequently decoded when your program is run. So if you are not prepared to believe in the representational power of coding schemes, you ought not to believe that any of your programs has ever done anything meaningful!

Next, we specify the initial set up of UTM's three tapes. Following this, we briefly consider the operation of UTM. You will appreciate that the construction of UTM described would be capable of simulating the operation of any TM, M, given any suitable input tape to M.

11.3.1 UTM's tapes

Our version of UTM is configured so that tape 1 is as shown in Figure 11.4.

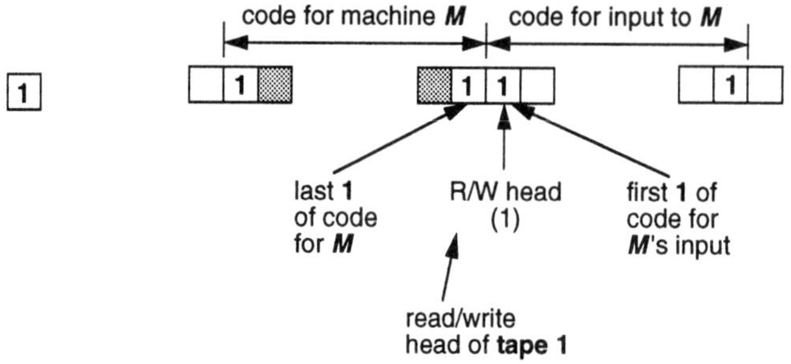

Figure 11.4 Tape 1 of UTM

As can be seen from Figure 11.4, tape 1 contains the code for the machine M, followed immediately by the code for M's input.

UTM will use its tape 2 as a 'work tape', on which to simulate M's operation on its input by carrying out the operations specified by the coded quintuples on the coded data. Thus, the first thing UTM does is to copy the coded input from tape 1 to tape 2, at which point tape 2 will be as specified in Figure 11.5.

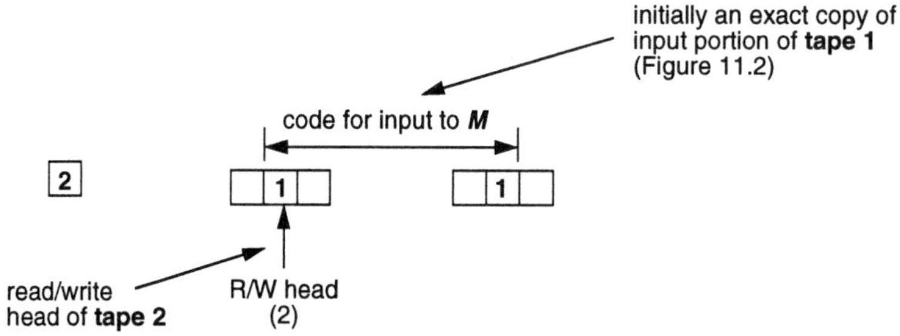

Figure 11.5 Tape 2 of UTM

Tape 3 of UTM will be used only to store a sequence of 0s denoting, at any stage, the current state of M. The organization of tape 3 is depicted in Figure 11.6.

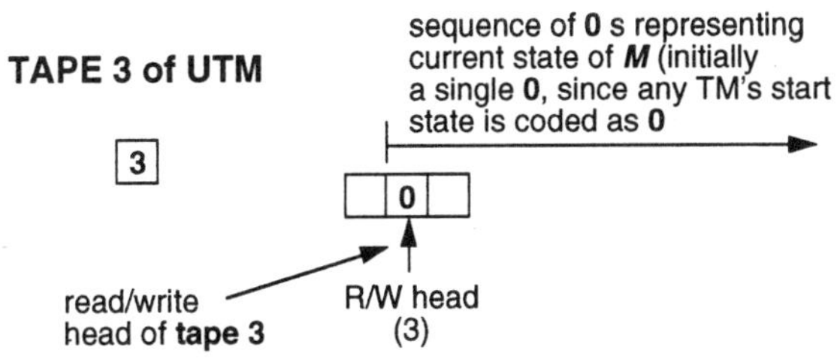

Figure 11.6 Tape 3 of UTM

To summarize:

tape 1
holds the coded *machine M*, followed by the coded input to *M*

tape 2
is used by UTM to work on a copy of *M*'s coded *input*

tape 3
is used to hold a sequence of 0s representing *M*'s *current state*

11.3.2 The operation of UTM

UTM operates as specified by the procedure in Table 11.5. I leave it to you to appreciate how the procedure could be represented as a TM. For clarification of the procedure in Table 11.5, you are advised to refer to the coding scheme and UTM's tape configurations described above.

A UTM based on the procedure in Table 11.5 is capable of carrying out the computation specified by any TM, given an initial set-up as described above. As input to such a machine, we code the TM according to our scheme, and then we can code an input tape to that TM using the same scheme. UTM will then simulate the computation performed by the original machine.

In particular:

- If *M*, the original machine, would produce a solution given a particular input tape, then UTM would *produce a coded version of that solution* (on its tape 2).
- If *M* would reach a state, *s*, in which it had no applicable quintuples for the current state and tape symbols, then UTM *would halt with the code for the state s on tape 3, and tape 2 would contain a coded version of M's tape configuration at the time M stopped*[1].
- If *M* would reach a situation where it **looped** indefinitely, repeating the same actions over and over again, then *UTM would also do the same*. We return to this last situation later in this chapter.

[1] This assumes that the 'while' loop in Table 11.5 terminates if no suitable quintuple can be found.

Table 11.5 The operation of UTM

copy code for M's data from tape 1 to tape 2	tape 2 is to be used as a work tape by UTM
write a 0 on tape 3 to represent the start state of M	the start state of M is represented by 0
while tape 3 does not contain exactly two zeros do	the halt state of M is represented by 00
find quintuple on tape 1 for current state	this involves UTM in proceeding along tape 1, comparing the first code in each quintuple (a sequence of zeros) with the sequence of zeros on tape 3
if quintuple found	tape symbols are represented by a possibly empty sequence of zeros
then if current symbol on tape 2 = quintuple current symbol	
then overwrite the current symbol code on tape 2	this can involve shuffling, since the code being replaced may not consist of the same number of zeros as the one replacing it
move the read head on tape 2 according to the quintuple direction	the tape 2 head must be moved to the next 1 to the left or right (or not at all), as appropriate
overwrite state code on tape 3 with quintuple state code	
endif	
endif	
endwhile	

We can now appreciate that we have described a three-tape deterministic TM, UTM, that can, if we accept **Turing's thesis**, carry out any **effective procedure**. We also know that from the three-tape version we could construct a deterministic 'standard' single-tape UTM, and our subsequent discussions will assume that this has been done.

11.3.3 Some implications of UTM

The existence of UTM makes Turing's thesis that TMs are the pinnacle of functional power even more compelling. We have seen that a TM that can 'run', as a kind of 'program', any other TM needs to be no more sophisticated than a standard TM. In a sense, *UTM actually embodies the effective procedure of carrying out the effective procedure specified by another Turing machine.*

Other designs of UTM may be suggested, based on different schemes for coding the machine M and its input. All are equivalent in that, since each UTM is a Turing machine, a UTM itself may be coded by the scheme for one of the other UTMs, and thus presented, with a coded version of one of its input tapes (i.e. the coded version of another machine, followed by the coded version of that machine's input), as input to that other UTM. In that sense also, UTM is truly *universal.*

In a more practical vein, UTM is a closer analogy to the stored program computer than the individual TMs we have considered so far. Each TM we looked at before was essentially a purpose built machine for computing one particular function. UTM, with its ability to carry out computations described to it in some coded form, is a counterpart of real computers that carry out computations described to them in the form of codes called programs. However, to revisit our argument from previous chapters, a given computer could only be as powerful as UTM if it had unlimited storage capabilities. Even then, it could not be *more* powerful.

11.4 THE RELATIONSHIP BETWEEN FUNCTIONS, PROBLEMS, SOLVABILITY AND DECIDABILITY

We have said much about the power of the TM. We spend much of the remainder of this chapter investigating its limitations. In the later stages of this book there have been many references to functions, to solving problems, and occasionally to effective procedure, but no clear definition of these terms has been given. We are now familiar enough with TMs and Turing's thesis to be able to provide these definitions.

11.4.1 Functions and computability

A **function** associates input values with output values in such a way that for each particular arrangement of input values there is but one particular arrangement of output values. Consider the arithmetic add (+) operator. This is a *function* because for any pair of numbers, x and y, the result of $x + y$ is always associated with a number z, that represents the value obtained by adding x and y. In the light of the previous section, it should be appreciated that, since any TM can be represented in binary form, it suffices to define the values (input and output) of functions in terms of numbers. This applies equally well to the language processing machines considered in this book as much as it does to those carrying out numerically-oriented operations.

We know that we can represent any of our **abstract machines** for language recognition (**finite state recognizers**, **push down recognizers**) as TMs (Chapter 7), then represent the resulting TM in such a way that its operation is represented entirely as the manipulation of binary codes. Thus, the notion of function is wide-ranging, covering associations between *strings* and *truth values* ('true' if the string is a sentence of a given language, 'false' if it is not), *numbers* and *other numbers* (MULT, DIV, etc.), *numbers* and *truth values* (COMPARE), and so on.

Calling a function an association between input and output values represents a very high level view of a function. We are usually also interested in *how* the association between the input and output values is made, i.e. the rules by which we derive a particular arrangement of output values from a particular arrangement of input values. More specifically, we are interested in characteristics of the *program* that embodies the 'rules' and produces the output values when presented with the input values.

From time to time, we have mentioned the notion of the **effective procedure**, which we can now say describes those procedures which are:

- deterministic
- finite in time and resources (space)
- mechanical
- represented in numeric terms.

It has been argued above that such effective procedures are precisely those that can be carried out by TMs, and in fact now we can say by one TM, which we call UTM.

Having a clearer idea of the notions 'function' and 'effective procedure' enables us to define what we call the **computable functions**, in Table 11.6.

Table 11.6 'Computable functions' and 'TM-computable functions'

The computable functions are those functions for which there is an effective procedure for deriving any correct output values when presented with any appropriate input values. They can therefore be called the effectively computable functions.

A TM-computable function is a function that can be computed by some TM.

So, Turing's thesis asserts that *the effectively computable functions and the TM-computable functions are the same.*

11.4.2 Problems and solvability

Associated with any function is a **problem**. In abstract terms, the problem associated with a function is a *question*, which asks 'what is the result of the function for these particular input values?'. For the '+' function, then, an associated problem is 'what is 3 + 4?'. The previous section suggested that the sentence recognition task for a given language could be regarded as a function associating strings with truth values. The associated problem then asks, for a given string 'what is the truth value associated with this string in terms of the given language?'. This is more usually expressed: 'is this string a sentence of the language or not?'.

A problem is **solvable** if the associated function is *computable*. We know now that 'computable' is the same as saying 'TM-computable'. So, a problem is solvable if it can be coded so that a TM could compute a solution to it in a finite number of transitions, or if a program run on an unlimited storage machine could do the same.

A problem is *totally solvable* if the associated function can be computed by some TM that produces a correct result for every possible assignment of valid input values.

An example of this is the '+' operator. We could define a TM, like the ADD machine, that produces the correct result for any pair of input values, by adding the numbers and leaving the result on its tape. Another totally solvable problem is the membership problem for the **context sensitive language** $\{a^ib^ic^i : i \geq 1\}$, since in chapter 7 we defined a TM that printed T for any string in $\{a,b,c\}^*$ that was a member of the language, and F for any such string which was not. The membership problem for $\{a^ib^ic^i : i \geq 1\}$ is thus totally solvable.

A problem is *partially solvable* if the associated function can be computed by some TM that produces a correct result for each possible assignment of input values for which it halts. However, for some input values, the TM will not be able to produce any result. The critical thing is that on any input values for which the TM halts, the result it produces is correct. This concept is best considered in the context of language recognition, and you may already have appreciated the similarity between the concept of *solvability* and the concepts of **deciding** and **accepting** languages discussed in Chapter 7. This similarity is not accidental, and we return to it later in the chapter. However, we will be considering one of the most important partially solvable problems of computer science in the next section.

A problem is *totally unsolvable* if the associated function cannot be computed by any TM. It is worth mentioning at this point that in discussing the concepts of solvability we never exceed the characteristics of *effective procedures* as defined in the previous section: we are still considering *deterministic*, *finite*, *mechanical* and *numeric* processes. For an abstract, simply stated, yet totally unsolvable problem, consider this:

> Define a TM that has as its input a non-packed tape (i.e. an arbitrary number of blank squares can appear between any two marked squares) on which there are *a*s, *b*s and *c*s, in any order. The machine should halt and print T if the leftmost marked symbol on its tape is a, and should halt and print F otherwise. The read/write head is initially located on the rightmost marked tape square.

The above machine cannot be defined.

Suppose we design a TM to address the above problem that moves left on its tape until it reaches an a, then prints T and halts. Does this mean the problem is partially solvable? The answer to this is 'no', since partial solvability means that the TM must produce a correct result *whenever it halts*, and our 'cheating' TM would not (though it would 'accidentally' be correct sometimes). No TM could be designed that would even partially solve the above problem. I leave it to you to convince yourself of this.

11.4.3 Decision problems and decidability

Problems that ask a question expecting a yes/no answer are sometimes known as **decision problems**. In seeking to solve a decision problem we look for the existence of a program (TM) to resolve each of a set of *questions*, where the formulation of each question depends on the assignment of specific values to certain parameters. For example:

- given two **regular grammars**, R_1 and R_2, are they **equivalent**?
- given a number, N, is N prime?
- given a TM, M, and a tape T, will M halt eventually when started on the tape T?

A *decision problem* is *totally solvable* if we can construct a TM that will provide us with the correct 'yes/no' response for each and every possible instantiation of the parameters. Thus, for example, the second decision problem above is totally solvable only if we can construct a TM that decides, for any number, if that number is prime or not. We could do this if we wished, so the second problem is totally solvable.

Of the other two problems, only one is totally solvable, and this is the first. In Chapter 4, we saw what we now know to be called effective procedures for converting any regular grammars into **non-deterministic FSRs**, for converting non-deterministic FSRs into deterministic FSRs, and for converting deterministic FSRs into their **minimal** form. If two regular grammars are equivalent, then their associated *minimal machines* will be exactly the same, if the states of one minimal machine are renamed to coincide with those of the other. If the states of one of the minimal machines cannot be renamed to make the two minimal machines exactly the same, then the two grammars are not equivalent. We could design a (complicated!) TM to do all this, and so *the equivalence problem for regular grammars is totally solvable.*

11.5 THE HALTING PROBLEM

Let us look again at the third of the three decision problems presented in the immediately preceding section:

given a TM, M, and a tape T, will M halt eventually when started on the tape T?

This problem is known as the **halting problem**, and was briefly alluded to in the discussion of the power of the FST at the end of Chapter 8. All of us have experienced the practical manifestation of this problem. We write a program, and run it. The program seems to be taking a long time over its computation. We decide it is stuck in an 'infinite loop', and interrupt the execution of the program. We have usually made some error in the design or coding of a loop termination condition. Even commercially supplied programs can sometimes suffer from this phenomenon. Some unexpected combination of values leads to a non-terminating repetition of a sequence of instructions. It would be useful if someone would design a program that examined other programs to see if they would always terminate, i.e. for all of their permissible input values. Such a program could form a useful part of the compiler, which could then give out an error message to the effect that a given program would not terminate for certain inputs.

However, as said before, a computer can never be more powerful than a TM, so if the halting problem, as represented in TM terms, is unsolvable, then by extension it is unsolvable even by a computer with infinite memory. We see next that the halting problem is indeed unsolvable in the general sense, though it is *partially* solvable, which is where we begin the investigation.

11.5.1 UTM_H partially solves the halting problem

Consider again our **universal Turing machine (UTM)**, as described earlier in this chapter. UTM simulates the computation of any machine, *M*, on any tape *T*. From the construction of UTM, we can see (as also discussed earlier) that this simulation is so faithful to *M* as to enter an indefinite loop if that is what *M* would do on the tape *T* in question. However, one thing is certain: if *M* would have reached its halt state on tape *T*, then UTM will also reach its halt state given the coded version of *M* and the coded version of *T* as *its* input. All we would need to do then, is to modify the UTM procedure (Table 11.5) so that it outputs a '1' and halts as soon as it finds the code '00' on tape 3 (indicating that the simulated machine *M* has reached its halt state).

Let us call the new version of UTM, described immediately above, UTM_H. As we have defined it, UTM_H *partially* solves the halting problem. Given any machine *M* and tape *T*, appropriately coded, UTM_H will write a 1 (on tape 2) and halt if *M* would have reached its halt state when presented with the tape *T* as its input. If *M* would have *stopped in an auxiliary state*, because no transition was possible, then UTM_H will not reach its halt state. We could further amend UTM_H to output a 0, then move to its halt state, if no applicable quintuple of M's could be found, and therefore *M* would have halted in a non halt state. However, if *M* would *loop infinitely* on tape *T*, then as defined, UTM_H has no alternative but to do the same.

It is clear that the critical situations for the halting problem are those in which *M* loops infinitely. If, in addition to our amendments specified above, we could show how to amend UTM_H so that it halts and write a 0 when *M* would have looped infinitely on tape *T*, we would be showing that the halting problem is totally solvable.

This last amendment is difficult to imagine, since various conditions can result in infinite loops, and a 'loop' in a TM could comprise numerous states, as a loop in a program may encompass numerous statements. At this point, then, it seems pertinent to try a different approach.

11.5.2 Reductio ad absurdum applied to the halting problem

Let us assume that we have already amended UTM_H so that it deals with both the halting and non-halting situations. (You may be becoming aware at this point that this is going to be a ***reductio ad absurdum*** proof, a technique we've used several times in this book.) This new machine, which we will simply call *H*, is specified schematically in Figure 11.7.

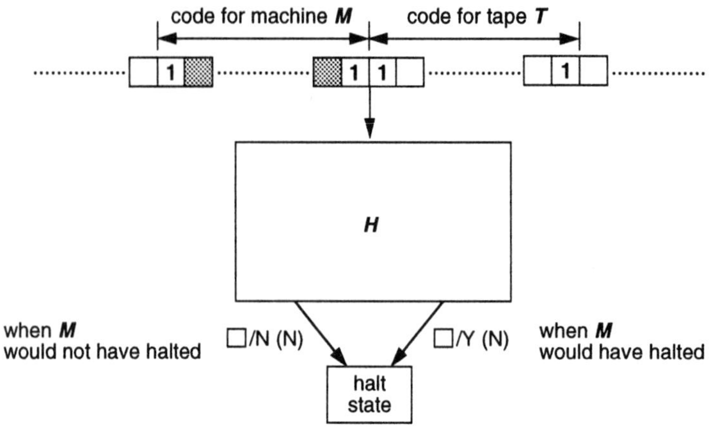

Figure 11.7 The machine *H* is assumed to solve the halting problem

Figure 11.7 defines *H* as a machine that prints Y and N rather than 1 or 0. Note that the two arcs entering *H*'s halt state are shown as having the blank as the current symbol. We assume that at that point *H* has erased everything from its tape, and would thus write Y or N on a blank square before terminating, leaving the read/write head pointing at the result.

So, *H* is assumed to:

- print Y and halt if *M* would *halt* on the input tape *T*, or
- print N and halt if *M* would *not halt* on the tape *T*.

In other words, *H* is assumed to totally solve the halting problem.

Next, we make what appears to be a strange amendment to *H*, to create a new machine called H_1, depicted in Figure 11.8.

In order to produce H_1, we would need to make straightforward amendments to H's behaviour in its halting situations. H_1 would:

- print Y and halt if *M* would *not halt* on the input tape *T*, or
- *loop infinitely* if *M* would *halt* on the tape *T*.

You should be able to see that, if *H* existed, it would be straightforward to make the necessary amendments to it to produce H_1.

The next thing we do probably seems even stranger: we modify H_1 to produce H_2, depicted in Figure 11.9.

H_2 copies the code for the machine *M*, then presents the two copies to H_1. Our scheme codes both machine and tape as sequences beginning and ending with a 1, between these 1s being simply sequences of 0s separated by 1s, so a coded machine could clearly be interpreted as a coded tape.

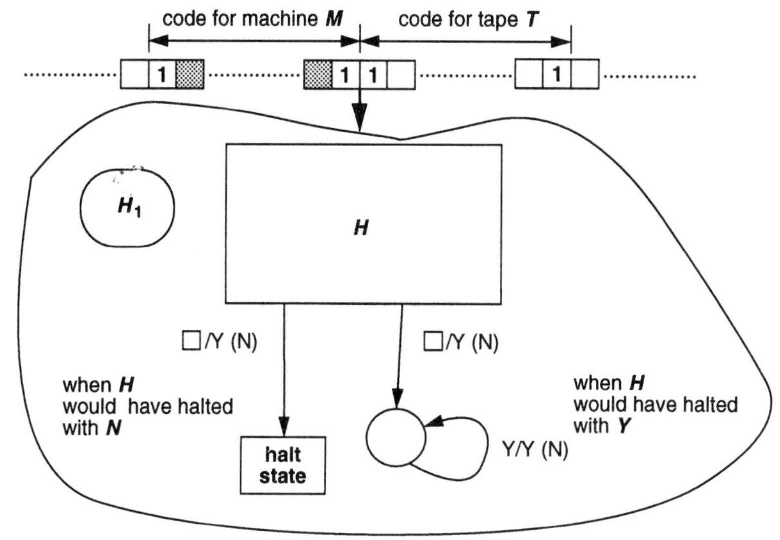

Figure 11.8 The TM H_1

Thus, instead of simulating the behaviour of *M* on its input tape, H_2 now simulates the behaviour of the machine *M* on a description of *M* itself (!). H_2's result in this situation will then be to:

- print Y and halt if *M* would *not halt* on a description of itself, or
- *loop infinitely* if *M* would *halt* on a description of itself.

The next step is the strangest of all. We present H_2 with the input specified in Figure 11.10.

Figure 11.10 shows us that H_2 has been presented with the binary code for itself to represent the machine, *M*. H_2 will first copy the code out again, then present the two copies to H_1. To H_1, the left hand copy of the code for H_2 represents a coded TM, the right hand copy the coded input to that TM. Thus, H_2's overall effect is to *simulate its own behaviour on an input tape that is a coded version of itself.* H_2 uses only the alphabet {0, 1, Y, N}, as it was derived from H_1, which also uses the same alphabet. Therefore H_2 could be applied to a description of itself in this way.

11.5.3 The halting problem shown to be unsolvable

Now we ask:

> Does H_2, as configured above, halt?

Well, suppose H_2 does halt:

> H_2 halts and prints Y if *M* would *not halt* on a description of itself

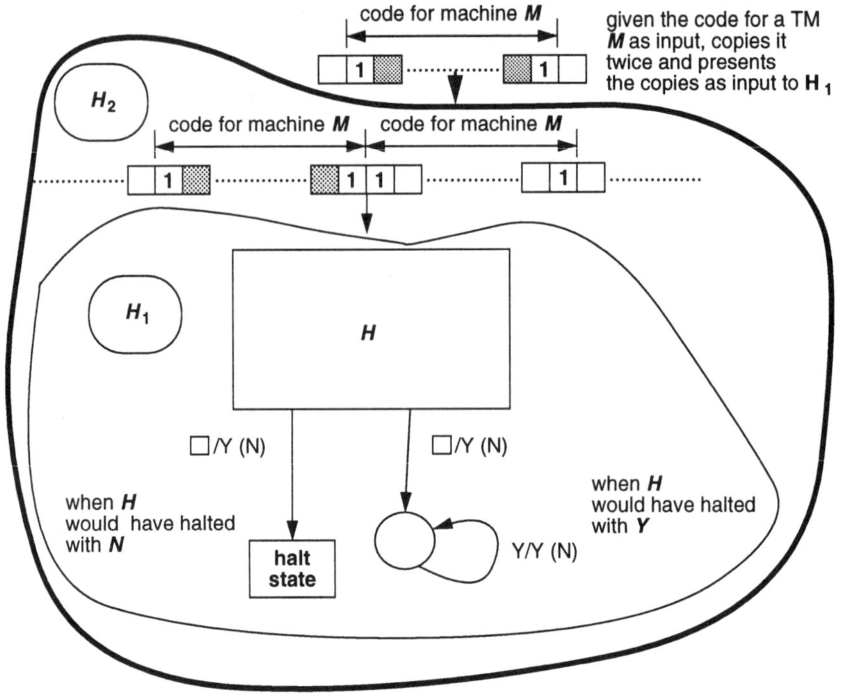

Figure 11.9 The TM H_2

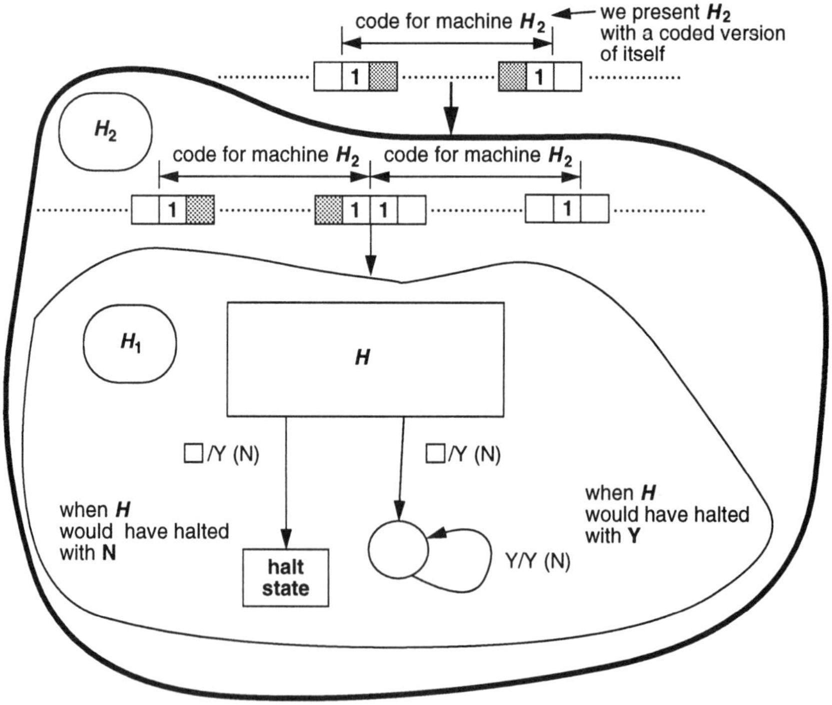

Figure 11.10 The TM H_2 is presented with a coded version of itself

However, in the situation here, M is H_2, so we have:

> H_2 halts and prints Y if H_2 would *not halt* on a description of itself

To paraphrase:

> *H_2 halts, given a description of itself as its input, if it does not halt, given a description of itself as its input*

This is clearly nonsense, so we must conclude that H_2 does *not* halt. However:

> H_2 *loops infinitely* if M would *halt* on a description of itself.

Again, in our situation here, M is H_2, so we have:

> H_2 *loops infinitely* if H_2 would *halt* on a description of itself.

To paraphrase once more:

> *H_2 does not halt, given a description of itself as its input, if it halts, given a description of itself as its input*.

We have devised a machine which halts if it does not halt, and does not halt if it halts. Where was our error? Every change we have made to our machines, from H onwards, requires the addition of a few quintuples. We are forced to go right back and reject our original assumption, as it is obviously the assumption itself that is at fault. The machine H that solves the halting problem cannot exist. *The halting problem is an unsolvable problem.*

However, to reiterate, the halting problem is *partially* solvable. It is solvable (e.g. by UTM_H, as described above) in precisely those cases when M *would* halt.

Again, we are unable to reject the above argument on the basis of the indirection involved in manipulating codes representing the machines and their tapes. We *cannot*, as computer users, refuse to believe in the representational power of codes. To do so is to denounce as meaningless any activity carried out by *real* computers.

11.5.4 Some implications of the unsolvability of the halting problem

The halting problem is one of the most significant results of mathematics. The general unsolvability of the halting problem indicates the ultimate futility of defining effective criteria for determining effectiveness itself. For example, an **algorithm** is an **effective procedure** that terminates for all its input values. There can therefore be no algorithm to decide, in the general case, whether some other procedure *is* an algorithm. The unsolvability of the halting problem implies that, in general, we cannot determine by algorithmic means whether or not some well-defined process will terminate for all of its values.

The halting problem also has practical implications for the enterprise of proving the correctness of programs. A program is said to be partially correct if whenever it terminates it produces a correct result. A program is said to be totally correct if it is partially correct *and* it terminates for each and every possible input value. The goal of proving programs totally correct is thus one that cannot be attained by algorithmic means, as to be able to do so would require a solution to the halting problem.

Many unsolvable problems of computer science actually reduce to the halting problem. That there is no computational device more powerful than the standard TM implies that effective procedures for analysing the behaviour of other effective procedures are doomed ultimately to simulating those procedures, at the expense of being caught in the never-ending loops of the simulated process, if such loops arise.

As an example of a problem that reduces to the halting problem, consider the *equivalence problem* for TMs, or for programs. Two TMs, M_1 and M_2, are equivalent if for each and every input value, they both yield the same result. Now assume that E is a TM that solves the equivalence problem for any two TMs. Suppose, for argument's sake, that E simulates the behaviour of each machine by carrying out the next applicable quintuple from M_1, followed by the next applicable quintuple from M_2, on coded representations of an equivalent input tape for each machine. Suppose that the M_1 simulation reaches its halt state first, having produced a result. E must now continue with the M_2 computation until that ends in a result. But what happens if M_2 would not terminate on the tape represented? In order to output F (i.e. the two machines are not equivalent), E would need to determine that M_2 was not going to halt. *E would need to solve the halting problem.*

The halting problem also manifests itself in many **decision problems** associated with programming. Some of these are:

- will a given program terminate or not? – halting problem;
- do two programs yield the same answers for all inputs? – this is essentially the TM *equivalence problem* that is shown to be unsolvable immediately above;
- will a given program write a given value in a given memory location?
- will a given machine word be used as data or as an instruction?
- what is the shortest program equivalent to a given program?
- will a particular instruction ever be executed?

The exercises ask you whether the above decision problems of programming can be represented as TM decision problems and subsequently proved to be generally impossible to solve. In all cases, the method of proof is the same: we show that if the given problem was solvable, i.e. there was a TM to solve it, then that TM would, as part of its activity, have to solve the halting problem.

The proof of the halting problem includes what seems like a peculiar form of self-reference. A formal system of sufficient representational power is capable of being used to represent itself. If it is capable of representing itself then it can be turned in on itself, so to speak, to lead to peculiar contradictions. Turing's results are analogous to similar results in the domain of logic established by the great mathematician Kurt Gödel. Here we simplify things greatly, but essentially Gödel showed that a system of logic capable of generating all true statements (what is called *completeness*) can be used to generate a statement P, which, in essence refers to itself, saying 'P is false'[2]. Such a statement can be neither *true* nor *false*, and is therefore inconsistent (if it is true, then it is false, and vice versa). In a way, such a statement says 'I am false'. In a similar way, our machine H_2, when given its own code as input, says: 'I halt if I do not halt, and I do not halt if I halt'!

The general unsolvability of the halting problem and Gödel's findings with respect to completeness leave computer science in a curious position. A machine powerful enough to compute everything we may ask of it is powerful enough to deal with representations of itself. This leads to *inconsistencies*. If we reduce the power of the machine so that inconsistencies cannot occur, then our machines are incomplete, and will not be able to compute everything we may reasonably expect of them.

It is worth briefly discussing the wider implications of the halting problem. The inability of algorithmic processes to solve the halting problem does *not* mean that machines are necessarily less intelligent that humans. However, you may think that *we* can look at the texts of our programs and predict that this or that particular loop will not terminate, as we often do when writing programs. This does not mean we can solve the halting problem in general, but only in certain restricted situations. There must come a point at which the size and complexity of a program becomes such that we are forced to 'execute' (e.g. on paper) the program. There is no reason to disbelieve that, for the restricted cases in which we can determine that a program would not halt, we could also write a program (and thus construct a TM) to do the same. The general halting problem embodies a level of complexity beyond the capabilities of machines and human beings.

11.6 COMPUTABLE LANGUAGES

In Chapter 7 we saw how from any **phrase structure grammar** we could construct a **non-deterministic TM** to **accept** the language generated by that grammar. In Chapter 10 we saw how any non deterministic TM could be converted into an equivalent deterministic TM. Thus, we conclude that the TM is the **recognizer** for the phrase structure languages in general. The phrase structure languages include all types 0, 1, 2 and 3 of the **Chomsky hierarchy**. However, as the earlier chapters of this book have shown, the TM is a more powerful computational device than we actually need for the more restricted types (**context free** and **regular**). Nevertheless, the phrase structure languages are the *computable languages*, using the term 'computable', as we do now, to

[2] Rather like the person who says: 'Everything I say is a lie'.

mean *TM-computable*. A computable language, then, is a formal language that can be accepted by some TM.

A question that arises, then, is 'are there formal languages that are *not* computable?' In the next section, we encounter a language that is not computable, in that there can be no TM to accept the language. This, in turn, means that there can be no phrase structure grammar to generate that language (if there were, we could simply follow the rules in Chapter 7 and construct from the grammar a TM recognizer for the language). This result will enable us to refine our hierarchy of languages and abstract machines, which brings us to the end of the book.

With respect to formal languages, the analogous concept to *solvability* is called *decidability*.

A language is *decidable* if some TM can take any string of the appropriate symbols, and determine whether or not that string *is* a sentence of the language. An alternative way of putting this is to say that *the membership problem for that language is totally solvable*.

A language is *acceptable*, which we also call *computable*, if some TM can determine if any string that *is* a sentence of the language is indeed a sentence, but for strings that are not sentences cannot necessarily make any statement about that string at all. In this case, *the membership problem for the language is partially solvable*.

In the final section, we summarize the decidability properties of the various types of formal language we have encountered in this book. However, for now we return to the question asked above: *are there formal languages that are not computable*? If a language is non computable, then it is not acceptable, and by **Turing's thesis** there is no algorithmic process that can determine, for *any* appropriate string, if that string is in the language.

11.6.1 An unacceptable (non computable) language

We now establish that there is indeed a non computable formal language. As you will see, the 'proof' of this is inextricably bound up with the **halting problem**, and also takes advantage of our TM coding scheme from earlier in this chapter.

Consider the following set X:

$$X = \{ 1x1 : x \in \{0, 1\}^+ \}$$

X is the set of all strings starting and ending in 1, with an arbitrary non-empty string of 0s and 1s in between. Now each string in this set either can, or cannot, represent the code of a TM. By considering a slight adaptation of the TM (sketched out in Chapter 10) that generates all strings in $\{a, b, c\}^+$ as part of its simulation of a non-deterministic machine, we know that the strings of this set could be generated systematically.

Now consider a **subset** Y of X defined as follows:

$$Y = \{x : x \in X \text{ and } x \text{ is the code of a TM with alphabet } \{0,1\}\}.$$

It would be straightforward to define a TM, or write a program that, given any string from X, told us whether or not that string was a valid TM code, i.e. of the format shown in Figure 11.11.

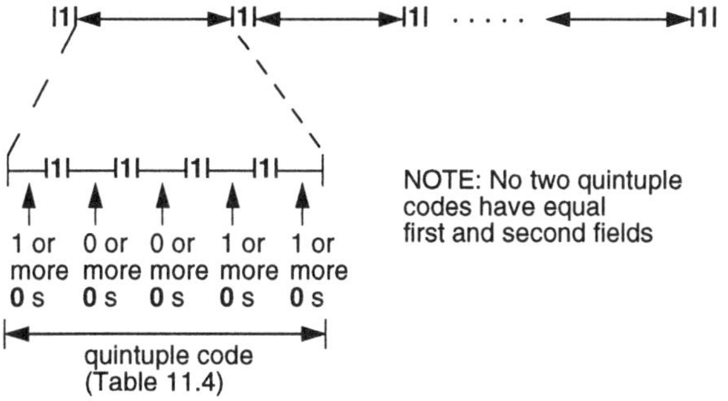

Figure 11.11 A binary code representing a TM

Note from Figure 11.11 that we are only interested in codes that represent deterministic machines, i.e. machines that have no more than one quintuple with the same 'current state' and 'current symbol'. We are also interested only in *binary TMs*, but we have already argued that all TMs can be reduced to binary form (cf UTM). This means that our 'current symbol' and 'write symbol' quintuple fields (i.e. the *second* and *third* fields of our quintuple representations) will not be allowed to contain more than two 0s.

Again, given that the set X can be generated systematically, and we can check for each string whether or not it represents a code for a TM, we can also see that there is an *effective procedure* for generating the set Y. Note that we are only interested in whether the codes are in the correct form to represent some TM, not in what the TM does. Most of the TM codes in Y would represent machines that do nothing of real interest, or indeed, nothing at all.

Given any code from the set Y we could recover the original machine. We can assume, for argument's sake, that for the alphabet, the code 0 represents 0, 00 represents 1, and all other codes are as we defined them earlier in the chapter. If y is a string in the set Y, we will call the machine whose code is y, M_y.

Now consider the following set, Z:

$Z = \{x : x \in Y$ and M_x does *not* **accept** $x\}$

Every string in Y represents a coded TM with alphabet $\{0,1\}$, and thus every string in Y can be presented as input to the machine whose code is that string. Thus, Z is the set of *all binary alphabet machines that do not accept the string represented by their own code*.

Now, we ask:

is Z an *acceptable* language?

Suppose that it is. In this case, some TM, say M_z, is the acceptor for Z. We can assume that M_z uses only a binary alphabet. Thus, M_z's code will be in the set *Y*. Let's call M_z's code *z*.

We now ask,

is the string *z* accepted by M_z?

Suppose that it is. Then *z* is *not* in Z, since Z contains only strings that are *not* accepted by the machine whose code they represent. It therefore seems that if *z* is accepted by M_z, i.e. is in the language accepted by M_z, then it isn't in the set Z. However, this is nonsense, because M_z is the acceptor for Z, and so any string it accepts *must* be in Z.

We therefore reject our assumption in favour of its negation. We suppose that the string *z* is not accepted by M_z. M_z is the acceptor for Z, and so any string M_z does not accept is not in Z. But this also cannot be correct! If M_z does not accept the string *z*, then *z* is one of the strings in Z, as it is the code for a machine (M_z) that does not accept its own code.

It seems that the string *z* is not in the set *Z* if it is in the set Z, and is in the set *Z* if it is not! The TM, M_z cannot exist, and we must conclude that *the language Z is not acceptable.* We have found an easily defined formal language taken from a two-symbol alphabet that is not computable. Such a language is sometimes called a totally undecidable language. We could generalize the above proof to apply to alphabets of any number of symbols, in effect showing that there are an infinite number of such *totally undecidable* languages.

11.6.2 An acceptable, but undecidable, language

One problem remains to be addressed, before the next section concludes the book by presenting an overall summary of the relationship between formal languages and automata. We would like to know if there are computable languages that are *necessarily acceptable, but not decidable.* For reasons that will be presented in the next section, any such languages must be properly type 0 in the Chomsky hierarchy, since the more restricted types of language in the hierarchy *are* decidable.

Here is a computable language that is acceptable, but not decidable. Given the sets *X* and *Y*, as specified above, we define the set *W* as follows:

$W = \{x : x \in Y$ and UTM_H halts when it applies x to $x\}$[3].

The set *W* is the set of codes of TMs that halt when given their own code as input. *W* is an *acceptable* language. *W* is *not* a *decidable* language because a TM that could tell us which valid TM codes were not in *W* (i.e. represent the code for machines that

[3] UTM_H was introduced earlier in the chapter. It halts and prints 1 when the simulated machine would have halted on the given tape.

do not halt when given their own code as input) would have to solve the *halting problem*.

Languages, like W, that are acceptable but not decidable are sometimes called *semi-decidable languages*.

11.7 COMPUTABLE LANGUAGES AND ABSTRACT MACHINES: THE BEGINNING

As implied above, associated with any language is what is called the membership problem for that language. Given a grammar G and a string s, the membership problem says: 'is s a sentence of the language $L(G)$?' From our discussion of **problems** and **solvability** earlier in this chapter, it should be clear that the membership problem for a language is solvable if the associated membership function for that language is (TM-) computable.

For all the phrase structure languages, the associated membership function is computable. *All phrase structure languages are computable (acceptable) languages.* However, we have seen that some type 0 languages are acceptable, but not decidable. However, we shall see that the other types (1, 2, 3) are *all* decidable.

Table 11.7 summarizes the decidability properties of the **regular, context free, context sensitive**, and **unrestricted** languages. In fact, since we would like to show only that types 1, 2, and 3 are decidable, we can specify the same (very inefficient!) method for all three types, assuming some initial minor amendments to the type 2 and 3 grammars.

In terms of formal languages, as presented in this book, we described each class of language in the Chomsky hierarchy, working from the regular languages up. We simultaneously worked up to the TM, by adding extra functionality to one type of abstract machine to yield a more powerful type of machine. For example, we showed how a machine that is essentially an FSR with a **stack** was more powerful than an FSR. We finally developed the Turing Machine, and showed that we need go no further. *There is no more powerful device for computation or language recognition than the TM.*

We might, as an alternative, have approached the subject by first presenting the TM, and then discussing how the TM gives us more power than we need for the more restricted languages and computations (such as *adding* and *subtracting*, which we saw being done by FSTs in Chapter 8). Then the abstract machines for the more restricted languages could have been presented as TMs that were restricted in some appropriate way. Given what we now know about the power of the TM, it seems only fitting to conclude this book by presenting, in Figure 11.12, this alternative view of *computable languages and abstract machines*.

Table 11.7 Decidability properties for the languages of the Chomsky hierarchy

Grammar type	General decidability	Justification
regular (type 3)	decidable	If necessary, remove ε from grammar using method described in Chapter 5.
context free (type 2)	decidable	Then apply the method below to the ε free part of the grammar.
context sensitive (type 1)	decidable	All productions are $x \rightarrow y$ where $\mid x \mid \leq \mid y \mid$. Thus, each step in a derivation either increases or leaves unchanged the length of the sentential form. Construct a non-deterministic TM to generate in parallel all sentential forms that do not exceed in length the length of the target string *s*. If s is one of the generated strings, print *T* and halt, if it is not, print *F* and halt. Convert the non deterministic TM into an equivalent deterministic TM.
unrestricted (type 0)	semi-decidable	Some productions may be of form $x \rightarrow y$ where $\mid x \mid \leq \mid y \mid$. The sentential form may thus lengthen and shorten during a derivation. There may therefore be no obvious point at which to give up if we do not manage to generate *s*, the target string. However, we know from Chapter 7 that all type 0 languages are acceptable.

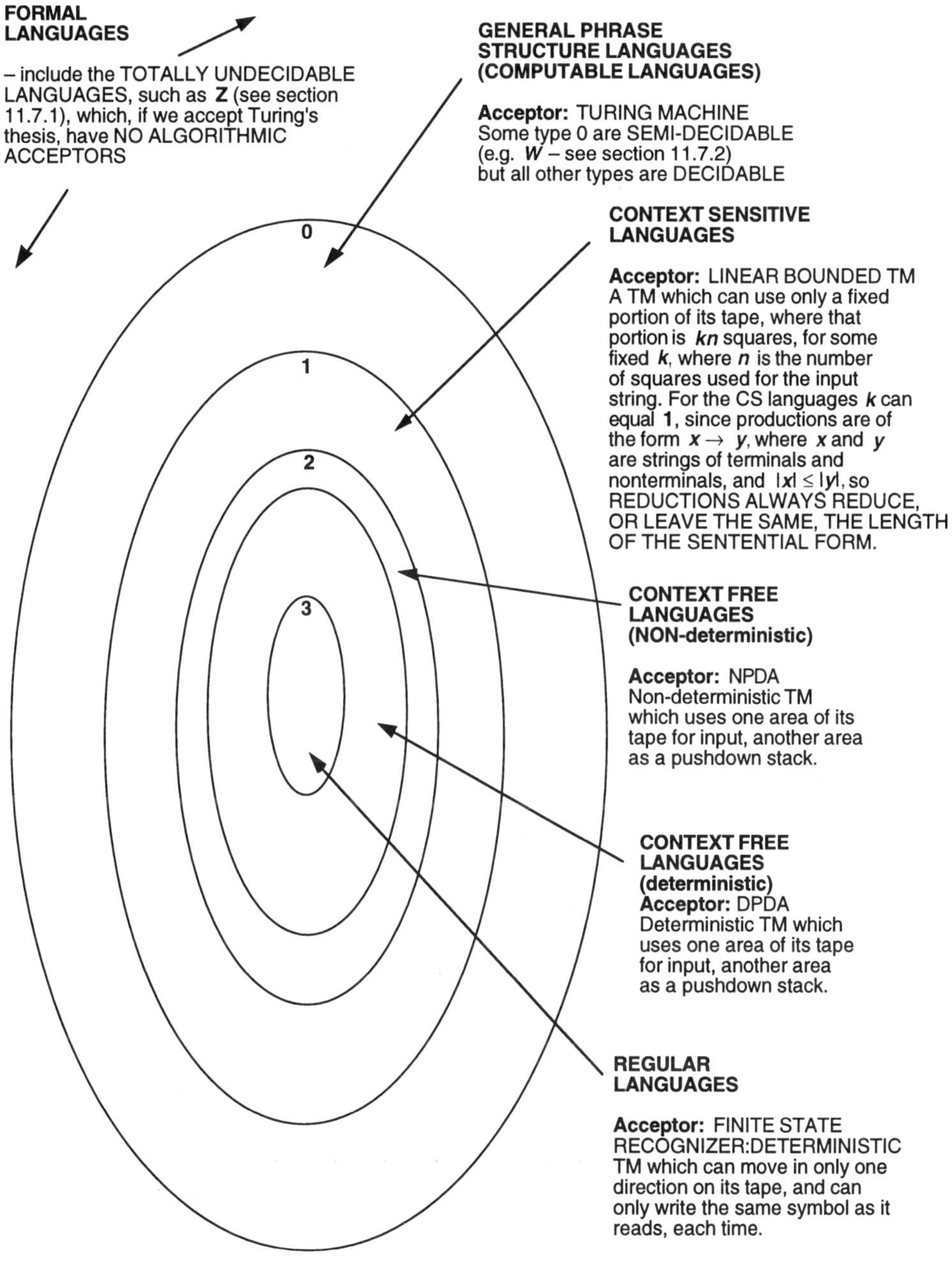

Figure 11.12 Computable languages and abstract machines

EXERCISES

1 Write a program representing a general **Turing machine** simulator. Your machine should accept as its input the **quintuples** of a Turing machine, and then simulate the behaviour of the TM represented by the quintuples on various input tapes. In particular, you should run your simulator for various TMs found in this book, and the TMs specified in Exercise 2 of Chapter 7.

Hint: the advice given for Exercise 6 of Chapter 5, in *Solutions to Selected Exercises* is also very relevant to this exercise

2† The printing problem asks if a TM, M, will print out a given symbol s, in M's alphabet, when started on a specified input tape. Prove that the printing problem is, in general, **unsolvable**.

Hint: this is a problem that reduces to the halting problem, as discussed earlier.

3 Show that the following (all taken from this Chapter) are all unsolvable problems. In each case first transform the statement of the problem so that it is couched in terms of Turing machines rather than programs. Then show that in order to solve the given problem, a TM would have to solve the **halting problem**.

(a) will a given program terminate or not? – halting problem
(b) will a given program write a given value in a given memory location?
(c) will a given machine word be used as data or as an instruction?
(d) what is the shortest program equivalent to a given program?
(e) will a particular instruction ever be executed?

4 Express the totally unsolvable problem in 11.4.2 in terms of programs, rather than TMs.

Hint: consider a non terminating program such as an operating system, for which the input can be regarded a stream of characters.

Glossary of terms

abstract machine

An abstract machine is a **function** or a collection of functions. For example:

> the **FSR** associates (symbol, **state**) pairs with sets of states, as in the tabular representation of the FSR suggested in Solutions to selected exercises, the comment on Exercise 3, Chapter 4.

The view of abstract machines as 'machines' rather than as functions enables us to consider the processing of sequences of input symbols over time, under the control of a **clock**. Thus, we can use them as the basis of a study of real computing machines.

accept

A **recognizer** essentially tells us if its input string is a member of a particular set. A string that is adjudged to belong to the set is said to be accepted by the machine.

acceptable language

A **formal language** which has an associated **TM** that, given any **sentence** of the language, terminates with an indication that the sentence is indeed a sentence of the language.

acceptance conditions

The configuration of an **abstract machine** that we expect to see when the machine halts, if that machine was given as its input an acceptable string.

- **FSR**: the acceptance conditions are that the input is **exhausted** and the machine is in a **state** designated as a **halt**, or **acceptance**, **state**
- **PDR**: as for FSR, but we may also specify the required conditions of the machine's stack
- **TM**: may include halt state and output configuration.

acceptance state

A **state** which an **FSR** or **PDR** must reach when it is signifying that it **accepts** a string.

algorithm

An **effective procedure** that terminates with a valid output for every appropriate input.

alphabet

A non-empty **finite** set of **atomic elements**.

ambiguity

A property possessed by a **grammar**, *G*, that is such that *L*(*G*) contains a **sentence** for which *G* can be used to construct two or more **derivation trees**.

arc

Specifies the successor relationship between **states** of an **abstract machine**, or **nodes** in a **tree**, and that a relationship exists between two nodes in a **graph**.

atom, atomic

A component of a symbolic expression that we do not attempt to analyse structurally, i.e. the building block of symbolic expressions (e.g. **terminal symbols** in **grammars**, symbols in **alphabets**).

backtrack

If a procedure reaches a dead end and recreates an earlier situation, when a choice between alternatives was taken, in order to explore one of those alternatives, this is known as backtracking. For example, a **non deterministic PDR** may return to a particular (**state**, input symbol, **stack**) configuration in order to try an alternative sequence of **transitions**.

Backus-Naur form (BNF)

An alternative representation of **context free grammars**. Useful for defining programming languages, as it enables **non terminals** (called syntactic categories in BNF) to have arbitrary length names. For examples of BNF notation in the definition of the Pascal language, see Chapters 2 and 3, and the solution to Exercise 7 of Chapter 2 in *Solutions to selected exercises.*

big O

A notation for expressing an approximation of the **time** taken or **space** used by a program or machine when carrying out a given task. O means ‘in the order of’.

blank

The status of every **tape square** of a **TM's** tape that is not occupied by a symbol. TMs can recognize blank squares, and can 'blank out' marked squares.

blank tape assumption

The assumption that if, in a TM's **input configuration**, the **head** is located on a **blank** tape square, the tape is occupied only by blanks.

bottom-up parsing

A bottom-up method attempts to build a **parse tree** from its **leaf nodes** (the **terminal string**) upwards, terminating when the tree is fully formed, and has S, the **start symbol** as its root. **Reduction parsing** is a bottom-up approach.

Chomsky hierarchy

A formal specification of the relationship between **phrase structure grammars**, in terms of four types, **type 0**, **1**, **2** and **3**. Each type, from 1 to 3, is properly contained within the type numerically preceding it.

Chomsky normal form (CNF)

A format into which the **productions** of any ε **free context free grammar** can be converted, without changing the **language generated by the grammar.** Formally, a CFG is in CNF if every production is of the form:

$x \rightarrow y$, where $x \in N$, and either $y \in T$ or $y = vw$, where $v,w \in N$

clock

Each **transition** made by an **abstract machine** is assumed to take place on receiving a signal emitted by an imaginary device. As we are interested in situations where the signals are 'transmitted' at regular intervals of time, we call the imaginary device a clock.

closed under an operation, closure

If we have a **set** of objects, and we show that a given operation applied to any **member** of the set produces an object that is also in the set, we say that the set is closed under that operation. For example, the set of natural numbers {1, 2, 3, 4,..} is 'closed under the operation +'.

complement

A **formal language**, L, is a **subset** of A^*, for some **alphabet** A. The complement of L, with respect to A, is the set $A^* - L$, i.e. the set of all **strings** in A^* that are not in L.

complexity

In this book, the term is used in two different ways:

- The complexity of an **abstract machine** is the number of **states** it consists of (for an **FSR**) or the number of **states** multiplied by the number of **alphabet** symbols (for a **TM**).
- The **time** complexity of a program is the number of basic operations the program carries out in relation to the length of the input.

computable

See **computable function**

computable function

A **function** that can be computed by a TM.

computable language

A language that can be **accepted** by a **TM**. Synonyms: **acceptable** language, **phrase structure language**, **type 0/unrestricted language**.

computation

A **function** associates input with output. Computation involves taking some input and actually producing the output specified by the function, by carrying out an **effective procedure**.

concatenation of strings

The concatenation of two **strings**, x and y, written xy, is the string formed by appending y onto the end of x. If $x = ab$ and $y = bcd$, then $xy = abbcd$.

concatenation of languages

The concatenation of two **formal languages**, L_1 and L_2, written L_1L_2, is the language resulting from concatenating every string in L_1 with every string in L_2, in turn. If $L_1 = \{a, bc, cd\}$ and $L_2 = \{a, ca\}$, then $L_1L_2 = \{aa, aca, bca, bcca, cda, cdca\}$.

context free (type 2)

A context free grammar has **productions** of the form $x \rightarrow y$, where $x \in N$ and $y \in (N \cup T)^*$.

A context free language is any language generated by a 'context free grammar'.

The **recognizer** for the context free languages is the **pushdown recognizer**.

context sensitive (type 1)

A context sensitive grammar has **productions** of the form $x \rightarrow y$, where $x \in (N \cup T)^+$ and $y \in (N \cup T)^*$, and $|x| \leq |y|$.

A context sensitive language is any language generated by a 'context sensitive grammar'.

The **recognizer** for the context sensitive languages is a TM that only needs to use the area of its **tape** occupied by the input string to process that string.

countably infinite

A set is countably infinite if it is **infinite**, but a program (TM) can print out its elements one by one in such a way that each element appears only once and each element is guaranteed to appear within a finite period of time.

decide, decidability, total d., partial d, und., semi-d.

A machine decides a language if it can indicate 'yes' for every string that is a sentence, and 'no' for every string in the **complement** of the language.

If a **TM** decides a language as above, the language is called a totally decidable language. **Types 1**, **2** and **3** of the **Chomsky hierarchy** are totally decidable languages. The type 0 languages are, in general, semi-decidable.

See also **solvability**.

decision problem

A **problem** that requires an answer for every **member** of a **set** of objects. The **halting problem** is a decision problem.

decision program

A program that can **decide** a language.

derivation, derive

The application of a sequence of **productions**.

derivation tree

A form of representing **derivations** using **context free grammars**. Since context free grammar **productions** have single **non terminals** on the **left hand sides**, each non terminal expands to a string of one or more **terminals** and/or non terminals. Derivations can thus be represented in **tree** form.

deterministic (FSR, PDR, CFL, TM)

A deterministic machine never has to make a choice about which **transition** to make, in a given situation.

A deterministic **context free language** (**CFL**) is a CFL for which a deterministic PDR can be defined.

ε generating non terminal

A **non terminal** appearing on the **left hand side** of a **production** that can be used as the first in the derivation of the **empty string**.

ε-free grammar

A grammar containing no ε **productions**.

ε-free production

A **production** that does not have the **empty string** on its **right hand side**.

ε production

A **production** with the **empty string** on its **right hand side**.

effective procedure

A procedure that:

- is deterministic
- involves finite time and resources (space)
- can be specified in terms of unambiguous rules
- is represented in numeric terms.

element (of a set)

An object that is a **member** of a **set**.

empty move, ε move

A **transition** made by a **PDR** or **FSR** without **reading** a symbol from the input string.

empty set, {}, ∅

A **set** containing no **elements**.

empty string, epsilon, ε, lambda, λ

The **string** that contains no symbols, and has a **length** of 0.

enumeration

The pairing off of the **elements** in a **set** with the natural numbers, in such a way that each element is associated with exactly one number.

equivalent

Of grammars and **recognizers**: a grammar, G, is equivalent to a recognizer, M, if $L(G)$ is exactly the same set as the set of **strings accepted** by M.

Of programs or TMs: two TMs, M_1 and M_2, are equivalent if for each and every input value, they both yield the same result.

exhausted

The input is exhausted when the **FST** or **PDR** has **read** every symbol.

exponential time

When an algorithm takes time $O(x^n)$ where n is the number of elements in the input (see **big O**).

finite

Limited in number. The **elements** of a finite **set** can be written out by a program (**TM**) that terminates, having written out all the elements.

finite language

A language consisting of a **finite** number of **strings**.

finite state recognizer (FSR), FS generator

An **abstract machine** that consists of a **finite** number of **states**, and makes a **transition** between states purely on the basis of the next symbol in the input string.

finite state transducer (FST)

A **finite state recognizer** with the additional requirement that it outputs a single symbol for each one it encounters in the input string.

formal grammar

Used in this book as synonymous with **phrase structure grammar**.

formal language

Any **subset** of the set A^*, where A is any **alphabet**.

function

An association between input values and output values, such that each configuration of input values is associated with only one configuration of output values. A function is essentially a specification of *what* is to be computed, but not necessarily *how* it is to be computed (see **computation**).

generator

An **abstract machine** that produces output without receiving any input.

graph

A **finite** set of ordered pairs of **nodes** of the form (x, y). For such a pair, we say there is an **arc** from x to y.

halt state

A **state** of an **abstract machine** in which the machine is expected to terminate its processing for valid inputs (or, in the case of **FSRs** and **PDRs**, for **acceptable strings**). For FSRs and PDRs, in this book the terms halt state and **acceptance state** are regarded as synonymous.

halting problem

The unsolvable **decision problem** that asks: can we provide a TM that will decide, for any **TM**, *M*, and input tape, *T*, whether or not *M* will halt if started on the **tape** *T*?

head

See **read/write head**.

index (of a string)

When we refer to the ith symbol in a **string** of **length** $\leq i$, the i is called the index. If x is a string we write it x_i, so if $x = abcded$, $x_4 = d$.

infinite

Limitless in number. Many infinite **sets** are **countably infinite**. Some sets, like the set of all **subsets** of the natural numbers, are not.

infinite language

A language that contains an **infinite** number of **sentences**.

ingoing arc

A directed **arc** entering a **state**.

input configuration of a Turing machine

A specification of:

- the position of the **read/write** head
- constraints applying to the **tape** symbols

of a **TM** before it begins its **computation**.

input string, input sequence

The **terminal string** presented to a **recognizer**. More generally, the initial sequence of symbols to be processed by an **abstract machine**.

instantaneous description

A description of:

- the contents of the **tape**
- the position of the **read/write** head
- the current **state**

of a **TM** at any given point in its **computation**.

intersection, $\cap$

Of two **sets**: the set of **elements** that occur in *both* of the sets.

language generated by grammar G [$L(G)$]

The set of **terminal strings** that can be derived using the **productions** of G, each **derivation** beginning with a production which has S, **the start symbol** of G, as its **left hand side**.

leaf node

In a **tree**, any **node** that has no successors (children).

left hand side

Of a **production**: the **string** to the left of the production arrow, $\rightarrow$.

length

Of a **string**: the number of symbols it contains (duplicates being counted). If x is a string, $|x|$ denotes its length, e.g. $|abcddadd| = 8$.

linear time

When an **algorithm** takes time $O(n)$, where n is the number of elements in the input (see big O).

loop

A sequence of **states** or **nodes** along a directed path, the first being the same as the last. Also used as a verb.

LR(1) language

A special case of the **LR(k)** languages. The **deterministic CFLs**.

LR(k) language

Languages that can be recognized by a **DPDR** (and are therefore **context free**) if that machine is allowed to look ahead in the input by no more than a fixed number, k, of symbols.

member

Any **element** of a **set** is a member of that set.

minimal FSR

A **deterministic FSR**, M, that is such that no deterministic FSR that **recognizes** the same language can have fewer **states** than M.

moment

An unspecified but finite period of time, used in discussing the time taken by **abstract machine** computations. Each signal from the **clock** is assumed to occur one moment after the previous signal.

multi-tape TM, k-tape TM

A TM that uses k **tapes** ($k > 1$), each of which has its own **read/write head**. Such a TM has instructions in the form of **sextuples** (rather than **quintuples**).

node

An object in a **tree** or a **graph** that is linked by **arcs** to other objects (nodes).

non deterministic (FSR, PDR, CFL, TM)

An **abstract machine** that can have a choice of applicable **transitions** in a given situation. A non deterministic CFL is a CFL for which a **deterministic PDR** cannot be found.

non proper, non properly

Of **sets**: the non proper **subsets** of a set include the set itself.

Of types of **formal language** in the **Chomsky hierarchy**: a language is not properly of a given type if it is possible to define a **grammar** of a subordinate type to generate that language.

non terminal symbol

A symbol that can appear in the **productions** of a **grammar**, but cannot appear in **sentences**.

null state

The **state** in a **deterministic FSR** which is added by the **subset method** to ensure that the machine is completely deterministic. From each state of the machine, for each **terminal symbol** for which there is not an **arc** going to a non null state, there will be an **outgoing arc** labelled with that terminal going to the null state. Then there is an arc that is both **outgoing** and **ingoing** to the null state for each terminal symbol.

outgoing arc

A directed **arc** leaving a **state**.

output configuration of a Turing machine

A specification of:

- the position of the **read/write** head
- constraints applying to the **tape** symbols

of a **TM** when it completes its **computation**.

packed tape

A **tape** on which no **blanks** appear between marked squares. Almost all our **TMs** in this book assume an initial configuration in which the input tape is packed.

palindrome

A **string** that equals the reverse of itself.

parse tree

A **derivation tree** that is built up in the process of **parsing**.

parser

A procedure that produces a structural account of a **string** according to some **grammar**.

parsing

The activity carried out by a **parser**.

phrase structure grammar (PSG), PS language (PSL)

A PSG is a **tuple** (N, T, P, S) where

- N is a **finite set** of **non terminal** symbols,
- T is a finite set of **terminal** symbols,
- $N \cap T = \{\}$,

- P is a set of **productions** defined as for **unrestricted grammar**,
- S is a **member** of N called the **start symbol**.

A PSL is a language generated by a PSG.

polynomial time

When an **algorithm** takes time $O(n^x)$, where n is the number of elements in the input (see *big O*).

pop

A **function** applied to **stacks**, which returns the symbol at the top of the stack. Actually two functions, as it also removes the top symbol. Used by the **push down recognizer**.

power

Of **strings**: a **function** to **concatenate** a string to itself a specified number of times. If x is a string, $x^0 = \varepsilon$, $x^1 = x$, and $x^i = xx^{i-1}$, all $i > 1$. So if $x = abcc$, $x_3 = abccabccabcc$.

problem

The question associated with a **function**, f, that asks 'what is the value of $f(x)$?'

production arrow, →

The symbol in between the **left hand** and **right hand** sides of **productions**.

production, production rule

A component of a **grammar** consisting of a **string** followed by a production arrow, followed by another string. A production $x \rightarrow y$ means 'the string x can be replaced by the string y'.

proper, properly

Of **sets**: A proper **subset** of a set cannot be the whole of the set.

Of types of **formal language** in the **Chomsky hierarchy**: A language is properly of a given type if it is not possible to define a **grammar** of a subordinate type to generate that language.

push

A **function** applied to **stacks**, which places a new symbol on top of the stack. Used by the **push down recognizer**.

pushdown recognizer

A **finite state recognizer** equipped with a **stack** that has **arcs** labelled with three components:

1. a symbol to be read from the input **string**
2. a symbol that may be found on the top of the stack
3. a string to be **pushed** onto the stack

The machine can make the **transition** specified by that arc only if (1) is the next symbol in the input string, and (2) is the symbol currently on the stack. The machine can then **pop** (2) from the stack, replacing it with (3), and make the transition. The push down recognizer is the recognizer for the **context free languages**.

queue

A data structure like a **stack**, but in which items are added to one end and removed from another.

quintuples

In general, a quintuple is a five element list. In this book, quintuples are used as an alternative representation of the **TM**, where each quintuple is of the form:

(current **state**, read symbol, write symbol, direction, new state).

However, **PDRs** can also be represented as quintuples (see the hints for Exercise 6, Chapter 5, in *Solutions to selected exercises*).

read/write head, r/w head

A **TM** is assumed to be equipped with a read/write head, which can sense the symbol on the current square of the **tape**, and overwrite that symbol before moving one tape square to the left or right.

reading

The **abstract machine** typically makes a **transition** for each symbol in the input **string**. We call this process reading the input.

recognizer

A machine that has the task of telling us if an input string belongs to a particular **set** is called a recognizer, or an **acceptor**. In this book, recognizing and accepting are regarded as synonyms, and are used interchangeably.

reductio ad absurdum

A proof technique. To prove a proposition, p, one assumes $\neg p$ to be true. By following a logically sound chain of inference from $\neg p$, one arrives at a contradiction.

Since a contradiction has been reached by following logically sound arguments from an original assumption, the original assumption must be false, i.e. one has shown $\neg\neg p$, which is p.

reduction parsing

A **bottom-up parsing** technique which exchanges the **left** and **right hand sides** of the **productions** of the **grammar**, resulting in what are called reductions. Parsing then begins with the input **string**, and attempts to find a sequence of reductions that will result in S, **the start symbol**, being the only remaining symbol.

reductions

See **reduction parsing**.

regular (type 3)

A regular grammar has **productions** of the form $X \rightarrow yY$, or $X \rightarrow z$ where $X, Y \in N$, $y \in T$ and $z \in T \cup \{\varepsilon\}$.

A regular language is any language generated by a regular grammar.

The **recognizer** for the regular languages is the **deterministic FSR**.

reject

A **recognizer** that has terminated without accepting an input **string** is assumed to have rejected the string.

repeat state theorem, vwx theorem

A theorem applying to **FSRs** and **FSTs** essentially saying that any FSR that processes a long enough **string** must go into a **loop**, and will continue to loop if the conditions that caused it to pass through the loop once are recreated.

right hand side

Of a **production**: the **string** to the right of the production arrow, $\rightarrow$.

semantics

Of an expression: what the expression means.

Of a program: the **computation** carried out by the program.

sentence

A **string** from a **formal language**. A **terminal string** generated by a **grammar**.

sentential form

Any **string** in $(N \cup T)^*$ that can be derived through the application of **productions** of a **grammar**, the first production applied being one with only S, **the start symbol** on its **left hand side**.

sequence

An ordered collection of **elements**, that permits duplicated elements. A **string** is a form of sequence.

set

An unordered collection of **elements** that does not allow duplicated elements.

set definition

The specification of a **set**, most commonly by specifying a **function** for generating objects along with a specification of the range of values to which the function is to be applied.

In this book set definitions are usually used to specify **formal languages**. For example, $\{a^i b^{i \text{ div } 3} : i \geq 1\}$ denotes the **infinite** set of **strings** of 1 or more *a*s followed by a number of *b*s which is the number of *a*s integer divided by 3 ({*a*, *aa*, *aaab*, *aaaab*, *aaaaab*, *aaaaaabb*, ..}).

set difference, (–), (\)

$A - B$ is the **set** of **elements** that are in A but not in B.

For example, $\{a, b, c\} - \{b, e, f\} = \{a, c\}$.

sextuples

The ***k*-tape TM** version of **quintuples**. As for quintuples, but with an extra designator, being a number between 1 and k, and denoting the **tape** on which the next operation is to take place.

shuffling

A task often performed by **TMs**, when a symbol is moved from one part of a **tape** to another, and all other symbols are moved to close up the **blank** that may result, and perhaps to make room for the symbol at its destination.

skipping

When a **TM** enters a **loop** that passes over all symbols, moving in one direction only, until it reaches a target symbol, we call this skipping over the symbols.

solvability

A **problem** is solvable if the associated **function** is **computable**.

space

The amount of storage required during a **computation**. For TMs, this is measured in terms of the number of **tape** squares required, perhaps expressed as a function of the number of squares required to represent the input.

stack

A popular data structure, used in this book by **push down recognizers**. Essentially a **string**, to which we add symbols at one end (called **pushing**), and remove values from the same end (called **popping**).

stack bottom marker, ⊥

Since the **pop** operation is undefined for empty **stacks**, the stack bottom marker is a special symbol used by **PDRs** to represent the bottom of the stack.

start (sentence) symbol

For a **terminal string** generated by a **grammar** to be a **sentence**, it must have been generated by a sequence of **productions** the first of which had a lone S, **the start symbol** of the grammar, on its **left hand side**.

start state

Abstract machines considered in this book have one or more **states** designated as start states. The machines are assumed to make their first **transition** from one of these states.

state

Used in two senses in this book:

- an **abstract machine** is represented as a directed **graph**, the **nodes** in the graph being called states
- the state of a machine is sometimes regarded as the internal configuration of all relevant details of the machine at a given point in its **computation** (for example, **instantaneous descriptions** of **TMs**).

string

A **finite sequence** of **atomic** symbols taken from an **alphabet**.

subset

A **set** which is the **empty set**, is equal to, or is contained by, another set is called a subset of that other set.

subset construction (algorithm) for FSRs

An **algorithm** that takes any **non deterministic FSR** and produces an **equivalent** deterministic FSR. It works by deterministically modelling the behaviour of several non deterministic **states** of the original machine in single states of the new machine.

substring

Any part, including ε, of a **string**. Formally, let s be any string, **taken from** an **alphabet**, A. Then the **members** of the **set** $\{y : x, y, z \in A^*, xyz = s\}$ are all of the substrings of s.

superset

A **set** that contains, or is equal to, another set is a superset of that other set.

syntax

The structure of an expression according to a set of formal rules.

syntax diagram

A diagrammatic form for representing **syntax**, relevant to the **context free languages**, and programming languages in particular.

taken from

It is often said that a **string** is a **sequence** of symbols over an **alphabet.** In this book the phrase 'taken from' is used in preference to 'over'.

tape

The one dimensional data structure used by the **TM**. It is assumed to be divided into squares. Each square can be occupied by a tape symbol or be **blank**. The tape is assumed to extend indefinitely at both ends, though at any time only a **finite** portion of it is 'marked' (occupied by symbols).

tape squares

See **tape**.

terminal node

A **leaf node** in the **derivation tree** or **parse tree** for a **sentence**, i.e. a node representing a **terminal symbol** or the **empty string**.

terminal string

A **string** of **terminal symbols**. See **sentence**.

terminal symbol

The symbols that can appear in **sentences** of a language.

time

With respect to **abstract machines**, assumed to be apportioned into discrete equal length moments. The time taken by a **computation** is usually measured in terms of the number of **transitions** a machine makes.

top-down

A top-down method of **parsing** attempts to build a **parse tree** from its root node (the node representing *S*, **the start symbol**) downwards, terminating when the target **sentence** has been obtained.

transducer

An **abstract machine** that processes input and produces output, and thus can be regarded as computing a **function**. In this book, the transducers studied are the **FST** and the **TM**.

transition, state transition

When a machine changes from one **state** to another (possibly the same) state.

tree

A tree is a **graph** where one **node**, *r*, is called the root node. *r* may have any number (including 0) of **outgoing arcs**, but no **ingoing arcs**. Each outgoing arc from *r*, if there are any, is an ingoing arc to the root of another tree.

tuple

A tuple is an ordered list of elements each of which can be simple objects, such as single symbols, or more complex objects such as **sets**. For examples, consider the (*N*, *T*, *P*, *S*) definition of **phrase structure grammar**, **quintuples** and **sextuples**.

Turing machine computable function

See **computable function**.

Turing machine (TM)

An augmented **finite state transducer** that uses a **tape** for input and output, and can move right and left on the tape, overwriting symbols on the tape. See **quintuples**.

Turing's thesis

The statement that every **effective procedure** can be carried out by a **TM**.

type 0, type 1, type 2, type 3 grammars and languages

See **unrestricted**, **context sensitive**, **context free**, **regular**, and **Chomsky hierarchy**.

unambiguous

A **grammar**, *G*, that is such that *L*(*G*) contains no **sentences** for which *G* can be used to construct two or more distinct **derivation trees** is called an unambiguous grammar.

union, $\cup$

The union of two **sets** is the set of **elements** in either or both sets.

unit production

A **production** of the form $X \to Y$ where $X, Y \in N$.

unit production graph

A **graph** representing **derivations** of **strings**, each derivation beginning with a **non terminal**, using only **unit productions**, and terminating the first time a non unit production is used.

universal Turing machine (UTM)

A **TM** that accepts as its input a description of any TM, *M*, and a description of an input **tape**, *T*, and simulates the behaviour of *M* on the tape *T*.

unrestricted (type 0)

An unrestricted **grammar** has **productions** of the form $x \to y$, where $x \in (N \cup T)^+$ and $y \in (N \cup T)^*$.
An unrestricted language is any language generated by an unrestricted grammar.
The **recognizer** for the unrestricted languages is the **TM**.

uvwxy theorem

The **repeat state theorem** for the **context free languages**. Essentially states that any sufficiently long **sentence**, *s*, of a CFL, *L*, is of the form *uvwxy*, where $uv^iwx^iy \in L$, all $i \geq 0$.

word

An alternative term for what in this book is called a **sentence**.

Further reading

The following are some suggested titles for further reading. Most of the items are accompanied by notes. In particular, some of the titles refer to articles that describe practical applications of some of the concepts in this book.
The bold numbers in parentheses refer to chapters in this book.

Beckman F.S. (1981) *Mathematical Foundations of Programming*. Addison-Wesley, Reading, MA.

*Encyclopaedic coverage of almost all aspects of computer science. The algorithm for minimization of FSRs (**4**) comes from Beckman. Also covers register machines and Wang machines (**9**). The programming problems relating to the halting problem are also adapted from Beckman (**11**).*

Brookshear J.G. (1989) *Theory of Computation: Formal Languages, Automata, and Complexity*. Benjamin/Cummings, Redwood City, CA.

*Chapter on complexity and Turing machines, including complexity of algorithms, and time complexity of language recognition problems (**10**). Does not mention context sensitive languages. The coding scheme for TMs, and the establishing of the undecidable languages in this book were based on Brookshear's approach (**11**). Much on LL(k) and LR(k) parsers (**5**). Uses quadruples, rather than quintuples, to describe TMs (**10**). Contains a list of NP problems in an appendix (**10**).*

Church A. (1936) An Unsolvable Problem of Elementary Number Theory. *American Journal of Mathematics*, **58**, 345–63.

*Church and Turing were contemporaneously addressing the same problems by different, but equivalent means. Hence, in books such as Harel, and Fenton and Hill we find references to the 'Church–Turing thesis', rather than 'Turing's thesis'. (**9, 10, 11**).*

Cohen D. I. A. (1986) *Introduction to Computer Theory*. John Wiley, New York.

*Covers some additional material such as: regular expressions, Moore and Mealy machines (in this book we use Mealy machines) (**4**). Discusses relationship between multi-stack PDRs (**5**) and TMs.*

Fenton N. and Hill G. (1993) *Systems Construction and Analysis: a Mathematical and Logical Framework*. McGraw-Hill, Maidenhead, UK.

*Contains chapters on formal language theory and complexity (**10**), the latter including an intuitive 'proof' of the halting problem (**11**) and discussion of P = NP problem (**10**).*

Floyd R.W. and Beigel R. (1994) *The Language of Machines: an Introduction to Computability and Formal Languages*. W.H. Freeman, New York.

*Includes a discussion of regular expressions (**4**), as used in the UNIX™ utility 'egrep'. Good example of formal treatment of minimization of FSRs (using equivalence classes) (**4**).*

Harel D. (1987) *Algorithmics: the Spirit of Computing*. Addison-Wesley, Reading, MA.

*Study of algorithms and their properties. Complexity, big-O (**10**), decidability (**11**). Discusses application of finite state machines to modelling simple systems (**8**). Focuses on 'counter programs': simple programs in a hypothetical programming language.*

Harrison M.A. (1978) *Introduction to Formal Language Theory*. Addison-Wesley, Reading, MA.

*Many formal proofs and theorems. Contains much on closure properties of languages (**6**).*

Hopcroft J.E. and Ullman J.D. (1979) *Introduction to Automata Theory, Languages and Computation*. Addison-Wesley, Reading, MA.

*Discusses linear bounded TMs for context sensitive languages (**11**).*

Hutchison D. and Silvester P. (1987) *Computer Logic: Principles and Technology*. Ellis-Horwood, Chichester, UK.

*Discusses use of FSTs as design tools for logical circuits (**8**).*

Jensen K. and Wirth N. (1975) *Pascal User Manual and Report*. Springer-Verlag, New York.

*Contains the BNF and Syntax chart descriptions of the Pascal syntax (**2**). Also contains notes referring to the ambiguity in the 'if' statement (**3**).*

Kain R.Y. (1972) *Automata Theory: Machines and Languages*. McGraw-Hill, New York.

*Formal treatment. Like Beckman develops Turing machines before other abstract machines. Discusses non-standard PDRs (**5**) applied to context sensitive languages.*

Minsky M.L. (1967) *Computation: Finite and Infinite Machines*. Prentice-Hall, Englewood Cliffs, NJ.

*A classic text, devoted to an investigation into effective procedures (**11**). More details on most things, of particular relevance is description of Shannon's two-state TM result (**10**), and reference to unsolvable problems (**11**). The 'proof' that FSTs cannot perform arbitrary multiplication (**8**) is based on the one here.*

Post E. (1936) Finite Combinatory Processes – Formulation 1. *Journal of Symbolic Logic*, **1**, 103–5.

*Post formulated a simple abstract string manipulation machine at the same time as did Turing (**9**). Cohen (see above) devotes a chapter to these 'Post' machines.*

Preece J. and Keller L. (eds.) (1990) *Human-Computer Interaction*. Prentice-Hall, London.

Human-computer interaction research and development uses grammars and state transition diagrams (Chapters 15 and 19).

Rayward-Smith V.J. (1983) *A First Course in Formal Language Theory*. Blackwell, Oxford, UK.

*The notation and terminology for formal languages we use in this book is based on Rayward-Smith. Very formal treatment of regular languages (plus regular expressions), FSRs (**4**), and context free languages and PDRs (**5**). Includes Greibach normal form (as does Floyd and Beigel), an alternative CFG manipulation process to Chomsky Normal Form (**5**). Much material on top-down and bottom-up parsing (**3**), LL and LR grammars (**5**), but treatment very formal.*

Rich E. (1984) *Artificial Intelligence*. McGraw-Hill, New York.

Artificial intelligence makes much use of representations such as grammars and abstract machines. In particular, machines called recursive transition networks and augmented transition networks (equivalent to TMs) are used in natural language processing.

Tanenbaum A.S. (1988) *Computer Networks* (2nd edn.). Prentice-Hall, London.

*Discusses FSTs for modelling protocol machines (sender or receiver systems in computer networks) (**8**).*

Turing A. (1936) On Computable Numbers with an Application to the Entscheidungsproblem. *Proceedings of the London Mathematical Society*, **42**, 230–265.

*The paper in which Turing introduces his abstract machine, in terms of computable numbers, not computable functions. Also includes his notion of a universal machine (**11**). A paper of remarkable contemporary applicability, considering that Turing was considering the human, rather than the machines, as computer.*

Winston P.H. (1984) *Artificial Intelligence* (2nd edn.) Addison-Wesley, Reading, MA. (see Rich)

Wood D. (1987) *Theory of Computation*. John Wiley, Chichester, UK.

*Describes several extensions to PDRs (**5**). Introduction to proof methods, including the pigeonhole principle (also mentioned by Harel) on which both the repeat state theorem (**6**, **8**) and the uvwxy theorem (**6**) are based.*

Solutions to selected exercises

CHAPTER 2

1 (a) **Regular**. Every **production** has a lone **non terminal** on its **left hand** side, and the **right hand** sides consist of either a single **terminal**, or a single terminal followed by a single non terminal.

(b) **Context** free. Every production has a lone non terminal on its left hand side. The right hand sides consist of arbitrary mixtures of terminals and/or non terminals one of which ($aAbb$) does not conform to the pattern for regular right hand sides.

2

(a)	$\{a^{2i}b^{3j} : i, j \geq 1\}$	i.e. *as* followed by *bs*, any number of *as* divisible by two, any number of *bs* divisible by 3
(b)	$\{a^i a^j b^{2j} : i \geq 0, j \geq 1\}$	i.e. zero or more *as*, followed by 1 or more *as* followed by twice as many *bs*
(c)	$\{\}$	i.e. the grammar generates *no strings at all*, as no derivations beginning with S produce a terminal string
(d)	$\{\varepsilon\}$	i.e. the *only string* generated is the *empty string*.

3 xyz, where $x \in (N \cup T)^*$, $y \in N$, and $z \in (N \cup T)^*$

The above translates into: 'a possibly empty string of terminals and/or non terminals, followed by a single non terminal, followed by another possibly empty string of terminals and/or non terminals'

5 For an **alphabet** A, A^* is the set of all strings that can be taken from A including the empty string, ε. A regular grammar to generate, say $\{a, b\}^*$ is:

$$S \to \varepsilon \mid aS \mid bS.$$

ε is derived directly from S. Alternatively, we can derive a or b followed by a or b or ε (this last case terminates the derivation), the a or b from the last stage being followed by a or b or ε (last case again terminates the derivation), and so on …
Generally, for any alphabet, $\{a_1, a_2, .., a_n\}$ the grammar:

$$S \to \varepsilon \mid a_1S \mid a_2S \mid .. \mid a_nS$$

is regular and can be similarly argued to generate $\{a_1, a_2, .., a_n\}^*$.

7 (b) The following fragment of the BNF definition for Pascal, taken from Jensen and Wirth (1975), actually defines all Pascal expressions, not only Boolean expressions.

<expression> ::= <simple expression> | <simple expression>
    <relational operator> <simple expression>
<simple expression> ::= <term> | <sign> <term> |
    <simple expression> <adding operator> <term>
<adding operator> ::= + | – | or
<term> ::= <factor> | <term> <multiplying operator> <factor>
<multiplying operator> ::= * | / | div | mod | and
<factor> ::= <variable> | <unsigned constant> | (<expression>) |
    <function designator> | <set> | not <factor>
<unsigned constant> ::= <unsigned number> | <string> |
    <constant identifier> | nil
<function designator> ::= <function identifier> |
    <function identifier> (<actual parameter>
        {, <actual parameter})
<function identifier> ::= <identifier>
<variable> ::= <identifier>
<set > ::= [<element list>]
<element list> ::= <element> {, <element> } | <empty>
<empty> ::=

Note the use of the **empty string** to enable an empty <set> to be specified (Chapter 5).

10 Given a **finite** set of strings, any string x from the set can be generated by regular grammar productions as follows:

$$x = x_1x_2..x_n, \; n \geq 1$$
$$S \to x_1X_1$$
$$X_1 \to x_2X_2$$
$$\cdot$$
$$\cdot$$
$$X_{n-1} \to x_n$$

For each string, x, we make sure the non terminals X_i are unique (to avoid any derivations getting 'crossed').

This applies to any finite set of strings, so any finite set of strings is a regular language.

CHAPTER 3

1 (b) $\{a^i b^j c^k : i, j, k \geq 1, i = j \text{ or } j = k\}$
i.e., strings of *a*s followed by *b*s followed by *c*s, where the number of *a*s equals the number of *b*s, or the number of *b*s equals the number of *c*s, or both

(c) Grammar *G* can be used to draw two different derivation trees for the sentence $a^3b^3c^3$, as shown in Figure SA.1. The grammar is thus ambiguous.

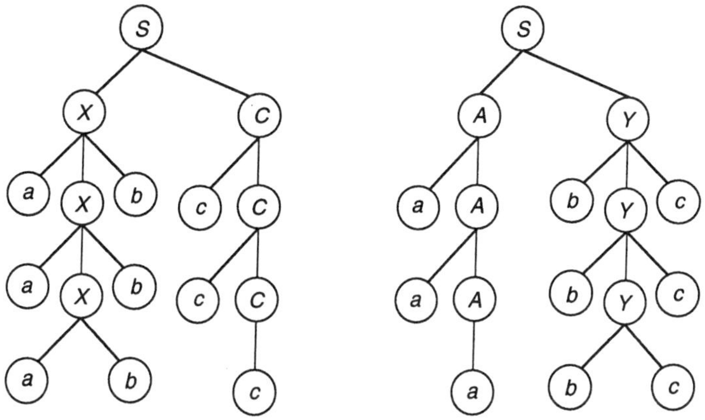

Figure SA.1

2 (b) As for the Pascal example, the *semantic implications* should be discussed in terms of demonstrating that the same statement yields different results according to which derivation tree is chosen to represent its structure.

CHAPTER 4

1 (a) The **FSR** obtained directly from the productions of the grammar is shown in Figure SA.2.

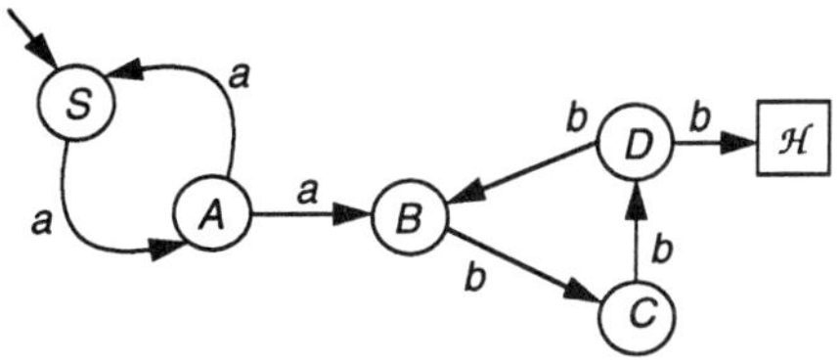

Figure SA.2

The above FSR is **non deterministic**, since it contains **states** (for example, state *A*) with more than one identically labelled outgoing arcs going to different destinations.

The **deterministic** version, derived using the subset method (null state removed) is in Figure SA.3.

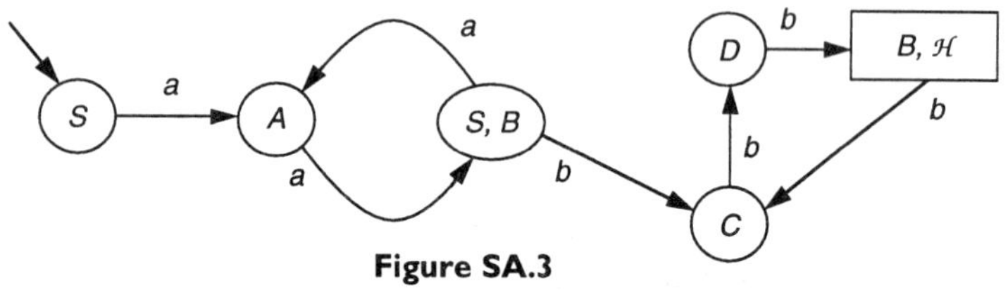

Figure SA.3

3 One possibility is to represent the FSR as a *two-dimensional* table (*array*), indexed according to (state, symbol) pairs. Table SA.1 represents the FSR of exercise 2.

Table SA.1

		TERMINALS	
		a	b
S	1	2, 3	–
T	2	4	3
A	3	–	5
T	4	2, 3, 4	5
E	5	–	5, 6
S	6	–	–

In Table SA.1, element (4, *a*), for example, represents the set of states directly reached from state 4 given the terminal *a*. Such a representation would be easy to create from the productions of a grammar that could be entered by the user, for example. The representation is also highly useful for creating the ,deterministic version. This version is also made more suitable if the language permits dynamic arrays (Pascal does not, but ADA and C, for example do). The program also needs to keep details of which states are **halt** and **start states**.

An alternative scheme represents the FSR as a *list of triples*, each triple representing one **arc** in the machine. In languages such as Pascal or ADA, this scheme can be implemented in *linked list* form. For example, consider the part of the FSR from exercise 2 shown in Figure SA.4.

This can be represented as depicted in Figure SA.5.

This representation is particularly useful when applying the *reverse* operation in the *minimization algorithm* (the program simply exchanges the first and third elements in

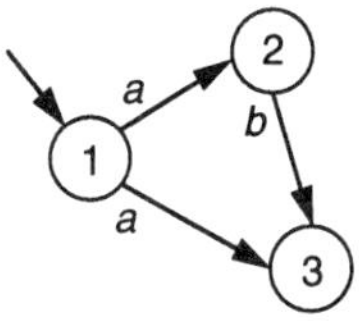

Figure SA.4

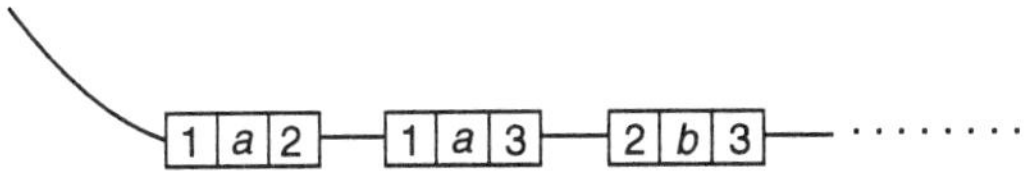

Figure SA.5

each triple). It is also a suitable representation for languages such as LISP, where the list of triples becomes a list of three element lists.

Since FSRs can be of arbitrary size, a true solution to the problem of defining an appropriate data structure would require *dynamic* data structures, even down to allowing an unlimited source of names. Although this is probably taking things to extremes, you should be aware of where you make such restrictions, and what their implications are.

CHAPTER 5

2 First of all, consider that a **DPDR** is not necessarily restricted to having *one* halt state. You design a machine, *M*, that enters a state that is a halt state after reading the first *a*, then remains in that state while reading any more *a*s (**push**ing them on to the **stack**, to compare with the *b*s, if there are any). If there are no *b*s, *M* simply stops in that halt state, otherwise on reading the first *b* (and **pop**ping off an *a*) it makes a transition to another state where it can read only *b*s. The rest of *M* is an exact copy of $M_3{}^d$, of Chapter 5. If there were no *b*s, any *a*s on the stack must remain there, even though *M* is accepting the string. Why can we not ensure that in this situation, *M* clears the *a*s from its stack, but is still deterministic?

5 The reasons are similar to why arbitrary **palindromic** languages are not deterministic. When the machine reads the *a*s and *b*s part of the string, it has no way of telling if the string it is reading is of the 'number of *a*s = number of *b*s' , or the 'number of *b*s = number of *c*s' type. It thus has to assume that the input string is of the former type, and **backtrack** to abandon this assumption if the string is not.

6 One possibility is to represent the PDR in a similar way to the *list* representation of the FSR described above (sample answer to exercise 3, Chapter 4). In the case of the PDR, the 'current state, input symbol, next state' triples would become **quintuples** of the form:

'current state, input sym, pop sym, push string, new state'

The program could read in a description of a PDR as a list (a *file* perhaps) of such 'rules', along with details of which states were *start* and *halt* states.

The program would need an appropriate dynamic data structure (e.g. linked list) to represent a stack. It may therefore be useful to design the stack and its operations first, as a separate exercise.

Having stored the rules, the program would then be set up so that its 'current state', say *C*, was indicated to be the start state. The program would then execute the algorithm in Table SA.2.

Table SA.2

```
can-go := true
while not(end-of-input) and can-go
   if there is a quintuple, Q, such that
            Q's current state = C, and
            Q's pop sym = the current symbol 'on top' of the stack, and
            Q's read sym = the next symbol in the input
   then
                        remove the next symbol from the stack
                        set up ready to read the next symbol in the input
                        push Q's push string onto the stack
                        set C to be Q's next state
   else                 can-go := false
   endif;
endwhile;
if end-of-input and C is a halt state
then return('yes')
else return('no')
endif.
```

As the PDR is assumed to be deterministic, the program can assume that only one quintuple will be applicable at any stage, and can also halt its processing of invalid strings as soon as an applicable quintuple cannot be found. The non deterministic machine is much more complex to model: I leave it to you to consider the details.

CHAPTER 6

3 Any FSR that has a loop on some path linking its start and halt states *in which there is one or more arcs not labelled with ε*, recognizes an **infinite language**.

4 In both cases, it is clear that the v part of the uvw form can consist only of *a*s or *b*s or *c*s. Then one simply argues that when the v is repeated the required numeric relationship between *a*s, *b*s and *c*s is not maintained.

5 The language specified in this case is the set of all strings consisting of two copies of any string of *a*s and/or *b*s. To prove that it is not a **CFL**, it is useful to use the fact that we know we can find a ***uvwxy*** form for which $|vwx| \leq 2^n$, and n is the number of non terminals in a **Chomsky Normal Form** grammar to generate our language. Let $k = 2^n$. There are many sentences in our language of the form $a^ib^ia^ib^i$, where $i > k$. Consider the vwx form as described immediately above. I leave it to you to complete the proof.

CHAPTER 7

1 This can be done by adding an arc labelled x/x (N) for each symbol, x in the alphabet of the particular machine (including the **blank**) from each of the halt states of the machine to a new halt state. The original halt states are then designated as non halt states. The new machine reaches its single halt state leaving the **tape/head** configuration exactly as did the original machine.

CHAPTER 8

1 (The 'or' **FST**). Assuming that the two input binary strings are the same length, and are interleaved on the tape, a bitwise or FST is shown in Figure SA.6.

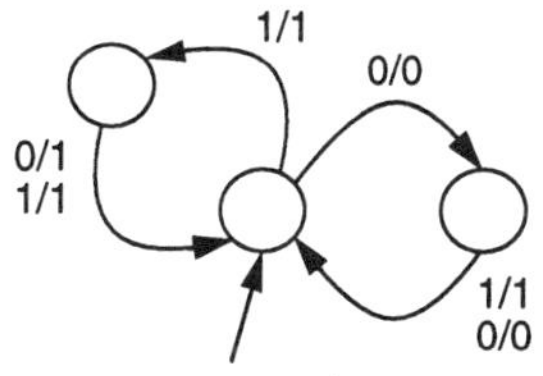

Figure SA.6

CHAPTER 9

4 **Functions** are discussed in more detail in Chapter 11. A specification of a function describes what is computed and does not go into detail about how the computation is done. In this case, then, the **TM** computes the function:

$f(y) = y \text{ div } 2, y \geq 1.$

5 (a) tape on entry:

$d1^n e, n \geq 0$ (or $d1^{x+1}e$)

tape on exit:

$df^n e 1^n$

i.e. the machine copies the 1s between d and e to the right of e, replacing original 1s by fs

(b) $2x + 3$ (or $2(x + 1) + 1$)), all $n \geq 0$

CHAPTER 10

2 Figure SA.7 shows part of a TM to execute the **quintuple** (A, 1, 0, R, B). The flowchart boxes relate to those from the flowchart in Chapter 10. Remember that the numeric designator following the direction specification on the arcs represents the number of the tape on which the next operation is to be carried out.

3 The **sextuple** (1, a, A, R, 2, 2) of the three tape machine M might be represented according to the schema shown in Figure SA.8.
Notes regarding the **shuffling** of the end of input marker are given in Table SA.3.

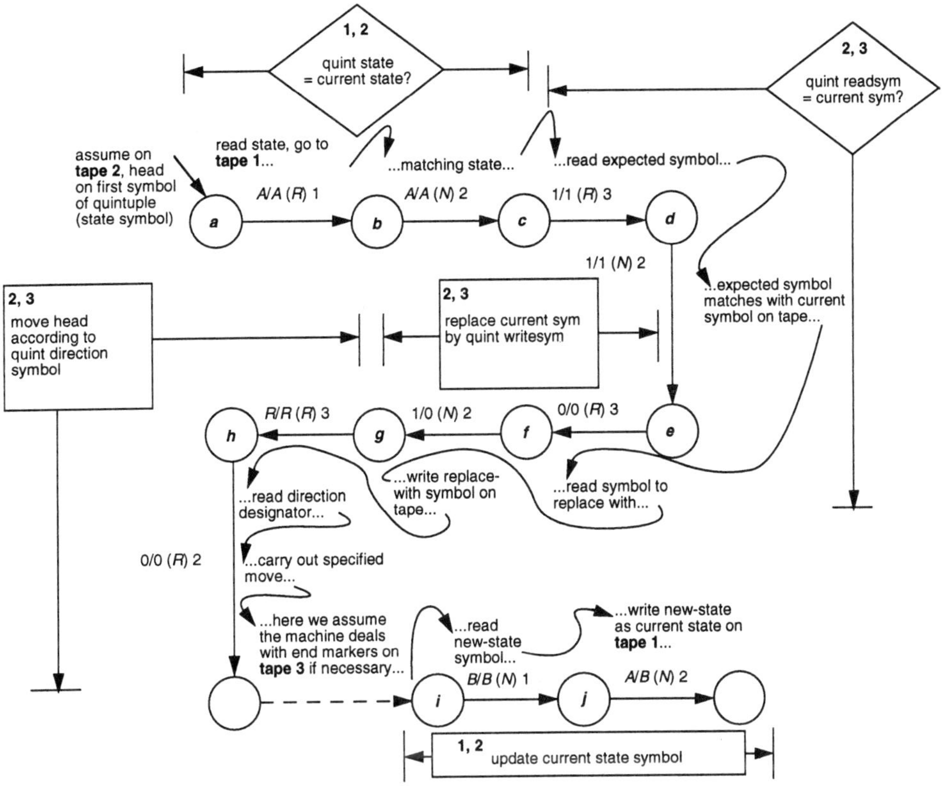

Figure SA.7

Table SA.3

States marked r, t and v, need an additional outgoing arc with current symbol ▩ leading to a sequence of states that 'shuffle' the ▩ to the right, as follows:-

state r

from here, S needs to ensure that the ▩ is moved right six squares,

state t

from here, the ▩ should be moved right four squares, and

state v

from here, the ▩ should be moved two squares to the right

Note: the number of squares the ▩ has to be shuffled along depends on the number of tapes there were on the original multi-tape machine.

Single sextuple of ***M***...

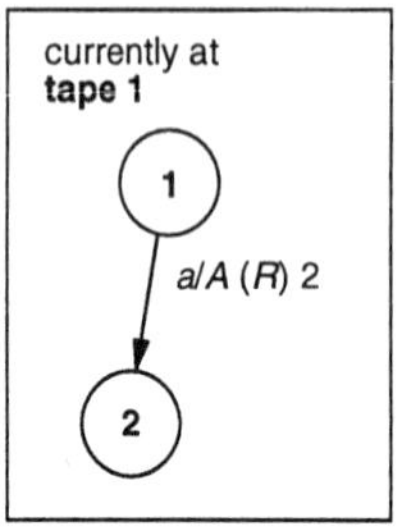

...becomes many quintuples of ***S***:

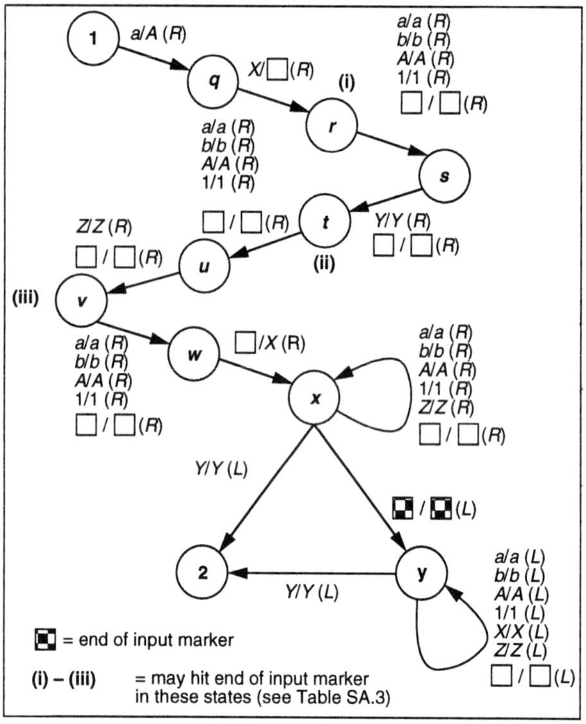

Note that we use the 'from state' label (**1**) and the 'to state' label (**2**) as the first and last states in the part of ***S*** we have constructed. We introduce new state labels for the other states of ***S*** that we create.
If we always do this, we are ensured that ***S*** will be linked exactly as ***M*** was.
In particular, what were the start and halt states in ***M*** become the start and halt states, respectively, of ***S***.

Figure SA.8

CHAPTER 11

2 Assume the TM, *P*, solves the printing problem by halting with output 1 or 0 according to whether *M* would, or would not, write the symbol *s*.

P would need to be able to solve the **halting problem**, or in cases where *M* was not going to **halt** *P* would not be able to write a 0, for 'no'.

Index